Investment Performance
measurement

THE FRANK J. FABOZZI SERIES

Investment Performance
measurement

BRUCE J. FEIBEL

John Wiley & Sons, Inc.

To Shari, Freda, and Shelly

For general information on our other products and services, or technical support, please contact our Customer Care Department within the United States at 800-762-2974, outside the United States at 317-572-3993 or fax 317-572-4002.

Wiley also publishes its books in a variety of electronic formats. Some content that appears in print may not be available in electronic books.

For more information about Wiley, visit our web site at www.wiley.com.

ISBN: 0-471-26849-6

10 9 8 7 6 5 4 3 2 1

contents

After we have set out the objectives for an investment, considered the challenges to reaching them, developed a strategy with the optimal chance of meeting our goals, allocated assets to asset classes and managers, and purchased the securities to build our portfolios, the next step is to check the results. Investment performance measurement is the quantification of the results achieved by an investment program. This book describes and demonstrates the techniques we use to measure investment performance.

Performance measures are statistics summarizing the rates of return achieved, estimates of the risk taken, and measures of the skill evidenced by the efficient use of risk. Once we have measured performance we are interested in measuring the contributions made by the securities, industries, asset classes, and other portfolio segments to the absolute and benchmark relative returns achieved. Together the returns and the insight gained as to how the returns were attained help foster the next round of asset allocation, manager selection, and security selection decisions. These decisions form a recurring investment cycle as the process starts again with the insight gained from the historical analysis, reevaluation of our future needs, and evaluation of the prospective opportunities.

Whether we are in the role of individual or institutional investor, delegate our investment decision making to others, or responsible for managing the portfolios, we are all interested in weighing the results of our activities. Historical risk and return statistics help form our expectations for future expected risk and return that we use in the process of constructing efficient portfolios. As investors, our goals for capital growth, income, and liquidity have to be synchronized with the realities presented by the capital markets, our abilities to select good managers, and the manager's ability to produce excess returns over time.

As part of a performance evaluation we compare the results we achieved to those earned by others with similar goals and constraints. We compare the performance of the managers we selected to managers with similar philosophies. Peer and benchmark relative performance are important to the investment manager. Investment managers are hired based in part on their relative past performance. As investment managers, the actual performance of our strategy provides insight into our strengths and helps adjust strategy for facing the future.

Performance measurement is an exciting and dynamic topic whose importance grows along with the increasing sophistication of investors and the strategies that they employ. The field lies at the nexus of the academic and the practical. Practitioners use ideas developed in the fields of finance, statistics, and accounting and blend them together with the realities presented by the cost of performing the analysis, data availability, technology, and, increasingly, tax and regulatory considerations to produce a meaningful analysis. Investors put a great deal of time and energy into the calculation, presentation, and interpretation of investment performance results. This commitment of resources and the serious consequences of the conclusions derived from performance results warrant a thorough examination of the subject.

Performance measurement is an important component of the body of knowledge for anyone involved in investing. This book provides someone who is interested in the topic with two things:

- A comprehensive and integrated survey of each of the steps taken to measure performance as well as a guide to the calculation, meaning, and interpretation of the various risk and return statistics commonly encountered by anyone responsible for selecting, monitoring, and evaluating the performance of investment managers.
- A reference to the calculation and presentation of historical risk and return statistics, detailed enough to be of use to practitioners charged with carrying out the analysis. In the illustrations that are used to explain the various concepts presented in the book, a spreadsheet format is used so that it is easier for the reader to replicate the calculations.

By reviewing both the concepts of performance measurement as well as examples of how they are used, we gain the insight necessary to understand and evaluate the management of investment funds.

The book has 20 chapters divided into five sections, each covering a consecutive step in the performance measurement process:

Part I: Measurement of the returns earned by portfolios, portfolio managers, peers, and benchmarks.

Part II: Measurement of the risks taken to earn these returns.

Part III: Measurement of the risk and return efficiency of the portfolio and other indicators of manager skill.

Part IV: Analysis of the contribution to return made by the security and segment components of the portfolio and attribution of benchmark-relative value added to management decisions.

Part V: Presentation and interpretation of returns calculated according to industry standards.

Although these sections provide worked examples illustrating particular techniques for analyzing performance, there is an important qualification accompanying these examples: we do not mean to imply that the methodology presented here is the only way to go about it.

Many of the statistics in this book can be calculated in different ways. This is especially true in the areas of risk measurement and performance attribution. There are also multiple definitions for some of the statistics of performance measurement. For example, practitioners use the term "alpha" in several different ways. We do not attempt here to inventory every variation in performance measurement methodology. Instead, we present fully worked examples representing a mainstream approach to implementing the major concepts in order to provide the reader with a hands-on experience in computing and applying the measures. There are many possible refinements to the examples presented here to meet the needs of a particular situation. The dynamic nature of the investments field and the creativity of its participants ensure that there will be a continuous stream of innovations in the measurement of performance.

acknowledgments

This book begins on a note of humility. *I* did not develop any of the methods that comprise the performance measurement body of knowledge. Many contributors have shaped the evolution of what now represents current practice in the field. I have tried to recognize and reference within the text their works, and recommend them as resources for further information. Those who want to keep current with developments in the field will be especially interested in *The Journal of Performance Measurement* (www.spauldinggrp.com) as well as various publications of the Association for Investment Management and Research (www.aimr.org). These resources have been especially helpful to me.

The book has benefited from conversations with many of my clients and colleagues. For sharing their insight and experience I thank Stephen Gaudette, Sherry Hui, Nigel Hutchings, Howard Mannion, Judy Mezzacappa, Andre Mirabelli, Sarah Ringle, Malcolm Smith, Mark Smith, Lyn Thompson, Patricia Warren, and Kurt Weisenbeck.

I would especially like to thank several people who have taken the time to comment on parts of this book as it was being written: Patti Coan, Frank Fabozzi, Christine Knott, Ken Kolber, Anthony Lombardo, Anil Madhok, Joe McDonough, Marc Rubenfeld, Linda Snodgrass, John Stahr, David Stockwell, and Stacey Urciuoli.

I thank all of my colleagues at Eagle Investment Systems for the opportunity, and in particular, David Palten and Lou Maiuri for their encouragement of this project.

I owe a special debt of gratitude to Danielle Newland for her help organizing, editing, suggesting examples, and in many other ways helping to convert the manuscript into a finished book.

Any errors or omissions are my own. It is my sincere hope that this book will provide you with information that helps you better understand and implement the process of analyzing investment performance. I welcome your feedback at feibels@yahoo.com.

Bruce J. Feibel
Brookline, Massachusetts

CHAPTER 1

Investment Performance Measurement

Investment is an initial forfeit of something we value in exchange for the anticipated benefit of getting back more than we put in. The difference between what we put in and what we got back is the *return*; we invest in order to yield this return. For financial assets return includes both the gain we receive when we finally either sell them to someone else, or they mature, as well as the income earned between the purchase and sale. Return is compensation for giving up the use of the capital in the interim. For most investments at the outset we cannot be sure of the value of the income and gains we will receive. The spectrum of instruments we could invest in provides a varying degree of return uncertainty. We can predict the return we will earn on a one-month T-bill with complete accuracy where we couldn't hazard a guess as to the return of an investment in an emerging markets stock fund. Financial theory and experience suggest that the highest return given a particular level of risk taken is likely to be achieved via the diversification of our assets across multiple security holdings. So we usually invest via a portfolio of securities, or a set of portfolios each managed to a particular objective. The higher the degree of return uncertainty, or *risk*, in a given investment, the more return we demand.

THE INVESTMENT PROCESS

Suppose we are starting out fresh with the responsibility for managing a pool of money. We can organize the tasks ahead of us into a series of steps:

1

■ Determine the goals of the investment based on the purpose of the funds and the constraints to be placed upon the investment, such as the requirement for income or the tolerance for short-term loss of principal.

■ Devise a strategy for meeting these goals. This includes the analysis of how well alternative scenarios for diversifying the investment across asset classes and funds can be expected to meet our goals and then the selection of the one with the most potential.

■ Implement the strategy. This includes the study and selection of various sets of managers and funds where the market expertise and philosophies together best fit our objectives. Once funded, the managers will set out to implement these strategies via the selection of securities and the optimal diversification among them to achieve the highest expected return given the level of risk.

■ Monitor and adjust the strategy. We periodically take stock of our situation by comparing the progress toward our original goals. We measure what was achieved and how we got there. We will observe the risk and return opportunities presented by the markets over the period and compare our results to those available and those realized by others in a similar situation. We will need to incorporate into our strategy the needs created by changes in our own situation and revise our expectations for the future. We will need to monitor the managers we hire to make sure they are managing the portfolio as expected.

Once we've made our investments, *Investment Performance Measurement* techniques quantify how much return we earned, how we earned it, and what risks we took along the way. Performance measurement is a backward-looking, or *ex-post*, undertaking. But the results inform our *ex-ante* decisions moving forward. It is important to differentiate the two because as investors we are interested in both forward- and backward-looking measures of risk and return. The difference is that with performance measurement we measure the past, while other branches of investments are concerned with forecasting future risk and return, to some degree by using past observations as a guide.

WHY MEASURE PERFORMANCE?

Performance measurement requires time, data, and other resources. So why do we do it? Depending on our perspective we could have several goals for the performance measurement process. For the purposes of this study we split up the world into *Investors* and *Investment Managers*.

Many times the two are the same person or team of people charged with the activity of investing. Anyone who has money to invest is an *investor*. The money can be the investor's own assets or someone else's for which they have fiduciary responsibility. Investors include all of us as individual investors, as well as pension plan managers, charity and foundation executives, corporate treasurers, trustees, investment custodians, and other institutional investor personnel and their supporting organizations.

Some investors build their own portfolios but most delegate this responsibility to professional investment managers. Investment managers research, develop, and implement investment strategies and are found at asset management firms, banks, mutual fund companies, and other types of organizations. Here we refer to the investment manager as someone who makes the day-to-day asset allocation, security selection, and other portfolio construction decisions in the management of a portfolio, whether they work as an individual or a member of a portfolio management team.

PERFORMANCE MEASUREMENT AND THE INVESTOR

Why do investors measure performance? As investors we use information derived from performance analysis to monitor the progress our savings are making toward our goals, select and evaluate the work of investment managers, and provide inputs for future asset allocation and manager selection decisions.

Monitoring Progress

Once we have allocated our assets, we monitor the ongoing performance of our own funds or those for which we have responsibility. For example, an individual investor saving for his retirement can measure the returns he is earning against the projected future value of these returns in order to determine whether his rate of savings or asset allocation needs to be readdressed. A corporate defined-benefit pension plan sponsor is interested in whether actual returns are consistent with the actuarial assumptions made in planning the benefits promised to retirees, company contributions to fund these benefits, and the fund's asset allocation. The potential cost to the company of having an underfunded plan makes the ongoing measurement and evaluation of investment performance a critical responsibility for the governors of the plan. This responsibility is paralleled at all institutional investors including insurance companies, endowments, and charities. The viability of these organizations depends a great deal upon their success as investors.

Manager Selection and Evaluation

Most investors delegate all or a portion of the management of funds to professional investment managers. If we are looking to hire a manager we might want to hire someone with a proven track record of successfully managing a strategy. Risk and return data are used to create these track records. Once we review and have hired a manager, regular performance measurement facilitates the review and judgment of the manager's success managing our money. Management fees are a significant cost to investors. Two managers investing in the same asset class and following a similar strategy can deliver widely different results. Even if we are not looking for market-beating results, risk or return measures outside of a standard range might indicate a problem in the way the fund is being managed. Performance measurement facilitates the ongoing communication between the client and manager about the clients changing objectives and the portfolios place within the strategy to meet them. And if the manager claims to have a strategy for market-beating returns, we need a way of quantifying whether he actually did. Ongoing analysis of historical risk and return is the only way to check that the manager's investment process is delivering what we are paying for. Pension consultancies, custodians, and investment research companies serve both institutional and individual investors by monitoring the relative performance of money managers. These organizations help investors analyze and evaluate manager performance.

Asset Allocation Inputs

The key decision that faces an investor is the selection of a proper saving, spending, and asset allocation strategy that provides a high probability of meeting their goals with an acceptable risk of loss. The investor situation and opportunities provided by the capital markets continuously change, so these decisions are periodically reviewed. The inputs to asset allocation plans are expectations for future return and risk, made in part through the analysis of the historical returns and relationship between the returns earned by different asset classes.

PERFORMANCE MEASUREMENT AND THE INVESTMENT MANAGER

The reasons for the investment manager to measure performance are just as compelling. Investment managers measure their historical performance to help evaluate and control their investment process and to facilitate the marketing of their services and communication with their clients.

Process Control

Returns are the product an asset manager delivers in exchange for the management fee. Passive managers are paid to deliver absolute market returns and active managers are paid even more to deliver that plus incremental benchmark relative return. Although investment management is an *ex-ante* process, where managers seek to improve their predictions of the factors impacting returns, ongoing measurement of risk and return provides necessary information as to whether the product is being delivered. In addition to measuring return, performance contribution and attribution analyses provide an understanding as to the sources of return. For example, if the manager overweighted a stock that subsequently outperformed, the impact of this decision on total portfolio performance over time can be quantified. The sum of such decisions is used to quantify the strengths and weaknesses of the manager's strategy.

Marketing and Client Service

Managers report performance as part of their regular periodic client communication. Investment managers routinely report the return, risk, and attribution statistics presented in this book to their clients. The data help clients monitor whether the manager is performing as expected given the capital market environment over the period. For institutional investors, the returns and risk measures facilitate a dialog about the manager's philosophy, investment process, and expectations for the future.

Fund managers also present their returns to prospects in the process of marketing their services. Many strategies are sold based on demonstration of a superior historical performance record. The performance measurement methodology and practices employed by managers are heavily influenced by industry standards for the presentation of performance to prospective institutional investors.

THE PERFORMANCE MEASUREMENT PROCESS

So far we have not made reference to the underlying assets whose performance we are measuring. This is by design, since performance measurement works much the same way across asset classes and management strategies. Performance measurement is a stage in the investment process common to all combinations of investor, vehicle, strategy, and asset class. Individual and institutional investors, investing via customized portfolios or commingled accounts, using a myriad of strategies and asset classes, use the tools presented in this book to measure and analyze investment performance. This is true for all combinations of strategy and implementation vehicle, including:

Investor	Vehicle	Strategies	Asset Classes
Pension Funds	Mutual Funds	Passive/Active	Cash & Equivalents
• Defined benefit	Institutional Separate	Quantitative/Fundamen-	Fixed Income
• Defined contribution	Accounts	tal	Equity
Insurance Companies	Institutional Commin-	Styles–Growth/Value	Real Estate
Endowments	gled Funds	etc.	Private Equity
Foundations	Partnerships & Hedge	Global/Domestic	Derivatives
Retail Investors	Funds	Overlay & Risk Mgmt.	Balanced Accounts
	Corporate Liquidity		
	Accounts		
	Wrap Accounts		
	Brokerage Accounts		

Other than the particulars of determining the current value of different security types, not a lot differentiates the measurement of the performance of a fixed income institutional separate account from that of an equity mutual fund. This is true even though they are different types of legal entities, servicing the needs of different types of investors.

After establishing the importance and utility of performance measurement as a subject, our next task is to inventory the key topics within the field. There are no strict boundaries separating the topics lying within the scope of performance measurement from other investment subjects. But we can establish some borders by defining the goal of performance measurement as:

> The calculation of return, risk and derived statistics stemming from the periodic change in market value of portfolio positions and transactions made into and within a portfolio, for use in the evaluation of historical fund or manager performance.[1]

Performance measurement is concerned with describing the results produced by the investor and manager, as opposed to what should have been done to produce different results, or what changes should be made to improve future results. Though the statistics are used in making forward-looking decisions, performance measurement is a backward-looking process. Using our definition, we can describe performance measurement as a set of procedures, linked in a process of several steps, illustrated in Exhibit 1.1, where the outputs of one step are used as the inputs to the next.

---

[1] In this book we use the terms "fund" and "portfolio" to mean any collection of assets.

EXHIBIT 1.1 Performance Measurement Process

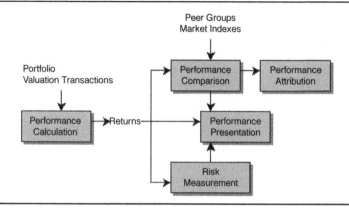

Performance measurement begins with the valuation of the assets within the portfolio. We take the actual portfolio positions, prices, transactions, and other inputs and then:

- Calculate the portfolio return and the manager's return, which could be different.
- Compare these results to those earned by our peers, market indices, and other benchmarks.
- Measure the absolute and benchmark relative risks taken to earn these returns.
- Calculate statistics representing manager skill by studying the patterns of returns produced by the manager and by relating returns to the risks taken.
- If we are interested in the sources of return, calculate the returns to the securities and segments of the portfolio and then measure the contribution to total return made by each. By comparing the relative contributions made by different securities to the total fund and benchmark return we can attribute value added over the passive market return as represented by the benchmark to the asset allocation and security selection decisions made by the manager.
- And finally, present the risk and return results according to regulatory and industry standards, including the combining of returns across all clients and funds invested in the strategy into composites that can be used for marketing a manager's services to prospective clients.

These are the subjects of this book. The topics are organized into five parts, each developing the next stage of the process. A description of each section follows.

PART I: RETURN MEASUREMENT

The measurement of performance starts with the calculation of return. The periodic change in the value of a portfolio and the resultant growth of assets over time is the most basic component of performance. We are interested in the total gain earned over the period as well as the benchmark relative gain attributable to the actions of the manager. By measuring return we can answer questions such as:

- How has the absolute value of the portfolio changed over time?
- What portion of the increase in value is attributable to the actions of the investment management firm or team?
- What was the impact of management fees, taxes, and currency fluctuation on the returns?
- How do these returns compare to those earned by the fund's peers and benchmark?
- How much value did the manager add over the benchmark?

In Part I of the book we cover the calculation and interpretation of rates of return. Single period rates of return are computed between portfolio valuation dates. Multiple period returns are calculated by compounding the single period returns. Topics in this section include the components of and calculation of single period returns, time value of money concepts, returns that take into account the timing of cash flows into or out of the portfolio, time and dollar weighted returns, the internal rate of return, the Modified Dietz return, cumulative returns, and procedures for calculating multiple period average and annualized returns. We also address the procedures for adjusting returns for the impact of fees, taxes, and exchange rate changes. We cover the calculation of rank and order statistics; look at how index returns are calculated and how they handle corporate actions and other constituent changes. Finally, we address the methods for determining the amount of value added over the benchmark.

PART II: RISK MEASUREMENT

The capital markets offer incremental returns only when investors assume heightened risk. After we have calculated the returns earned to the portfolio, we measure the risk taken to achieve those returns. The volatility of returns over time is the main indicator of the risks taken. Where the benchmark is set to indicate the level of risk we expected to take, then we also measure how well the fund tracked the benchmark over the period. By measuring risk we hope to answer these questions:

- How much total risk was taken to achieve the returns?
- What was the probability of achieving a return below the return required to meet our objectives?
- Did the portfolio track its benchmark as required?

In Part II of the book we discuss alternative definitions of risk, define forward- versus backward-looking risk, and the available methods of inferring the risks taken from the time series of historical returns. We will also examine the evaluation of absolute risk in a mean-variance framework where risk is proxied by the standard deviation of returns. We then look at measures where risk is defined as the potential of losing money, or downside risk. Finally, we cover the methods used to determine the incremental risk taken by the manager over the risk implied by the benchmark, or benchmark relative risk. We examine the use of regression analysis and tracking error to measure relative risk.

PART III: EFFICIENCY AND SKILL MEASUREMENT

Once we have measured the returns and risks taken, we can evaluate the composite risk and return efficiency of the portfolio. We are interested in whether the fund is being managed efficiently, and in the case of actively managed portfolios, discovering evidence of the manager's skill. The statistics representing efficiency and skill are used to help answer questions that include:

- Did the fund return as much as other funds, or the benchmark, that exhibited a similar degree of risk?
- How did the investment perform on a risk-adjusted basis?
- Were manager deviations from benchmarks rewarded on a risk-adjusted basis?
- What was the manager's risk-adjusted value added over the period?
- Is there any evidence of manager skill in the historical return series?

In Part III we look at measures of the efficiency of the portfolio in a mean-variance framework, including the Sharpe ratio, M^2 return, and the Information Ratio. We look at the measurement of value added via the calculation of the portfolio's Alpha and Beta in the context of the Capital Asset Pricing Model (CAPM). We then cover some methods to analyze the time series of returns to determine whether there is statistical evidence of manager value added over the period.

PART IV: PERFORMANCE ATTRIBUTION

By comparing fund and benchmark returns, we can determine whether the manager has added value over the period. We are also interested in *how* the value added was achieved. For example, if we overweighted the technology segment of a diversified equity portfolio during a period when technology stocks were in favor, this decision added incremental value. Using performance contribution and attribution analysis techniques, we can quantify the value added by this and similar decisions. Performance attribution is used to help answer questions such as:

- How did the different securities and segments within the fund perform over the period?
- What was the impact of using instruments that modify segment exposures such as currency forward contracts and futures?
- How were the contributions to total fund return attributable to these securities and portfolio segments?
- How much did the fund's asset allocation relative to the benchmark, as well as other decisions, contribute to the value added?
- Were the management factors that contributed to value added over the benchmark in accordance with the manager's stated investment style?

To understand how fund performance was achieved, we first need to calculate the returns for the securities that comprise the portfolio. In this section we look at the calculation of security and portfolio segment returns. We cover the calculation of performance on an effective exposure basis for funds employing derivatives. We then look at how individual security returns contribute to the portfolio return. We show how portfolio segment and security level returns and weights within the portfolio or index are used to derive statistics describing how the portfolio holdings combined to produce the absolute and benchmark relative return. We also examine the methodology for ascribing the value added to decisions made by the manager to allocate assets to attractive securities or segments.

PART V: PERFORMANCE PRESENTATION

The investments industry, via the Association for Investment Management and Research (AIMR), has developed global standards for the presentation of performance to prospective investors. Even if we were not in a position of being a prospective purchaser of investment manager services, the standards are important because they effectively govern the methodology used by the industry to calculate and present returns. In this section we cover the calculation and interpretation of the numbers presented according to AIMR standards to help answer questions including:

- What does a manager do to meet the standards?
- How do we interpret the composite returns presented by managers?
- How have all of the portfolios entrusted to the manager performed on average?
- How closely have the manager's portfolios managed with the same strategy performed?

In this section we summarize the industry standards for the presentation of performance measurement results to investors. Given the degree of influence of the standards not just on performance presentation, but also other aspects of performance measurement, attention is paid to the calculation and interpretation of the required statistics including composite returns, and equal- and asset-weighted composite dispersion statistics.

SUMMARY

The statistics of performance are generic to most investment situations. Return is the ratio of capital gains and income to capital invested. Absolute risk statistics measure the variability in return. Relative risk measures the variability in benchmark relative return. Composite risk/return measures relate the returns earned to the risks taken. Contribution statistics are market value weighted returns to the security and segment components of a portfolio and benchmark. Attribution statistics are the benchmark relative contributions to return. Each set of statistics builds on the others and provides successively more information to the performance analyst. The examples in the following chapters illustrate specific implementations of these generic techniques, which represent the most commonly encountered applications. But the concepts behind each of these measures can be modified to reflect the requirements suggested by the investment under consideration. We start with the measurement of return.

Return Measurement

Single Period Return

A t the end of the year 2001, the 5-year average annual return earned by the Fidelity Magellan fund, one of the largest U.S. mutual funds, with net assets of over 75 billion dollars, was 10.28% before taxes.[1] After subtracting the impact of taxes on dividend distributions to shareholders, the return was 8.83%. The equivalent average return for similarly managed Large Cap portfolios was 6.73%. The 5-year average return for the S&P 500 was 10.70%. If we were an investor in the Magellan fund, we could use these statistics to evaluate whether or not we are happy with its performance. But what do these numbers mean? How can we adjust the numbers to account for the timing of the investor's investments into the fund? How can we calculate the returns for our own portfolios? These are some of the topics covered by the chapters in Part I of this book.

RETURN

We can best explain the concept of return with a simple example. Suppose we invest $100 in a fund. Our investment goes up in value and we get $130 back. What was the return on this investment? We've gained $30. Taking this *dollar return* and dividing it by the $100 invested, and multiplying the decimal result 0.3 by 100 gives us the return expressed as a percentage:

$$\left(\frac{30}{100}\right) \times 100 = 30\%$$

---

[1] Source: Fidelity Investments, www.fidelity.com.

A *rate of return* is the benefit we have received from an investment over a period of time expressed as a percentage. Returns are a ratio relating:

How much was gained or lost
given
How much was risked

We interpret a 30% return as a gain over the period equal to almost 1/3 of the original $100 invested. Although it would seem that no special knowledge of investments is required to calculate and interpret rates of return, several complications make the subject worthy of further attention:

- Selection of the proper inputs to the return calculation.
- Treatment of additional client contributions and withdrawals to and from the investment account.
- Adjusting the return to reflect the timing of these contributions and withdrawals.
- Differentiating between the return produced by the investment manager and the return experienced by the investor.
- Computing returns spanning multiple valuation periods.
- Averaging periodic rates of return.

Why do we use rates of return rather than absolute dollar gains to describe the performance of an investment? There are several reasons that returns are the preferred statistic for representing investment performance:

- A return summarizes a lot of information into a single statistic. This includes data on the market value, income earned, and transactions made on all of the investments in the fund.
- Returns are ratios, and it is usually faster and easier for us to interpret a proportion between two things than to use the underlying data.
- Returns are unaffected by the relative size of portfolios. For example, if we put $100 at work and gain $10 we have earned the same return as the investor that put $1 million at work and ended up with $1.1 million. Returns are much more useful for comparing the performance of different funds, funds to indices, and managers to other managers.
- Returns calculated for different periods are comparable; we can compare the returns earned in one year to those earned in prior years.

■ The return earned on two investments can be compared to show the relative gains earned over the period. For example, a fund that earned 10% in a year produced twice as much gain as a fund that earned 5% during the year.

■ The interpretation of the rate of return is intuitive. Return is the value reconciling the beginning investment value to the ending value over the time period we are measuring. We can take a reported return and use it to determine the amount of money we would have at the end of the period given the amount invested:

Investment made × (1 + Decimal return) = Accumulated value

For example, if we were to invest $100 at a return of 10% we would have $110 at the end of the period:

$$\$100 \times (1.10) = \$110$$

Adding one to the decimal return before multiplying gives a result equal to the beginning value plus the amount earned over the period. Multiplying the investment made by the return of 0.1 will give the amount earned over the period ($10).

Let's look closer at the calculation of return. In our introductory example we earned a $30 gain on an investment of $100. By dividing the gain by the amount invested we derive the 30% return using

$$\text{Return in percent} = \left(\frac{\text{Gain or loss}}{\text{Investment made}} \right) \times 100 \qquad (2.1)$$

Suppose that instead of investing and then getting our money back within a single period, we held an investment worth $100 at the beginning of the period and we still held on to it at the end of the period when it was valued at $130. We can calculate the return by:

1. Taking the ratio of the ending value to the beginning (130/100 = 1.3) and
2. Subtracting one from the ratio to take away the portion representing the original investment. This leaves the relative growth over the period (1.3 − 1 = 0.3).
3. Multiplying this result by 100 transforms the decimal fraction into a percentage gain (0.3 × 100 = 30%).

We calculate the same return whether we buy and then liquidate an investment within a period or we carry an investment over from a prior period and hold it. The smallest unit of time we use to measure return is called a single *measurement period*, or simply *period*. When we measure the return on an investment we buy and hold across periods, we treat the beginning market value as if it were a new investment made at the beginning of the period and the ending market value like it were the proceeds from the sale of the investment at the end of the period.

It does not matter which of the two forms of return calculation presented so far we use because the two methods are equivalent:

$$\left(\frac{\text{Gain or Loss}}{\text{Investment made}} \right) \times 100 = \left[\left(\frac{\text{Current value}}{\text{Investment made}} \right) - 1 \right] \times 100$$

$$30\% = \left(\frac{130 - 100}{100} \right) \times 100 = \left[\left(\frac{130}{100} \right) - 1 \right] \times 100$$

We can prove they are the same by deriving the second form from the first:

$$\left(\frac{\text{MVE} - \text{MVB}}{\text{MVB}} \right) \times 100 \rightarrow \left(\frac{\text{MVE}}{\text{MVB}} - \frac{\text{MVB}}{\text{MVB}} \right) \times 100 \rightarrow \left(\frac{\text{MVE}}{\text{MVB}} - 1 \right) \times 100$$

where MVE = market value at the end of the measurement period and MVB = market value at the beginning of the measurement period.

Using the first form, the numerator of the rate of return calculation is the *unrealized gain or loss:* the difference between the starting and ending market value. In either form the denominator is the *investment made* or *investment base*. The amount in the denominator represents the *money at risk*, or *principal*, invested during the period. In the first period, the investment made is equal to the amount originally invested in the fund. In subsequent periods, it is equal to the ending market value of the previous period. The market value at the end of the investment period plus the income earned over the period equals the *accumulated value* for the period. Exhibit 2.1 shows the calculation of monthly return where we invest $100 on December 31 and it grows to $110 at the end of January and then $120 at the end of February.

EXHIBIT 2.1 Percentage Return versus Dollar Return

	A	B	C	D
1	Month Ending	Market Value	Dollar Return	Percent Return
2	12/31	100		
3	1/31	110	10	10.00
4	2/28	120	10	9.09
5			↑	
6			=B4-B3	=((C4/B3)*100)

Notice that even though the dollar return is the same $10 in each monthly period, the percent return is lower in the second month (10/110 = 9.09%) than it was in the first month (10/100 = 10.00%). The reason for the lower return in the second month is that the amount at risk in the fund for the second month equals not only the original investment of $100 but also the additional $10 gained in the first month. Given the same dollar gain, but more money put at risk, the lower the return that will be credited to the investment.

Now that we have looked at the basic calculation of returns, in the next three sections we step back to look deeper into the component inputs to the return calculation, the market value and cash flows into or out of the portfolio.

MARKET VALUE

The market value represents the current amount that a third party would be willing to pay the fund for the assets held. The process of determining the current value of portfolio is called *valuation* or *mark-to-market*. By using the market value of the investment to calculate returns, we recognize a gain on the investment even though it is not actually *realized* by selling the investment, i.e., we do not have to wait until we liquidate a portfolio in order to calculate the performance of the portfolio. To calculate returns that include unrealized gains, we need to value the fund at the end of each measurement period. For an investment fund, these dates are the periodic *valuation dates*. Most funds are valued at regular frequencies. A return calculated between two valuation dates is called a *single period, holding period,* or *periodic* return. The periodicity of single period returns is related to the frequency of valuation. For example, single period returns are available on a daily basis for mutual funds that are valued every night, but may be available only monthly for institutional separate accounts, or quarterly for an investment in a real estate partnership. For commingled funds, valuations are performed at least as often as participants are allowed to move money into or out of the fund. The fund valuations as of the beginning and end dates are used to calculate the return between these two dates.

We calculate market value by starting with accounting data. The accounting data include a record of the transactions made during the period and the positions held at the beginning and end of the period, which reflect these transactions. When there are no transactions into or out of the investment account, a single period return is calculated using the beginning and ending valuations. Fund market values are determined by summing up the market values of the underlying investments within the fund. If we are calculating the returns on a position in a commingled investment, such as a mutual fund, the market value equals the sum of the shares owned multiplied by the unit value of each share on the valuation date. A unit value is calculated by dividing the sum of the individual security market values by the number of units or shares outstanding. Market values are determined on a trade date, accrual-based accounting basis.

With *trade date accounting* we include securities in the fund valuation on the day the manager agrees to buy or sell the securities, as opposed to the day they are settled, or exchanged for cash. The trade date valuation is made because it is the date upon which the manager assumes ownership of the security. Security prices can also move considerably between trade date and settlement date. The commitment to buy or sell the securities is recorded as a receivable or payable on the fund's books between trade date and settlement date. In the calculation of total fund value, the net payable offsets any cash that might be committed to the purchase of the securities. Likewise we account for income on the day that it is earned, or *accrued*, rather than received. We include in the valuation any receivables or payables, including dividends and interest receivable.

The *market value* of each security is the amount you would expect to receive if the investment were sold to a willing buyer on the valuation date. It is calculated using observed market prices for instruments such as exchange-traded equities. An estimate of the value based on the market price of similar assets is required for private placements and other assets where it is not possible to get a market quotation for the asset. For example, bonds that do not trade often are marked to market with reference to bonds of a similar character that did trade. Although it is possible, for liquidity reasons, that we might not realize the observed market price used in the valuation if we were to actually sell the security, we avoid introducing subjective estimates of trading impact into return calculations. We assume that the disposal of a large block of stock or other potentially illiquid asset will take place over time, and not via a forced sale. We also do not adjust for estimated explicit costs of disposing the asset, such as commissions, when we are valuing the portfolio. Basically, we assume that the portfolio is an ongoing concern.

Security market values used in performance include a measure of income earned or accrued income on the investment. *Accrued income* is income earned but not yet received. For example, if one were to sell a bond between coupon dates, you will receive interest sold in addition to the principal value of the bond on trade date. Interest sold is a credit for the interest accrual since the last coupon date. Because the accrual would be part of the proceeds if the security were sold on valuation date, it is included in the market value calculation. Returns that reflect both the change in market value and the income earned during the period are called *total returns*.[2] In a similar manner, total fund market value is adjusted for accrued receivables and payables at the fund level. For example, the accrued management fee payable to the investment manager is subtracted from the total market value.

The principles of market quote-based, trade date, accrual accounting, and mark to market valuation are used to value all securities in the fund, resulting in the single period return calculation formula:

Percent Rate of Return

$$= \left[\left(\frac{\text{Ending Market Value} + \text{Ending Accrued Income}}{\text{Beginning Market Value} + \text{Beginning Accrued Income}} \right) - 1 \right] \quad (2.2)$$
$$\times 100$$

Note that we include the accrued income in both the numerator and the denominator of the return. Income is included in the numerator because it is part of the gain over the period. We include income in the denominator because it is part of the capital put at risk at the beginning of the period. If we only include income in the numerator, we will overstate the return during the period.

TRANSACTIONS WITHIN THE FUND

Is it is also important to look at what is not included in the calculation of portfolio return. The *cost of investments* established on the initial purchase of a security and by subsequent investments is *not* considered in performance measurement after the first period's return calculation. Exceptions to this practice are certain securities, such as commercial paper and other cash equivalents, which are valued at their amortized cost. It is the change in the market value of our investments that determines the increase in our wealth over the period. The cost of invest-

---

[2] For a discussion of the use of total return versus yields in performance measurement see Robert Anthony, "How to Measure Fixed-income Performance Correctly," *Journal of Portfolio Management*, Winter 1985.

ments is, however, an important consideration in the measurement of after-tax performance, which is covered in Chapter 6. For each subsequent period, the ending market value for the previous period is used as the starting market value for the next period. The justification for this practice is that we assume that the investment cycle begins afresh with each valuation period, and it is the current market value at the beginning of the period that is put at risk in the next period.

Our return calculation makes no reference to gains realized on security sales during the period. In fact the fund beginning and ending market values include both *unrealized* and *realized gains and losses* generated by trading within the fund during the measurement period. Consider a fund with this record of activity:

December 31, 2000
 ▪ Owns 100 shares Stock A priced at $1 per share = $100 MVB

January 31, 2001
 ▪ Stock A is worth $110 for a (10/100 = 10%) return in January

February 28, 2001
 ▪ Stock A is worth $115 for a (5/110 = 4.55%) return in February

March 1, 2001
 ▪ 50 shares of Stock A are sold for $1.15 per share, a net amount of $57.50.
 ▪ The realized gain on the sale is $7.50 ($57.50 – $50 = $7.50)
 ▪ 10 Shares of Stock B at $5.75 a share are purchased with the proceeds

March 31, 2001
 ▪ Stock A is worth (50 shares × $1 = $50)
 ▪ Stock B is worth (10 shares × $5 = $50)
 ▪ The total fund is worth $100, for a (–15/115 = 13.04%) loss in March.

Exhibit 2.2 shows that we do not explicitly use the realized gain of $7.50 in the return calculation for March. The realized gain on the sale of Stock A was committed to the purchase of Stock B, which was then valued at the end of the period. The point of this example is that even though we *explicitly* calculate the unrealized market value change during period, this market value change *implicitly* includes any realized gains/losses on securities sold during the period.

It is possible that the manager would take the sale proceeds and not turn them over into a new investment. In this case, we still do not include the realized gain explicitly in the return calculation. Instead, we include the cash received on the sale in the total fund market value calculation.

EXHIBIT 2.2   Reinvestment of Gain Impact on Returns

	A	B	C	D	E	F
1	Date	MV Stock A	MV Stock B	Total MV	Gain/Loss	% Return
2	31-Dec-2000	100.00	0.00	100.00		
3	31-Jan-2001	110.00	0.00	110.00	10.00	10.00
4	28-Feb-2001	115.00	0.00	115.00	5.00	4.55
5	01-Mar-2001	57.50	57.50	115.00		
6	31-Mar-2001	50.00	50.00	100.00	-15.00	-13.04
7					↑	↑
8					=D6-D5	=((E6/D5)*100)

EXHIBIT 2.3   Holding Gains in Cash

	A	B	C	D	E	F
1	Date	MV Stock A	Cash	Total MV	Gain/Loss	% Return
2	31-Dec-2000	100.00	0.00	100.00		
3	31-Jan-2001	110.00	0.00	110.00	10.00	10.00
4	28-Feb-2001	115.00	0.00	115.00	5.00	4.55
5	01-Mar-2001	57.50	57.50	115.00		
6	31-Mar-2001	50.00	57.90	107.90	-7.10	-6.17
7					↑	↑
8					=D6-D5	=((E6/D5)*100)

Exhibit 2.3 illustrates the fact that we do not need to know about the transactions *within* the fund during the valuation period in order to calculate fund level performance. Transactions within the fund during the period do not affect the return calculation as they have an equal and opposite impact on performance—a purchase of one security is a sale of another (cash). This is also true of income received during the period. Income received on a security is an outflow from that security but an inflow of cash. To calculate fund performance, when there are no transactions that involve moving money into or out of the fund during the period, we only need to know the market value of all of the securities plus cash at the beginning and the end of the holding period.

CASH FLOWS

So far we have looked at the calculation of a single period return for situations where only the market value of our holdings at the end of the period is made available for investment at the beginning of the next period. Individuals and institutional investors also make occasional or periodic contributions to and withdrawals from investment accounts. These net contributions are *not* included as components of investment return; they represent an increase of capital at risk but not a capital gain on our investment. For this reason, when a fund receives new money it is not possible to measure performance by simply observing the change in market value.

EXHIBIT 2.4   Cash Flows

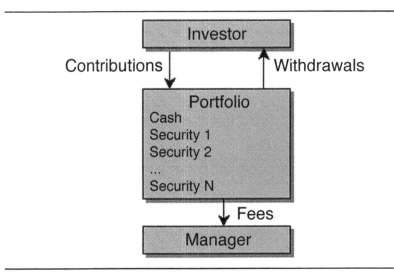

These asset transfers into and out of the fund are sometimes called *cash flows*. Cash flow is a generic term for different transaction types with the economic effect of adding to or taking away from the investment in the fund. For a defined-benefit pension plan the cash flows include periodic corporate contributions to fund the plan and withdrawals to service retirees. For a mutual fund, cash flows include purchases or liquidations of fund shares and exchanges of shares between funds. Exhibit 2.4 shows the transaction relationships between the investor, the manager, and the fund.

The value of the cash flow is the amount of money deposited or withdrawn. A positive cash flow is a flow into the fund. A negative cash flow is a flow out of the fund. Notably, cash flows are not always made in cash, but can be made via the contribution of stock or other assets to the fund. An example of this is when a fund is transitioned to a new investment manager. The monetary value of these "in-kind" contributions is measured at the current value of the assets transferred at the time of the contribution. In these situations it is important to use the market value instead of the original cost. If the original cost were used, the return calculation for the first period after the contribution would count the entire return to date as earned in the first period after the transfer. So the term *cash flow* refers to a transfer of assets into or out of the portfolio, valued at the market value of these assets at the time of the transfer, regardless of whether or not the transaction was actually made in cash.

The calculation of gain/loss must compensate for the fact that the increase in market value is not entirely due to investment gain during the period. For example, suppose we have a fund with an MVB of $100 and a MVE of $130. What is the gain if we invested an additional $10 during the period? We started off with $100 and ended up with $130. We subtract out the additional investment before calculating the gain of $20:

$$\text{Gain/loss} = (\text{Current value} - \text{Original investment} - \text{Net cash inflows} + \text{Net cash outflows}) \tag{2.3}$$

In terms of our example, the gain is $20 (130 − 100 − 10 + 0). The $20 gain/loss during the period combines two amounts: the gain on the original $100 and the gain on the additional $10 invested. If instead of having a net inflow we had a net outflow because we took money out of the fund during the period, the second component would be the gain earned up until the money was withdrawn.

RETURN ON INVESTMENT

When there are cash flows, in addition to modifying the numerator, we need to modify the denominator of the return calculation to account for additional capital invested or withdrawn during the measurement period. We can modify this calculation to account for additional investment or withdrawals; the result is the *Return on Investment* (ROI) formula. ROI is the gain or loss generated by an investment expressed as a percentage of the amount invested, adjusted for contributions and withdrawals:

$$\text{ROI in percent} = \left[\frac{(\text{EMV} + \text{NOF}) - (\text{BMV} + \text{NIF})}{\text{BMV} + \text{NIF}}\right] \times 100 \tag{2.4}$$

where NOF is the Net Outflows and NIF is the Net Inflows.

Exhibit 2.5 shows the calculation of ROI in terms of our example where there was an inflow of $10 during the period.

EXHIBIT 2.5 Return on Investment

	A	B	C	D	E
1	MVB	In Flows	Out Flows	MVE	Return on Investment %
2	100.00	10.00	0.00	130.00	18.18
3		=(((D2+C2)-(A2+B2))/(A2+B2))*100			
4					

The first expression (EMV + NOF) is used in place of the ending market value used in the ROR calculation. We adjust the ending market value for any withdrawals from the fund. Notice that this will increase the numerator amount and the resulting return. Withdrawals are treated as a *benefit* to performance. In the second expression, we are subtracting the amount invested in order to calculate the gain. The inflows are treated as investments, which reduce the gain. Contributions are treated as *costs* to performance.

The amount invested (BMV + NIF) is the ROI denominator. Increasing the BMV by the contributions results in a lower return (since we are dividing the same gain by a larger number).

Is 18.18% the proper return for the period where BMV = 100, EMV = 130, and there was a NIF = 10? Note that there is an implicit assumption that the NIF was available for investing, or at risk, for the complete period. If the additional inflow were made at the beginning of the period, the investor did not have use of the money for the whole period. He would expect a higher fund return to compensate for this than if he did have access to the money over the period. So, returns should take into account the timing of the additional cash flows. If the investment were made sometime during the period, the investor did have use of the capital for some part of the period. For example, if the measurement period were a month and the $10 contribution came midway through the month, the fund had $100 of invested capital for the first half of the month and $110 for the second half. The gain of $20 was made on a smaller invested balance; therefore the return credited should be higher than 18.18%.

While ROI adjusts for fund contributions and withdrawals, it does not adjust for the *timing* of these cash flows. Because of the assumption that contributions were available for the whole period ROI will give the same return no matter when in the period the flows occur. Another drawback of the ROI as a measure of investment performance is that it does not adjust for the *length* of the holding period. The ROI calculation gives the same result whether the gain was earned over a day, a year, or 10 years. For these reasons, we need a measure of return where we consider both the timing of cash flows and the length of the period where the assets were at risk. Both adjustments are derived from time value of money concepts.

COMPOUNDING

Let's say we invested $100 today and ended up with $200 ten years from now. Yet, what if our colleague put the same $100 to work and ended up with $200 at the end of the first year? We both doubled our money, but clearly it would not be correct to credit both situations with the same performance. When we calculate returns, we take into account the time value of money.

Returns can be equated to the interest rates used in the calculation of the future value of a fixed income investment. Unlike returns, however, interest rates may be known ahead of time, so we can project the future value at the beginning of the period. The future value of an investment equals the present value plus the interest and other gains earned over the period:

$$FV = PV \times (1 + R)^N \qquad (2.5)$$

where FV is the value at end of period, PV is the current value of the investment, R is the rate of per period interest, and N is the number of valuation periods.

In return calculations, we calculate this rate R using observations of the beginning and ending market values. To calculate the MVE of an investment during a single period, we multiply the MVB by 1 plus the interest rate:

Ending market value $=$ Beginning market value $\times (1 + $ Interest rate$)$

The difference between the start and end value is the income earned. In a *Simple Interest* scenario, the income earned is not reinvested to earn additional interest in the following periods. For example, if an MVB = $1000 is put to work for four months at an interest rate = 5% per month, we calculate an ending value of $1200:

End value $=$ Beginning value
$$\times [1 + (\text{Rate in percent}/100) \times \# \text{ of time periods invested}]$$

$$1000 \times [1 + (0.05 \times 4)] = 1200$$

We use simple interest calculations if the investor withdraws the income earned at the end of each period. In this example, the total gain over the four months = $200. Divided by the $1000 invested gives a 20% return for the four-month period. This equals the monthly periodic dollar return multiplied by four.

Compounding is the reinvestment of income to earn more income in subsequent periods. If the income and gains are retained within the investment vehicle or *reinvested*, they will accumulate and contribute to the starting balance for each subsequent period's income calculation. Exhibit 2.6 shows that $100 invested at 7% for ten years, assuming yearly compounding, will result in an ending value of $196.72.

To illustrate the compounding process, we can step through the calculations for the first four years:

1. The original investment is $100.
2. $100 × (1 + 0.07) = $107 to invest at the start of the second year.
3. $107 × (1 + 0.07) = $114.49 to invest at the start of the third year.
4. $114.49 × (1 + 0.07) = $122.50 to invest at the start of the fourth year.
5. $122.50 × (1 + 0.07) = $131.08 to invest at the start of the fifth year.

Or $100 × (1 + 0.07)^4 = $131.08. A rule of thumb to use when projecting values when compounding income is that investments at 7% income earned per year double in ten years, *before* the addition of any more principal.

Let's return to the question of evaluating the return earned on two investments with the same dollar gain over different time periods. If we had two investments both earning the same dollar gain of 100 on an investment of 100, but the first fund took ten years to accomplish what the second fund did in one, and we assume that the investment income and gains compounded yearly, we would ascribe an annual return rate of 7.18% to the first and 100% to the second fund as shown:

	A	B	C	D
1	**MVB**	**Periods**	**Return**	**MVE**
2	100	10	7.18%	200.00
3	100	1	100.00%	200.00
4	=RATE(B3,0,-A3,D3,-1)			
5				

EXHIBIT 2.6   Compound Interest

	A	B	C	D	E	F	G	H
1	Year	BMV	Interest Rate	EMV	Principal	Interest	Interest on Interest	% of Value
2	0			100.00	100.00			
3	1	100.00	0.07	107.00	100.00	7.00	0.00	
4	2	107.00	0.07	114.49	100.00	14.00	0.49	0%
5	3	114.49	0.07	122.50	100.00	21.00	1.50	1%
6	4	122.50	0.07	131.08	100.00	28.00	3.08	2%
7	5	131.08	0.07	140.26	100.00	35.00	5.26	4%
8	6	140.26	0.07	150.07	100.00	42.00	8.07	5%
9	7	150.07	0.07	160.58	100.00	49.00	11.58	7%
10	8	160.58	0.07	171.82	100.00	56.00	15.82	9%
11	9	171.82	0.07	183.85	100.00	63.00	20.85	11%
12	10	183.85	0.07	196.72	100.00	70.00	26.72	14%
13								
14		=D11		=B12*(1+C12)		=C12*$B$3*A1	=D12-(E12+F12)	=G12/D12

EXHIBIT 2.7   Interest on Interest

	A	B	C	D	E	F	G	H
1	Year	BMV	Interest Rate	EMV	Principal	Interest	Interest on Interest	% of Value
2	0			100.00	100.00			
3	10	100.00	0.07	196.72	100.00	70.00	26.72	14%
4	20	196.72	0.07	386.97	100.00	140.00	146.97	38%
5	30	386.97	0.07	761.23	100.00	210.00	451.23	59%
6						↑		
7		=D4		=B5*(1+C5)^10		=C5*$B$3*A5	=D5-(E5+F5)	=G5/D5

Standard investments industry performance calculations and presentations assume both reinvestment and compounding. With compound interest we assume the accumulation of gains earned in each period is reinvested in the successive period. Because of the reinvestment assumption, cash withdrawals, investment expenses, taxes, and other factors that impede this compounding process may result in lower realized returns than the return that is actually presented to investors. The reinvestment assumption is not realistic for all investors. For example, any taxable investor investing outside a vehicle that is shielded from taxes, such as a 401(k)-plan account, will have to pay taxes on income distributions from the fund. The taxes reduce the income available for reinvestment in the next period. Given this fact, one of the trends in performance measurement is to incorporate these factors that lower the reinvestment amount into the return calculation.

Factoring in taxes and expenses is important because the power of investing lies in the *compound interest*, the interest on the interest earned in prior periods. Given a 10-year investment earning a 7% return, the interest on interest component comprises 14% of the ending value. Exhibit 2.7 shows that if we invest for 30 years at 7%, the interest on interest will approach 60% of ending value.

When interest earnings are withdrawn after each period, the simple interest calculation is a better measure of the situation. If income is left to earn more income, then the compound interest calculation is the better measure. Compound interest is assumed in almost all investment applications. With interest rates we usually assume that interest is reinvested at the same interest rate for subsequent periods. The difference between working with returns instead of interest rates is that in return calculations, while we also assume that the income is reinvested, we recognize that the periodic returns will fluctuate over time.

While we understand that earning a higher return over the holding period will increase the ending investment value, the frequency of compounding also impacts the ending value. Exhibit 2.8 shows that holding the rate the same; the more frequent the compounding within the period the higher the ending value.

EXHIBIT 2.8   Future Value and Compounding Frequency

	A	B	C	D	E
1	Frequency	MVB	Periods	Return	MVE
2	Yearly	1000.00	1.00	0.07	1070.00
3	Monthly	1000.00	12.00	0.07	1072.29
4	Daily	1000.00	365.25	0.07	1072.50
5	Continuously	1000.00	-	0.07	1072.51
6			=FV(D4/C4,C4,0,B4*-1)		
7				=EXP(D5)*B5	
8					

The inverse is also true; the more frequent the compounding assumption, the lower the return credited for the same pattern of market values.

Interest rates are usually quoted on a yearly or *annual* basis. We can adjust the quoted annual interest rate to account for more frequent compounding:

$$MVE = MVB \times \left[1 + \frac{r_{period} \times m}{m}\right]^{m \times periods} \tag{2.6}$$

where r is the periodic interest rate and m is the times per period that interest is paid or compounds.

For example, if a \$100 investment yielded 3% for 6 months (i.e., MVB = 100 and MVE = 103), the value at the end of a year, assuming semiannual compounding and reinvestment of the interest, is \$106.09:

$$106.09 = 100 \times \left[1 + \frac{0.03 \times 2}{2}\right]^{2 \times 1\ year}$$

As we continue to increase the compounding frequency m, the compounding formula converges on a limit where the returns are *continuously compounded*. Calculation of future value with continuous compounding simplifies the compounding formula to Equation (2.7).

$$MVE = MVB \times e^{r_{period} \times nperiods} \tag{2.7}$$

Where e is the exponential constant 2.71828...

IMPACT OF CASH FLOW TIMING ON RETURN

Given the fact that money has a time value, let's return to a question we considered earlier: What is the proper holding period return to attribute to a fund where the MVB equals $100, we invest an additional $10 during the period, and the MVE equals $130?

No matter when in the period the investment is made, the dollar gain is (130 − 100 − 10 = $20) for the period. The return over the period depends on the timing of the additional investment. The return could be as low as 18.18% or as high as 20%. If the $10 were invested right at the *beginning of the period*, capital employed equals the original investment of $100 plus the additional investment of $10:

$$\left(\frac{130 - 100 - 10}{100 + 10}\right) \times 100 \to \left(\frac{130 - 110}{110}\right) \times 100 \to \left(\frac{20}{110}\right) \times 100 = 18.18\%$$

If the additional investment were right at the *end of the period*, the capital employed during the period is just $100, so the return is 20%:

$$\left(\frac{130 - 100 - 10}{100}\right) \times 100 \to \left(\frac{130 - 110}{100}\right) \times 100 \to \left(\frac{20}{100}\right) \times 100 = 20.00\%$$

Given the same gains, returns are higher when the investment is made at the end of the period. In the second scenario, the additional contribution is not included in the denominator. The same numerator divided by a smaller denominator leads to the higher return. The higher return is justified when the contribution is made at the end of the period because the capital at risk during the period was lower but we earned the same dollar gain.

This example shows that it is important to track the timing of contributions or withdrawals to an investment account in order to accurately calculate returns. We always adjust the numerator for the additional contributions or withdrawals during the period. We either include the full amount of the contribution in the denominator, none of it, or a partial amount, depending on the timing of the cash flow. When the denominator of a return calculation is adjusted for contributions or withdrawals, we call the denominator the *Average Capital Employed*, or the *Average Invested Balance*.

In addition to the consideration of the time value of money, the *market timing* of the investor contributions and withdrawals will affect realized returns. For example, suppose we are investing via a mutual fund and during the month the fund's net asset value (NAV) per share varies between 10.00 and 12.00:

Date	NAV per share
5/31	10.00
6/10	12.00
6/20	10.00
6/30	11.00

The monthly return that will be published for the fund for the month will be (11/10 = 10%). Exhibit 2.9 shows the calculation of holding period returns for all of the possible holding periods within the month.

For the investor in period one who had perfect foresight and withdrew on 6/10 to earn a 20% return, the month was a good one. For the investor who lacked timing skill, the investment at the high on 6/10 and withdrawal at the bottom on 6/20 led to a −16.67% return. This spread of 36.67% represents the return differential due to the timing of the cash flows, which were at the *discretion of the investor*. Actions of the investment manager would have had no impact on this differential return.

Commingled funds have many investors. Some have a buy and hold strategy, some are trading in and out of the fund, and others have a regular program of buying or selling new shares of the fund. In a time when the market moved up, down, and back up, the returns earned by different investors could be quite different depending on the cash flows and return volatility. Although this example would represent an unusually volatile period, the point is that actual returns as experienced by the investor can vary depending on investment timing decisions.

In the Exhibit 2.9, the advertised return for the period would be the 10% return measured from the start of the period to the end. Even though different investors experienced different returns, the investment manager for the mutual fund had no control over these timing decisions; therefore 10% is an accurate representation of manager performance.

EXHIBIT 2.9 Cash Flow Timing and Returns

	A	B	C	D	E
1	Period	Return From	Calculated As	% Return	
2	1	5/31 – 6/10	((12 / 10) – 1) x 100	20.00	
3	2	5/31 – 6/20	((10 / 10) –1) x 100	0.00	Published Return
4	3	5/31 – 6/30	((11 / 10) – 1) x 100	10.00	
5	4	6/10 – 6/20	((10 / 12) –1) x 100	-16.67	
6	5	6/10 – 6/30	((11 / 12) – 1) x100	-8.33	
7	6	6/20 – 6/30	((11 / 10) – 1 x 100	10.00	

EXHIBIT 2.10   Manager 1 Timing Decision

	A	B	C	D
1	**Segment**	**MVB**	**Return**	**MVE**
2	Cash	10	1.00	10.05
3	Equity	100	-10.00	90.00
4	Total	110	-9.05	100.05
5				
6			=((D4/B4)-1)*100	=SUM(D2:D3)

EXHIBIT 2.11   Manager 2 Timing Decision

	A	B	C	D
1	**Segment**	**MVB**	**Return**	**MVE**
2	Cash	0.00	1.00	0.00
3	Equity	110.00	-10.00	99.00
4	Total	110.00	-10.00	99.00
5				
6			=((D4/B4)-1)*100	=SUM(D2:D3)

TIMING OF INVESTMENT MANAGER DECISIONS

We also consider the timing of manager decisions when calculating returns. Consider two managers who start with the same holdings at the beginning of the month valued at $100. Both receive a client contribution of $10. Their strategies differ only in that Manager 1 has a strategy of timing the market, that is buying before anticipated market rallies and selling before anticipated falls. The market moves down 10% during the month.

Manager 1 leaves the contribution in cash. Exhibit 2.10 shows the calculation of his return equal to -9.05%. Exhibit 2.11 shows that Manager 2 invests the contribution in equities at the beginning of the month and experiences a -10.00% return. The 95 basis point (-9.05% - -10%) positive difference in returns is the *differential return*, or *value added*, attributable to Manager 1's timing decision.

SEGREGATING INVESTOR AND MANAGER TIMING DECISIONS

The preceding sections illustrate a performance measurement problem: except in the case where the investor and the manager are the same, decisions made by the investor and the investment manager must be segregated to properly attribute responsibility for returns achieved.

The ideal statistic for measuring the return experienced by the investor would include effects of both:

■ The timing of investor decisions to invest in the fund.
■ The decisions made by the manager to allocate assets and select securities within the portfolio.

The first effect is attributable purely to decisions made by the investor. The second can also be considered to be attributable to the investor because he made the decision to hire the manager. The actual returns experienced by the investor are affected by a combination of the two effects.

Conversely, the ideal statistic for measuring the return produced by the investment managers would consider only their decisions about asset allocation and security selection, as they usually have no control over the timing of external cash flows.

Because of the need to isolate the timing of investor decisions we need two different measures of return. In the next two chapters we discuss the industry standard calculations for measuring:

■ Money-Weighted Returns—the return experienced by the investor.
■ Time-Weighted Returns—the return produced by the manager.

PRECISION OF RETURN CALCULATIONS

Before we move on to address these two types of returns, one important point to make about returns is the degree of precision employed when communicating returns. While we *calculate* returns to whatever precision we can, for the sake of accuracy, we sometimes see returns *presented* to the hundredth and sometimes even more specific decimal precision. Displays of this level of precision may give users of the data a false impression. Investment performance measurement is not an exact science and the numbers are not statistically valid to high levels of precision. Returns are calculated using valuations, which can range in precision from actual market prices in the liquid equity markets to extrapolations from recent sales data for a real estate fund. Performance results can be sensitive to many seemingly unimportant decisions, for example, the time of day used to capture prices or exchange rates. Valuation, record keeping, methodology selection, and data quality matters also affect the accuracy of performance calculations.

In practice we report returns without a confidence interval or estimate of potential measurement error. But it is important to keep in mind the idea of a range around the reported return in situations where we are comparing returns. It is possible that the returns were calculated with a different source of security valuations, different degrees of precision with regard to the treatment of investor cash flows, and other differences. This "noise" factor around the returns is also important when evaluating comparative performance in situations where active return differentials are small, such as for many fixed income strategies. We should keep in mind the fact that returns are really estimates of performance.

CHAPTER 3

Money-Weighted Return

The *Money-Weighted Return* (MWR), or *Dollar-Weighted Return*, is used when we need to measure the performance as experienced by the investor. MWR is a performance statistic reflecting how much money was earned during the measurement period. This amount is influenced by the timing of decisions to contribute to or withdraw money from a fund, as well as the decisions made by the manager of the fund. The MWR commingles the effects on return of the efforts of both the manager and the investor. Money-Weighted Returns are contrasted with statistics used to measure manager performance—*Time-Weighted Returns* (TWR)—which are discussed in Chapter 4.

MONEY-WEIGHTED RETURN

MWR is the return an investor actually experiences when making an investment. It reconciles the beginning market value and additional cash flows into the portfolio to the ending market value. The timing and size of the cash flows in between have an impact on the ending market value:

Transaction	Before Asset Value	Effect on Performance
Contribute	Goes Up	Positive
Contribute	Goes Down	Negative
Withdraw	Goes Up	Negative
Withdraw	Goes Down	Positive

EXHIBIT 3.1   Weighting Cash Flows

	A	B	C	D
1	Date	Time into Total Period	Months Invested	Period Weight
2	12/31	0	12	1.00
3	1/31	1	11	0.92
4	2/28	2	10	0.83
5				▲
6			=12-B4	=C4/12

To reflect these transactions, the MWR takes into account not only the amount of the flows but also the timing of the cash flows. Different investors in a portfolio will invest different amounts and make their investments on different dates. Because of the differences in cash flow timing and magnitude, it is not appropriate to compare an MWR calculated for different investors.

When there are no cash flows the MWR calculation is the same as the ROI calculation and there is no need for a cash flow adjustment.

$$\text{MWR no cash flows} = \left(\frac{\text{Gain or Loss}}{\text{Investment made}} \right) \times 100$$

If there is a cash flow, we need to take into account the amount and the timing of the flow. To account for the timing of the flow, we calculate a weighting adjustment. Exhibit 3.1 shows that if we are calculating an MWR for a 1-year period and there are two cash flows, the first at the end of January and the second at the end of February, the flows will be weighted by 0.92 for the January month end flow (the flow will be available to be invested for 92% of the year) and 0.83 for the February month end flow (the flow will be available to be invested for 83% of the year).

INTERNAL RATE OF RETURN

Suppose we invest $100 at the beginning of the year and end up with $140 at the end of the year. We make cash flows of $10 each at the end of January and February. What is the appropriate return for this situation?

The MWR that we are looking for will be the value that solves this equation:

$$100 \times (1 + MWR) + $$
$$10 \times (1 + MWR)^{0.92} + $$
$$10 \times (1 + MWR)^{0.83} = 140$$

The return that causes the beginning value and intermediate cash flows to grow to the ending value is the *Internal Rate of Return* or *IRR*. The return is the value that solves for IRR in the equation:

$$MVE = MVB \times (1 + IRR) + CF_1 \times (1 + IRR)^1 \ldots CF_N \times (1 + IRR)^N \quad (3.1)$$

where CF is the amount of the cash flow in or out of the portfolio and N is the percentage of the period that the CF was available for investment, or period weight.

The IRR is an MWR. It is approximately equal to a weighted average of the returns for each subperiod within the total period measured, where the weights are a product of the length of the subperiod and the amount of money at work during the subperiod, which is equal to the MVB plus the net cash flows for the subperiod. The IRR is the rate of return implied by the growth in the observed market values of the fund, as well as additional cash flows. It explains the growth in assets over the time period being measured. The IRR is a constant rate over the measurement period; this means that we assume that each dollar invested grows at the same rate, no matter when it was invested.

The inputs to the calculation are simply the beginning and ending market values, the cash flows into or out of the portfolio, and the date that these cash flows occurred. Notice that the problem of calculating an IRR is the reverse of that for calculating the future value of an investment. Here, the ending value is known and the return is unknown. Unlike the formula we used to create future value given a return, we cannot directly calculate the return given the beginning and ending values. Because we cannot use algebra to rearrange the terms of the equation to derive the solution, the IRR is calculated using a trial and error process—an initial guess is made and then we iteratively try successive values until the beginning market value equals the sum of the discounted cash flows plus the ending market value. Techniques have been developed to perform the iteration efficiently and converge on a solution. Exhibit 3.2 shows the calculation of the IRR using the Microsoft Excel solver.

EXHIBIT 3.2 Internal Rate of Return

	A	B	C	D	E	F
1	Date	Months Invested	Period Weight	Value	Future Value of Flow	
2	Dec-31-2000	12	1.00	100	117.05	=D2*((1+E8)^C2)
3	Jan-31-2001	11	0.92	10	11.55	=D3*((1+E8)^C3)
4	Feb-28-2001	10	0.83	10	11.40	=D4*((1+E8)^C4)
5	Dec-31-2001			140	140.00	=SUM(E2:E4)
6						
7		IRR calculated using solver		Difference:	0.00	=D5-E5
8				IRR:	0.1705	
9				Percent Return:	17.05	=E8*100

The IRR that resolves the flows used in Exhibit 3.2 is 17.05%. The steps taken to set up the spreadsheet were:

1. Inserted rows 2–5, which represent the beginning market value of 100, the two cash flows of 10, and the ending market value of 140.
2. Added cell E5, which is the sum of the future value of the cash flows.
3. Added cell E7, which is set as the difference between the ending market value and the sum of the future values.
4. Executed the Excel solver utility, with parameters set to change the value in cell E8 until the difference value in cell E7 was 0.

In terms of our original example:

$$100 \times (1 + 0.1705) +$$
$$10 \times (1 + 0.1705)^{0.92} +$$
$$10 \times (1 + 0.1705)^{0.83} = 140$$

In this example, each cash flow is compounded at 17.05% for the whole portion of the year invested; this illustrates the assumption made by using the IRR that the rate of return is constant within the period.

We can calculate an IRR for single periods of less than a year. The period weight used for each of the cash flows is the percentage of the total period under consideration. For example, a cash flow on the 5th of a 30-day month would be weighted at $[(30 - 5)/30] = 0.8333$ of the month.

Exhibit 3.3 shows the calculation of the monthly IRR where MVB = 1000 on 12/31, MVE = 1200 on 1/31, and we have two cash flows, 400 into the portfolio on 1/10, and 100 out of the portfolio on 1/20.

If the cash flows are out of the portfolio, the cash flow adjustment is negative. A time of day assumption must also be taken into account in the IRR calculation; in this example we are using a beginning of day assumption. If the cash flow out of the portfolio took place at the beginning of day on the 20th, the cash was not available for investment for 12 full days in the month. Solving for the IRR in this situation we get a −8.02% return for the month.

EXHIBIT 3.3 IRR for Periods Less than a Year

	A	B	C	D	E	F
1	Date	Days Invested	Period Weight	Value	Future Value of Flow	
2	31-Dec-2000	31	1.00	1000	919.85	=D2*((1+E8)^C2)
3	10-Jan-2001	22	0.71	400	376.97	=D3*((1+E8)^C3)
4	20-Jan-2001	12	0.39	-100	-96.82	=D4*((1+E8)^C4)
5	31-Jan-2001			1200	1200.00	=SUM(E2:E4)
6						
7				Difference:	0.00	=D5-E5
8				IRR:	-0.0802	
9				Percent Return:	-8.02	=E8*100

IRR is an MWR: it takes into account both the timing and the size of cash flows into the portfolio. It is an appropriate measure of the performance of the investment as experienced by the investor. But there are some drawbacks to using the IRR formula. The main problem with the IRR formula is that it cannot be calculated directly and needs to be solved via iteration. This was a problem when computer CPU time was very expensive and needed to be conserved. The need to save computing time led to the development of various IRR estimation techniques that did not require the iterative algorithm. One of these return calculation methods, the Modified Dietz method, is still the most common way of calculating periodic investment returns.

MODIFIED DIETZ RETURN

The Modified Dietz return is a simple interest estimate of the MWR. The formula is named for its developer, Peter Dietz, who was associated with the Frank Russell pension consulting company, as well as being the author of one of the first books on the subject of performance measurement.[1] The Modified Dietz formula provides a computational advantage over the IRR in that it is a closed form solution, it does not require iterative trial and error to solve for the return. The Modified Dietz calculation is the same as the ROI calculation, except the cash flows used to calculate the invested balance in the denominator are adjusted to reflect the time they have been available for investment in the portfolio:

$$\text{Modified Dietz return} = \left(\frac{\text{MVE} - \text{MVB} - \text{CF}}{\text{MVB} + \text{Adjusted net cash flows}} \right) \times 100 \quad (3.2)$$

Where CF is the net amount of the cash flows.

The cash flows are adjusted to reflect the percentage of time they were available to the manager of the portfolio. The adjusted cash flows are calculated as:

$$\begin{aligned} &\text{Adjusted net cash flows} \\ &= \text{Sum}(\text{CF}_i \times \text{Cash flow adjustment factor}) \end{aligned} \quad (3.3)$$

---

[1] Peter Dietz, *Pension Funds: Measuring Investment Performance* (New York: The Free Press, 1966).

EXHIBIT 3.4   Modified Dietz Return

	A	B	C	D
1	Date	Days Invested	Day Weight	Value
2	31-Mar-2001	30	1.00	100
3	20-Apr-2001	10	0.33	10
4	30-Apr-2001			120
5				
6	Dollar Value Added:		10	=D4-D2-D3
7	Average Invested Balance:		103.33	=D2+(C3*D3)
8				
9	Modified Dietz Return:		9.68	=(C6/C7)*100

Where CF_i are the the individual cash flows. Similar to the IRR, in the Modified Dietz calculation, an adjustment to the cash flows is made by weighting the flows by the number of days they were available for investment during the period. (The original Dietz method, not currently used in practice, makes the assumption that all cash flows occurred midway through the period.)

$$\text{Cash flow adjustment factor} = \left(\frac{\text{Days in the period} - \text{Day of the flow}}{\text{Days in the period}} \right) \qquad (3.4)$$

For example, Exhibit 3.4 shows the calculation of a Modified Dietz return for this situation:

Begin market value + Accrued income	MVB	100
End market value + Accrued income	MVE	120
Sum (Client contribution/withdrawal)	CF	10 on the 20th of a 30-day month

To calculate the Modified Dietz return, first we calculate the adjustment factor:

$$\frac{30 - 20}{30} = 0.33$$

Then we adjust the cash flow by multiplying the amount of the cash flow by the adjustment factor:

$$0.33 \times \$10 = \$3.33$$

We then add the modified flow to the denominator to calculate the Modified Dietz return:

$$9.68\% = \left(\frac{120 - 100 - 10}{100 + 3.33}\right) \times 100$$

Rates computed with either the exact IRR or the Modified Dietz method are Money-Weighted Returns. MWR results *are* effected by the timing and magnitude of the cash flows during the period.

CHAPTER 4

Time-Weighted Return

One reason to calculate returns is to help rate the performance of the investment manager. Many times a tremendous dispersion in returns exists between the best and worst performing managers investing within a given asset class and similar strategy. Because returns compound over time, there is a considerable advantage to the investor in selecting the manager who demonstrates more skill (or luck?) by delivering higher returns than his peers. As we saw in Chapter 2, investors can experience different returns while investing in the same fund depending on the timing and magnitude of their cash flows into and out of the portfolio. The IRR and Modified Dietz returns are not appropriate measures of manager return because they are impacted by these cash flows. They are measures of the fund performance, but do not provide a good measure of the performance of the fund's manager.

Here we shift our attention to measuring the return earned by the manager. Since the manager has no control over the timing and amount of investor flows, we need a performance measure that negates the effect of these cash flows. Instead, we want to measure the performance of capital committed to the manager for the whole period, as this is the measure of manager performance. To measure manager performance on this basis, we need to adjust the return calculation to eliminate the effect of cash flows.

TIME-WEIGHTED RETURN

A rate of return is the percentage change in the value of an asset over a given period of time. Total returns are calculated by dividing the capital gain/loss and income earned by the value of the investment at the beginning of the period. The *Time-Weighted Return* (TWR) is a form of total return that measures the performance of a dollar invested in the fund for the complete measurement period. The TWR eliminates the timing effect that external portfolio cash flows have on performance, leaving only the effects of the market and manager decisions. TWRs are used to make legitimate comparisons of manager performance, both to other managers with a similar style and to the market. To calculate a time-weighted return, we break the measurement period into shorter subperiods, calculate the returns for the subperiods, and then compound them together to derive the TWR for the period. The subperiod boundaries are determined by the dates of each cash flow.

Taking these steps we can calculate a TWR:

1. Start with the market value at the beginning of the period.
2. Move forward through time toward the end of the period.
3. Note the value of the portfolio the instant before a cash flow into or out of the portfolio.
4. At each valuation date, calculate a *subperiod return*, which is the return for the subperiod since the last cash flow.
5. Use the market value at the end of the period to calculate the subperiod return for the last period.
6. Compute the TWR, equal to the product of (1 + the subperiod returns).

The last step is called *geometric linking*, or *chain linking* of the returns. Chain linking has the same function as compounding in the future value calculation: each subperiod ending value including income earned is invested into the next period's return. Chain linking is used instead of the future value formula to employ the compounding because the periodic returns are usually different for each subperiod:

$$\text{Time-weighted return} = [(1 + R_1) \times (1 + R_2) \times \ldots (1 + R_N) - 1] \times 100 \qquad (4.1)$$

where R_N are the subperiod returns.

We often use the word *geometric* when we are referring to the compounding process. Geometric mathematical operations relate to proportions, whereas *arithmetic* operations refer to differences. We use multiplication when we work with proportions and addition when we work with differences. To illustrate, in an arithmetic sequence 3, 6, 9, 12 we add the fixed number 3 to derive the next result. In a geometric sequence we multiply to get 3, 9, 27, 81. Fortunately for us, investing is a geometric process!

The TWR assumes compounding and reinvestment of gains and income earned in prior subperiods. The expression (1 + the subperiod decimal return) is called a *wealth relative, return relative*, or *growth rate*.

The growth rate represents the increase in capital over the subperiod, which is the ratio of the ending market value to the beginning market value. For example, if a portfolio is worth $100 at the beginning of the subperiod, and $105 at the end of the subperiod before the next cash flow, the subperiod return is 5% and the growth rate for the subperiod equals 1.05. The TWR requires as inputs the date and value of each cash flow into and out of the portfolio and the values of the fund at the beginning and end of each subperiod bracketed by the cash flow dates.

The next three sections illustrate the steps to calculate a TWR where we want to evaluate the performance of an investment manager over a month where the fund the fund values were:

Date	End of Day Valuation
5/31	1000
6/9	1100
6/19	1200
6/30	1200

And there were two cash flows during the month:

Date	Cash Flow
6/10	200
6/20	−100

1. Divide into Subperiods Based on Cash Flow Dates

The first step in the TWR calculation is to divide the period we are interested in into subperiods, where the subperiods are separated by the cash flow dates. The next step is to note the value of the portfolio the instant before the cash flow. If we are working with a beginning of day assumption for the timing of the cash flows, we use the valuation for the night prior to the date of the cash flow into or out of the portfolio:

Date	Begin of Day Valuation	Cash Flow	End of Day Valuation
5/31			1000
6/9			1100
6/10	1100	200	
6/19			1200
6/20	1200	−100	
6/30	1200		1200

In this case, there are two cash flows and three subperiods, from:

1. 5/31 to the end of day 6/9
2. 6/10 to the end of day 6/19
3. 6/20 to the end of day 6/30

Note that there are (1 + the number of cash flow dates) subperiods.

2. Calculate Subperiod Returns

Single period returns are calculated for each subperiod. The assumption regarding the time of day that cash flows are made available to the manager controls the treatment of the cash flow adjustments in the formula. Here we assume that cash flows occur at the beginning of the day, so we adjust the market value for the beginning of the day by the cash flow in order to form the denominator of the return calculation. Cash flows into the portfolio are added to the denominator, cash flows out of the portfolio are subtracted. If there is more than one cash flow during the day we net the flows together in order to calculate the cash flow adjustment:

$$\text{Subperiod return (start of day flow assumed)} = \frac{\text{MVE}}{\text{MVB} + \text{Net cash inflows}} \qquad (4.2)$$

The numerator in the calculation is the ending market value for the subperiod. The denominator is the beginning market value adjusted for the cash flow in or out of the portfolio. This cash flow adjustment is required to adjust the valuation just prior to the cash flow for the amount of the flow. The purpose of the *cash flow adjustment* is to negate the effect of the contributions/withdrawals from the return calculation.

The subperiod returns calculated in terms of our example are 10%, −7.69%, and 9.09%. Exhibit 4.1 summarizes the calculation of the subperiod returns.

EXHIBIT 4.1   Subperiod Returns

	A	B	C	D	E	F	G
1	Sub Period	Return From	BMV	CF	EMV	Percent Return	Growth Rate
2	1	5/31 – 6/10	1000	0	1100	10.00	1.10
3	2	6/10 – 6/20	1100	200	1200	-7.69	0.92
4	3	6/20 – 6/30	1200	-100	1200	9.09	1.09
5				=((E4/(C4 + D4))-1)*100		=1+(F4/100)	
6							

EXHIBIT 4.2   Time-Weighted Return

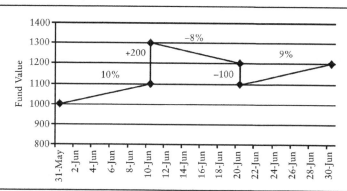

3. Link the Subperiod Returns

The percentage return for the month is calculated by chain linking the subperiod returns:

$$[(1 + 0.10) \times (1 + (-0.0769)) \times (1 + 0.0909) - 1] \times 100 = 10.77\%$$

By calculating returns in this manner, we have completely eliminated the impact of cash flows into or out of the portfolio. TWR is used in performance measurement applications where we are interested in isolating just the decisions of the portfolio manager. These applications include the comparison of manager performance to benchmarks. Exhibit 4.2 shows how the TWR eliminates the effect of cash flows from the example return calculation.

There are some exceptions to the general rule that TWR is the appropriate measure of investment manager performance. In some situations, the portfolio manager does have discretion over the timing of cash flows.

The development of the TWR was an important milestone in investment analysis. A study commissioned in 1968 by the Bank Administration Institute (BAI), recommended the TWR as the appropriate method of calculating a return for the purpose of manager evaluation and comparison.[1] The BAI study, authored by leading academics, is the most influential document developed in the field of investment performance measurement. Although some aspects are dated, such as certain techniques for dealing with portfolios measured infrequently, the recommendations of

---

[1] Bank Administration Institute, *Measuring the Investment Performance of Pension Funds for the Purpose of Inter-Fund Comparison*, Bank Administration Institute, Park Ridge, Illinois 1968.

the BAI study remain the template for the measurement of portfolio performance.

ESTIMATING THE TIME-WEIGHTED RETURN

We have seen how the TWR method best calculates the returns used to evaluate the performance of investment managers. In fact, to enhance the comparability of returns earned by different investment managers, AIMR standards require the use of a TWR. There is, however, a potentially significant hurdle to implementing this method: the time-weighted return methodology requires valuation of the portfolio before each cash flow and, unfortunately, these periodic valuations are not always available. There are two reasons for this. There is a cost to obtaining market prices for all of the securities held by a portfolio. The process of performing a valuation, including bank reconciliation of cash and positions, and the determination of income entitlement and other procedures, imposes costs that many long term investors, such as pension plans, might not want to bear any more frequently than they have to. Many investment vehicles, such as institutional separate accounts, are currently valued only on a monthly frequency, but the investor may deposit or withdraw from the account at any time during the month. Industry trends are to perform valuations more frequently and daily valuation is becoming increasingly common. AIMR has suggested that they will likely require valuation before any cash flow for returns calculated for the purposes of marketing presentations by 2010. This effectively means daily valuation for many cases. Until daily valuation is universally available, approximations of the true TWR are required whenever there is a cash flow but no valuation available for the preceding period.

When we are interested in evaluating manager performance and a valuation is not available to net out the effect of each cash flow, we can make an estimate of the TWR. Various methods have been used to make the estimate. For example, in one method the return on a corresponding market index was used to approximate the return of the fund over the period. This and other methods are no longer used in practice. The most common method of approximating a TWR is the linked MWR approach. The procedure for estimating the true TWR using the *Linked MWR Method* is to:

1. Calculate the MWR for each subperiod between valuation dates. We usually do this by calculating a monthly IRR or Modified Dietz return, assuming that the portfolio is valued at each month's end.

EXHIBIT 4.3   TWR Measurement Error

	A	B	C	D	E	F	G	H	I
1	Case	MVB	MV 15th	CF 15th	MVE	TWR	MWR (Dietz)	% Difference	Diff. as % TWR
2	1	100	102	0	105	5.00	5.00	0.00	0%
3	2	100	98	0	106	6.00	6.00	0.00	0%
4	3	100	90	0	110	10.00	10.00	0.00	0%
5	4	100	102	4	110	5.85	5.88	-0.03	1%
6	5	100	98	4	112	7.61	7.84	-0.24	3%
7	6	100	90	4	114	9.15	9.80	-0.65	7%
8	7	100	102	15	125	8.97	9.30	-0.33	4%
9	8	100	98	15	128	11.01	12.09	-1.08	10%
10	9	100	90	15	130	11.43	13.95	-2.52	22%
11			=(((C10/B10)*(E10/(C10+D10)))-1)*100					=((E10-B10-D10)/(B10+(0.5*D10)))*100	

2. Compound the subperiod MWRs over longer periods using the same chain linking method we used to link subperiod returns into a true TWR.

When we calculate the TWR in this way, we are assuming the rate of return was constant over the subperiod, instead of calculating the actual return earned. This linked MWR estimate of TWR provides a reliable approximation of the TWR in situations where the cash flows are small relative to the portfolio size and there is not a large amount of return volatility in the period. If the cash flows are large and/or there is large volatility within the period, the MWR estimate of TWR is inaccurate.

It is important to note that the linked MWR is an *estimate* of the TWR over the longer period, because even though the cash flows are weighted within the subperiod they will affect the resulting returns. The linking process does not in any way average or remove the effect of the cash flows from the cumulative return calculation as in a true TWR. In some situations, the TWR calculated using the linked MWR estimation method could be closer to the MWR than the true TWR.

We can analyze the measurement error using combinations of the cash flow size as a percentage of the beginning balance and the volatility of the investment during the period. For example, suppose we have a portfolio where the valuation is performed only on a monthly basis but cash flows can occur during the month. We can calculate the MWR using the Modified Dietz method and use it as the estimated TWR for the month in a long-term return calculation. Exhibit 4.3 illustrates the error embedded in the MWR estimate with combinations of cash flow size and volatility.

Here we assume that the cash flows occur half way into the month. Notice that the MWR becomes a progressively worse approximation of TWR as we increase the cash flows as a percentage of beginning market value and the relative changes in market value over the period. But the linked MWR estimate of the TWR does provide a reasonable approximation of the exact TWR for many cases.

ELIMINATING DISTORTION CAUSED BY LARGE CASH FLOWS

An expedient solution to calculating an estimated TWR using the MWR and removing the error associated with large cash flows is to calculate a special valuation when there are large cash flows and to calculate subperiod returns for the periods flanking the large cash flow date. To do this, analysts monitor the portfolio for cash flows and identify situations where the MWR is being materially influenced by the cash flows. This is usually done using some threshold net transaction value, such as 10% of the beginning of period portfolio value. This is sometimes called the *Stop the Clock* method of calculating subperiod returns. A special valuation is used for the period ending just before the cash flow. The subperiod returns are linked together as in the TWR calculation in order to calculate the periodic return. If there are additional cash flows in between the subperiods demarcated by large cash flows, they are day weighted using either the IRR or Modified Dietz method.

Exhibit 4.4 shows how we can approximate the true TWR by calculating two subperiod Modified Dietz returns and then linking them to form the monthly return given a portfolio with this pattern of valuations and cash flows:

Date	End of Day Valuation
2/28	1000
3/9	1050
3/19	1500
3/31	1800
3/10	300
3/20	50

EXHIBIT 4.4　Linked MWR Estimate of TWR

	A	B	C	D	E	F	G	H	I
1	Date	MVB	Cash Flow	Cash Flow % of MVB	MVE	Subperiod Percent TWR	Subperiod Growth Rate	Dietz Day Weighted Flows	Stop the clock Weighted Flows
2	2/28				1000				
3	3/9		=C4/E2		1050				
4	3/10	1050	300	30%	1350	5.00	1.05	212.90	=(12/22)*C6
5	3/19				1500				
6	3/20	1500	50	4%	1550	11.11	1.11	19.35	27.27
7	3/31		=C6/(B4+C4)		1800	16.13	1.16		=(12/31)*C6
8								232.26	
9		True TWR:	35.48	=(PRODUCT(G3:G8)-1)*100					
10		Modified Dietz Return:	36.52	=((E7-E2-C4-C6)/(E2+H8))*100					
11		Dietz Return 2/28 - 3/9:	5.00	=((E3-E2)/(E2))*100					
12		Dietz Return 3/9 - 3/31:	29.04	=((E7-E4-C6)/(E4+I6))*100					
13		Stop the Clock Dietz Return:	35.50	=((1+C11/100)*(1+C12/100)-1)*100					

The true TWR in this situation is 35.48% for the month. The stop the clock version of the Modified Dietz return of 35.50% is a better approximation of the TWR than the 36.52% unmodified Modified Dietz calculation. If the valuations were actually available before each of the cash flows we would use the TWR formula and not an estimation method. The MWR approximation methods are used only when we do not have portfolio valuations available to calculate a true TWR.

COMPARING THE TWR AND THE MWR

Now that we have discussed the two types of returns used to measure portfolio return, it is useful to contrast their meaning and interpretation. Exhibit 4.5 compares the TWR and MWR.

EXHIBIT 4.5   Properties of the Time- and Dollar-Weighted Return

	Money-Weighted Returns	Time-Weighted Returns
Measures	The average growth rate of all dollars invested over the period	The growth rate of a single dollar invested over the period
Usage in analyzing investment results	Appropriate measure of investor or fund performance Appropriate for determining whether assets can fund obligations	Appropriate for measuring performance of vehicle or manager Appropriate for market comparison Appropriate for comparing managers
Effect of external cash flows	Reflects both the timing and amount of dollars at work over the period	Eliminates the effect of both timing and amount of money at work
Statistic represents	The return that reconciles MVB, CF, and MVE	The return of $1 invested in the portfolio from begin to end
Ordering of investment pattern	Does matter	Does not matter
Calculation drawbacks	Iteration required for IRR calculation	Valuation is required before each flow

CHAPTER 5

Multiperiod Return

The returns we have calculated so far are single period returns. While these are useful, we are usually interested in measuring performance over time periods longer than a day or month, which are the most common valuation frequencies. We can calculate single-period returns across valuation dates by compounding the single period returns into cumulative returns. In addition, returns calculated for multiple periods often are presented as an average of the single period returns over the period, usually on an annual average basis. This chapter deals with the compounding and averaging aspects of multiperiod return calculation.

CUMULATIVE RETURN

We have already seen the compounding process at work when we took the subperiod returns calculated using the TWR method and chain linked them together to create the TWR. When we link more than one return in order to derive a longer period return we are calculating a *Cumulative Return*. Cumulative returns can be created for any historical time period appropriate for performance analysis. Some examples of cumulative return periods include month-to-date, year-to-date, first quarter of the year, 1-year, 3-year, since-account-inception, and so on.

To compound the periodic returns, we first take each return and convert it into a growth rate, where the growth rate equals (1 + the decimal return). Then we multiply the growth rates together to determine the cumulative return.

$$
\begin{aligned}
&\text{Cumulative return} \\
&= [(\text{Growth rate}_1) \times (\text{Growth rate}_2)\ldots - 1] \times 100
\end{aligned} \tag{5.1}
$$

EXHIBIT 5.1   Cumulative Returns

	A	B	C	D	E
1				**Growth Rates**	
2	**Year**	**Return**	**Single Period**	**Compounded**	**Cumulative Return**
3	1	0.09	1.09	1.090	9.000
4	2	0.06	1.06	1.155	15.540
5	3	-0.02	0.98	1.132	13.229
6	4	0.08	1.08	1.223	22.288
7	5	-0.04	0.96	1.174	17.396
8				=PRODUCT(C3:C7)	=(D7-1)*100

EXHIBIT 5.2   Returns Using Growth Rates

	A	B	C	D	E
1	**Year**	**Compound Growth Rate**	**Period**	**Percent Periodic Return**	
2	0	1.00000	Y0 to Y1	9.00	=((B3/B2)-1)*100
3	1	1.09000	Y0 to Y3	13.23	=((B5/B2)-1)*100
4	2	1.15540	Y1 to Y4	12.19	=((B6/B3)-1)*100
5	3	1.13229	Y2 to Y4	5.84	=((B6/B4)-1)*100
6	4	1.22288	Y2 to Y5	1.61	=((B7/B4)-1)*100
7	5	1.17396	Y2 to Y5	3.68	=((B7/B5)-1)*100

Exhibit 5.1 shows the calculation of a cumulative 5-year return given a series of yearly returns equal to 9%, 6%, –2%, 8%, and –4%. The cumulative 5-year return is equal to 17.396%.

Growth rates compounded over multiple periods are called *cumulative growth factors*. These growth factors are useful in order to calculate the cumulative return over multiple periods without needing to know the intermediate returns or growth rates.

Given the beginning value of an investment, we can calculate the ending market value by multiplying it by the cumulative growth factor. For example, $100 invested into a fund with a compound 5-year return of 17.40% will result in an ending value of $117.40:

$$100 \times (1.174) = 117.40$$

Growth rates also can be used to derive the return between any two dates:

$$\left[\left(\frac{\text{End period growth rate}}{\text{Begin period growth rate}} \right) - 1 \right] \times 100 \tag{5.2}$$

Exhibit 5.2 shows the calculation of returns over each of the possible holding periods, given the growth rates from Exhibit 5.1.

We calculate cumulative returns when we are interested in the performance of investments over long-term time periods. Note that cumulative returns incorporate the assumption that investment gains are reinvested into the portfolio and compounded over time. The appreciation at the end of each period, as measured by the return, is treated as if it were income that is reinvested in the portfolio in the next period.

COMPRESSING PERIODS

Single period returns are usually calculated on a daily or monthly periodic frequency. The single period returns can be compressed into long-term returns by compounding. For example, the daily returns calculated over the course of a month can be compressed into a monthly return. Compounding 12 monthly returns will give the same result as if the daily returns were compounded over a year. In a similar fashion, monthly returns can be compressed into yearly returns for purposes of calculating multiyear returns, etc. In the previous example, we used five yearly frequency returns to derive the 5-year cumulative return. If the yearly returns were calculated using a daily frequency return we could have chain linked the approximately 1250 (250 trading days × 5 years) returns and derived the same result. It is sometimes easier to work with the compressed monthly, quarterly, or yearly returns even if they were originally calculated on a daily basis.

ARITHMETIC MEAN RETURN

In evaluating investment performance we are sometimes interested in comparing average, or mean, investment returns. Average returns can be used to contrast the performance of different investment managers or funds over time. There are two methods of calculating the average of a series of returns: the arithmetic and geometric methods.

As a measure of the average return, a mean return can be calculated by taking the sum of the periodic returns and dividing it by the number of returns:

$$\text{Arithmetic mean return} = \frac{\text{Sum(Periodic returns)}}{\text{Count of returns}} \tag{5.3}$$

The periodicity of the returns must be the same for each of the returns, i.e., all of the returns must be daily, monthly, or yearly frequency. The arithmetic mean return is usually used in historical portfolio risk measurement, covered in Part II. But the arithmetic mean return cannot be used in all applications. For example, we may want to use an average yearly return to project the future value of an investment. One problem with using arithmetic mean returns is that they do not take into account the compounding of returns over time.[1] For example, if we have two yearly returns:

Year	Return
1	10%
2	20%

The arithmetic mean return is 15% [(20 + 10)/2]. The compound 2-year return is 32%:

$$[(1.10) \times (1.20) - 1] \times 100 = 32.00\%$$

If we take the arithmetic mean return and plug it into the compounding formula we will get a different result than we did using the actual periodic returns:

$$[(1.15) \times (1.15) - 1] \times 100 = 32.25\%$$

Use of the arithmetic mean return to reconcile the beginning to ending investment value would overstate the ending value. The average return we need to use for this application must be lower than the arithmetic mean return in order to account for the compounding process between periods.

GEOMETRIC MEAN RETURN

When we multiply the average yearly return by the total number of years the result will not equal the compounded return because it does not take into account the interest earned on interest. In the previous example, the 20% return in the second year earned on the first year's 10% return is not accounted for by the arithmetic average. To account for the interest on interest in the calculation, instead of taking the arithmetic mean return we can calculate the geometric mean return. The

---

[1] For more on the use of the arithmetic and geometric mean see Mahamood Hassan, "Arithmetic Mean and Geometric Mean of Past Returns: What Information do These Statistics Reveal?" *Journal of Investing*, Fall 1995.

Geometric Mean Return is the *n*th root of the compound return, where *n* = the number of periods used to calculate the cumulative return. Taking this root is the inverse of multiplying or compounding the returns.

$$\text{Geometric mean return} = (\sqrt[N]{(1 + \text{Cumulative return})} - 1) \times 100 \quad (5.4)$$

Exhibit 5.3 shows that the calculation of the geometric average yearly return derived from a two-year compound return of 32% equals 14.89%.

In Excel, to take the *n*th root, we raise the compound growth rate to the (1/n) power.

$$(\sqrt[2]{1.32} - 1) \times 100 \rightarrow (1.1489 - 1) \times 100 = 14.89\%$$

Inserting the geometric mean return into the compound growth formula will yield the compound return for the period:

$$\text{Compound return} = \{[1 + (\text{Geometric mean return}/100)]^N - 1\} \times 100$$

Taking the geometric mean return of 14.89%, we can derive the 32% compound return for two months:

$$\{[1 + (14.89/100)]^2 - 1\} \times 100 \rightarrow [(1.1489)^2 - 1] \times 100 \rightarrow$$
$$(1.32 - 1) \times 100 \rightarrow 32\%$$

or

$$[(1.1489 \times 1.1489) - 1] \times 100 = 32\%$$

Exhibit 5.4 shows that by using geometric mean return we can compound it for the same number of periods used to calculate the cumulative return and reach the same result as if we had used each of the actual periodic returns.

EXHIBIT 5.3   Geometric Mean Return

	A	B	C	D	E
1				Growth Rates	
2	Year	Return	Single Period	Compounded	Cumulative %
3	1	0.10	1.10	1.10	
4	2	0.20	1.20	1.32	32.00
5		=PRODUCT(C3:C4)			
6			Arithmetic yearly average:	15.00	
7			Geometric yearly average:	14.89	
8			=((D4^(1/2))-1)*100		
9					

EXHIBIT 5.4   Using the Geometric Average Return

	A	B	C	D
1	Year	Actual Return	Geometric Average Return	
2	1	15.00	5.342	=(((1+(B6/100))^(1/3))-1)*100
3	2	7.00	5.342	=C2
4	3	-5.00	5.342	→ =C2
5				
6	Year 1-3 in %	16.898	16.898	=((1+C2/100)*(1+C3/100)*(1+C4/100)-1)*100
7		↖ =((1+B2/100)*(1+B3/100)*(1+B4/100)-1)*100		
8				

EXHIBIT 5.5   Averaging Using Log Returns

	A	B	C	D	E
1	Using Discrete Returns				
2	Year		Return	Growth Rate	
3	1		15.000	1.150	
4	2		7.000	1.070	
5	3		-5.000	0.950	
6		Geometric Average:	5.342	→ =(PRODUCT(D3:D5)^(1/3)-1)*100	
7					
8	Using Log Returns				
9	Year	Return	Growth Rate	LN(Growth Rate)	
10	1	15.000	1.150	0.140	
11	2	7.000	1.070	0.068	
12	3	-5.000	0.950	-0.051	=LN(C12)
13			Average:	0.0520	=AVERAGE(D10:D12)
14			$e^{average}$:	1.0534	→ =EXP(D13)
15			Geometric Average:	5.342	=(D14-1)*100

While the arithmetic mean return can be added to derive the arithmetic sum of the fund returns over a period, the geometric mean growth rates can be multiplied to derive the compound multiperiod return. Because geometric mean returns are meant to be compounded, to reflect the growth in the asset over time, they will always be less than or equal to the arithmetic mean return. The geometric mean will only equal the arithmetic mean if growth has been constant over the period.

Using Continuous Returns

To calculate the multiperiod geometric average return, we take the product of the single period growth rates and then calculate the nth root of the result, where n represents the number of periods. An alternative to this calculation is to use continuously compounded returns. We do this by taking the arithmetic average of the natural logs of the growth rates, and then taking the base of the natural logarithm e to the power of the result. Exhibit 5.5 shows how to calculate the geometric average return using the log returns method.

By taking the log of the single period growth rate, we calculated a continuously compounded return for each period. Raising e to the average of the continuously compounded growth rates yields the geometric average return.

EXHIBIT 5.6   Annualizing Sub Year Returns

	A	B	C	D
1		Rate	Percent Rate	
2			=((1.06)^(1/12))-1	
3	Monthly rate:	0.005	0.487	
4	Yearly rate:	0.060	6.000	
5			=((1+B3)^12)-1	

ANNUALIZING RETURNS

Returns are typically presented on a yearly or *annual basis*. This is done because it is easier to compare investment returns if the time period is the same for each investment, i.e. we cannot compare a cumulative return of 10% to another of 12% if the first was earned over 15 months and the second over 12 months. To analyze the difference in returns between any two investments, it is helpful to hold the time period constant. Yearly or annual presentations are standard. Cumulative returns that have been calculated using more or less than a year of holding period returns can be restated to an annual basis. The geometric mean return when calculated for a 1-year period is called an *Annualized Return*, average annual return, or compound annual return. By restating returns to an annual basis, we facilitate the comparison of returns on portfolios with different inception and ending dates.

Interest rates are typically quoted on an annual basis. Exhibit 5.6 shows that if the investor purchases a fixed income instrument with a maturity period of one month and a monthly compounding frequency, the rate quoted will be the annual rate of 6% and not the monthly rate of approximately 0.487%.

If we have a return for a period less than a year, and we need to turn it into an annual return, we can compound it by raising the holding period growth rate to the power equal to the number of periods in the year:

$$[(1 + \text{period rate})^{\# \text{ of periods}} - 1] \times 100$$

We would need to continue to reinvest at the single period rate of approximately 0.5% per month to produce the annual return of 6%. The main problem with quoting interest rates and returns that are annualized based on a frequency of less than a year is that they are hypothetical projections of the annual return, as there is no guarantee that the investor will be able to reinvest at 0.5% per month to realize the 6% return for the year as in this example.

EXHIBIT 5.7   Annualizing Sub Year Returns

	A	B
1	**1M Percent Return**	**12M Percent Return**
2	20.00	791.61
3		
4	=(((1+A2/100)^12)-1)*100	

EXHIBIT 5.8   Annualizing Returns

	A	B	C
1	**Period**	**Return**	**Percent Return**
2	3 Year Compound:	0.191	19.100
3	Annualized 3-Year:	0.060	6.00
4			
5		=((1+B2)^(1/3))-1	=B3*100

As an extreme example of the problem in using annual returns created in this way, suppose the market had a great month and is up 20%. Exhibit 5.7 shows the conversion to an annual basis results in a 792% compounded annual return. Most times when we present returns for analysis we do not annualize until the series of periodic returns contains one year of observations.

If the holding period return is greater than a year, the rate is usually restated to an annual basis using the inverse of the compounding formula used above. The inverse of taking a number and raising it to a power n is to take the nth root of the number:

$$\text{Yearly rate} = [\sqrt[\text{\# of periods}]{(1 + \text{period rate})} - 1] \times 100$$

Exhibit 5.8 shows that if an investment earned 19.1% over a 3-year period, the return can be quoted as an annual average return of 6%:

$$(\sqrt[3]{1.191} - 1) \times 100 = 6.00$$

Notice that we calculate the annualized return by first taking the nth root of the cumulative growth rate, or 1.191 in our example, as opposed to taking the nth root of the cumulative return. The nth root of the growth rate is the geometric average growth rate. To transform it into the geometric average return we subtract 1 and multiply by 100. The annual average of a 3-year 19.1% compound return is 6.00%.

EXHIBIT 5.9 Annualizing Odd Year Returns

	A	B	C
1	**Period**	**Return**	**Percent Return**
2	12/31/1999 - 4/30/2001	0.1400	14.00
3	Annualized 16 month:	0.1035	10.35
4		↑	=((1+B2)^(365.25/B6))-1
5			
6	Days in period:	486	◄— =366+31+28+31+30

Sometimes we need to calculate an annualized return for cumulative periods that are not exact multiples of a year. To calculate annualized returns for such periods, we count the actual number of days in the cumulative period and divide it by 365.25 to calculate an annualized equivalent:

Annualized return

$$= \left[\left(\sqrt[\frac{\text{Number of days}}{365.25}]{\text{Linked growth rates}} \right) - 1 \right] \times 100 \tag{5.5}$$

Exhibit 5.9 shows that the annualized equivalent of a 14% return earned over 16 months equals 10.35%.

Accepted presentation methodology for periods over a year is to present annual average returns using the geometric mean. The return is presented with the time period used in the calculation. For example, a 15.00% geometric mean return calculated based on a 2-year compounded return is presented as a "2-year average annual return." Presentation of fund performance usually includes an average annual return for several periods greater than a year: 3-year, 5-year, 10-year, since-fund-inception, and so on, where each return is expressed on an annualized basis.

Whenever there is variability in periodic returns, the geometric mean return will always be lower than the arithmetic mean return. The arithmetic mean treats equal positive and negative returns equally. For example, a positive 50% and then a negative 50% return offsets each other using an arithmetic average:

$$\frac{0.50 - 0.50}{2} = 0$$

In reality, a positive 50% gain in period one followed by a 50% decline in period two leads to a decrease in investment value over the two periods. For example, if we started with $100, a positive 50% and then a negative 50% return would lead to an ending value of $75. Exhibit 5.10 shows how the geometric mean return accounts for this decrease.

EXHIBIT 5.10   Geometric Mean Return Reconciles Values

	A	B	C	D	E	F
1	Year	MVB	Return	Growth Rate	MVE	
2	1	100	0.50	1.50	150.00	
3	2	150	-0.50	0.50	75.00	=B3*D3
4					→	
5		Compound Return:	-25.00		75.00	=B2*(1+C5/100)
6		Arithmetic Average:	0.00			
7		Geometric Average	-13.40		75.00	=100* (1+(C7/100))^2

COMPOUND ANNUAL INTERNAL RATE OF RETURN

The time weighted return is the appropriate measure of manager return for situations where the manager does not control the timing and magnitude of cash flows. If the manager does have control over cash flows, then the MWR is a better measure of return than the TWR for the performance of the manager. For example, private equity funds pool the resources of investors to invest in nonmarket traded securities issued by companies. These include venture capital and other types of private investment. In these funds, an investor might make a long-term commitment to invest in a partnership set up by the private equity manager to make the actual investments. The manager might call on the investor for capital drawing down this commitment over a period of years as they decide to provide funding to companies. At the later stages of the partnership, the manager returns cash to the investors as they sell stakes in the portfolio companies. In addition to handling these cash flows, the MWR also provides a good solution for calculating returns to portfolios where the values of the investments on cash flow dates are difficult to determine. Again, using private equity as an example, the cash flow dates might be made over a period wherein the portfolio companies that the partnership is investing in are difficult to value. To take the timing of these cash flows into account and get around the problem of having to value illiquid assets, we use the IRR to calculate the return for such portfolios.[2]

We can compound an annual equivalent IRR for periods greater than a year. To accomplish this, all we need to do is adjust the cash flow weights so that they are multiples of a year.

In Exhibit 5.11 we calculate a 5-year IRR of 10.01%. This is equivalent to an annualized IRR of 1.93%.

---

[2] For more on return calculation for these vehicles see David Tierney and Richard Bailey, "Opportunistic Investing," *Journal of Portfolio Management*, Spring 1997.

EXHIBIT 5.11 Compound Annual IRR

	A	B	C	D	E	F	G
1	Year	Days	Flow	Value	Weight	Future Value	
2	0	0	400	0	5.00	440	=FV(F10,E2,0,-C2,0)
3	1	365	100		4.00	110	=FV(F10,$E$2,0,-C3,0)
4	2	730	100		3.00	110	=FV(F10,$E$2,0,-C4,0)
5	3	1095	-50		2.00	-55	=FV(F10,$E$2,0,-C5,0)
6	4	1461	-50		1.00	-55	=FV(F10,$E$2,0,-C6,0)
7	5	1826		550		550	→
8							
9					Difference:	0	=F7-D7
10	Total Days:	1826			*Annual Return:	0.01926	
11					Annual % Return:	1.92582	=F10*100
12					Growth Rate:	1.01926	=1+F10
13					Years:	5.00	=((B7-0)/365.25)
14					Compound Return:	10.01	=((F12^F13)-1)*100

MULTIPLE PERIOD RETURN ANALYSIS

We can use a multiperiod example to show how the difference between the MWR and the TWR shows the impact of cash flows on performance. Although we use the TWR to evaluate performance of an investment manager, the MWR is still important for measuring the growth in the assets of the fund over time. If there were no cash flows during the period the TWR and the MWR will be equal. When there are cash flows, the MWR and TWR will differ because the MWR takes cash flows into consideration while the TWR eliminates their effects.

We can demonstrate these points with an example when a manager is responsible for two portfolios managed using the same strategy, and both funds have the same returns. Clients A and B in Exhibit 5.12 earn the same yearly returns over five years. Client A makes no cash flows other than a $1000 initial investment. Cell B9 shows the calculation of the TWR equal to −0.80%.

Exhibit 5.13 shows the calculation of the MWR for Client A. Because there are no cash flows, the MWR and the TWR for client A are equal. The cash flow pattern for Client B differs in that he made an initial investment of $200 and subsequent investments of $200 at the beginning of the next four years. Because Client B has more money at work in periods where the returns are higher, his MWR is higher than that for Client A. Exhibit 5.14 shows the calculation of the IRR for Client B. The annualized MWR is 2.56%, significantly higher than the annualized TWR equal to −0.16%.

EXHIBIT 5.12   MWR versus TWR

	A	B	C	D	E	F
1			Client A		Client C	
2	Year	Return	BMV=$1000	Return	BMV=$1000	
3	1	(8.00)	920.00	8.00	1,080.00	
4	2	(4.00)	883.20	4.00	1,123.20	
5	3	-	883.20	-	1,123.20	
6	4	4.00	918.53	(4.00)	1,078.27	
7	5	8.00	992.01	(8.00)	992.01	
8	5-year Cumulative		=((1+B3/100)*(1+B4/100)*(1+B5/100)*(1+B6/100)*(1+B7/100)-1)*100			
9	TWR	-0.80		-0.80		
10	MWR	-0.80	=F43	-0.80		
11	5-year Annualized		=((1+((C7-1000)/1000))^(1/5)-1)*100			
12	TWR	-0.16		-0.16		
13	MWR	-0.16	=F40	-0.16		
14						
15	**MWR**		Client B		Client D	
16	Year	Return	$200 per year	Return	$200 per year	
17	1	(8.00)	184.00	8.00	216.00	
18	2	(4.00)	368.64	4.00	432.64	
19	3	-	568.64	-	632.64	
20	4	4.00	799.39	(4.00)	799.33	
21	5	8.00	1,079.34	(8.00)	919.39	
22	5-year Cumulative					
23	TWR	-0.80		-0.80		
24	MWR	13.45	=F58	-13.18	=F74	
25	5-year Annualized					
26	TWR	-0.16		-0.16		
27	MWR	2.56	=F55	-2.79	=F71	

EXHIBIT 5.13   IRR Calculation for Client A

	A	B	C	D	E	F	G
29	Client A						
30	Year	Days	Flow	Value	Weight	FV	
31	0	0	1,000		5.00	992.01	=FV(F39,E31,0,-C31,0)
32	1	365	0		4.00	0.00	=FV(F39,E32,0,-C32,0)
33	2	730	0		3.00	0.00	=FV(F39,E33,0,-C33,0)
34	3	1095	0		2.00	0.00	=FV(F39,E34,0,-C34,0)
35	4	1461	0		1.00	0.00	=FV(F39,E35,0,-C35,0)
36	5	1826		992.01		992.01	=SUM(F31:F35)
37							
38					Difference:	0.00000	=F36-D36
39	Total Days:	1826			*Annual Return:	(0.0016)	Calc Using Solver
40					Annual % Return:	(0.16)	=F39*100
41					Growth Rate:	0.99840	=1+F39
42					Years:	5.00	=((B36-0)/365.25)
43					Compound Return:	(0.80)	=((F41^F42)-1)*100

Order of Returns Affects the MWR but not the TWR

Exhibit 5.12 also illustrates another interesting property of multiple period returns. While the order of the returns experienced does not matter when we are calculating a TWR, it does influence the MWR, when there are cash flows. This is because the MWR is the single interest rate that reconciles the beginning and end value of an investment made, given the pattern of cash flows. In the example, we can see that Clients

C and D experience the same yearly returns as Clients A and B, except that the order of the returns is reversed. Instead of earning negative returns in the early years, the manager earned positive returns, and vice versa. Because there are no cash flows, the MWR for Clients A and C are equal to the TWR. And because the order of returns does not matter when we are calculating the TWR (i.e., TWRs are commutative), the TWRs for Clients A and C are equal. But the MWR *is* influenced by the order of returns when there are cash flows. Notice that the MWR for Client D, who had the same pattern of cash flows as Client B, is significantly lower than the MWR for Client B. This is because Client D had more money invested in years when the returns were negative. Exhibits 5.14 and 5.15 show the calculation of the IRR for Clients B and D.

EXHIBIT 5.14   IRR Calculation for Client B

	A	B	C	D	E	F	G
44	Client B						
45	Year	Days	Flow	Value	Weight	FV	
46	0	0	200		5.00	226.89	=FV(F54,E46,0,-C46,0)
47	1	365	200		4.00	221.24	=FV(F54,E47,0,-C47,0)
48	2	730	200		3.00	215.73	=FV(F54,E48,0,-C48,0)
49	3	1095	200		2.00	210.36	=FV(F54,E49,0,-C49,0)
50	4	1461	200		1.00	205.11	=FV(F54,E50,0,-C50,0)
51	5	1826		1,079.34		1,079.34	=SUM(F46:F50)
52							
53					Difference:	(0.0000)	=F51-D51
54	Total Days:	1826			*Annual Return:	0.0256	Calc Using Solver
55					Annual % Return:	2.56	=F54*100
56					Growth Rate:	1.02556	=1+F54
57					Years:	5.00	=((B51-0)/365.25)
58					Compound Return:	13.45	=((F56^F57)-1)*100

EXHIBIT 5.15   IRR Calculation for Client D

	A	B	C	D	E	F	G
60	Client D						
61	Year	Days	Flow	Value	Weight	FV	
62	0	0	200		5.00	173.63	=FV(F70,E62,0,-C62,0)
63	1	365	200		4.00	178.61	=FV(F70,E63,0,-C63,0)
64	2	730	200		3.00	183.73	=FV(F70,E64,0,-C64,0)
65	3	1095	200		2.00	188.99	=FV(F70,E65,0,-C65,0)
66	4	1461	200		1.00	194.43	=FV(F70,E66,0,-C66,0)
67	5	1826		919.39		919.39	=SUM(F62:F66)
68							
69					Difference:	0.0000	=F67-D67
70	Total Days:	1826			*Annual Return:	(0.0279)	Calc Using Solver
71					Annual % Return:	(2.79)	=F70*100
72					Growth Rate:	0.97212	=1+F70
73					Years:	5.00	=((B67-0)/365.25)
74					Compound Return:	(13.18)	=((F72^F73)-1)*100

CHAPTER 6

Adjusting Returns for Impact of Fees, Taxes, and Currency

The returns we have calculated so far are typical of most of the returns calculated for investment analysis and return presentations to investors. They are fund level returns that describe the growth in assets due to the gains and income earned within the portfolio. These returns were, however, calculated without considering the factors that serve to reduce the gross return on investments: management fees, expenses, sales charges, and taxes. In addition, foreign investors will experience either a gain or a loss on foreign exchange that will impact the return on investments made into vehicles that are denominated in another currency. We can adjust the return calculations to take these factors into account, but there is no standard return calculation that will meet the needs of every situation. This is because investment vehicles differ as to their treatment of management fees and expenses. The way that sales charges paid by the investor are handled also depends on the vehicle. Taxes compound the problem because the taxes paid by an individual depend on the individual's personal circumstances.

But even though the calculations need to be modified to fit the situation, it is worth reviewing the adjustment of returns for these factors because of their practical importance. So we will review some generic ways of adjusting returns for investment related expenses and taxes, and then look at the specific situation of mutual funds. Given that mutual funds are the most widely held vehicle for investing, the techniques presented here are applicable to a wide audience, but the concepts can be modified to fit the situation at hand.

MANAGEMENT FEES AND EXPENSES

The costs of investing include the explicit costs of trading, management fees, and the operational costs of investing, such as accounting, custody, shareholder servicing, trustee, and other costs. The explicit costs of trading are embedded in the calculation of return because we include the broker commission, fees, and trading taxes into the cost of the investment established on trade date. The difference between the amount paid and the value of the security at the end of the day includes the effects of these trading costs. This serves to reduce the single period returns by the commission and trading fees. So we do not need to explicitly recognize trading costs in the calculation of the fund level return.

In the case of mutual funds, the accrued liability for the management fee and other investment expenses reduce the reported daily NAV.[1] So returns calculated using the per-share NAV explicitly include the effect of these fees, i.e. mutual fund returns are *net-of-management fee and expense returns*. For many types of accounts however, including institutional separate accounts, we do need to explicitly factor these fees into the calculation in order to determine the equivalent return.

Management Fees

The investment advisor manages the fund in exchange for a periodic *management fee*. While the return calculated before the subtraction of the management fee is useful in measuring the manager's investment skill, it is the after-fee return or *net-of-fee return* that is actually experienced by the investor. There are many algorithms for determining the management fee on an investment. Vehicle specific industry custom as well as negotiation between the manager and the client together form the way that fees are determined. In many situations, the calculation of the fees depends on the manager's stated fee schedule. Fee schedules are usually tiered by assets under management, for example:

Total Assets Under Management	Annual Fee
First $1,000,000	1.00%
Next $1,500,000	0.70%
Over $2,500,000	0.35%

[1] For background on mutual funds see Robert Pozen, *The Mutual Fund Business* (Cambridge, MA: The MIT Press, 1998).

The fee schedule might also have a cap or a floor. And there are many variations to the way management fees for investment vehicles are structured. For example, hedge funds and other investment partnerships are investment vehicles marketed to high net worth individuals and institutional investors. These partnerships are typically structured so that there is both a net asset-based management fee and a performance-based incentive fee. *Performance based fees* are calculated as a percentage of the profits earned by the fund during the period. Structures where 1–2% of the net assets plus 10–20% of the fund profits are paid each year to the advisor as compensation are common. Sometimes there is a hurdle rate applied to the incentive fee; for example, the manager receives 20% of the profits over and above the hurdle rate of return, where the hurdle rate is either a fixed percentage or tied to a market benchmark. *Wrap accounts* are accounts usually holding one or more funds where a financial advisor charges a fee for asset allocation and other advice. The wrap fees are usually based on assets under management, rather than on transactions made. The wrap fee can be deducted from the market value to calculate a net-of-fee return on the wrap fee account in a similar way as the management fee is deducted to calculate a net of management fee return for an individual fund. While the algorithms for calculating the fees might change from situation to situation, the calculation of returns remains much the same.

There are also different ways of administrating the collection of fees. In some cases, fees are accrued within the portfolio on a daily or monthly basis. In this case the fee is treated in the same way as the accrual of income on a bond, except that the management fee accrual is a negative to the investor. In other cases fees are calculated on a periodic basis based on assets under management at the end, the beginning, or on an average for the period. Fees might be accrued daily but paid only quarterly. Sometimes the management fee is not paid out of the fund itself, but is paid by the investor separately.

No matter how the fees are determined and paid, we are interested in analyzing fund returns that are calculated both gross-of and net-of management fees. If fees are calculated based on the market value at the end of the measurement period, one way to calculate a single period net-of-management-fee return is:

1. Use the fee schedule to calculate the dollar value of the management fee. Ideally this would be done on an accrual basis for proper matching of the expenses to the income and gains earned.
2. Calculate a basis point return adjustment by dividing the dollar value of the fees by the market value of the fund.

3. Subtract the basis point fee return adjustment from the gross of fee return.

Exhibit 6.1 shows the calculation of a quarterly net-of-management-fee return over several quarter ends. One advantage of this method is that it can be applied whether or not the management fees are actually paid from the investment account.

Expenses

We can extend this methodology in order to calculate returns net of the other expenses of investing. Many of these types of expenses, such as custody fees, are withdrawn directly from the investment account. Exhibit 6.2 shows how to calculate a return net of these effects by subtracting them from the numerator of the return calculation.

The impact on return can be thought of as a negative income accrual. One assumption made here is that the management fees and other expenses can be separately identified.

These examples showed how fees and expenses serve to reduce single period returns, but the difference between gross and net performance compounds over time. We calculate a multiperiod net return by compounding the periodic net returns.

EXHIBIT 6.1   Returns Net of Management Fees

	A	B	C	D	E	F	G
1	Quarter	End Market Value	Gross of Fee Return	Quarterly Fee	Fee % of EMV	Net of Fee Return	
2	Year Begin	100,000.00					
3	1	100,000.00	0.00	250.00	0.2500	(0.25)	(0.25)
4	2	103,000.00	3.00	253.75	0.2464	2.75	2.7462
5	3	108,150.00	5.00	260.19	0.2406	4.76	4.7474
6	4	105,987.00	(2.00)	257.48	0.2429	(2.24)	(2.2381)
7			↓		↑	↓	
8			=((B6/B5)-1)*100		=(D6/B5)*100	=(C6-E6)	
9		=(100000*($C$13/100))+((B6-100000)*($E$13/100))					
10							
11	Year		5.99			4.97	
12		Fee Schedule - Percent of End of Period Assets:					
13		First $100,000:	0.250	Over $100,000:	0.125		

EXHIBIT 6.2   Returns Net of Expenses and Fees

	A	B	C	D	E
1		Market Value	Return		
2	BMV:	1,000.00	Gross of Fee and Expense:	17.50	=((B3-B2+B4)/B2)*100
3	EMV:	1,100.00	Gross of Fee:	14.00	=((B3-B2+B4-B5-B6)/B2)*100
4	Income:	75.00	Net of Fee:	4.00	=((B3-B2+B4-B5-B6-B7)/B2)*100
5	Custody Expenses:	25.00			
6	Other Expenses:	10.00			
7	Management Fees:	100.00			

TAXES

Nontaxable institutional investors including pension funds, charities, and endowments have the benefit of seeing their income and investment gains compound from period to period unencumbered by taxes. Unfortunately, this is not the case for investors investing outside of tax-deferred accounts, such as corporations, insurance companies, nuclear decommissioning trusts, and others. These investors are subject to taxes on their income earned and capital gains. Taxes often serve to reduce returns more than any other factor. *Capital gains* are the difference between the amount paid for a security, or investment in a portfolio of securities, and the amount realized upon sale. A tax liability is established only when the investor actually sells the security; that is, taxes are recognized on a cash basis. Because income and gains earned in one period are only available for investment in the next period at a rate of (1 – the effective tax rate), taxes can significantly reduce the long-term returns realized. Managers of taxable accounts consider the impact of taxes as a key input to the investment process. Taxes can be minimized and deferred to future periods by investing in securities with nontaxable income, minimizing turnover, selling high cost tax basis lots first, and many other techniques.[2]

Given the effect of taxes, investors are interested in measuring the impact of taxes on their returns and monitoring and comparing the efforts of their managers to control these impacts. To calculate an *after-tax return*, we modify the single period return calculation formula by reducing the value added from income and gains earned over the period by the tax liabilities generated during the period.

$$\text{Tax adjusted return} = \frac{\text{Income} + \text{Gains} - \text{Tax on income} - \text{Tax on realized gains}}{\text{Capital at risk}} \quad (6.1)$$

We subtract tax liabilities instead of tax payments because taxes are typically paid in cash from outside the investment account. An investor might not pay the tax on a gain earned in one year until the following year. To calculate after-tax returns over multiple time periods, we compound, average, and annualize single period after-tax returns in the same manner as we do pretax returns.

---

[2] For a summary of the subject of investment tax considerations see Robert Jeffrey, "Tax Considerations in Investing," in *The Portable MBA in Investment* (New York: John Wiley and Sons, Inc., 1995).

While the modification of the single period return formula is conceptually straightforward, there are several return measurement considerations:

- Determining the tax liability to subtract from the gains and income earned.
- Separating tax liabilities due to investor and investment manager decisions.
- Accounting for the potential for taxes on unrealized gains embedded in the portfolio.

Determining the Tax Liability

The calculation of the actual tax liability owed by an investor is a subject all its own. All levels of government impose taxes and the rules change every year. Complicating the analysis of a single investment is the fact that there is an interaction between the taxes generated by one investment with the taxes generated by others. For example, gains on one investment can usually be used to offset losses to another. Or the investor might have tax loss carryforwards from prior periods that can be used to offset gains in the next. The taxation of investments is a complex topic and is more in the realm of tax accounting than performance measurement. But we can make practical attempts to estimate the after-tax returns. If the purpose of calculating the after-tax return is to gain insight into the tax management efficiency of the manager, making certain assumptions in order to simplify the calculations is acceptable. Some of the assumptions commonly made include:

- Each investment portfolio exists in isolation from the rest of the portfolios forming the investor's total tax situation.
- Taxes are recognized when the liability is generated rather than when they are paid.
- The liability is recognized on an accrual basis for income and on the date of the sale for capital gains.
- The maximum tax rate applies to all income and gains.

Making these assumptions has the added benefit of making after-tax returns calculated for different portfolios and managers more comparable. But we should keep in mind the fact that these assumptions mean that the return that we calculate only approximates the investor's actual realized after-tax return. Exhibit 6.3 shows the calculation of the basic single period after-tax return.

EXHIBIT 6.3 After-Tax Return

	A	B	C	D	E	F
1	BMV:	100.00		Pre Tax Gain:	15.00	=B2+B3
2	Realized Gain:	10.00		Investment Made	100.00	=B1
3	Change in Market Value:	5.00		Pre Tax Return:	15.00	=(E1/E2)*100
4	EMV:	105.00			→	
5				Post Tax Gain:	13.00	=E1-((B6/100)*B2)
6	Tax Rate:	20.00		Investment Made	100.00	=B1
7				Post Tax Return:	13.00	=(E5/E6)*100

Here, we have a BMV of 100, an EMV of 105, and we realized 10.00 of gains during the period. Cell F3 shows the calculation of the pretax return, 15.00%. The gain of 15 equals the realized gain of 10 plus the unrealized gain of 5. We assume that the rest of the proceeds from the sale generating the gain were invested in a new security during the period. To calculate the post-tax return, we subtract the tax liability of 2.00 (10 realized gain × 20% tax) generated from the sale. We can modify the calculation presented here to calculate a money weighted return, for example, by day weighting the cash flows to calculate a Modified Dietz return. The 2% difference between the pre- and post-tax returns is the *tax burden*.

The calculation of the tax liability depends on the specific investor situation, such as tax bracket, instrument type, locale of the investor, and holding period of the investment. For example, the federal tax rate applicable to the gain on the sale of a common stock is currently lower if the stock was held for more than one year. In addition to the federal tax, the investor will need to pay a state, and possibly a local tax on the sale of the gain depending on where she or he lives. U.S. Treasury bond income received is taxable only at the Federal level; there is no state or local tax levied. No federal or state tax is deducted for municipal bond income. Once we have mapped the applicable tax rates for each combination of instrument, holding period, etc. we can generalize the calculation of the applicable tax rates using Equation (6.2).

$$\text{Tax rate} = \text{Fed tax rate} + [\text{State tax rate} \times (1 - \text{Federal tax rate})] \\ + [\text{Local tax rate} \times (1 - \text{Federal tax rate})] \qquad (6.2)$$

Investor versus Manager Decisions

When we calculate after-tax returns, we face a situation analogous to the one that led us to the requirement for two pretax returns, the TWR used to evaluate managers and the MWR used to measure funds. Suppose we are evaluating the performance of a manager of a separately managed portfolio, which is a portfolio with one investor. The manager might sell securities held by the fund, which will generate a taxable gain, for two reasons. The first reason he might sell securities is to execute the fund's investment strategy. If the strategy is to invest in undervalued companies, he will periodically sell stocks that become fully valued and reinvest the proceeds in new picks. The taxes generated by these transactions are attributable to the manager; we should subtract these capital gains taxes from the numerator of the return calculated to measure the manager. The second reason the manager will sell securities is to raise cash to fund client withdrawals. While the client will have to pay just as much tax as he would on a sale due to manager trading decisions, the taxes on securities sold to fund the withdrawal are attributable to the investor's decision to withdraw money. The tax liabilities generated in the process of funding client withdrawals are *nondiscretionary capital gains*. These taxes should not be deducted from the return earned by the manager. When we calculate an after-tax return on the fund, we subtract only the taxes from sales due to managerial decisions. When we calculate an after-tax return earned by the client, we subtract the impact of all taxes.

Unfortunately, isolation of the nondiscretionary capital gains is not possible via direct examination of the portfolio accounting. Transactions performed for multiple reasons are commingled together. Various methods have been proposed for removing the effect of client generated tax liabilities. AIMR suggests a method where we adjust the numerator of the return calculation upward for the impact of these gains.[3] To calculate an after-tax return that removes the effect of the nondiscretionary capital gains, we

1. Calculate the ratio of gains (realized and unrealized) to assets (including withdrawals).
2. Multiply the client withdrawal amount by this gain ratio and the capital gains tax rate.
3. Add this adjustment factor back to the numerator of the return calculation.

We will return to the subject of adjusting the return for taxes on gains and income later in this chapter, in the section on mutual fund performance.

Accounting for Future Taxes on Unrealized Gains

Here we have calculated a return that takes into account the effect of capital gains taxes generated by security sales. Because capital gains taxes

---

[3] For a summary of the AIMR after-tax return recommendations and some alternative methods see *Invitation to Comment: Redrafting the After-Tax Provisions of the AIMR-PPS Standards* (Charlottesville, VA: Association for Investment Management and Research, 2001).

are only realized upon the sale of a security, one way to defer taxes is to minimize turnover and hold securities within the portfolio for as long as possible. But because the investor will eventually withdraw his money, or liquidate the portfolio, there is a potential tax on the unrealized gains lurking in every taxable portfolio. Because of this tax overhang, investors also are interested in a measure of return that takes the potential taxes into account. We calculate such an *after liquidation* after-tax return by assuming that the investor sold all the securities in the account on the end date. To do this we calculate an assumed tax liability equal to the unrealized gain multiplied by the applicable tax rates, and then subtract the result from the numerator. Mutual funds must follow specific SEC directions for calculating both before- and after-liquidation returns that are presented to investors in advertisements and other materials. Although the post-liquidation return is useful to the investor in identifying funds with large embedded unrealized capital gains, it is not always meaningful for the purpose of comparing investment managers. One reason is that the difference in time since the inception date of the portfolio, or *vintage year*, will influence the cost paid for the securities and therefore the unrealized gain embedded in the funds being compared.

MUTUAL FUND RETURN CALCULATION

Although the treatment of investment expenses and taxes is specific to the vehicle and investor situation, the calculation of returns for mutual funds forms a case study for calculating returns that include the effects of fees and taxes. Mutual funds are vehicles for commingled investment that are marketed to the retail investor. Mutual funds and other similar products require performance calculations that reflect the impact of unitized valuations, dividend distributions, loads and other sales charges, expenses and expense subsidies, and taxes. This section illustrates the calculation of returns adjusted for each of these factors. In the United States, the SEC has specified the calculation and reporting requirements for advertised mutual fund performance. The assumptions embedded in these return calculations are explored in this section to guide interpretation of these returns and modification of the formulas to meet the needs of a particular investor. There are several kinds of mutual funds; here we address return measurement for the most common type, open-end investment companies. An open-end mutual fund sells shares to investors and stands ready to redeem those shares at the fund's current market value per share. The principles of mutual fund performance can be used to calculate performance on many kinds of unitized products with mutual-fund like characteristics.

EXHIBIT 6.4 Mutual Fund Balance Sheet

	A	B	C	D	E
1	Assets		Liabilities		
2	Investments at Cost	$700.00	Accrued management fee	$50.00	
3	Cash	10.00	Other accrued expenses	30.00	
4			Total Liabilities		80.00
5			Equity		
6			Paid in by investors	500.00	
7			Undistributed realized gains	30.00	
8			Unrealized gains	100.00	
9			Total Equity		630.00
10	Total Assets	$710.00	Total		$710.00
11					
12	Net Asset Value	$630.00	=B10-E4		
13	Shares Outstanding	100.00 →			
14	Net Asset Value Per Share	6.30	=B12/B13		

Mutual funds pool the investments of multiple individual participants and invest the proceeds in a portfolio of securities. Mutual funds and other commingled pools provide diversification and the benefits of professional investment management to investors. Shareholders receive a proportionate share of the capital gains and income earned on the fund's holdings. Investors buy shares of open-end funds directly from the investment company at the Net Asset Value (NAV) per share. The NAV per share is calculated each day by first calculating the gross assets of the fund, which is the sum of the market value of each of the securities and the cash holdings of the fund. The *net asset value* of the fund is then calculated by taking the gross assets and subtracting accrued liabilities to the fund including the fee payable to the management company and other expenses such as custody and transfer agency fees. Exhibit 6.4 illustrates the calculation of the fund's NAV per share. At the end of each day, the net asset value per share is calculated by dividing the net asset value of the fund by the shares outstanding, including new shares purchased using new contributions into the fund that day. The new contributions are added to the equity capital of the fund.

$$\text{NAV per share} = \frac{\text{Total assets} - \text{Total liabilities}}{\text{Shares outstanding}} \qquad (6.3)$$

When an investor makes a contribution into a mutual fund, the fund company creates new shares with a value equal to the NAV at the end of the day the contribution was made. Mutual funds employ *forward pricing*, where the contribution is made at the NAV struck at the end of the day the contribution was made. This has a beneficial impact on the return measurement process in that the NAV per share does not have to be adjusted by cash flows in order to calculate a time weighted return. We can calculate a time weighted return on a mutual fund without knowing the total market value of the fund or the size and timing of cash flows. The cash flow impact has already been netted out of the return because additional shares are issued proportional to each contribution. For example, suppose we have a fund where a shareholder contribution is received on Day 1 for $10. The shareholder receives shares equal to the contribution divided by the Day 1 NAV of $10, or one share. The money is made available to the fund manager the next day, and the additional share is included in the next day's NAV calculation. Exhibit 6.5 demonstrates the calculation of the NAV per share and return when there are contributions into the portfolio.

If there were no dividend distributions to shareholders from the fund, we could calculate mutual fund returns with the ROI formula using the change in NAV per share. We do this by dividing the ending NAV per share by the beginning and transforming it into a return, as in Exhibit 6.6.

Mutual fund returns measured via the change in the fund's NAV per share are inherently TWRs. When new contributions are made into the fund new shares are issued at the market value of the fund, and when withdrawals are made shares are retired. Because of this the NAV of the fund is equivalent to a wealth ratio relative to the original investment in the fund. The contributions and withdrawals do not affect the return calculated. But there is one complication: Because funds periodically pay out income and capital gains to the investor, we need to adjust for these distributions when we calculate a multiperiod return.

EXHIBIT 6.5   NAV Calculation with Contributions

	A	B	C	D	E	F	G
1	Day 1						
2	Net Assets		Shares		NAV Per Share	10.00	=B5/D5
3	NAV Begin	100.00	Begin Shares	10.00			
4	Cash Flow	0.00	New Shares	0.00			
5	NAV End	100.00	End Shares	10.00			
6							
7	Day 2						
8	Net Assets		Shares		NAV Per Share	11.00	=B11/D11
9	NAV Begin	100.00	Begin Shares	10.00	=D5		
10	Cash Flow	10.00	New Shares	1.00	=B10/F2		
11	NAV End	121.00	End Shares	11.00	=D9+D10		
12							
13					Return using values & flows:	10.00%	=(B11/(B9+B10))-1
14					Return using NAVs per share:	10.00%	=(F8/F2)-1

EXHIBIT 6.6   Returns Calculated Using NAV Per Share

	A	B	C	D
1	Date	NAV Per Share	Return %	
2	31-Dec	10.00		
3	31-Jan	11.00	10.00	=((B4/B3)-1)*100
4	28-Feb	12.00	9.09	
5	31-Mar	13.00	8.33	
6	30-Apr	14.00	7.69	
7	31-May	15.00	7.14	

Distributions

Capital gains and income earned by the fund are returned to the share-holder in the form of periodic dividend *distributions*. Income distributions are made up of the income earned on the underlying investments in the portfolio, including dividend and interest accruals. Accrued expenses are deducted and then the net amount is distributed to the shareholder as a dividend. Each investor receives a total dividend equal to their shares outstanding on the ex-dividend date multiplied by the per share dividend amount. The *ex-dividend date*, or *ex-date*, is the date when new investors into the fund are no longer entitled to the recently declared dividend. The frequency of the distributions varies depending on the type of portfolio, but all mutual funds must distribute most of their gains to shareholders by the end of each year. The NAV of the portfolio will fall on the day the fund goes ex-dividend by the amount of the dividend (in addition to the market value change for that day). Published mutual fund returns will be calculated assuming that the investor reinvests these distributions into new shares of the fund.

RETURN BEFORE EXPENSES AND TAXES

We can use this algorithm to calculate the cumulative return for a mutual fund, where we assume that capital gains and income distributions are reinvested into new shares:

1. Calculate begin shares using an assumed investment of $1000.
2. Calculate reinvestment shares for each distribution.
3. Calculate end of period market value using accumulated shares and end of period NAV.
4. Calculate the growth rate and transform into a return.

For example, suppose we have the dividend and NAV history from Exhibit 6.7 and we want to calculate a cumulative return for the period 12/31 to 5/31.

EXHIBIT 6.7   Dividend and NAV History

	A	B	C
1		Per Share	
2	Date	Dividend	NAV
3	31-Dec	0.000	10.000
4	31-Jan	0.250	10.000
5	28-Feb	0.000	11.000
6	31-Mar	0.250	12.000
7	30-Apr	0.000	13.000
8	31-May	0.250	13.000

First, we calculate begin shares. We can use a hypothetical investment of $1000 as the beginning value:

$$\text{Begin shares} = \frac{1000}{\text{NAV per share at start date}} \quad (6.4)$$

	A	B	C
1	Amount Invested:	1000.00	
2	Purchase date NAV per Share:	10.00	=B1/B2
3	Begin Shares:	100.00	

Next, for each dividend we calculate the reinvestment shares:

$$\text{Reinvestment shares} = \frac{\text{Per share distribution} \times \text{Accumulated shares}}{\text{Reinvest date NAV}} \quad (6.5)$$

	A	B	C	D	E	F	G
1			Per Share				
2	Date	Dividend	NAV	Begin Shares	Distribution Amount	Reinvest Shares	End Shares
3	31-Dec	0.000	10.000	100.000	-	-	100.000
4	31-Jan	0.250	10.000	100.000	25.000	2.500	102.500
5	28-Feb	0.000	11.000	102.500	0.000	0.000	102.500
6	31-Mar	0.250	12.000	102.500	25.625	2.135	104.635
7	30-Apr	0.000	13.000	104.635	0.000	0.000	104.635
8	31-May	0.250	13.000	104.635	26.159	2.012	106.648
9							
10				=G7	=B8*D8	=E8/C8	=F8+D8

Finally, we calculate the ending market value and return:

$$\begin{aligned}&\text{Ending market value} \\ &= (\text{Begin shares} + \text{Total reinvest shares}) \times \text{Ending NAV}\end{aligned} \quad (6.6)$$

$$\text{Periodic return} = \left(\left(\frac{\text{Ending market value}}{1{,}000}\right) - 1\right) \times 100 \quad (6.7)$$

Exhibit 6.8 shows the cumulative returns to this fund. In terms of our example, the cumulative return is 38.64% assuming reinvestment of the dividends on each ex-dividend date. Because of the hypothetical beginning investment of 1000, this method of calculating a return is slightly different from that in the previous chapters, but in fact the results are the same TWR.

EXHIBIT 6.8 Returns Calculated Using NAV Per Share and Dividend

	A	B	C	D	E	F	G	H	I
1		Per Share							
2	Date	Dividend	NAV	Begin Shares	Distribution Amount	Reinvest Shares	End Shares	End Amount	To Date Percent Return
3	31-Dec	0.000	10.000	100.000	-	-	100.000	1000.000	-
4	31-Jan	0.250	10.000	100.000	25.000	2.500	102.500	1025.000	2.50
5	28-Feb	0.000	11.000	102.500	0.000	0.000	102.500	1127.500	12.75
6	31-Mar	0.250	12.000	102.500	25.625	2.135	104.635	1255.625	25.56
7	30-Apr	0.000	13.000	104.635	0.000	0.000	104.635	1360.260	36.03
8	31-May	0.250	13.000	104.635	26.159	2.012	106.648	1386.419	38.64
9						↓			
10				=G7	=B8*D8	=E8/C8	=F8+D8	=G8*C8	=((H8/1000)-1)*100

RETURN AFTER SALES CHARGES

Frequently the investor must pay a sales charge for purchasing shares in a mutual fund. The sales charges, or *loads*, may be applied either when the investor buys the shares or when they are sold. Front-end loads are applied to the initial purchases of fund shares. Back-end loads are applied when they are sold. A fund may be offered with multiple share classes, each of which has a different sales charge and expense distribution structure. Investors are interested in calculating returns reflecting these sales costs.

Front-End Load-Adjusted Returns

Some funds have *front-end loads*, which are sales charges levied upon the initial purchase of shares in a fund. A portion of the investor's initial contribution is paid as a load reducing the initial contribution and the remainder is used to purchase shares in the fund. The load amount usually depends on the size of the initial contribution, and it usually declines as the size of the initial investment increases. The price that the investor pays for the shares is adjusted from the NAV to an *offer price* by the percentage amount of the sales charge. To calculate the return that reflects the smaller initial investment, we

1. Calculate the offer price using the begin NAV and sales charge.
2. Calculate begin of period shares using the offer price and assumed investment of $1000.
3. Calculate reinvestment shares for each distribution.
4. Calculate the growth rate and transform into a return.

For example, if we took the same NAV and dividend information from the previous example, and assumed that there was a 5.75% initial sales charge, we would calculate the return by:

EXHIBIT 6.9   Front-End Load Fund Returns

	A	B	C	D	E	F	G	H	I
1			Per Share						
2	Date	Dividend	NAV	Begin Shares	Distribution Amount	Reinvest Shares	End Shares	End Amount	To Date Percent Return
3	31-Dec	0.000	10.000	94.250					
4	31-Jan	0.250	10.000	94.250	23.563	2.356	96.606	966.06	-3.39
5	28-Feb	0.000	11.000	96.606	0.000	0.000	96.606	1,062.67	6.27
6	31-Mar	0.250	12.000	96.606	24.152	2.013	98.619	1,183.43	18.34
7	30-Apr	0.000	13.000	98.619	0.000	0.000	98.619	1,282.05	28.20
8	31-May	0.250	13.000	98.619	24.655	1.897	100.515	1,306.70	30.67
9									
10				=G7	=B8*D8	=E8/C8	=F8+D8	=G8*C8	=((H8/1000)-1)*100

First, calculating the offer price using the begin NAV and sales charge:

$$\text{Offer price} = \frac{\text{NAV per share}}{(1 - \text{Front-end load})} \tag{6.8}$$

In terms of our example:

	A	B	C
1	Front End Load %:	5.75	
2	Amount Invested:	1000.00	
3	Purchase date NAV per Share:	10.00	=B3/(1-B1/100)
4	Offer price per share:	10.61	
5	Begin Shares:	94.25	=B2/B4
6			

Starting with the same $1000 initial investment, the front-end load has the effect of reducing the shares purchased. The lower base is used to calculate the reinvestment shares on subsequent dividend distributions, as in Exhibit 6.9.

The cumulative return in this case is 30.67%, versus 38.64% in the no load example with the same NAV and distribution history. Not only does the load immediately impact the return, having the effect of putting the investment underwater from the start, but the difference compounds as dividends are received and reinvested in subsequent periods.

Back-End and Deferred Loads

Funds that levy the sales charge when the investor redeems their shares are *deferred-load*, or *back-end load,* funds. The investor pays no sales charge on purchase and all of the initial contribution goes to purchase fund shares. Most back-end loads are structured as *contingent deferred sales charges* (CDSC). CDSC is a back-end load that declines over time. For example, if you sell mutual fund shares after one year, the sales charge may be 4% and after three years the charge may decline to 2% and then to 0% after five years. The process of calculating the return on a portfolio with a deferred load is to:

1. Calculate beginning of period shares using an assumed investment of $1000.
2. Calculate reinvestment shares for each distribution.
3. Calculate the ending market value prior to the levy of the sales charge.
4. Adjust the ending market value by subtracting the sales charge.
5. Calculate growth rate and transform into a return.

Continuing with the same NAV and distribution history as in the prior examples, suppose the fund has a back-end sales charge of 5% on shares held one year or less.

The first step is to calculate the beginning of period shares. As with the no load example, this is equal to the assumed investment of $1000 divided by the NAV at the end of the day the contribution is made. Any dividends received are assumed to be reinvested and reinvest shares are calculated and accumulated to the end of the period.

For calculating returns on a fund with a CDSC charge, we assume that the shares are going to be sold at the end of the calculation period. The ending market value is the ending NAV per share times the end shares. We then adjust the ending market value by the amount of the load and use the resulting number in the return calculation.

To calculate the adjusted ending market value:

1. Find the lower of the NAV at the end of the period or the NAV at the beginning of the period:

$$\text{CDSC NAV} = \text{Lower of (Begin NAV, End NAV)} \qquad (6.9)$$

2. Calculate the back end fee:

$$\begin{aligned} &\text{CDSC sales charge} \\ &= [\text{Beginning shares} \times (\text{CDSC NAV} \times \text{Load \%})] \end{aligned} \qquad (6.10)$$

3. Calculate an Adjusted Ending Market Value:

$$\begin{aligned} &\text{Adjusted ending market value} \\ &= (\text{End shares} \times \text{Ending NAV}) - \text{CDSC sales charge} \end{aligned} \qquad (6.11)$$

4. Calculate the return by dividing the adjusted EMV by the assumed initial investment:

$$\text{Periodic return} = \left[\left(\frac{\text{Adjusted EMV}}{1,000} \right) - 1 \right] \times 100 \qquad (6.12)$$

EXHIBIT 6.10   Back-End Load-Adjusted Return

	A	B	C	D	E	F	G	H	I
1		Per Share							
2	Date	Dividend	NAV	Begin Shares	Distribution Amount	Reinvest Shares	End Shares	End Amount	To Date Percent Return
3	31-Dec	0.00	10.00	100.00					
4	31-Jan	0.25	10.00	100.00	25.00	2.50	102.50	1,025.00	2.50
5	28-Feb	0.00	11.00	102.50	0.00	0.00	102.50	1,127.50	12.75
6	31-Mar	0.25	12.00	102.50	25.63	2.14	104.64	1,255.63	25.56
7	30-Apr	0.00	13.00	104.64	0.00	0.00	104.64	1,360.26	36.03
8	31-May	0.25	13.00	104.64	26.16	2.01	106.65	1,386.42	38.64
9						↓			
10				=G7	=B8*D8	=E8/C8	=F8+D8	=G8*C8	=((H8/1000)-1)*100
11									
12	NAV for sales charge:	10.00		=MIN(C8,C3)		Adjusted ending market value:	1336.42	=H8-C14	
13	Back end sales charge %:	5.00	→			Back end load adjusted return:	33.64	=((H12/1000)-1)*100	
14	Back end sales charge $:	50.00		=(1000/C3)*C12*(C13/100)					

Exhibit 6.10 illustrates the calculation of a return for a fund with a back-end load. The back-end load-adjusted return is 33.64%. Notice that the back-end sales charge is not levied on shares received via the process of reinvesting dividends. In addition, the use of the lower of the begin or the end NAV results in a lesser sales charge on a loss experienced by the investor if the NAV falls instead of rises over the measurement period.

RETURN AFTER EXPENSES

The net asset value of the fund is reduced by various costs of running the mutual fund. The primary expense is the *management fee*, which the investment management organization sponsoring the mutual fund charges in exchange for managing the fund. This management fee is usually presented in annual terms as a percentage of net assets, or *expense ratio*. As the fund assets grow, the percentage fee sometimes falls as incremental new assets are added to the fund. The increments are referred to as *breakpoints*. The management fee is calculated using the breakpoint schedule, accrued, and then subtracted from the net asset value of the fund each day. The management fee accrual acts as a liability on the fund's balance sheet. The value of the liability is the amount that the fund owes to the management company in between the actual payment dates.

Because the NAV includes the effect of the management fee, mutual fund returns are intrinsically *Net of Fee* returns. Investors also want to understand the effect of the management fee and calculate returns before the application of the fee, or *Gross of Fee* returns. Because the fee has already been embedded in the NAV, we need to gross up the NAV by the amount of the fee, expressed in per share terms, and then calculate the return.

EXHIBIT 6.11   Gross of Fee Returns

	A	B	C	D	E	F	G	H	I	J
1			Per Share Expense Factor							
2	Date	Dividend	Per Share Expense Factor	NAV	Begin Shares	Distribution Amount	Reinvest Shares	End Shares	End Amount	To Date Percent Return
3	31-Dec	0.00	-	10.00	100.00					
4	31-Jan	0.25	0.008330	10.00	100.00	25.83	2.58	102.58	1,025.83	2.58
5	28-Feb	0.00	0.008330	11.00	102.58	0.85	0.08	102.66	1,129.27	12.93
6	31-Mar	0.25	0.009163	12.00	102.66	26.61	2.22	104.88	1,258.54	25.85
7	30-Apr	0.00	0.009996	13.00	104.88	1.05	0.08	104.96	1,364.46	36.45
8	31-May	0.25	0.010829	13.00	104.96	27.38	2.11	107.06	1,391.84	39.18
9						↓				
10			=D7*$C$11		=H7	=(B8+C8)*E8	=F8/D8	=G8+E8	=H8*D8	=((J8/1000)-1)*100
11	Monthly Expense Ratio:	0.000833								

Gross of Fee Returns

To calculate a gross of fee return:

1. Transform the expense ratio to a per share accrual factor.
2. Calculate begin of period shares using an assumed investment of $1000.
3. Calculate reinvestment shares for each distribution.
4. Treat the accrual of the expense as a nontaxable distribution and calculate reinvestment shares for the accrual.
5. Calculate the growth rate as the ratio of the ending market value and the assumed $1000 investment.
6. Transform the growth rate into a return.

For example, suppose that the fund we have been using as an example has an annual management fee of 1.00%. In this example, we divide the annual fee by 12 to form a monthly expense accrual per share of 0.0833%:

$$\text{Percent expense accrual} = \left(\frac{\text{Annual \% factor}/100}{\text{Months in period}} \right) \times 100 \qquad (6.13)$$

	A	B	C	D
1	Annual management fee%:	1.00		
2	Monthly fee factor:	0.083333		
3			=((B1/100)/12)*100	

We then calculate the return in the same fashion as in the previous examples, with the exception that we treat the expense factor as a dividend, which has the effect of grossing up the fund return.

In Exhibit 6.11 we calculate a cumulative gross of fee return of 39.18%, as opposed to 38.64% for the net of fee return. Notice that because the effect of the grossing up process on the return calculation is the same as that of a dividend, we can add the per share expense factor to the dividend in the calculation of the distribution amount. Then, reinvested shares and the return are calculated in the usual manner. In this example, the expense is accrued on a monthly basis; in practice, the expenses are accrued and factored into returns on a daily basis.

Management Fee Subsidies

Occasionally fund companies will subsidize a portion of the management fee for a period of time to facilitate the marketing of the fund. When there is a subsidy, the net-of-fee return will be higher than it would have been without the subsidy, because of the smaller expense accrual. We can calculate a return excluding the effect of the subsidy by treating the subsidy in the opposite way of an expense, i.e., as a negative dividend.

12B-1 Fees

Fund companies have devised other sales charge structures that are not straight front-end or back-end load schemes. There are funds and share classes of funds that pay brokers trailing commissions called, after the SEC rule that allowed them, *12b-1 fees*. Some funds have several share classes each with a different allocation of the fees. Each class of shares has a separate NAV calculated at the end of each day. 12B-1 fees have the effect of moving loads into the expense structure of the fund as they are accrued and netted into the daily NAV calculation in the same way as management fees and other expenses.

Other Expenses

In addition to the management fee, several other expenses are accrued on a daily basis and act to reduce the NAV and the returns. These include operating expenses such as custody and shareholder servicing charges. Returns can be grossed up by any of these fees or by the total of all of the expenses in order to calculate gross-of-expense returns. The process is the same as for calculating the gross-of-management fee returns, a daily expense factor is calculated and added to the distribution amount in order to calculate reinvest shares.

RETURN AFTER TAXES ON INCOME AND CAPITAL GAINS

Mutual funds are often held in taxable accounts. Mutual fund shareholders are subject to three main types of taxes:

1. Taxes on income earned by the fund.
2. Taxes on the gains derived from securities sold by the fund.

3. Taxes on gains derived from the redemption of the fund shares.

The first two tax liabilities are generated when the fund pays out income earned and realized gains to the investor. Two similar funds differing only in the degree of turnover might have the same pretax returns, but the fund with more turnover might have a lower after-tax return due to the taxes on realized gains. The third type of tax is due when the investor sells his shares back to the fund. We can compare funds on an after-tax basis by calculating after tax returns. Because every investor has a unique tax situation, the after-tax return experienced by two investors in the same portfolio will be different. Tax rates depend on where the investor lives and what tax bracket he is in. The final taxes due and the aggregate after-tax return experienced by the investor depend on activity across her investments. For example, gains realized on one holding are offset with losses on others before the calculation of taxes due by the investor. Because of the investor specific nature of calculating after-tax returns, we have two choices. We can calculate an after-tax return that takes into account the specifics of the tax situation faced by a particular investor or we can use a set of assumptions that are reasonable approximations for many investors. An example of an assumption would be the tax rates used to calculate the returns.

This section shows how to calculate the two after-tax returns that mutual fund companies report in their prospectuses. To enhance comparability across fund companies, the SEC has mandated that these returns follow a standard calculation methodology.[4] The SEC methods make some assumptions, those relevant to our task are:

- Only federal taxes are levied; state and local taxes are ignored.
- The tax rates applicable are the highest federal tax rates on income, short-term, and long-term capital gains.

The return calculations illustrated here can be modified to facilitate the analysis of after-tax returns for a particular investor situation.

Taxes on Distributions

The mutual fund itself is a nontaxable entity, it pays no income and capital gains taxes itself. Instead, it passes these tax liabilities through to the individual shareholder. It is the *distribution* of income and capital gains to the shareholder that generates the tax liability. These distributions are made on a periodic basis, where substantially all of the income and gains are passed

---

[4] For more information on the SEC requirements for calculating after-tax returns see *Disclosure of Mutual Fund After-Tax Returns*, Securities and Exchange Commission, Washington, D.C., 2001.

through to the investor by the end of each year. Income distributions are comprised of a proportional share on the income earned via dividend and interest accruals on the securities held by the fund. When the fund sells securities, the realized gains are also passed through to the investor. The U.S. tax code currently applies a lower tax rate on capital gains earned on sales of securities held longer than a year than on gains on securities held for shorter periods. Because of this fund companies break the distributions into *short-term capital gains* and *long-term capital gains* distributions.

Taxes on Redemption of Fund Shares

Holdings within the fund are marked to market each day in the course of the NAV calculation. When the investor withdraws money from the fund, he is, in effect, selling his shares back to the fund company. The proceeds from the sale are calculated using the NAV per share on the date of the sale. The increase in the NAV is attributable to the unrealized gains embedded in the current holdings of the fund. The investor must pay a tax on the difference between these proceeds and the original cost basis of the shares. If the investor accumulated shares in the fund over time, the tax is calculated on a lot-by-lot basis. Even if the investor bought his shares all in one go, should he reinvest dividend distribution proceeds he will have accumulated shares at more than one price.

So mutual fund after-tax returns depend on both the timing of the sale of securities held by the fund and the timing of the sale of the fund shares back to the investment company. The former decisions are controllable by the fund manager and the latter decision is the responsibility of the investor. We can isolate the two types of decisions via the use of two different after-tax return calculations:

- After-tax preredemption returns subtract the tax due on distributions from the fund to the investor.
- After-tax post redemption returns also subtract the tax due when the investor sells shares back to the fund company.

After-Tax Preredemption Returns

After-tax preredemption returns or *preliquidation* returns take into account the tax that investors have to pay when they receive a fund distribution. Preredemption refers to our assumption that the investor continues to hold the shares at the end of the measurement period. These returns are calculated by adjusting the income and capital gain distributions by the applicable tax. We then reinvest the net-of-tax distribution into the fund in subsequent periods. To calculate an after-tax preredemption return for any period:

1. Calculate begin of period shares using an assumed investment of $1000.
2. Calculate the after-tax distribution amount for each distribution where:

After-tax distribution = Pre-tax distribution × (1 − Tax rate)

3. Reinvest the after-tax distribution into the fund by determining reinvestment shares.
4. At the end of the period calculate the compound growth rate as the ratio of the ending market value to the assumed $1000 investment.
5. Transform the growth rate into a return.

Exhibit 6.12 illustrates the calculation of an after-tax, preredemption return for a mutual fund.

EXHIBIT 6.12   After-Tax Preredemption Returns

	A	B	C	D	E	F	G
1					Per Share		
2			Pre Tax		Post Tax		
3	Date	Income Dividend	ST Capital Gain	LT Capital Gain	Income Dividend	ST Capital Gain	LT Capital Gain
4	31-Dec	0.000	0.000	0.000	0.000	0.000	0.000
5	31-Jan	0.250	0.000	0.000	0.150	0.000	0.000
6	28-Feb	0.000	0.000	0.000	0.000	0.000	0.000
7	31-Mar	0.000	0.100	0.150	0.000	0.060	0.120
8	30-Apr	0.000	0.000	0.000	0.000	0.000	0.000
9	31-May	0.100	0.100	0.050	0.060	0.060	0.040
10						↓	
11					=B9*(1-$E$13/100)	=C9*(1-$E$14/100)	=D9*(1-$E$15/100)
12							
13			Tax rate on income %:		40.00		
14		Tax rate on ST capital gains %:			40.00		
15		Tax rate on LT capital gains %:			20.00		

	H	I	J	K	L	M	N
1							
2							
3	NAV	Begin Shares	Post Tax Distribution Amount	Reinvest Shares	End Shares	End Amount	To Date Percent Return
4	10.000	100.000					
5	10.000	100.000	15.00	1.500	101.500	1,015.00	1.50
6	11.000	101.500	0.00	0.000	101.500	1,116.50	11.65
7	12.000	101.500	18.27	1.523	103.023	1,236.27	23.63
8	13.000	103.023	0.00	0.000	103.023	1,339.29	33.93
9	13.000	103.023	16.48	1.268	104.290	1,355.78	35.58
10					↓		
11		=L8	=(E9+F9+G9)*I9	=J9/H9	=K9+I9	=L9*H9	=((M9/1000)-1)*100

Notice that the tax levied on the distributions has the effect of reducing the multiperiod return. This is because we reinvest *after-tax* dollars into the fund at each distribution date. The investment of fewer after-tax dollars translates into a lower compound return.

RETURN AFTER TAXES ON REDEMPTION GAINS

After-tax, post redemption returns reflect not only the tax on distributions made to the shareholder, but also the tax liability generated upon the sale of fund shares. We estimate the second tax liability in the same way as we do the first: we subtract the cost basis of the fund shares held from the proceeds and then multiply the gain by the appropriate tax rate. One notable aspect of performing this calculation is that because we are assuming reinvestment of fund shares, the shares sold at redemption need to be broken up into lots, where each lot has a different cost basis depending on the share price on each reinvestment date. We do this because the tax rate on short-term gains to individuals is higher than that on long-term gains and we need to reference the date each share was purchased to determine whether the holding period of the lot was short- or long-term. To calculate an after-tax post redemption return we:

1. Calculate begin of period shares using an assumed investment of $1000.
2. Calculate the after-tax distribution amount for each distribution.
3. Determine reinvestment shares for each after-tax distribution.
4. Calculate the gain on the initial and reinvested shares where:

$$\text{Gain} = (\text{NAV}_{\text{end}} - \text{NAV}_{\text{reinvestment date}}) \times \text{Incremental reinvest shares} \tag{6.14}$$

5. Characterize each gain as short-term or long-term depending on the holding period.
6. Separately, sum the gains and losses for all short-term shares (lots) and then all long-term shares (lots).
7. Apply long- and short-term gain netting rules and then calculate the tax liability:

$$\text{Tax liability} = (\text{Net gain} \times \text{Tax rate}) \tag{6.15}$$

8. Adjust the ending market value by the tax liability:

$$\text{Adjusting ending market value} = [(\text{End shares} \times \text{Ending NAV}) - \text{Tax liability}] \tag{6.16}$$

9. Calculate the growth rate as the ratio of the adjusted ending market value and the assumed $1000 investment.
10. Transform the growth rate into a cumulative return.

Exhibit 6.13 illustrates the calculation of after-tax, post redemption returns for an investment in a mutual fund sold two years after the initial investment, where shares were also accumulated via the reinvestment of after-tax distributions.

We calculate an after-tax post redemption return equal to 29.43%. Notice that the after-tax gain is calculated by comparing the investment, or reinvestment NAV for each lot received upon reinvestment to the NAV on the date the investor is assumed to sell the fund shares. For example, the calculation of the $1.52 gain on the shares received as part of the 3/31 distribution was determined by:

$$\text{Gain} = [(\text{NAV}_{end} - \text{NAV}_{\text{distribution date}}) \times \text{Reinvest shares}]$$
$$= (13 - 12) \times 1.52 = 1.52$$

EXHIBIT 6.13   After-Tax Post Redemption Return Calculation

	A	B	C	D	E	F	G
3	Date	Income Dividend	ST Capital Gain	LT Capital Gain	Income Dividend	ST Capital Gain	LT Capital Gain
4	31-Dec-99	0.00	0.00	0.00	0.00	0.00	0.00
5	30-Jun-00	0.25	0.00	0.00	0.15	0.00	0.00
6	31-Dec-00	0.00	0.00	0.00	0.00	0.00	0.00
7	31-Mar-01	0.00	0.10	0.15	0.00	0.06	0.12
8	30-Jun-01	0.00	0.00	0.00	0.00	0.00	0.00
9	31-Dec-01	0.10	0.10	0.05	0.06	0.06	0.04
10							
11					=B9*(1-$E$13/100)	=C9*(1-$E$14/100)	=D9*(1-$E$15/100)
12							
13			Tax rate on income %:	40.00			
14			Tax rate on ST capital gains %:	40.00			
15			Tax rate on LT capital gains %:	20.00			

	H	I	J	K	L	M	N	O	P
3	NAV	Begin Shares	Post Tax Distribution Amount	Reinvest Shares	End Shares	End Amount	ST Gain	LT Gain	
4	10.00	100.00						300.00	=($H$9-H4)*I4
5	10.00	100.00	15.00	1.500	101.50	1,015.00		4.50	=($H$9-H4)*K5
6	11.00	101.50	0.00	0.000	101.50	1,116.50			
7	12.00	101.50	18.27	1.523	103.02	1,236.27	1.52		=($H$9-H7)*K7
8	12.50	103.02	0.00	0.000	103.02	1,287.78			
9	13.00	103.02	16.48	1.268	104.29	1,355.78	0.00		
10						Total Gain:	1.52	304.50	=SUM(O4:O9)
11			=(E9+F9+G9)*I9	=J9/H9	=K9+I9	Tax:	0.61	60.90	=O10*(E15/100)
12									
13		Tax adjusted EMV:	1294.27	=M9-(N11+O11)			=N10*(E14/100)	=O10*(E15/100)	
14		After tax Post red return %:	29.43	=((J13-1000)/1000)*100					
15									

Under the current tax code, if the length of time between these two dates is greater than a year the lower, long-term, tax rate is applied. Because the tax depends on the length of the holding period, the assumed tax on the distribution depends on the period for which the return is being calculated. For example, when we calculate a 3-year return at the end of 2003, the 3/31/2001 distribution will instead be treated as a long-term distribution. The short-term gain on the 3/31/2001 distribution will become a long-term gain starting on 3/31/2002.

Netting Gains and Losses

Exhibit 6.13 shows the calculation of an after-tax post redemption return when there was a gain on each of the fund shares accumulated during the period. We could have a situation where there is a mix of long- and short-term gains and losses earned on different share lots sold at the end of the period. Because losses can be written off against other gains, they become a benefit for the purpose of calculating a tax liability. The return calculation mirrors the tax rules where the investor is allowed to net long- and short-term gains and losses together before the calculation of the tax liability. We incorporate the netting rules by calculating the cost basis and gain/loss for each share on a lot-by-lot basis. This results in a short- or long-term gain/loss value for each lot of shares sold. Once the total short- and long-term gain/loss amounts have been calculated for each tax lot, we apply the rules to determine the amount and taxable nature of the total gain/loss. The netting rules are:

1. If there is both a short- and a long-term gain—do not add the two amounts together. Each amount must be taxed independently of one another at a separate rate. The total long-term gain is taxed at the long-term tax rate. The total short-term gain is taxed at the short-term tax rate. Both the short- and long-term tax liabilities adjust the ending proceeds.

2. If there is a long-term gain and a short-term loss—sum and then compare the two amounts. If the net amount is positive then the long-term gain was greater than the short-term loss. The net amount is taxed at the long-term tax rate. If the net amount is negative, the long-term gain was less than the short-term loss. The net negative amount is taxed at the short-term tax rate to determine the tax benefit to the ending proceeds.

3. If there is a long-term loss and a short-term gain—sum the two amounts and compare. If the net amount is positive the long-term loss

was less than the short-term gain. Therefore, the net amount is taxed at the short-term tax rate. If the amount is negative, the long-term loss was greater than the short-term gain. The net negative amount is taxed at the long-term tax rate to determine the tax benefit.

There are several other considerations for special situations when calculating returns according to the SEC rule, but this example shows how after-tax returns are calculated for most situations.

ADJUSTING RETURNS TO THE INVESTOR'S BASE CURRENCY

Most investment portfolios are managed in one currency. Even if the portfolio invests in foreign securities, it accepts contributions and valuations are performed in a single home or *base currency*. However, investors in these funds might have different base currencies than the portfolio or investment firm's base currency. These investors in funds that are managed overseas are interested in measuring their performance in their own home base currency. The net return to these investors is the fund return, adjusted for the change in foreign exchange rates, or *exchange rate returns*.

There are several ways to convert a return from one base currency to another. First, we could take each of the holdings and cash flows into the fund, as measured in the fund's base currency and multiply these values by the exchange rate from the base currency to the target currency. We could then calculate the fund's return using the standard TWR and MWR formulas. This is the most accurate method of converting returns, because it allows for transactions to be done at different exchange rates. Column I in Exhibit 6.14 shows how to convert returns using this method.

EXHIBIT 6.14   Converting Returns to a Different Currency

	A	B	C	D	E	F	G	H	I	J	K
1		**U.S. Dollars**						**Canadian Dollars**			
2	Day	MVE	Return		USD/CAD Rate	Currency Return		MVE	Return		Return
3	0	1,000.00			0.62			620.00		=((H5/H4)-1)*100	
4	1	1,000.00	0.000	=((B5/B4)-1)*100	0.63	1.613	=((E5/E4)-1)*100	630.00	1.613		1.613
5	2	980.00	-2.000		0.62	-1.587		607.60	-3.556		-3.556
6	3	960.00	-2.041		0.64	3.226	=B5*E5	614.40	1.119		1.119
7	4	990.00	3.125		0.67	4.688		663.30	7.959		7.959
8	5	1,000.00	1.010		0.64	-4.478		640.00	-3.513		-3.513
9											
10	5-Day		0.00			3.226			3.226		3.226
11				=((E8-E3)/E3)*100			=((1+C8/100)*(1+F8/100)-1)*100				
12											
13						=((1+C10/100)*(1+F10/100)-1)*100					

The market values of a fund managed in U.S. dollars over five days are in Column B. In Column H we have converted them to Canadian dollars using the exchange rates in Column E. The exchange rates here are quoted such that if the exchange rate increases, a foreign investor with a U.S.-dollar-based investment will experience a gain measured in his home currency. For example, the exchange rate of 0.62 on Day 2 indicates that 1 U.S. dollar is worth 0.62 Canadian dollars. So we multiply the market value of the holding in U.S. dollars by the exchange rate in order to determine the value in Canadian dollars. Exchange rates are not always quoted in this way; if the exchange rates were instead quoted as Canadian dollars per U.S. dollar then we would divide by the exchange rate to determine the value. Once we have converted the values we calculate the fund's return in Canadian dollars in the same way as we do the return in U.S. dollars. On Day 2 we record a loss of 3.556%. This loss is due to a combination of the decrease in market value as well as the decrease in the U.S./Canada exchange rate. On Day 3 the Canadian dollar is worth 1.587% less than it was on the day before. We can isolate the currency loss by calculating a *currency return*, equal to the change in exchange rates divided by the beginning exchange rate.

$$\text{Currency return} = \left(\frac{\text{End exchange rate} - \text{Begin exchange rate}}{\text{Begin exchange rate}} \right) \times 100 \qquad (6.17)$$

Another way to calculate the return converted to Canadian dollars is to instead take the return in U.S. dollars and multiply it by the currency return. This return will approximate the return calculated by the first method in all situations except if there were cash flows into the fund at different exchange rates during the day (Just as if we had cash flows into the fund at different values in base currency during the day).

$$\begin{aligned}&\text{Currency converted return}\\ &= (1 + \text{Fund return}) \times (1 + \text{Currency return}) - 1\end{aligned} \qquad (6.18)$$

In Column K we calculate the currency return using this method. One advantage of using this method is that we don't actually need to convert each day's returns in order to convert a multiple period return to a different base currency. In Cell K10 we convert the 5-day return in U.S. dollars, which was 0.00%, to Canadian dollars by multiplying by the 5-day exchange rate return, 3.226%. This is a useful shortcut when we convert returns over long periods of time.

CHAPTER 7

Measuring Relative Return

After calculating the return on our fund, or a fund we are managing on behalf of someone else, the natural next step is to think about whether or not we are happy with the result. The periodic returns we calculate quantify how our investments have performed. To determine whether or not we are satisfied with our performance given the general market conditions, we need to have a basis of comparison. Performance comparisons are individualized according to investor or fund-specific objectives and constraints. Return requirements, tolerance for risk, income, and liquidity requirements guide the investment policy for the portfolio. The investment policy guides the allocation to asset classes, managers, and strategies. Given a basis of comparison, we might need to temper our spending and capital accumulation projections, adjust our investment strategy, change our investment manager, or make other changes. There are three possible reference points for comparison.

- A target or projected return for the portfolio.
- The return earned by funds with a similar purpose and strategy.
- The market return for the asset class, as represented by a market index or benchmark customized for the strategy.

The first option is straightforward. We compare the results to the target return. But given that markets fluctuate, if we had an absolute long-term average goal in mind, we would not expect to earn that target return in any one period. For example, if the market is down 20% in a period and our fund is down 15%, while none of us has a long-term investment objective of losing money, we would be happy with our performance on a relative basis. So the peer group and benchmark comparison alternatives are of value even for funds with specific return objectives. In this chapter we look at the process for comparing our returns to those earned by other funds or peer groups.

The second option seeks to compare our performance to that earned by similar funds. Here we demonstrate the construction of peer group universes and the calculation of peer group average returns, which are commonly used as a basis for comparison. Finally, market indices and other benchmarks are commonly used to measure the success of an investment strategy. The selection of the manager's benchmark is an important consideration. The benchmark serves to ensure that the interests of the fund and manager are aligned. We also discuss at a summary level the methodology behind the third option—the creation and calculation of returns for market indices and other comparison benchmarks.

This chapter covers the techniques for making performance comparisons. By comparing the returns earned to the market or peer returns for the period, we can find out if our absolute performance was reasonable. For measuring the performance of the manager, however, it is the *relative* performance that is of interest. The chapter closes with a discussion of the methodology for determining the relative value added by the manager over time.

PEER GROUPS

Human nature makes us want to know not just how we did, but how well we did relative to other investors or *peers*. We want to know how our fund performance compares to funds with similar goals and constraints. Institutional and individual investors compare their performance to other investors even though periodic performance will vary due to differences in asset allocation and other decisions. Rightly or wrongly, besting the peer group averages is frequently touted as an indication of skill on behalf of the manager. Managers with superior performance attract assets, and managers with subpar performance lose clients. This is true even if it is a questionable practice to chase after past performance, i.e., buy last year's hot manager or strategy.

Assuming investment decisions were made based on the specific circumstances of the investor, returns will vary from fund to fund for legitimate reasons. These legitimate differences notwithstanding, we want to know if our performance is in line with that of investors who are, more or less, comparable to us. For example, the plan sponsor of a large public employee pension plan is interested in comparing the performance of the plan to that of other public funds of a similar size. If we have hired a manager to invest for us, we want to know how our manager or advisor has performed relative to his competitors.

Peer group analysis is the process of comparing the performance of a fund or its managers to the performance of similar funds and their managers. Peer group analysis is a straightforward process. We compare returns and other performance statistics of similarly managed portfolios in order to draw inferences based on the relative performance. We assume that the objectives and constraints imposed on the managers of these portfolios are similar enough to provide valid inter-fund comparisons. The straightforward nature of the process notwithstanding, a review of the tools and techniques employed in a peer group analysis is justified because of the extreme practical importance. Money management is a competitive, dynamic industry. There are minimal barriers to entry. Transitioning assets to a new manager is easy. Whether past performance says anything about future performance or not, managers with superior relative past performance attract assets based on their track records. This phenomenon occurs in the arenas of both institutional and retail funds management. Funds that receive a five-star rating from Morningstar, a mutual fund research and publishing company, attracts more investors than other funds. Morningstar rankings are based on a calculation of risk-adjusted return as compared to a peer group ranking of funds with similar styles.

PERFORMANCE UNIVERSE

We call the group of funds used for performance comparison a *performance universe*. A universe is a list of portfolios similar to ours and includes their returns and other statistics over different time periods. We can create our own universe, or we can obtain precompiled performance data from universe publishers. There are separate universes available for funds marketed to institutional and retail investors. Publishers of retail fund universe data include Morningstar, Lipper, and Micropal. We can use their data to compare mutual funds. Pension consultants, custodians, and publishers maintain institutional fund universes. Some publishers of institutional fund universe databases include Russell-Mellon, Wilshire (TUCS), and the WM Company. In addition to the published universes, pension consultants, fund companies, and other organizations maintain inhouse universes for research and competitor analysis.

While each performance universe has its own distinguishing characteristics, the methodology used to create and rank funds within them are largely the same. The main task of a universe publisher is to periodically gather data on the funds in which it is interested. Some of the universe publishers independently calculate the returns; others obtain returns precalculated by managers, plan sponsors, or their custodians. The retail universes calculate their own returns using the published NAVs and distribution data. Quarterly periodic returns are the norm for institutional universe products, but some are updated more frequently.

The first step in comparing our fund to a peer group is to select the appropriate universe. Within each universe funds are grouped by category into *subuniverses*. Subuniverses are created by filtering the universe of funds to derive a list of comparable portfolios by:

- Asset class and strategy. For example, domestic equity, international equity, and real estate.
- Type of investor. For example, funds managed on behalf of corporate or public defined benefit plans, endowments, and foundations.
- Type of manager. For example, funds managed by asset management firms, banks, or insurance companies.

Within the appropriate subuniverse, funds can be further filtered to create a customized list of appropriate funds for comparison. For example, we could take one of the institutional fund universe data sets for funds that are being managed on behalf of corporate pension plans and then filter it to exclude funds under a certain size, and then exclude funds that do not yet have a three-year track record. We can then compare and contrast the funds. For example, we could compare the performance of our small-capitalization company separate account manager to all of the small-capitalization funds that are included in the universe.

We can rank and compare the performance of the funds in the narrowed resulting list. We can compare performance by any return, risk, or risk-adjusted return statistic. Data are available over several time periods; so we could, for example, compare funds by year-to-date cumulative return, or three-year annualized returns. In addition to performance statistics we can compare other characteristics of the fund, such as the fund's asset allocation weightings, average credit quality, or duration.

Rank and Order Statistics

We are interested in our *relative* performance within the universe. Was our fund a top performer? Or was it a middling or poor performer? We use rank and order statistics to evaluate the relative performance of a fund within a universe. *Rank and order statistics* like medians, quartiles, and percentiles provide a way of describing the relative position of a particular observation within a data set. Suppose we are interested in a peer group comparison of 1-year returns for a group of funds and that our fund had a 6.21% return in the period. Exhibit 7.1 shows the set of 1-year returns for a universe of 20 funds, sorted from high to low. We chose 20 for clarity of the examples, and while it depends on the market and strategy, the typical universe has more funds.

Once the returns are sorted, we can evaluate our relative position. The first step is to determine the median return. The *median* is the return for the middle fund in the universe. Half of the funds will have performance above and half below the median. By looking at the performance of our fund versus the median we can see whether our fund performed better or worse than the average fund. Exhibit 7.2 shows the median universe return was 3.56%.

Note that by constructing the universe in this way we are *equal weighting* each portfolio return in the comparison. That is, we are not weighting the funds by their asset size or other criterion. We determined the median by looking for the middle observation in the sorted array of returns. We find the rank position of the middle value by taking $(N + 1)/2 = 10.5$ where N is the total number of return observations. If the total number of funds is an even number, then we can take the median as the average of the two middle observations. If N is odd, the middle observation serves as the median. In our case the median lies halfway between the tenth and eleventh observations.

EXHIBIT 7.1   Peer Group Universe Returns

	A	B	C	D	E
1			1-year Return		
2	Fund	% Return		Fund	% Return
3	1	14.20		11	3.11
4	2	8.85		12	2.96
5	3	8.45		13	2.69
6	4	6.86		14	2.23
7	5	6.28		15	1.68
8	6	**6.21**		16	1.34
9	7	6.10		17	-0.78
10	8	5.21		18	-2.69
11	9	4.33		19	-3.66
12	10	4.00		20	-4.14

EXHIBIT 7.2   Universe Median

	A	B	C	D	E	F	G	H	I	J	K	L	M	N	O	P	Q	R	S	T
1	1	2	3	4	5	6	7	8	9	10	11	12	13	14	15	16	17	18	19	20
2	14.20	8.85	8.45	6.86	6.28	**6.21**	6.10	5.21	4.33	4.00	3.11	2.96	2.69	2.23	1.68	1.34	-0.78	-2.69	-3.66	-4.14
3																				
4									Groups:	2.00										
5								Median Position:	10.50		→	=(COUNT(A2:T2)+1)/K4								
6								Median Return:	3.56			=(J2+K2)/2									

We can further refine the comparison by splitting the data set into four groups, or *quartiles*. The *first quartile return* is the middle return earned by the funds that performed better than the median return. In investments industry practice, first quartile performance denotes the performance of the *best quartile*. Performance within the first quartile indicates that the fund was a top 25% performer for the period. 25% of the return observations will be higher than the first quartile return and 75% will be below. In other contexts, first quartile is used to reference the worst performing quartile. The Excel quartile function uses the convention 1 = worst and 3 = best quartile.

The *third quartile return* is the performance of the fund halfway between the median return and the fund with the poorest performance for the period. Performance below the third quartile return indicates that the fund performance ranked in the bottom quartile. A measure of the dispersion, or variability, around the median return is the *semi-inter-quartile range*, which is the difference between the first and third quartile returns. The semi-interquartile range is an appropriate measure of variability when we are using the median as the indicator of the middle return. We discuss measures of dispersion where the average return is instead measured by the mean in Chapter 20.

Exhibit 7.3 illustrates the calculation of universe quartile returns. Notice that the position of the best quartile return is 5.25 values from the top return ((20+1)/4). We used linear interpolation to calculate the return that corresponds with this position by taking the return at the sixth position (6.21%) and adding 0.75 × the difference between the fifth and sixth returns, or 0.05 (0.75 × (6.28 – 6.21)). This method is consistent with the way we calculated a median return by averaging the two middle observations. There are other ways of interpolating a return that falls at a noninteger rank. For example, the Excel quartile function returns 6.23%, which strikes us as strange because it is closer to the sixth observation than the fifth.

We can also determine the quartile ranking of a fund without calculating a quartile return. Equation (7.1) shows how we can take the rank position to calculate the quartile ranking of a portfolio.

EXHIBIT 7.3   Universe Quartile

	A	B	C	D	E	F	G	H	I	J	K	L	M	N	O	P	Q	R	S	T
1	1	2	3	4	5	6	7	8	9	10	11	12	13	14	15	16	17	18	19	20
2	14.20	8.85	8.45	6.86	6.28	**6.21**	6.10	5.21	4.33	4.00	3.11	2.96	2.69	2.23	1.68	1.34	-0.78	-2.69	-3.66	-4.14
3																				
4					Groups:	4.00								Groups:	4.00					
5			Best Quartile Position:			5.25		=(COUNT(A2:T2)+1)/E4			Worst Quartile Position:			5.25			=(COUNT(A2:T2)+1)/O4			
6			First Quartile Return:			6.26		=F2+0.75*(E2-F2)			Third Quartile Return:			1.43			=P2+0.25*(O2-P2)			

EXHIBIT 7.4   Determining Quartile from Rank

	A	B	C	D
1	Rank:	6.00		
2	Quartile:	2.00	⟶	=CEILING((B1^4)/('20+1),1)

$$Quartile\ ranking\ =\ Ceiling\left(\frac{Rank\ position \times 4}{Number\ of\ observations + 1}\right) \qquad (7.1)$$

Where ceiling is a function taking the result and rounding it up to the next highest integer value. Exhibit 7.4 uses this formula to determine that our fund falls within the second quartile.

We did this by taking the rank order of the portfolio, multiplying it by the number of groups, and dividing the result by the total number of observations + 1. We then round the result up to the next highest integer value, which equals 2, or second quartile.

We can collect the funds into any number of groupings. *Quantile* is the generic term for these groupings, where quartiles = 4, quintiles = 5, decile = 10, percentiles = 100, and so on. Analysts commonly group portfolios into quintiles, or five groups, and deciles, or 10 groups, in addition to quartiles. We can generalize Equation (7.1) to find the Quantile rank of a portfolio:

$$Quantile\ ranking\ =\ Ceiling\left(\frac{Rank\ position \times Number\ of\ groups}{Number\ of\ observations + 1}\right) \qquad (7.2)$$

A generic algorithm for calculating percentile returns is to:

1. Sort the array of returns from highest to lowest.
2. Compute the location of the N-tile within the array by:

$$Quantile\ location\ =\ \left(\frac{Percentile}{100}\right) \times (Number\ of\ observations + 1) \qquad (7.3)$$

3. If the quantile location is an integer value, then the percentile equals the value at that location. If it is not then we use linear interpolation to obtain the value. We do this by taking the two returns that bound the N-tile location, take the difference between them, and multiply by percentile value. Then we add this result to the lower value.

EXHIBIT 7.5   Quantile Returns

	A	B	C	D	E	F	G	H
1	Number of Observations:		20					
2	Return		Percentile	Rank	Remainder	Lower Return	Higher Return	Difference
3	Best Decile:	8.81	10	2.10	0.90	8.45	8.85	0.40
4	Best Quintile:	6.74	20	4.20	0.80	6.28	6.86	0.58
5	Best Quartile:	6.26	25	5.25	0.75	6.21	6.28	0.07
6	Median:	3.56	50	10.50	0.50	3.11	4.00	0.89
7	Worst Quartile:	1.43	75	15.75	0.25	1.34	1.68	0.34
8					↓			
9		=(E7*H7)+F7		=(C7/100)*($D$1+1)				=G7-F7

EXHIBIT 7.6   Universe Comparison

	A	B	C	D	E	F
1	Fund	Quarter	YTD	2001	2000	1999
2	Return	29.71	20.84	24.20	13.07	17.20
3	%-tile	10	9	45	32	24
4						
5	Universe					
6	5th Decile	31.20	22.70	29.75	18.50	22.02
7	First Quartile	18.97	13.00	28.04	15.14	18.93
8	Median	12.33	8.30	23.55	12.72	15.90
9	Third Quartile	7.01	4.79	20.59	11.12	13.90
10	95th Decile	4.76	-2.80	18.62	10.05	0.70

Exhibit 7.5 shows the calculation of various quintiles for our sample universe.

To calculate the n-tiles, we first converted them into percentiles. A percentile return $P\%$ for a data set is the value that is greater than or equal to $(1 - P\%)$ of the returns, but is less than $P\%$ of the returns (holding to our convention that the best quantile is the highest return).

PEER GROUP ANALYSIS

Exhibit 7.6 is a representative universe total return comparison table. The fund is ranked within the universe over several time periods.

A common way of analyzing funds within a peer group is with the aid of a floating bar chart similar to that in Exhibit 7.7. The X-axis represents several calendar time periods and the Y-axis is the percentage return. In this chart the floating bars are broken up into quartile sections representing the universe returns for each time period. Then, we locate the fund return within the quartile section.

Notice that the length of each bar and the size of the quartile section within it are indicators of the *dispersion*, or spread of returns, within the universe during the period. For example, there was a bigger dispersion of returns within the universe in 1999 than in 2000 or 2001. And for the year-to-date there is a greater division between the best return and the first quartile return than for the other quartiles, where the returns are grouped more closely together. The bar charts can also be created for cumulative periods and for risk and risk-adjusted return statistics.

PEER COMPARISON CONSIDERATIONS

There are several factors to keep in mind when using a peer group universe as a basis for performance comparison.

■ Determining the portfolios to include in the universe is a subjective process. Participation in the universe collection process is often voluntary, and no universe has the complete population of assets under management. Some universes represent a very small proportion of the total assets under management for a particular investor base or strategy.

■ Peer group comparisons should be on a risk-adjusted basis. We expect to earn higher returns given the risk taken, but performance comparisons are frequently made on an absolute return basis without any adjustment for the risk taken. Some of the suppliers of peer group data also provide measures of risk taken and composite measures of risk-adjusted return, such as Sharpe Ratios. The most popular retail fund peer group ranking measures are done using risk-adjusted returns.

EXHIBIT 7.7   Calendar Period Peer Group Comparison

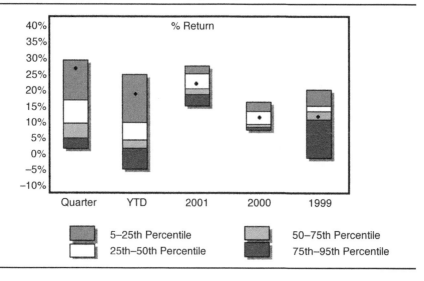

■ The comparisons are very sensitive to the proper classification of portfolios in universes. Besides the risk of outright misclassification, the universe might have very broad portfolio definitions where a category like "large company domestic equity" could contain portfolios managed according to many different styles. Many managers employ a range of styles, and grouping them into a particular category can be misleading. Funds differ as to their liberty to hold cash balances, allocate assets, invest outside the benchmark, use derivatives, hedge currency, and other factors. The problem is especially acute when trying to rank portfolios such as hedge funds, which use a wide variety of investment strategies. The objectives, constraints, and strategies of the peer group portfolios need to be as closely aligned as possible to provide a good analysis. Some universes address this problem by classifying managers according to the strategy implied by the holdings in their portfolios.

■ The returns and other statistics need to be calculated in the same way. For example, it would be inappropriate to compare funds where some of the returns are time weighted and others are dollar weighted. As we have seen in Part I, and will see again in Part II on risk measurement, there is more than one way to calculate these statistics.

■ Over time, the comparison will probably suffer from *survivorship bias*. Survivorship bias develops in performance universe data when the universe returns are created looking backward from the current period, and funds that disappeared over the time period are not included in the comparison. For example, the three-year return comparison would not include all funds that existed three years ago, but only those that continued to exist until the present period. If this is the case, survivorship bias is likely to lead to understated peer group comparisons, as poorer performing funds are closed or merged into other funds. The longer the period, the more the comparisons will be impacted by survivorship bias. Because the number of funds in the peer group shrinks as the return period increases, the statistical significance of the peer group comparisons decreases as the time period lengthens.

Given these considerations many people feel that performance comparisons should be made against a market index, or similar benchmark, and not a peer group universe. The reality is that peer comparison is a significant component of the performance measurement process. We are all interested in performance relative to our peers and the comparison can at least provide interesting input for further analysis. In addition, there are some strategies for which no market index or benchmark exists.

MARKET INDICES

Practitioners have come to accept that a peer group universe does not fulfill all of the requirements for a good measure of relative performance. Jeffrey Bailey set out the criteria of a good performance comparison benchmark, which is "unambiguous, investable, measurable, appropriate, and specified in advance."[1] Peer group universes do not enjoy all of these ideal characteristics. For example, we cannot invest in an asset called "the median manager return." But we still need to understand whether our investments have done as well as they should have, given the returns provided by the capital markets during the period. A performance benchmark is the standard by which we judge the success or failure of an investment strategy. We usually benchmark a fund against the performance of a market index. We can compare not only the return, but also the risk experienced by the investor in the fund against that of the index. An index represents the average price level of a particular asset class or market. Periodic changes in the index represent the average performance of the underlying securities. An appropriate index for a particular fund represents the performance of the universe of assets that are eligible for portfolio construction according to the manager's mandate and specific strategy. For example, the S&P 500 index represents the performance of U.S. large capitalization stocks. We could use the S&P 500 as the benchmark to judge the performance of funds that invest in the U.S. large-cap stock asset class. The appropriate market index return is the return that can be earned by the investor at low cost where there are index funds that parallel the performance of the index. It therefore makes a good benchmark of active manager performance.

Indices are published by many different organizations. Suppliers of market indices include financial data publishers (S&P, Dow Jones), pension consultants (Frank Russell, Wilshire), and brokerage firms (Lehman Brothers, Morgan Stanley). Some of the providers publish complete families of indices that represent the performance of the global stock and debt markets. There are multiple, competing index families that represent the performance of every major asset class, and new indices are continually developed. Taking the global equity markets as an example, there is an index for each country that is popularly used as the primary reference for the performance of that particular country's stock market. These indices, such as the Dow Jones in the U.S. and the DAX in Germany, are predominantly used within the local marketplace. Because these indices differ in their construction methodology there is the

---

[1] Jeffrey Bailey, "Are Manager Universes Acceptable Performance Benchmarks?" *Journal of Portfolio Management*, Spring 1992.

demand by global investors for a consistently constructed set of indices representing each market around the world. MSCI (Morgan Stanley Capital International), FTSE (Financial Times-London Stock Exchange), and others provide these global index families.

Investors also customize the market indices to reflect their own unique objectives and constraints. For example, funds that are restricted from investing in tobacco stocks will take the market index and subtract the contribution to return of the tobacco stocks in order to derive an appropriate benchmark for their situation. Balanced fund mandates are benchmarked using an index calculated as the sum of the weighted returns of several cash, fixed income, and equity indices. There are many other types of custom benchmarks. We use the more generic term *benchmark* rather than *index* to encompass both market indices and custom benchmarks.

Benchmark selection is one of the most important decisions made by the investor. The benchmark selection decision influences the entire investment process from the construction of portfolios to the evaluation of performance. The benchmark employed at the total fund level as well as the benchmarks used to guide management of funds investing in particular asset classes, or with particular styles, heavily influences the management of these funds. Benchmarks are important inputs to performance measurement and evaluation. Along with the fund returns, index returns are the primary inputs to performance attribution and risk analysis.

Given its importance to performance measurement, how do we determine the correct benchmark for a portfolio? The benchmark depends a great deal on the investor's objectives and constraints or the fund's stated strategy. Therefore, the benchmarking decision is usually made well before the measurement of performance. We then take the fund's benchmark as a given when performing any kind of comparison, attribution, or risk analysis. For an institutional or private client separate account, the benchmark is part of the investment policy statement, along with the requirements of the fund for liquidity, income, permissible investments, and other information providing guidance to the manager. For those more interested in this important topic, Web sites of the various benchmark providers are a good place to start researching the composition of the various indices.

EQUITY INDEX RETURN CALCULATION

Each index publisher has different methods for defining the universe of securities that are eligible for inclusion in the index and for selecting the actual constituent securities from this universe. Once these decisions have been made the weighting scheme of the securities selected within the index is the next decision. There are several ways to weight securities within the index. Taking an equity index as an example, we could equal weight each stock in the index. Although some indices are equal weighted, use of an equal-weighted index as a benchmark implies that the investor equal weights stocks within a portfolio. Instead we could weight each index constituent according to its proportionate market capitalization. The market capitalization of a stock is equal to the shares outstanding, multiplied by the current market price. The total return for a market cap-weighted index is calculated by weighting each stock return by its proportional market cap. Most of the indices used as manager performance benchmarks are market capitalization weighted, and the examples here use a market cap-weighting methodology. In a market cap-weighted index, larger companies have a greater impact on the total index return than smaller companies. To calculate the market cap we need to determine the number of shares outstanding for each stock. To maintain an index that represents the investable marketplace, we can subtract from the total shares outstanding the shares that are closely held or government owned. To reduce double counting we can adjust the share balance by shares that are crossheld by other companies, i.e., two companies that hold stock in each other. Each of the publishers has a different methodology for figuring these adjustments. While our examples focus on a basic equity index, indices constructed to gauge the performance of other asset classes adjust the basic methodology to handle the characteristics of the specific asset class.[2]

Once we have determined the weighting scheme, we can begin calculating index returns. Single period index returns for a basic equity index are calculated by taking the periodic market value of each constituent, weighting each constituent return, and then calculating the total index level. Suppose we are starting a new index and our index construction methodology filters the universe of stocks down to three stocks with a total beginning market cap of 31,500:

Stock	Shares	Price	Market Cap
A	1,000.00	12.00	12,000.00
B	3,000.00	3.50	10,500.00
C	2,000.00	4.50	9,000.00
Total			31,500.00

At the start of the measurement period we initialize the index level to an arbitrary base value, or *level*, say 1000. At the end of the next day we record the change in market value of the three stocks and calculate an index return for the day. Exhibit 7.8 shows the return calculation for Day 1.

---

[2] For more information on the construction of indices see Frank Fabozzi (ed.), *Professional Perspectives on Indexing* (New Hope, PA: Frank J. Fabozzi Associates, 1997).

EXHIBIT 7.8   Index Return Calculation

	A	B	C	D	E	F	G	H	I	J
1	Day 0					Day 1				
2	Stock	Shares	Price	Market Cap		Stock	Shares	Price	Market Cap	Return
3	A	1,000.00	12.00	12,000.00		A	1000.00	12.37	12,370.00	3.08
4	B	3,000.00	3.50	10,500.00		B	3000.00	3.62	10,860.00	3.43
5	C	2,000.00	4.50	9,000.00		C	2000.00	4.45	8,900.00	-1.11
6	Total			31,500.00		Total			32,130.00	
7										
8		Index Level:	1000.00				Index Level:	1020.00	→ =(I6/D6)*C8	
9							Return:	2.00	=((H8/C8)-1)*100	

The Day 1 index level is equal to 1020. We calculated the level by taking the ratio of the beginning and end market value (32,130/31,500 = 1.02). This gives the growth rate for the index on Day 1. Multiplying the growth rate by the initial index level of 1000 yields the index level at the end of Day 1 (1000 × 1.02 = 1020). We then calculated the index return by taking the ratio of the two daily index levels, 2.00% (1020/ 1000 − 1). The index return is also equal to the prior day index level multiplied by (1 + total return for the day). There is an implicit reinvestment assumption in the index calculations; the gains in one period are reinvested into the index in the next period.

The change in index levels in a weighted average index represents the weighted average stock price change in the market for the day. It is a summary statistic highly influenced by stocks with large price changes and stocks with large percentage weights within the index.

We calculate index levels in addition to returns in order to build a time series that can be used to determine the performance of the market between any two dates. We can calculate multiperiod cumulative index returns by taking the ratio of the index levels between any two dates.

$$\text{Cumulative index return} = \left[\left(\frac{\text{Index level end of period}}{\text{Index level begin of period}} \right) - 1 \right] \times 100 \quad (7.4)$$

We can restate the cumulative index return to an annual basis in the same way we do fund returns:

$$
\begin{aligned}
&\text{Annualized index return} \\
&= \left[(1 + \text{Cumulative index return})^{\frac{365.25}{\text{\# of days}}} - 1 \right] \times 100
\end{aligned}
\quad (7.5)
$$

Exhibit 7.9 shows the calculation, using levels, of compound cumulative and annualized returns for an index over several periods.

EXHIBIT 7.9   Multiperiod Returns Using Index Levels

	A	B	C
1	Year Ending	Value Without Dividends	Value With Dividends
2	1995	631.20	1223.11
3	1996	756.70	1497.66
4	1997	988.16	1989.67
5	1998	1236.81	2527.35
6	1999	1476.54	3055.86
7	2000	1345.96	2817.84
8			
9	Cumulative Returns		
10	1/1996 to 12/2000	113.24	130.38
11	1/1997 to 12/2000	77.87	88.15
12	1/2000 to 12/2000	-8.84	-7.79
13			
14		=((B7/B6)-1)*100	
15	Annualized Returns		=((((1+B10/100)^(365.25/1826))-1)*100
16	1/1996 to 12/2000	16.35	
17	1/1997 to 12/2000	15.50	
18	1/2000 to 12/2000	-8.84	

It is important to note that multiperiod index returns are inherently time-weighted returns. We link the index growth rates, calculated using index levels, in the same way as we do the subperiod growth rates calculated between cash flow dates for the portfolio. To calculate a dollar weighted index return, we could create a portfolio that purchases shares in the index level in proportion to the contribution and calculate a return on the dollars invested in this portfolio.

EQUITY INDEX MAINTENANCE

Stock indices need to be maintained to reflect the decision to add or delete constituents from the index and the effects of corporate actions. To show the maintenance of the index for this activity, we first look at a stock split, which does not need to be explicitly handled in the index return calculation. When a stock splits, the number of shares outstanding goes up and the price goes down in the same proportion. For example, the stock of Company B in our index splits 2 for 1 effective after the close of trading on Day 1, leaving 6000 shares outstanding at the begin of Day 2. Exhibit 7.10 shows that because the shares and price change proportionately, we do not have to make a formal adjustment to the index calculation for a constituent stock split.

Changes in Capitalization

We do, however, need to account for outstanding capitalization changes, for example, if one of the companies in the index issues new shares.

Suppose that Company A issues 200 new shares effective at the close of market Day 2. We need to account for these new shares in the calculation of the index return Day 3. One way to account for a market capitalization change is to calculate an adjusted beginning market cap for the return calculation on Day 3. Exhibit 7.11 shows how to adjust the ending market cap (32,450) upward for the impact of the new shares issued for Company A.

We do this by adding the market value of the new shares (shares × price) to the ending market capitalization on Day 2. The Day 2 adjusted ending market value is used in the denominator of the Day 3 index return calculation in cell H28. This is analogous to the way we add a purchase to the denominator for the daily security level return calculation for portfolios that are trading. We can use the same adjustment methodology when a security is added to or dropped from an index.

Let's take a closer look at the calculation of an index level. We are interested in creating a series of numbers (index levels) that represents the change in values of a fixed set of constituents defined on the base date, where each constituent is weighted by its market capitalization within the market as a whole. If there were no share changes from day to day we could calculate the index using this formula:

EXHIBIT 7.10   Index Return with Stock Split

	A	B	C	D	E	F	G	H	I	J
11	Day 1					Day 2				
12	Stock	Shares	Price	Market Cap		Stock	Shares	Price	Market Cap	Return
13	A	1,000.00	12.37	12,370.00		A	1,000.00	12.79	12,790.00	3.40
14	B	3,000.00	3.62	10,860.00		B	6,000.00	1.81	10,860.00	0.00
15	C	2,000.00	4.45	8,900.00		C	2,000.00	4.40	8,800.00	-1.12
16	Total			32,130.00		Total			32,450.00	
17										
18		Index Level:	1020.00				Index Level:	1030.16	=(I16/D16)*C18	
19	Company B 2:1 Split						Return:	1.00	=((H18/C17)-1)*100	

EXHIBIT 7.11   Index Return with Capital Change

	A	B	C	D	E	F	G	H	I	J
21	Day 2					Day 3				
22	Stock	Shares	Price	Market Cap		Stock	Shares	Price	Market Cap	Return
23	A	1,000.00	12.79	12,790.00		A	1,200.00	12.79	15,348.00	0.00
24	B	6,000.00	1.81	10,860.00		B	6,000.00	1.81	10,860.00	0.00
25	C	2,000.00	4.40	8,800.00		C	2,000.00	4.40	8,800.00	0.00
26	Total			32,450.00		Total			35,008.00	
27										
28		Index Level:	1,030.16				Index Level:	1030.16	=C28*(I26/C33)	
29	Company A Issues 200 New Shares						Return:	0.00	=((H28/C28)-1)*100	
30		New Shares:	200.00							
31		Price:	12.79	=C23						
32	Market Cap Adjustment:		2,558.00	=C30*C31						
33	Adjusted Capitalization:		35,008.00	=D26+C32						

Capitalization weighted index level

$$= \frac{\text{Sum(Current stock price} \times \text{Current shares)}}{\text{Sum(Prior stock price} \times \text{Prior shares)}} \times \text{Prior index value} \quad (7.6)$$

But we also need to take into account periodic additions and deletions from the index, including the addition of shares due to a new stock issue by one of the current index constituents. We saw how to do this by adjusting the prior day market capitalization by the new issue when calculating the current day's return. Another way of handling capitalization changes is via the introduction of a *capitalization adjustment factor* that corrects for the constituent changes and impacts of corporate actions. To use this method we take the following steps:

1. The starting denominator equals the beginning total market capital divided by the starting index level, in our case 1000.
2. Divide each day's total market cap by the prior day divisor when there are no new or deleted index constituents and no corporate actions requiring adjustment.
3. When there is a capital change, calculate a divisor adjustment factor equal to:

   Current day adjustment factor

   $$= \frac{\text{Prior day market cap} + \text{New component market cap}}{\text{Prior day market cap}} \quad (7.7)$$

4. Multiply the prior day divisor by the adjustment factor to get today's divisor.

Exhibit 7.12 shows the calculation of the index levels and returns for each day using the index divisor approach.

EXHIBIT 7.12 Index Level Calculation Using Divisor Adjustment

	A	B	C	D	E	F	G
1							
2		Day 0	Day 1	Day 2	Day 3		
3	Market Capitalization:	31,500.00	32,130.00	32,450.00	35,008.00		
4	Divisor:	31.500	31.500	31.500	33.983		=D4*E9
5	Index Level:	1,000.00	1,020.00	1,030.16	1,030.16		=E3/E4
6	Return:		2.00	1.00	-	→	=((E5/D5)-1)*100
7							
8	Additional Market Cap:				2,558.00		
9	Adjustment Factor:				1.08		=(D3+E8)/D3

EXHIBIT 7.13 Total Return Index

	A	B	C	D	E
1					
2		Day 3	Day 4		
3	Market Capitalization:	35,008.00	35,008.00		
4	Dividend:	-	700.16		
5	Divisor:	33.98	33.98		=B5*C10
6	Index Level:	1,030.16	1,050.86		=(C3+C4)/C5
7	Return:	-	2.01	→	=((C6/B6)-1)*100
8					
9	Additional Cap:	2,558.00	-		
10	Adjustment:	1.08	1.00		=(B3+C9)/B3

Indices that are calculated in this way are called *Laspeyres chain indices*. A Laspeyres index is the value of a basket of, in this case, securities where the value of each successive weighted basket of securities is linked together over time. The relative market caps of the individual securities within the index determine the security weights. The number of shares used to determine the weights is fixed at the base period, i.e., only the change in price serves to change the relative weight of the securities within the index over time. The adjustment factor reconciles the prior day index value to the new day's market capitalization and protects the time series of index levels from changes in the components of the index and corporate actions. We can contrast the Laspeyres index to the *Paasche index*, where we do adjust the number of shares of each security within the index periodically. Most stock market indices are Laspeyres indices.

One advantage of the divisor approach is that it makes it easy to account for day-to-day market capitalization adjustments. The adjustment factor is used to account for many types of corporate actions, including secondary share offerings, stock repurchase programs, rights offerings, and spin-offs. In addition to corporate actions the adjustment factor is changed to account for new additions to or deletions from the index caused by mergers, bankruptcies, and corporate reorganizations.

The index levels calculated so far are *price only indices*; they do not include income earned on the securities within the index. An index that includes both price appreciation and dividend income is a *total return index*. If we are calculating a total return index we include the daily dividend accruals in the calculation. Exhibit 7.13 shows how to use the divisor approach to calculate a total return index.

Fixed Income Indices

Fixed income indices are more difficult to select and construct than equity indices, for several reasons. First, there are many types of bonds, with varying maturities, credit quality, and other differentiating factors.

The market index appropriate for one investor might have a very different collection of these bonds than that for another investor, and that index might not be representative of a weighted average of the bond market as a whole. To facilitate the selection of an index matching the characteristics of the portfolio, the fixed income index families offer a variety of subindices, which can be combined in different ways to provide a proper benchmark. Lehman Brothers, JP Morgan, Merrill Lynch, and other providers compile the major fixed income benchmark families.[3]

CUSTOMIZED BENCHMARKS

Benchmarks can also be customized to reflect the investor's tolerance for risk as well as restrictions with respect to particular asset classes, hedging, instruments, industries, and other factors. A benchmark created to reflect a passive version of a particular strategy is called a normal portfolio. A *normal portfolio* is a benchmark completely customized for the evaluation of a particular portfolio or strategy. The constituent selection and weighting methods are agreed on at the inception of the investment between the manager and the client. The return and risk profile of the normal portfolio is used to measure the performance of the manager.

We can also manipulate the market indices in various ways to customize them for the needs of a particular investment strategy. Some common ways of doing this are discussed in the following sections.

Blended Benchmark

Portfolios that contain securities from several different asset classes are sometimes called *balanced funds*. We can benchmark a balanced fund using the weighted average return for indices representing each asset class. For example, for a fund whose risk and return objectives indicate a 50/50 split between equity and fixed income, we might calculate a benchmark return equal to 50% of the S&P 500 return and 50% of the Lehman Aggregate index return. We could leave the weights fixed at 50/50 each period, or let them float with the market between periodic *rebalancing* dates. For example, if we start out with a 50/50 benchmark and the equity market rises while bonds remain flat, in the next period we would expect our fund to be comprised of proportionately more equity than fixed income. If we keep a static 50/50 benchmark in the next period we might imply that the fund should be rebalanced to the

---

[3] Lev Dynkin, Jay Hyman, Vadim Konstantinovsky, and Nancy Roth, "MBS Index Returns: A Detailed Look," *Journal of Fixed Income* (March 1999), provide a guide to the methodology behind the construction and calculation of a fixed income index.

benchmark by selling stocks and buying bonds. We could instead allow the benchmark weights to *float* with the market until a periodic rebalancing date. For example, we could let the benchmark float in between quarters and then rebalance it to the fixed weights at quarter end.

Liability Benchmarks

Many portfolios are set up to fund a specific liability, for example the future payment of benefits promised by a corporate defined-benefit pension plan. Insurance companies have fixed income portfolios designed to fund the liabilities created by their products. One of the main considerations in the management of these portfolios is that the growth in liabilities is matched with the growth in assets. The main influence of price change in fixed income portfolios is the change in interest rates. The value of the assets will vary inversely to the change in liabilities as interest rates fluctuate. To monitor the change in assets versus the change in liabilities, we can benchmark these portfolios against a custom liability benchmark comprised of zero coupon government bonds or treasury strips that match the dollar and time to maturity characteristics of the liability structure. The custom benchmark is a portfolio that is constructed and valued in a similar way as a market index. The portfolio is valued periodically and single-period returns are calculated in the same manner as for a market benchmark. The relative performance of the portfolio versus the custom benchmark will indicate whether the portfolio is structured to neutralize the effects of interest rate changes.[4]

Market Index Less a Component

Benchmarks can also be customized to reflect the investor's restrictions with respect to particular asset classes, instruments, industries, and the like. Instead of building up a new index from the stock level, we can adjust the return of an index by the contribution to return from certain stocks in the index. For example, a large corporate pension plan might use as its benchmark the return of the S&P 500 index excluding the company's own stock. Or a fund that applies social screens, like excluding tobacco companies, will calculate its index less these stocks.

Market Index Plus Hurdle Rate or Less Management Fee

One of the disadvantages of using a market index as a basis for performance comparison is that the index is not a real portfolio that must pay

---

[4] For more on liability benchmarks see Ronald Ryan, "Managing a Fixed Income Portfolio Versus a Liability Objective," in *Managing Fixed Income Portfolios*, Frank J. Fabozzi (ed.) (New Hope, PA: Frank J. Fabozzi Associates, 1997).

management fees and other expenses. We can compare the gross-of-fee return to the index, or we can use as a custom benchmark the market index return adjusted downward in proportion to the management fee. We do this by periodically subtracting a basis point management fee from the index return and chain linking the adjusted returns. For some investment strategies, we might choose to do the opposite and add basis points to create a *hurdle rate* out of the basic index return. The hurdle rate created from a benchmark will vary along with the market and better reflect the actual opportunities available to the investor than a fixed percentage return benchmark.

Currency Conversion

Suppose we are a Canadian investor with a U.S. portfolio, and we are using the S&P 500 as a benchmark. Our return in Canadian dollar base currency will not only be affected by the local U.S. dollar change in security values, but also the change in the U.S./Canada exchange rate. We can adjust the returns on the S&P 500 to reflect this by re-basing the S&P 500 return into Canadian dollars. We do this using the same methodology to currency convert fund returns presented in Chapter 6.

VALUE ADDED

The goal of the manager of an active strategy is to produce returns above the benchmark return or *value added*. Many times the management fees paid by the client and the compensation of the investment manager depend on the amount of value added. So once we have determined the fund and benchmark returns for the period, the next thing that we do is to calculate the value added. Value added is sometimes called *excess return*. Here we will reserve the term "excess return" to refer to the return above the risk free rate, a figure that we use in the calculation of the Sharpe ratio and other statistics based on the Capital Asset Pricing Model, which are covered in Part II. In this book, value added refers to the difference between the fund and the benchmark return.

Single Period Value Added

Suppose that a fund had a 15% return and the benchmark returned 10% over a one-month period. What was the value added by the manager? Most people would answer 5%. We could stop there and call the arithmetic difference between the fund and benchmark return "value added." But let's take a closer look. What if we made two 100-dollar investments at the beginning of the period, one into the fund and one into an index fund that tracked the benchmark? At the end of the month we would have $115 in the fund and $110 by investing in the benchmark. Investing in the fund gave us an extra $5. We could measure value added by taking the $5 gain and dividing by the $100 initial investment. The result would be 5%.

But there is an argument that we should measure the value added gained against not the beginning investment, but against the ending value that we would have achieved if we had simply invested the money into the index fund. Using this definition, we would calculate a value added equal to 4.55% ((115/110) − 1). Another way to calculate the same figure is to divide the single period growth rates:

$$\left(\frac{1.15}{1.10} - 1\right) \times 100 = 4.55\%$$

We could call the first definition *arithmetic value added*, because we are subtracting the benchmark return from the fund return in order to derive the percentage gain. The arithmetic value added in our example was 5%.

$$\text{Arithmetic value added} = \text{Fund return} - \text{Benchmark return} \qquad (7.8)$$

The second definition we could call *geometric value added*, because we are taking the ratio of the two growth rates in order to derive the gain.

$$\text{Geometric value added} = \left[\left(\frac{(1 + \text{Fund return})}{(1 + \text{Benchmark return})}\right) - 1\right] \times 100 \qquad (7.9)$$

Both figures are correct; they just have a different interpretation. Arithmetic value added is the difference between the fund return and the benchmark return for the period. Geometric value added is the ratio of the rate of growth in the two investments over the period. The geometric value added is the return that reconciles the amount of extra dollars we would have had after investing in the active fund versus investing in the benchmark.

Multiperiod Value Added

The arithmetic and geometric value added figures provide an interesting example of how we need to be careful when using return differences to analyze performance.

Suppose the fund and benchmark earned the same returns in Month 2 as in Month 1. In Exhibit 7.14 we illustrate the calculation of value added for this situation. For both months, the single period arithmetic value added is 5% and the geometric value added 4.55%.

The cumulative fund return after two months equals 32.25%, and the benchmark return is 21.00%. The arithmetic value added over the two months is the difference between them, or 11.25%. We calculate multiple period value added by independently compounding the fund and benchmark returns and then subtracting the multiperiod benchmark return from the multiperiod fund return. The multiperiod geometric value added is 9.30%. We calculate it by taking the ratio of the multiperiod growth rates. The 9.30% figure has the same economic interpretation as the single period value added, it represents the additional dollars gained by investing in the fund over and above those we would have received by investing in the benchmark.

Now suppose we took the single period value added figures and compounded them over the two periods. Exhibit 7.15 illustrates the problem with doing this. Cell B8 is the compounded single period arithmetic value added. It does not equal the difference between the compounded returns calculated in cell B5. We cannot take single period arithmetic value added figures and compound them over time to derive the value added over multiple periods.

Notice that we can, however, compound the single period geometric value added figures to reconcile the multiperiod geometric value added. Cell B9 shows how we can do that. One reason why the geometric value added is sometimes preferred over the arithmetic value added is that we can compound the benchmark growth rate with the value added and derive the fund return. We can see this in cell B13.

EXHIBIT 7.14   Arithmetic versus Geometric Value Added

	A	B	C	D	E
1	Month 1				
2		Return	BMV	EMV	
3	Fund:	15.00	100.00	115.00	=C3*(1+B3/100)
4	Benchmark:	10.00	100.00	110.00	=C4*(1+B4/100)
5	Arithmetic Value Added:	5.00	=B3-B4		
6	Geometric Value Added	4.55	=((1+B3/100)/(1+B4/100)-1)*100		
7					
8	Month 2				
9		Return	BMV	EMV	
10	Fund:	15.00	115.00	132.25	=C10*(1+B10/100)
11	Benchmark:	10.00	110.00	121.00	=C11*(1+B11/100)
12	Arithmetic Value Added:	5.00	=B10-B11		
13	Geometric Value Added	4.55	=((1+B10/100)/(1+B11/100)-1)*100		
14					
15	Two Month Cumulative				
16	Fund:	32.25	=((1+B3/100)*(1+B10/100)-1)*100		
17	Benchmark:	21.00	=((1+B4/100)*(1+B11/100)-1)*100		
18	Arithmetic Value Added:	11.25	=B16-B17		
19	Geometric Value Added	9.30	=((1+B16/100)/(1+B17/100)-1)*100		

EXHIBIT 7.15   Compound Value Added

	A	B	C	D
1				
2		Two-Month	Month 1	Month 2
3	Fund:	32.25	15.00	15.00
4	Benchmark:	21.00	10.00	10.00
5	Arithmetic Value Added:	11.25	5.00	5.00
6	Geometric Value Added	9.30	4.55	4.55
7	**Compounded Value Added**			
8	Arithmetic:	10.25	=((1+C5/100)*(1+D5/100)-1)*100	
9	Geometric:	9.30 ➤	=((1+C6/100)*(1+D6/100)-1)*100	
10			Does not equal 11.25	
11				
12	**Fund Return = Bench + Value Added**			
13		32.25 ➤	=((1+B4/100)*(1+B6/100)-1)*100	

In summary, the geometric value added is the value that causes the benchmark return to grow to the fund return over a period. Although most people derive value added arithmetically as the difference between the fund and benchmark return, value added is an inherently geometric concept, wherein the relative growth rates compound over time to produce the multiperiod incremental gains over the benchmark. We can use value added analysis to compare the fund to the benchmark or the fund to other funds. We can compare the performance of two funds over different economic cycles by comparing the value added over different periods of time.

Risk Measurement

CHAPTER 8

Risk

art I of this book showed us how to measure the return earned on an investment portfolio, the return for its benchmark, and the value added by the manager over the benchmark. Once we have calculated the returns, we are interested in assessing the results. Exhibit 8.1 presents us with a short history of returns for a fund and its benchmark and Exhibit 8.2 with summary statistics for the 13-month period.

EXHIBIT 8.1   Single Period Returns

Month	Fund	Benchmark	Value Added
1	7.00	5.76	1.24
2	5.00	4.18	0.82
3	-4.00	-3.11	-0.89
4	4.50	4.00	0.50
5	4.00	3.87	0.13
6	-3.00	-2.36	-0.64
7	8.00	5.55	2.45
8	0.10	-3.12	3.22
9	1.00	-0.50	1.50
10	-5.00	-2.74	-2.26
11	2.00	6.33	-4.33
12	4.00	2.03	1.97
13	7.00	5.89	1.11

EXHIBIT 8.2   Multiperiod Returns

	Fund	Benchmark	
Cumulative Return:	33.87	28.00	
Annualized Return:	30.90	25.60	

	Monthly	Cumulative	Annualized
Arithmetic Value Added:	0.37	5.87	5.30
Geometric Value Added:	0.36	4.58	4.22

We can see that the monthly periodic returns have been mostly positive, the cumulative absolute return is positive, and the fund outperformed its benchmark by a healthy margin over the period. In light of this we may conclude that we are happy with the performance of the portfolio.

But we have left out of our evaluation an important consideration: risk. Capital market theory and history indicate that there is a tradeoff between risk taken and the returns achieved. Risk produces return: If we take on no risk, we should not expect to earn a return over that compensating for the time value of money. Given a diversified portfolio and long-time horizon, we expect to achieve a higher return for taking on risk. This point raises some questions about the performance of our sample portfolio:

- To earn the value added, did the manager take on more risk than we wished to tolerate?
- How efficiently did the portfolio use risk in order to deliver return?
- Were there alternative portfolios that delivered similar returns with less risk?

To answer these questions, we need to measure risk as well as return. Part II of the book is about the measurement of the investment risk taken, in the past, in order to earn a return. To most of us, the *return* and the measurement of it by observing the change in market value over time are intuitive concepts. This is not the case for risk. Our awareness of what is risky depends on our individual situation, and the methods used to quantify risk might not be self-evident. Given this, in this chapter we start by looking at alternative definitions of investment risk and then derive various measures of risk appropriate for the situation.

The most commonly used indicator of investment risk is the volatility of periodic returns. Chapter 9 is about the measurement of historical volatility, principally via the statistic standard deviation. There are some drawbacks to the use of standard deviation as a return measure. Where risk is defined as the probability of incurring a loss larger than one can tolerate, and some other situations, we measure risk by evaluating the proportion of returns that fall below a threshold required return or downside risk. We cover risk measurement in a downside framework in Chapter 10. For funds managed to a specific benchmark, the benchmark is an indication of the level of volatility that we expect to experience. We would expect a fund that is benchmarked against an emerging markets index to be more volatile than one benchmarked against the S&P 500. Just as we are interested in isolating the value added from the fund return when we evaluate manager returns, we are interested in separating out the benchmark relative volatility from the absolute volatility. Chapter 11 covers some measures of how well the variability in fund returns tracks the variability in benchmark returns, which allows us to depict fund-specific volatility. In Part III we unite the return measures covered in Part I with the risk measures developed in Part II to relate risk and return together in the measurement of efficiency and skill. We will use the fund and benchmark in Exhibit 8.1 to illustrate the statistics of risk and risk-adjusted return measurement.

DEFINING RISK

Returns give us a measure of only a single dimension of investment performance. To reach a meaningful conclusion as to the success or failure of an investment strategy, we also consider the other dimension: the risks taken in the course of earning those returns. But before we can measure this, we need to be able to define what it is we are attempting to measure.

Risk is scenario dependent: what we would consider risky depends on the requirements and constraints presented by the investor's situation. Here are three examples where risk is defined in different ways:

- An individual investor saving money to pay for a young child's college education is concerned with the possibility of not having saved enough money to fund the future tuition. The risk of not having enough to fund a liability due in the future is called *shortfall risk*. Capital growth over the long term would be the main goal of an investment program designed to fund this future goal. As the spending target date is many years down the road, we are less concerned with a lack of investment income or periodic negative returns. But we would want to make sure the risk we do take on is rewarded in terms of long-term return.
- A corporate treasury department has as a requirement the maintenance of a fund that meets the short-term needs of the corporation to pay bills and other expenses. The goals for such a fund would be to provide the corporation with a high degree of liquidity and some income. Stability in principal is the main investment objective for these funds. We would be willing to trade off any possibility of long-term appreciation in these assets in exchange for short-term safety. There is no tolerance for the risk of principal loss in this situation. Loss of principle can be equated with experiencing a negative return during a period.

■ An active fund manager has as his main goal to perform well enough over time to attract and retain clients but remain within the risk tolerance specified by the client. Here the client communicates his risk tolerance via the setting of the benchmark and will judge the manager based on the efficient use of benchmark relative risk in order to achieve value added. The value added can be compared with the excess risk to measure whether the manager budgeted his *active risk* well, where active risk is defined as the risk associated with positioning the portfolio in a different way than the benchmark.

MEASURING RISK

When we make our investments, it is the expected return along with the *uncertainty* in expected return that we use to gauge the appropriateness of a particular asset class or fund to a particular situation. Different investments or combinations of investments have different levels of uncertainty associated with them. Two funds might have had a similar average periodic return, for example 5%. But there is a clear difference in the two investments if Fund A had steady returns of 5% a year and Fund B had a history where half of the time the returns were 0% and the other half of the time 10%. Assuming that past history can be used as a guide to the future our projected savings would be more uncertain with Fund B. This is because Fund B has a wider dispersion of possible outcomes than Fund A. In a similar way, if our definition of risk is risk relative to the benchmark, we expect to earn a higher return in exchange for making active decisions that change our risk relative to the benchmark. If a fund held the same securities in the benchmark in the same proportion as the benchmark, we would expect to earn the benchmark return. In this situation there is no active risk. But if instead the manager overweights attractive securities relative to the benchmark, then we would expect a higher return given the risk of these decisions not working out, leading to underperformance. In both absolute and relative risk situations, given the same average expected return, most investors would prefer the more certain to the less certain choice. So we can equate risk with the uncertainty as to the outcome of our investments. One investment is riskier than another if it has a greater dispersion of possible outcomes.

In performance measurement we are interested in quantifying past performance. So how can we relate a concept of risk defined as *future* uncertainty when we are actually measuring *past* activity? This is a valid question, some would say there is no risk in past returns because these returns have already happened and we knew what they were! In fact, to quantify ex-post risk, we need to come up with a measure of uncertainty. When we turn from evaluating future risk to the measurement of past risk, we use as our proxy for uncertainty the volatility of the periodic returns. Return *volatility* is the variability of the periodic returns over time. There are several measures of variability. One indication of volatility is the range between the highest periodic return achieved and the lowest. If this range were very large then we would say that the investment was riskier than one with a smaller range, and we would hope to have earned a higher long-term return on this investment given the degree of return uncertainty.

So given that we should expect higher returns only in exchange for taking risk, if volatility were a good proxy for risk then we would expect volatility to be correlated with return. In fact the history of returns to various asset classes provides us with evidence that volatility is a good proxy for risk. In exchange for taking on volatility investors have been rewarded with a higher long-term average return. Exhibit 8.3 shows average annual returns to several asset classes from 1925–2000 as compiled by Ibbotson and Associates.[1] The asset classes with the highest average annual return have also been the ones with the greatest dispersion in annual returns. We can see that while small company stocks had the highest average return, 17.3%, the range of yearly returns experienced by investors in this asset class ranged 200.9% from low to high annual return. That is in one-year small company stocks lost 58% of their value but in at least one other year the asset class returned approximately 143%. This is a much larger differential from that experienced by investors in, for example, long-term government bonds. The returns to this asset class range 49.5% from low to high, and the average return was 5.7%.

EXHIBIT 8.3   U.S. Capital Market Risk and Returns 1925–2000

Asset Class	Annual Returns			
	Average	High	Low	Range
Small Company Stocks	17.3	142.9	-58.0	200.9
Large Company Stocks	13.0	54.0	-43.3	97.3
LT Corp Bonds	6.0	42.6	-8.1	50.7
LT Gov't Bonds	5.7	40.4	-9.2	49.5
Intermediate Gov't Bonds	5.5	29.1	-5.1	34.2
U.S. Treasury Bills	3.9	14.7	0.0	14.7

Source: Stocks, Bonds, Bills and Inflation® 2001 Yearbook, © 2001 Ibbotson Associates, Inc. Based on copyrighted works by Ibbotson and Sinquefield. All rights reserved. Used with permission.

---

[1] Ibbotson Associates, *Stocks, Bonds, Bills, and Inflation 2001 Yearbook* (Chicago: Ibbotson Associates, 2001).

This history shows us how volatility measures uncertainty. If history is an accurate guide to the future and we invested in small company stocks, we would be much less certain of having a particular ending market value at the end of the period as compared to an investment in Treasury bills.

CLASSIFYING RISK MEASURES

While our primary definition of risk is the variability in the historical return series, we can tailor our risk measures to the investor situation. There are three main classes of historical risk statistics: absolute risk measures, downside risk measures, and benchmark relative risk measures.

Absolute Risk

Absolute risk is defined as the total variability in returns. By total variability we mean two things. First, it is the total dispersion of returns that we are interested in measuring. The primary measure of absolute risk is the standard deviation of periodic short-term returns. Second, when we measure the risk of a fund by using standard deviation, we include both the variability inherent in the underlying asset class, as represented by the benchmark, as well as any extra-benchmark volatility introduced by an active manager.

Downside Risk

There are investment strategies specifically designed to reduce the risk of extreme losses as well as strategies with a higher than average risk of extreme losses. An example of a strategy with a risk of extreme losses would be one that employs leverage by borrowing money to invest. Several risk measures exist to isolate this downside risk. Downside risk measures also provide a better indication of risk when the assumptions underlying the use of standard deviation do not hold.

Relative Risk

Absolute returns to an actively managed portfolio include two components: the return delivered by the capital markets over the period and the value added over the benchmark earned by the manager. We isolate the value added over the benchmark in order to assist in judging the efforts of the manager. We make the same distinction in risk measurement. The total variability in returns, or absolute risk, includes both the volatility inherent in the markets over the period and the volatility introduced or tempered by the manager. We are interested in isolating the degree of this relative risk in order to put the benchmark relative return into perspective. We can measure the degree of association between the fund and benchmark return variability using regression analysis and other tools.

FORWARD- VERSUS BACKWARD-LOOKING RISK

The relative volatility of different investments is a major factor in our investing decisions. Past volatility is used as a proxy for absolute risk in several ways. We use measures of historical volatility to estimate future volatility. For example, based on the historical returns, we can see that we might not be too confident in earning around 17% in any one year in small company stocks, even though that is our long-term average return. We would be progressively more confident in achieving the average return to other asset classes. This confidence comes in exchange for a lower long-term average return. Historical volatility also informs our estimate of the probability of experiencing a short-term loss. We have a higher probability of losing money in any one year in an asset class with a wider dispersion of returns than one with a smaller dispersion.

Past volatility helps us estimate future volatility, but the same caveat about past returns not necessarily providing a good indication as to future return applies to risk measurement as well. So while past volatility helps us to estimate future volatility, *performance measurement* is strictly concerned with measurement of past volatility rather than the estimation and management of future volatility. *Forward-looking* risk estimation (ex-ante risk) is the process of forecasting the expected risk of the current portfolio. As part of the portfolio management process, we evaluate the risk of making changes to the current portfolio versus the expected gains.

Backward-looking (ex-post risk) risk is the measurement of the historical risk experienced by the investor in the portfolio or the benchmark relative risk produced by the manager. Historical risk statistics become less relevant to the forecasting of future risk as fund composition, manager style, capital markets relationships, and other factors change. As an extreme example, take the case of a fund that was invested in Treasury bills in the past but currently holds stocks. We would agree that *any* statistics representing the past risks of investing in this fund are now irrelevant. Another example would be a balanced fund with a low historical risk of large capital losses resulting from an initial asset allocation to bonds. This fund is more at risk of sustaining a capital loss after an extended bull market in stocks. This is because of the increase in the relative weight to equities as stocks rose in value, assuming there is no rebalancing back to the initial asset allocation by selling stocks and buying bonds. In addition, risk postures may change as the manager's strategy evolves, for example, by raising or lowering the cash allocation in a fund.

The estimation of the anticipated risks implied by the current composition of the portfolio is a different discipline than the measurement
of historical risk. To estimate current and predict future risks, we would
focus mainly on the measurement of the risk implied by the *current* fund
holdings. Even here we usually assume that the current composition of
the fund will remain stable over the term predicted. In addition to past
volatility, there are additional techniques for estimating risk that depend
on the type of portfolio. For example, if we had a bond fund, we would
calculate the fund's average duration, credit quality, and other risk factors specific to fixed income securities. These would give us an indication as to the risk of loss due to unexpected interest rate changes or
quality downgrades. For an equity portfolio, we look at the average P/E,
market capitalization, country exposure, industry exposure, and other
equity risk factors to gauge future volatility. A concentrated investment
in technology stocks is expected to be more volatile than a more diversified portfolio. In addition to looking at the current characteristics of the
portfolio, Value at Risk (VaR) is another technique used to quantify an
estimate of forward-looking risk. VaR uses the current fund holdings,
together with the volatility and correlation of returns among these holdings, to derive estimates of expected future risk. Because of their forward-looking nature, characteristics analysis, VaR, and other tools are
more the provenance of risk *management* than risk *measurement*.

While backward-looking risk informs the estimation of forward-
looking risk, and forward-looking risk is an important investment consideration, it is the former that we are concerned with in this book.
When we are measuring performance, we are interested in quantifying
the past history of an investment, and this includes the risk and risk-
adjusted return track record of the fund or manager. Backward-looking
risk measures represent the actual volatility experienced by an investor
in the fund during the period measured.

While return volatility is a good proxy for risk in many situations,
there are definitions of risk that are not as well captured by the return
volatility. For example, to an investor relying on the income produced
by an investment to fund current spending, potential for the investment
not to provide the required periodic income would be the relevant definition of risk. So, it is important to distinguish between volatility as a
measure of risk versus a *definition* of risk. But periodic return volatility
is the usual proxy for the risks experienced while investing.[2]

---

[2] For a history of the development of the concept, measurement, and management of
risk see Peter Bernstein, *Against The Gods, The Remarkable Story of Risk* (New
York: John Wiley & Sons, 1996).

CHAPTER 9

Absolute Risk

We invest via diversified portfolios to maximize the return we expect to earn given a particular tolerance for risk. We measure the level of risk taken by way of summary statistics that describe the variability of periodic returns, or return *volatility*, around the average return enjoyed. The primary measure of volatility used in the investments industry to represent risk is the standard deviation of return around the mean return. The mean, standard deviation, and other descriptive statistics are used to depict the total, or *absolute risk* inherent in a pattern of historical returns. We differentiate absolute risk from the measurement of risk concerned with deviations from target or benchmark returns, which are the subjects of Chapters 10 and 11. In this chapter, we first examine the calculation and use of statistics that describe the historical time series of returns and then measure the average, or middle return, about which the periodic returns have varied, and then look at statistics that measure the degree of variability around the average. For standard deviation to accurately describe the variability in a return series the distribution must be approximately normally distributed. The chapter closes with a discussion of the properties of the normal distribution and statistics that indicate a departure from normality.

RANGE OF RETURNS

Exhibit 8.3 in the previous chapter shows one way to indicate the volatility of historical returns for an investment, which is by looking at the range of periodic returns that have been experienced. We can summarize the dispersion of a return series by sorting the return series and taking the difference between the highest and lowest return in order to calculate the range of returns:

$$\text{Range} = \text{Highest return} - \text{Lowest return} \qquad (9.1)$$

The range is the difference between the highest and lowest return observed. The high and low returns for our sample fund, from Exhibit 8.1, are 8.00% and −5.00% and the range is equal to 13.00%. The corresponding range for the benchmark is 9.45%. The range comparison is an easily calculated and understood representation of the relative volatility of the two funds.

HISTOGRAM

One problem with using ranges is that they are they are highly susceptible to outliers. For example, the range of yearly T-bill returns for the period 1926 to 2000 was from −0.02% to 14.71%. However, the −0.02% return which occurred in 1938, was the only year a negative return was experienced. The 14.71% return occurred in 1981 and this was the only year in which T-bill returns were greater than 11.24%.[1] So using the range of returns to estimate risk leaves out information as to the historical probability of achieving a particular return. Often the best way to gain insight into the dispersion of returns, as well as their relative frequency, is to visualize the range of returns by means of a graph. By grouping the returns into return ranges, we can then draw a *frequency distribution*, or *histogram*, of the returns. The histogram shows the relative frequency with which the returns fall into the different return buckets, or class intervals. It shows where in the range of observed returns the periodic returns are concentrated and where they have been experienced infrequently.

We create a histogram by taking the series of returns and dividing them into a number of *bins* or *class intervals*. There is no hard and fast rule as to the number of bins. If there are too few bins, the shape of the return distribution cannot be inferred from the chart. The greater the number, the more accurately the graph will depict the return distribution. But as we add more bins, gaps will begin to appear where there are bins with no returns. Once we have decided on a number that does a good job of communicating the underlying distribution, we subtract a value slightly above the lowest return from a value slightly below highest return and divide the difference by the number of bins. This gives us the interval between bins. We create the bins by successively adding the intervals starting from the low return.

---

[1] Ibbotson Associates, *Stocks, Bonds, Bills, and Inflation 2001 Yearbook* (Chicago: Ibbotson Associates, 2001).

EXHIBIT 9.1 Histogram Sample Fund and Benchmark

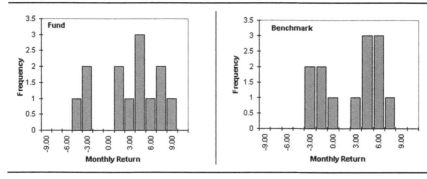

EXHIBIT 9.2 Large Cap U.S. Stock Monthly Returns 1971–2000

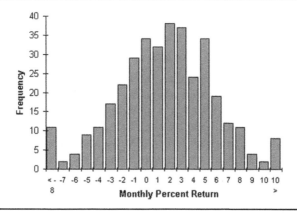

Source: Stocks, Bonds, Bills and Inflation 2001 Yearbook, © 2001 Ibbotson Associates, Inc. Based on copyrighted works by Ibbotson and Sinquefield. All rights reserved. Used with permission.

Exhibit 9.1 shows the histogram of returns for our sample fund and benchmark. Although in a real situation we would hesitate to draw conclusions based on 13 months of returns, we can see a similar distribution of returns for both entities. A histogram of the monthly large capitalization U.S. stock returns from January 1971 to December 2000, shown in Exhibit 9.2, is more informative.

Notice that the returns cluster around an average return of approximately 1% a month. Also the frequency of returns experienced drops as we move toward the high and low ends, except where it turns up again at either end.

EXHIBIT 9.3   Arithmetic Mean Return

	A	B	C	D
1	**Month**	**Fund**	**Benchmark**	**Difference**
2	1	7.00	5.76	1.24
3	2	5.00	4.18	0.82
4	3	-4.00	-3.11	-0.89
5	4	4.50	4.00	0.50
6	5	4.00	3.87	0.13
7	6	-3.00	-2.36	-0.64
8	7	8.00	5.55	2.45
9	8	0.10	-3.12	3.22
10	9	1.00	-0.50	1.50
11	10	-5.00	-2.74	-2.26
12	11	2.00	6.33	-4.33
13	12	4.00	2.03	1.97
14	13	7.00	5.89	1.11
15				
16	Arithmetic Mean:	2.35	1.98	0.37
17		=SUM(B2:B14)/COUNT(B2:B14)		

MEAN RETURN

While the histogram provides a nice graphical representation of the dispersion in returns, in any financial analysis we will need summary statistics describing dispersion. Exhibit 9.2 is an example of a phenomenon where the returns for most investment strategies tend toward an average. It is the variability around this average return that we are interested in measuring. The first step in understanding the dispersion of returns is to calculate the average of the single period returns. *Average* is a generic term for statistics describing the middle of a data set. The *Arithmetic Mean Return* is the simple average of the returns. To calculate the average return, we sum the observed returns and divide by the number of returns in the series:

$$\text{Arithmetic mean return} = \frac{\text{Sum}(RP_i)}{N} \qquad (9.2)$$

where RP_i are the individual monthly portfolio, or fund returns and N is the count of returns.

Exhibit 9.3 shows the calculation of the monthly arithmetic mean return, which is 2.35% for our sample fund and 1.98% for the benchmark. On average, the fund outdid the benchmark by 0.37% per month.

We showed the calculation of the mean return used in risk measurement in order to differentiate the *arithmetic* mean return from the *geometric* mean return. The geometric mean return is the primary measure of investment performance. The geometric mean return accounts for the compounding of returns that occurs as the gains earned in one period are invested forward into succeeding periods. It can be used to reconcile the beginning value of an investment to the ending value. By contrast the arithmetic mean return is a simple average of the periodic returns. It is a representative return, consolidating each of the return observations into a single number meant to be representative of the time series of returns. The arithmetic mean return does not account for the reinvestment of periodic gains and income. For this reason the arithmetic mean return will always be higher than, or equal to, the geometric return.

The arithmetic mean return is useful, however, in the analysis of the distribution of periodic returns that implies investment risk because it provides the center around which the periodic observed returns are distributed. However, with some adjustments to the inputs, geometric returns also could have been used in the measurement of historical risk. For the benefit of consistency, we use arithmetic returns in the risk measurement demonstration examples in this book.

One problem with the mean is that, like the range, it is highly influenced by outliers, which are observations far from the average return. Sometimes the calculation of a mean including outliers can give a misleading impression as to the average return experienced over the period. One method of calculating a mean that avoids the outlier problem is to calculate a *trimmed mean*. A percentage of high and low outliers are excluded from the calculation of a trimmed mean.

RETURN DEVIATIONS

Each monthly return in Exhibit 9.3 differs to some extent from the arithmetic mean of the monthly returns. In some months the fund performed better than its own average and in some months worse. The amount of superior or inferior performance varies from month to month. It is the average degree of this variation in the performance history that we seek to summarize when we measure absolute investment risk. A fund with a smaller degree in variation of monthly returns around its mean exhibits less risk than a fund with a greater variation. The differences between the periodic returns and the mean return are *return deviations*. Return deviations represent the distance that each fund return lies from the average return. These deviations are calculated as the difference between each observation and the arithmetic average return:

$$\text{Return deviation} = RP_i - \overline{RP} \qquad (9.3)$$

EXHIBIT 9.4 Deviations from Mean Return

	A	B	C	D
1	**Month**	**Fund Returns**	**Deviation**	
2	1	7.00	4.65	
3	2	5.00	2.65	
4	3	-4.00	-6.35	
5	4	4.50	2.15	
6	5	4.00	1.65	
7	6	-3.00	-5.35	
8	7	8.00	5.65	
9	8	0.10	-2.25	
10	9	1.00	-1.35	
11	10	-5.00	-7.35	
12	11	2.00	-0.35	
13	12	4.00	1.65	
14	13	7.00	4.65	
15				=B14-$B$16
16	Arithmetic Mean:	2.35		
17	Sum positive deviations:	23.02	=AVERAGE(B2:B14)	
18	Sum negative deviations:	-23.02		
19	Sum of Deviations:	0.00		

Where RP_i are the individual return observations and $\overline{RP}$ is the mean of the return series. In Exhibit 9.4 we calculate the deviations from the mean return for our sample fund.

One property of the arithmetic mean return is that it is a balancing point. The sum of the distances of the returns above the mean return equals the sum of the distances of the returns that fall below the mean return. The mean return is the point where the sum of the return deviations equals zero. We see in Exhibit 9.4 that the deviations of both the positive and negative deviations from the mean are 23.02% for the fund. The same calculations performed for the benchmark show a sum of deviations equal to ±21.70%.

MEAN ABSOLUTE DEVIATION

It would be good if we could find a single statistic that encapsulates the idea of the range but avoids the problem of outliers by taking into account all of the deviations from the mean return rather than just the two biggest deviations, as in the range. An intuitive way to attempt to encapsulate in a single statistic the total variability of a series of returns would be to take the average of all of the return deviations. However, we cannot take the simple average because the sum of the return deviations is zero. To correct for this, we can instead take the absolute value of the deviations and then average them. The average of the absolute values of the return deviations is called the *Mean Absolute Deviation* (MAD) or *Mean Deviation*.

EXHIBIT 9.5 Mean Absolute Deviation

	A	B	C	D	E
			Absolute		Absolute
1	Month	Fund Return	Deviation	Index Return	Deviation
2	1	7.00	4.65	5.76	3.78
3	2	5.00	2.65	4.18	2.20
4	3	-4.00	6.35	-3.11	5.09
5	4	4.50	2.15	4.00	2.02
6	5	4.00	1.65	3.87	1.89
7	6	-3.00	5.35	-2.36	4.34
8	7	8.00	5.65	5.55	3.57
9	8	0.10	2.25	-3.12	5.10
10	9	1.00	1.35	-0.50	2.48
11	10	-5.00	7.35	-2.74	4.72
12	11	2.00	0.35	6.33	4.35
13	12	4.00	1.65	2.03	0.05
14	13	7.00	4.65	5.89	3.91
15		=ABS(B14-$B$16)			
16	Arithmetic Mean:	2.35		1.98	
17	Mean Absolute Deviation:	3.54		3.35	
18		=AVERAGE(E2:E14)			

$$\text{Mean absolute deviation} = \sum \text{ABS}(RP_i - \overline{RP}) \times \frac{1}{N} \qquad (9.4)$$

The Mean Absolute Deviation is the arithmetic mean of the absolute value of the difference between each of the observed returns and the arithmetic mean of the returns. Exhibit 9.5 illustrates the calculation of the Mean Absolute Deviation for our sample fund and benchmark, equal to 3.54% and 3.35%, respectively.

Using the mean absolute deviation we can see that although the fund had a higher arithmetic mean return over the period, it also had a higher dispersion of returns around the mean. Because we are using the variability in returns as a surrogate for risk, this is our first indication that it is possible that the fund exhibited more risk over the period.

STANDARD DEVIATION

While the mean absolute deviation is a functional description of the variability in a series of returns, it is not commonly used in performance analysis. This is because there are measures of variability with better statistical properties than the mean absolute deviation that also convey the same information. We use the deviations from the mean in the calculation of the most commonly used statistic representing return dispersion, the standard deviation of returns. *Standard deviation* is a measure of how widely the actual returns were dispersed from the average return. When calculating standard deviation, instead of taking the absolute value of each deviation, we square each of the deviations. This has the same effect as taking the absolute value in that it turns all of the deviations into positive numbers. The squared deviations are summed and then divided by the number of returns to give the *variance*. We typically avoid using variance as a measure of ex-post risk because it is measured in squared returns, rather than returns. In other words we cannot directly compare the variance to the return in order to assess reward to risk. We can, however, compare the standard deviation to the return to make a direct comparison. Standard deviation is the square root of the variance. To calculate the standard deviation of a return series:

1. Square each difference between the periodic returns and the arithmetic mean return.
2. Sum the squared differences.
3. Divide the sum of the squared differences by the number of returns.
4. Take the square root of the result.

$$\text{Standard deviation} = \sqrt{\frac{\sum (RP_i - \overline{RP})^2}{N}} \tag{9.5}$$

Equation (9.5) is the formula for standard deviation, where RP_i is the individual portfolio return observations, $\overline{RP}$ is the arithmetic mean return, and N is the count of returns. Note that because we are squaring the deviations, the standard deviation is affected more by outliers than the mean absolute deviation. Exhibit 9.6 illustrates the calculation of standard deviation for our fund, equal to 4.13%. The standard deviation for the benchmark is lower, 3.65%.

Standard deviation is the primary statistic used to describe the variability in a pattern of returns. Because this variability is a proxy for risk, standard deviation of the periodic returns is the chief proxy for risk used in the management and analysis of investments. A higher standard deviation indicates a wider dispersion of returns around the mean return. A portfolio that has twice the standard deviation of another fund has twice the volatility as that fund.

There are a few considerations we should keep in mind when using the standard deviation and related measures of risk. These include the number of observations used to form the statistic and the underlying periodicity of the data used.

EXHIBIT 9.6   Standard Deviation

	A	B	C	D
			Difference to	Squared
1	**Month**	**Fund Returns**	**average**	**Difference**
2	1	7.00	4.65	21.59
3	2	5.00	2.65	7.00
4	3	-4.00	-6.35	40.37
5	4	4.50	2.15	4.61
6	5	4.00	1.65	2.71
7	6	-3.00	-5.35	28.66
8	7	8.00	5.65	31.88
9	8	0.10	-2.25	5.08
10	9	1.00	-1.35	1.83
11	10	-5.00	-7.35	54.08
12	11	2.00	-0.35	0.13
13	12	4.00	1.65	2.71
14	13	7.00	4.65	21.59
15				
16	Arithmetic Average:	2.35		
17	Count of returns:	13.00		
18	Sum squared differences:	222.23		
19	Standard deviation	4.13	⟶ =SQRT(B18/B17)	
20				
21	Benchmark	3.65		

Length of Time Period

The examples in this section of the book use 13 months of monthly returns as inputs. We use a small number of observations to facilitate the study of the calculation and interpretation of the various statistics. A practical analysis, however, will usually involve longer time periods. But how many return observations should we use? Most commonly, practitioners will use three years of monthly data, or 36 monthly observations, to analyze the historical risk of the investment strategy. The choice of the time period has implications as to both the number of observations used and the exposure to all phases of the market cycle. If we have a short time period, the statistics may be highly unstable as they are sensitive to the addition or deletion of additional periods. The results will have a low statistical validity. In addition, if we are making inferences based on, say, the standard deviation, these inferences may be invalid if the time period does not represent different phases of market cycles, in our case periods of both high and low volatility. Here we are also implicitly equal weighting each return observation when calculating the risk statistics. For example, if we are calculating a 3-year trailing standard deviation, the return from 36 months ago contributes equally to the calculation as last month's return. There are alternatives to equal weighting, for example, by using weighted moving averages, where the most recent time periods would have a higher weighting in the calculation. We use the weighting techniques more in the estimation of ex-ante, or future risk, than in the measurement of historical risk.

A related issue is the use of the sample vs. population version of the standard deviation. When deriving averages used in the risk statistics, such as the average of the return deviations used in the standard deviation, we divided by the total number of returns in the data set, or N. Dividing by N gives the average when we are calculating risk statistics for the entire *population* of returns we want to describe. When we are using statistics such as the standard deviation to identify the characteristics of a complete data set, we use the population version of these statistics. Sometimes we calculate the risk statistics using a part of the population, or a *sample* set of returns. When we calculate risk statistics using a sample, but intend to use the statistics to make judgments about the entire population, we divide by $N-1$ instead of N. If we were to recalculate the examples in this chapter by dividing by $N-1$ instead of N we *would* get meaningfully different absolute results. This is because we chose to use only 13 observations to facilitate the study of each measure. The adjustment for samples is not a major consideration in the analysis of risk, because we usually use a large enough number of return observations that, dividing by either N or $N-1$, gives approximately the same result. Regardless, none of the relative rankings and inferences made based on differences between the fund and benchmark risk would change. If we were taking risk statistics calculated using two different sources and then using them in a comparison, it is useful to know whether the population or sample method was used.

Measurement Frequency

Assume we are calculating daily single period time-weighted returns. To calculate a 1-year cumulative return, we could link either the approximately 250-trading-day returns or the twelve monthly returns. In either case, we would get the same 1-year return because time-weighted returns can be compressed—the daily returns for one month equal the one month return and so on. This property does not extend to risk measures. The periodicity of the underlying returns impact the risk calculations.

For example, because returns usually fluctuate less on a daily basis than on a monthly basis, the standard deviation of a series of daily returns is usually smaller than the standard deviation of monthly returns, over the same time period. Risk statistics are commonly computed using daily, weekly, monthly, or quarterly periodic return frequencies. It is inappropriate to compare risk statistics that were calculated using a different underlying periodicity. Choice of the return frequency is dependent on the availability of the underlying fund returns, which is in turn dependent on the valuation frequency. Traditionally, valuation was only available on a monthly basis for most investment vehicles, except mutual funds. As daily valuation of investment portfolios has become more prevalent outside of the mutual fund industry, daily frequency risk measurement is now possible. Assuming that we experience risk on a daily basis, risk statistics calculated using monthly inputs might not represent the risk implied by the daily returns. In addition, it is possible that the relative rankings of portfolios or strategies would change with the use of more or less frequent data. Using daily observations allows for the measurement of the true volatility experienced by the investor.

Arithmetic versus Geometric Risk Statistics

So far we have calculated the standard deviation of the periodic returns around the arithmetic mean return. We could have instead calculated the standard deviation of the returns around the geometric mean return. To do this we first calculate the natural logs of the growth rates of the single period returns, and then take the standard deviation of these growth rates. In practice most analysts use the arithmetic methodology to calculate historical risk statistics, but the geometric statistics are also valid.

ANNUALIZED STANDARD DEVIATION

For the same reason that it is helpful to state return in annual equivalents, we can state risk on an annualized basis. The method we use to annualize risks is different from that used to annualize returns. The annualized version of the standard deviation statistic is sometimes called *volatility*. To annualize the standard deviation, we multiply the standard deviation by the square root of the number of returns in a year given the periodicity of the data.

$$\text{Annualized standard deviation} = \left(\sqrt{\frac{\sum (RP_i - \overline{RP})^2}{N}} \right) \times \sqrt{P} \qquad (9.6)$$

where P is the number of return periods per year.

Our example, Exhibit 9.6, uses monthly data, so we multiply the standard deviation of the monthly returns (4.13%) by the square root of twelve, which is approximately 3.46, in order to annualize the returns. The annualized standard deviation of our sample is 14.32% for the fund and 12.63% for the benchmark. If the return observations were quarterly we would multiply by the square root of four, weekly the

square root of 52, and if daily by the square root of the number of trading days in a year for the market where the investment trades.

We multiply standard deviation by the square root of the periodicity
to transform the periodic statistic into a statistic comparable with the
annualized arithmetic return. In this example, we used monthly returns
to calculate a mean monthly return. We calculate the annual equivalent
of the arithmetic mean return by multiplying the periodic arithmetic
mean return by the number of returns in a year as given by the frequency of the data. We multiply the arithmetic mean monthly return by
12 in order to calculate an *annual equivalent arithmetic mean return.*

$$\text{Annual arithmetic mean return} = \left(\frac{\text{Sum}(RP_i)}{N}\right) \times P \qquad (9.7)$$

where P is the number of return periods per year or *periodicity* of the
returns. It is the annual arithmetic mean return about which the standard deviation of arithmetic returns varies. The annual mean returns for
our sample data are 28.25% for the fund and 23.80% for the benchmark. If the return observations were quarterly, we would multiply the
quarterly average by 4, weekly by 52, and if daily by the number of
trading days in the year. This is approximately 250, but depends on the
holiday schedule for the market where the asset trades.

We took the monthly return and multiplied it by 12 in order to calculate the annual mean return. In the same way, we could take the
monthly variance and multiply it by 12 in order to calculate the annual
variance. Because the standard deviation is the square root of the variance, we are being consistent by multiplying the standard deviation by
the square root of 12 to form the annualized equivalent. This method of
conversion is sometimes called the *square root of time rule,* which
assumes that risk compounds with the square root of time. But this rule
may not always be true. Different studies covering different asset classes
have found results where variability increased by more than and less
than the standard deviation of time. For example, the standard deviation of daily returns compounded into a yearly series using the square
root rule may overstate or understate the annual standard deviation as
calculated using monthly inputs. Using market returns as an example,
the standard deviation of monthly large cap U.S. stocks from 1971–
2000 was approximately 4.43%. The annual equivalent was 15.33%
(4.43% multiplied by 3.46). The standard deviation of the annual
returns for the same period was actually a bit higher, 15.84%.[2] In other

---

[2] Ibbotson Associates, *Stocks, Bonds, Bills, and Inflation 2001 Yearbook.*

cases volatility will be higher for short-term periods than for long-term periods, i.e. the standard deviation of monthly returns compounded into yearly equivalents will be higher than the standard deviation of the annual returns.

The square root of time rule makes the assumption that changes in the series of returns are random, i.e., that the periodic returns are not serially correlated. *Serial correlation* is an indication that there is a trend in the time series of returns, for example, that a period with positive returns was more likely to be followed by another period with positive returns than one with negative returns. If the returns exhibit serial correlation, then using the square root of time rule to estimate risk over multiple periods will underestimate the actual risk. There are other methods of scaling risk where serial correlation is present.

NORMAL DISTRIBUTION

The histogram shows how the observed returns are distributed around the mean return. Returns are continuous statistics, i.e., they can take any value within the range of returns. Returns are *normally distributed* when return observations equally distant from the mean return have the same relative frequency of observation. In a normally distributed return series, most of the returns are close to the average return, and there are relatively few extremely high and low returns. The normal distribution can be described with an equation that calculates the area under the bell-shaped curve that could be drawn over the histogram of a normally distributed population of returns. Exhibit 9.7 illustrates a return series with a normal distribution.

EXHIBIT 9.7   Normal Distribution

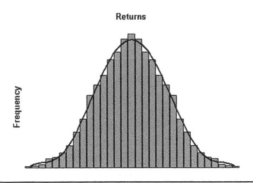

EXHIBIT 9.8   U.S. Large Company Stocks Monthly Return Dispersion 1971–2000

	A	B	C	D	E	F
		From	To	Count	Cumulative	Cumulative %
1	1 Std Deviation	-3.28	5.53	268	268	74%
2	2 Deviations	-7.68	9.93	72	340	94%
3	3 Deviations	-12.09	14.33	17	357	99%
4	> 3 Deviations	< -12.09	> 14.33	3	360	100%
5	Total					
6						
7	Mean: 1.12			Standard Deviation: 4.40		

Source: Stocks, Bonds, Bills and Inflation 2001 Yearbook, © 2001 Ibbotson Associates, Inc. Based on copyrighted works by Ibbotson and Sinquefield. All rights reserved. Used with permission.

The normal distribution is an accurate description of the dispersion of values around the mean for many things, such as the heights and weights of the population of people.

One property of standard deviation for a normally distributed population is that we can use the standard deviation together with the mean to mathematically describe the distribution of the time series of returns, as evidenced by the histogram:

- About 68% of the observed returns will be within a range of one standard deviation above and below the mean return.
- About 90% of the returns will be within ±1.65 standard deviations.
- About 95% of the returns will be within ±2 standard deviations.
- Almost all of the returns will be within ±3 standard deviations.

We can look at the history of monthly Large Cap U.S. Stock returns to examine these rules of thumb. The mean monthly return for the period from January 1971 to December 2000 was 1.12% and the standard deviation was 4.40%. Exhibit 9.8 shows that the dispersion of monthly Large Cap U.S. Stock returns comes close to the distribution described by the normal distribution.

It is interesting that there were three months we could call extreme events, where the returns were more than three distributions away from the mean return. In this case, these were all on the negative side (October 1974 16.57%, October 1987 –21.52%, and August 1998 –14.46%). The standard deviation of returns without including these months is 4.09%. This shows how outliers influence the standard deviation.

When we use the rules of thumb associated with the standard deviation, we are using the normal distribution to determine the probability of experiencing particular returns different from the mean return. It is these probabilities that represent investment risk.

EXHIBIT 9.9   Risk Implied by VaR

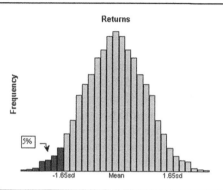

HISTORICAL VALUE AT RISK

One way to use the normal distribution is to convert percentage risk into dollar risk. When we are communicating the risks associated with an investment, it is useful to convert the standard deviation in percentage terms into dollar terms. *Value at Risk* (VaR) is the estimate of the maximum dollar loss we could expect to experience, over a given time horizon, with a stated level of confidence. VaR is the dollar loss at a particular percentile location of the returns distribution. For example, suppose we have a portfolio currently worth $100,000. We are told we have a monthly VaR of $10,000, with a confidence level of 5%. We would interpret this to mean "We do not expect losses to exceed more than 10% (10,000/ 100,000) of the portfolio's value in more than 1 out of 20 months." VaR is stated in terms of the dollar value of the portfolio, so it is a more intuitive measure of risk than standard deviation for many investors.

To calculate VaR, we first select a confidence level. For example, if we wanted to be able to say that 95% of the time losses in a particular period do not fall below a certain level, we would consider as risky those returns that fell 1.65 standard deviations below the mean return as indicated in Exhibit 9.9.

We chose 1.65 standard deviations because we would expect 90% of the returns to fall within ±1.65 standard deviations from the mean. The 10% is split between the upper and lower tails of the distribution; that is, 5% of the returns are expected to fall 1.65 standard deviations below the mean and 5% of the returns 1.65 standard deviations above the mean. Given the confidence level, we can determine the historical VaR by multiplying an assumed investment made times the return at the point in the distribution 1.65 standard deviations below the mean return. Equation (9.8) shows how we do this using the standard deviation of returns.

$$\text{Historical value at risk} = \text{Investment} \times [\overline{RP} - 1.65 \times \text{stdev}(\overline{RP})] \quad (9.8)$$

Exhibit 9.10 illustrates the calculation of VaR for our sample fund and benchmark. We can see that with a $10,000 investment in the fund we would expect to lose no more than $446.82 in any one month, 95% of the time.

This means that 95% of the time we would expect to achieve a monthly fund return equal to or greater than –4.47%. We calculate the return at 1.96 standard deviations below the mean by multiplying the standard deviation by 1.96 and subtracting the result from the mean return, which is at zero standard deviations. We derive the VaR in dollar terms by multiplying the result by the initial investment of 10,000. VaR does not imply that this is the lowest return achieved; we would expect 5% of the periodic returns to fall below this amount with a greater resulting dollar loss.

The approach to calculating VaR covered here is an application of standard deviation in a backward-looking absolute risk measurement framework. VaR is more commonly used on a forward-looking basis. One way to calculate VaR on a forward-looking basis is to take the current portfolio holdings, as well as estimates as to the return variability and return correlation amongst those holdings, and generate a distribution of possible future market values. We generate the estimates of future variability and correlation by relying on history as a guide and there are many methods of doing this.

EXHIBIT 9.10 Value at Risk

	A	B	C
1	**Month**	**Fund**	**Benchmark**
2	1	7.00	5.76
3	2	5.00	4.18
4	3	-4.00	-3.11
5	4	4.50	4.00
6	5	4.00	3.87
7	6	-3.00	-2.36
8	7	8.00	5.55
9	8	0.10	-3.12
10	9	1.00	-0.50
11	10	-5.00	-2.74
12	11	2.00	6.33
13	12	4.00	2.03
14	13	7.00	5.89
15			
16	Monthly Average:	2.35	1.98
17	Standard Deviation:	4.13	3.65
18	Investment:	10000.00	10000.00
19	5% VaR of 10,000:	-446.82	-403.47
20	=C18*((C16/100)-(1.65*(C17/100))) ◥		

OTHER DISTRIBUTIONS

One caveat to using the VaR calculated by using the mean and standard deviation is that we are assuming the returns are normally distributed. To use the rules of thumb associated with standard deviation, i.e., 68% of the returns are expected within a range of one standard deviation above and below the mean, the individual returns need to be reasonably normally distributed around the mean return.

The normal distribution is symmetrical around the mean return. The return history may have a greater number of extreme high or low returns than the normal distribution would indicate. Some investment strategies are designed to produce asymmetric, or nonnormal, return distributions. Strategies that employ option contracts are examples of investments that produce a nonnormal distribution. For example, the use of purchased put options reduces the risk of losses, while leaving the potential for gains, in exchange for a lower average return reflecting the cost of the put options. Written call options have the opposite effect. The upside potential of the fund is truncated in exchange for the option premium increasing the average returns. There are many more examples of strategies that are designed to produce a nonnormal return distribution.[3] In these cases the distribution of returns is *asymmetrical*. Additionally, the return distribution might take on different shapes depending on the frequency of observation or the time period being measured. There are families of other possible distributions that a series of returns might take. Having said that, many strategies are well served by standard deviation because the pattern of returns approaches a normal, or lognormal, distribution.

Standard deviation is not an accurate description of the dispersion of returns when the return distribution is asymmetrical. One quick indication that the distribution of returns might be nonnormal is if the median return is higher or lower than the mean return. The median return is the middle return in an ordered array of the returns from high to low. (See Exhibit 7.2 in Chapter 7). For a perfectly symmetrical distribution, the mean and median returns are about the same. Two important ways in which a return distribution might be nonnormal are when the distribution exhibits skewness or kurtosis. We can measure these properties in order to determine whether the distribution is normal or not.

---

[3] For more on this see Richard Bookstaber and Roger Clarke, "Problems in Evaluating the Performance of Portfolios with Options," *Financial Analysts Journal* (January/February 1985).

EXHIBIT 9.11   Positive Skewness

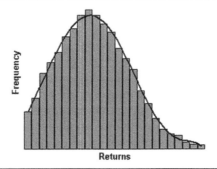

EXHIBIT 9.12   Negative Skewness

SKEWNESS

If there are more returns on the right side of the historic return distribution than the normal, we say that the distribution is *skewed* positively to the right as in Exhibit 9.11.

The histogram of a *positively skewed* return distribution has more returns extending to the right than the normal distribution. If returns are positively skewed, the mean return is higher than the median return because of the effect that the positive outliers have on the mean. If returns are positively skewed, standard deviation will underestimate the proportion of returns above the mean and overestimate the proportion of returns below the mean.

When there are more returns extending to the left side of the return distribution than the normal distribution implies, the distribution is *negatively skewed* as in Exhibit 9.12.

The negatively skewed return histogram looks like it has a tail extending to the left. If returns are negatively skewed, the median return is higher than the mean return because of the effect that the negative outliers have on the mean. If returns are negatively skewed, standard deviation will overestimate the proportion of returns above the mean and underestimate the proportion of returns below the mean. This is important because we have been using the standard deviation as a measure of return uncertainty. If the return series has negative skewness, we could underestimate the risk of below mean returns by using standard deviation to describe the dispersion in returns.

We are interested in the degree of skewness present in the return distribution in order to assess normality, and thus the appropriateness of standard deviation as a description of the variability. The *skewness* statistic is a measure of the degree of asymmetry in the spread of returns around the mean return. We can measure the degree of skewness using:

$$\text{Skewness} = \sum \left(\frac{RP_i - \overline{RP}}{\text{Standard deviation } (RP_i)} \right)^3 \times \frac{1}{N} \qquad (9.9)$$

To calculate skewness:

1. Take the difference between each monthly return and the arithmetic average return.
2. Divide the difference by the standard deviation of returns.
3. Cube the result.
4. Sum the cubed differences.
5. Divide the sum of the cubed differences by the count of returns.

Exhibit 9.13 illustrates the calculation of skewness equal to −0.44 for the example fund and −0.32 for the benchmark. A perfectly normal return distribution has a skewness of zero. Unfortunately, skewness is not measured in units of return, as are the mean and standard deviation. The skewness statistic can only be interpreted as a measure of the shape of the return distribution. The higher the absolute value of skewness the more the set of returns is biased toward the upper or lower tail of the normal distribution. If the return distribution is skewed to the right tail, skewness will be positive. Positive skewness reveals that there are positive return outliers. In other words, positive skewness indicates that when gains did occur, they were greater than anticipated, and losses smaller than anticipated, by the normal distribution. If the return distribution is skewed to the left tail, skewness is negative indicating that there are negative return outliers in the set. The relative skewness of two strategies shows the chances of experiencing a large return "surprise" or an outlier. Skewness is highly influenced by any outliers. For example, the skewness of large company stock returns for the period from January 1971 to December 2000 was –0.36, but by excluding outlier returns more than 3 standard deviations from the average changes the skewness to –0.02.

KURTOSIS

A nonnormal distribution also might have more or fewer returns in the center of the distribution than the normal distribution. *Kurtosis* is the degree to which the histogram of a return series is more peaked or flatter than that described by the normal distribution. The degree of kurtosis can be calculated by Equation (9.10).

$$\text{Kurtosis} = \sum \left(\frac{RP_i - \overline{RP}}{\text{Standard deviation } (RP_i)} \right)^4 \times \frac{1}{N} \tag{9.10}$$

To calculate kurtosis we:

1. Take the difference between the monthly returns and the arithmetic average return.

EXHIBIT 9.13 Skewness

	A	B	C	D	E
	Month	Fund	(Deviation/Std Dev)²	Benchmark	(Deviation/Std Dev)²
1					
2	1	7.00	1.42	5.76	1.11
3	2	5.00	0.26	4.18	0.22
4	3	-4.00	-3.63	-3.11	-2.72
5	4	4.50	0.14	4.00	0.17
6	5	4.00	0.06	3.87	0.14
7	6	-3.00	-2.17	-2.36	-1.69
8	7	8.00	2.55	5.55	0.94
9	8	0.10	-0.16	-3.12	-2.74
10	9	1.00	-0.04	-0.50	-0.32
11	10	-5.00	-5.63	-2.74	-2.17
12	11	2.00	0.00	6.33	1.69
13	12	4.00	0.06	2.03	0.00
14	13	7.00	1.42	5.89	1.23
15					=((B14-$B$16)/$B$17)^3
16	Arithmetic Mean Return:	2.35		1.98	
17	Standard Deviation:	4.13		3.65	
18	Skewness:	-0.44		-0.32	
19			=SUM(C2:C14)/COUNT(B2:B14)		
20					

EXHIBIT 9.14   Kurtosis

	A	B	C	D	E
1	Month	Fund	(Deviation/Std Dev)⁴	Benchmark	(Deviation/Std Dev)⁴
2	1	7.00	1.59	5.76	1.15
3	2	5.00	0.17	4.18	0.13
4	3	-4.00	5.58	-3.11	3.80
5	4	4.50	0.07	4.00	0.09
6	5	4.00	0.03	3.87	0.07
7	6	-3.00	2.81	-2.36	2.01
8	7	8.00	3.48	5.55	0.91
9	8	0.10	0.09	-3.12	3.83
10	9	1.00	0.01	-0.50	0.21
11	10	-5.00	10.01	-2.74	2.81
12	11	2.00	0.00	6.33	2.02
13	12	4.00	0.03	2.03	0.00
14	13	7.00	1.59	5.89	1.32
15				=((B14-$B$16)/$B$17)^4	
16	Arithmetic Mean Return:	2.35		1.98	
17	Standard Deviation:	4.13		3.65	
18	Kurtosis:	1.96		1.41	
19	Excess Kurtosis:	-1.04		-1.59	
20	=B18-3		=SUM(C2:C14)/COUNT(B2:B14)		

2. Divide the difference by the standard deviation of returns.
3. Raise each difference to the 4th power.
4. Sum the resulting differences.
5. Divide the sum of the differences by the count of returns.

The kurtosis for a perfectly normal return distribution is equal to 3. To simplify the interpretation of kurtosis, we sometimes report only the *excess kurtosis*, which is equal to the kurtosis minus three.

$$\text{Excess kurtosis} = \left[\sum \left(\frac{RP_i - \overline{RP}}{\text{Standard deviation } (RP_i)} \right)^4 \times \frac{1}{N} \right] - 3 \qquad (9.11)$$

Like skewness, the kurtosis has no meaning in terms of return; it is just a measure of the shape of the return distribution. The return distribution given by our example has excess kurtosis of −1.04 for the fund and −1.59 for the benchmark. Exhibit 9.14 demonstrates the calculation of kurtosis.

Positive excess kurtosis indicates a more peaked than normal, or *leptokurtic,* return distribution. A more peaked distribution has more instances of returns close to mean and more frequent large positive or negative returns than a normal distribution of returns. So positive excess kurtosis indicates a *fatter tailed* distribution than normal. A fat-tailed distribution is notable in terms of volatility because it indicates that we would expect to see more frequent extreme higher or lower returns than the normal distribution would indicate. Negative excess kurtosis indicates a flatter than normal return distribution or a *platykurtic distribution*. We can see the distribution of large company stocks is fatter tailed by looking at the histogram in Exhibit 9.2. This is quantified by calculating an excess kurtosis equal to 2.36.

TESTING FOR A NONNORMAL DISTRIBUTION

Together skewness and kurtosis can tell us whether we might be surprised by extreme returns. For example, a skewness near −1 and excess kurtosis greater than 1 together indicate that we would experience more large negative returns than standard deviation would indicate. We are interested in whether taken together the skewness and kurtosis statistics indicate whether or not the distribution of returns was normal or not. The Jarque-Bera (JB) test can be used for this purpose.

$$\text{Jarque-Bera test} = \left(\frac{N}{6}\right) \times \left[\text{Skewness}^2 + \frac{(\text{Excess kurtosis})^2}{4}\right] \quad (9.12)$$

The JB test compares the skewness and kurtosis values to the expected values if the distribution were normal. A JB test result of greater than (about) 6 on a large data set indicates that the return distribution may not be normally distributed. The sample fund and index both have JB statistics well below 6, but our example uses only 13 monthly fund and index returns, and the JB test is not useful for such a small number of observations.

We can, however, perform the JB test on the series of monthly returns to large company stocks from 1971 to 2000. The JB Test result for this asset class is 91.52, indicating that the distribution of returns departs from normality. The same calculation, excluding the three monthly returns that are outliers, is 3.17.

EXHIBIT 9.15 Jarque-Bera Test for Normality

	A	B	C	D
1			Fund	Index
2		N:	13	13
3		Skewness:	-0.44	-0.32
4		Excess Kurtosis:	-1.04	-1.59
5		JB Statistic:	1.01	1.58
6		=(D2/6)*((D3^2)+(D4^2/4))		
7				

Large Company Stocks			Large Company Stocks ex Outliers	
N:	360		N:	357
Skewness:	-0.36		Skewness:	-0.02
Excess Kurtosis:	2.36		Excess Kurtosis:	0.46
JB Statistic:	91.52		JB Statistic:	3.17

Taken together, the skewness and kurtosis statistics indicate that we should expect some more extreme returns than the standard deviation would indicate for this asset class. We can compare these statistics for different investments to get an idea as to the relative risk associated with extreme events.

CHAPTER 10

Downside Risk

Standard deviation is a good measure of the variability in a series of returns where the returns were normally distributed. A standard deviation of 10% indicates that we expect to see returns at the mean return ±10%, 68% of the time and ±20%, 95% of the time. While standard deviation describes the variability in returns above and below the mean return, because our intuitive definition of risk is informed by the risk of losing principal, we are usually more interested in the risk implied by the returns that are *below* the mean return. However, because a normal distribution implies an equal number of returns above and below the mean return, standard deviation can help us differentiate the downside risk of two investment strategies. A fund with a 20% standard deviation has experienced less volatility via both upside gains and downside losses than one with a 30% standard deviation.

Standard deviation is not a good measure of return variability if the distribution of returns is skewed or otherwise nonnormal. If the distribution of returns were not normally distributed, we would expect to experience a different number of returns than indicated by the normal distribution at a particular point in the distribution. For example, if we have a strategy that employs put options, we would not expect to see the large negative losses that we would otherwise have incurred. Besides the problem with nonnormal distributions, there are more criticisms of standard deviation as the surrogate risk statistic. In this chapter we present these criticisms and then review some modifications to the risk measurement framework designed to address these shortcomings.

PROBLEMS WITH STANDARD DEVIATION

If we accept that we can equate the variability in returns around the mean return with "risk," then standard deviation of returns is an acceptable measure of risk. But considering the variability of return around the mean return might not be how we would all conceptualize the risk of investing. There are two reasons for this:

■ The center around which standard deviation is calculated is the mean historical return.
■ Standard deviation treats positive and negative return deviations from the mean with equal weight.

First, return deviations that comprise the standard deviation are calculated using the mean return as a reference return. The mean return is a measure of the average return in the return history. The concept of standard deviation treats as a contribution to risk any returns that fall on either side of this mean return. Investors may, however, have a different focal point for riskiness. For example, we may be investing in large company equities that have had a mean annual return of 13%. To reach our goals, however, we might expect to earn a minimum return of 10% per year. In this case, we would consider annual returns below 10%, not 13%, as risky.

The second criticism is that standard deviation treats positive return deviations in the same way as negative deviations. For many of us it is counterintuitive that returns that are *above* the average return should make a positive contribution toward a measure of riskiness. For example, if the average monthly return for an investment were 1% and there comes a month when the return is 10%, we might consider this a fortuitous rather than a risky event. But the 10% return will have the same impact as a –10% return on the standard deviation of returns. The volatility created by losses certainly has more of an impact on how we feel about an investment than the volatility created by gains in excess of the mean return. This second criticism is tempered when the returns are normally distributed: If half of the returns are above the mean return and half below the mean return, any ranking of portfolios based on upside and downside risks will be the same. But this is not the case if the returns are not normally distributed or if the investor has a target return that is different than the mean return.

ABSOLUTE RISK VERSUS DOWNSIDE RISK

To deal with these objections, analysts have developed a *downside* risk measurement framework. Downside risk statistics function by counting as risky only those returns that are below a specified reference return.

EXHIBIT 10.1   Standard Deviation

	A	B	C
1	**Month**	**Fund 1**	**Fund 2**
2	1	7.00	-10.00
3	2	5.00	-9.70
4	3	-4.00	-10.20
5	4	4.50	-9.89
6	5	4.00	-10.40
7	6	-3.00	-10.09
8	7	8.00	-10.61
9	8	0.10	-9.70
10	9	1.00	-10.40
11	10	-5.00	-9.89
12	11	2.00	-10.61
13	12	4.00	-10.09
14	13	7.00	-10.82
15			
16	Target Monthly Return:	0.00	0.00
17			
18	Cumulative Return:	33.87	-75.25
19	Growth of $1000:	1338.71	247.47
20			
21	Standard Deviation:	4.13	0.35
22	Downside Deviation:	1.96	10.19

As an illustration of the problems with standard deviation that led to the development of downside risk measures, consider an investor who defines a risky event as one where the returns in any period are negative. To this investor, risk is the possible loss of principal. Exhibit 10.1 shows two alternative portfolios for this investor. Fund 1 has a standard deviation of return equal to 4.13%, while that of Fund 2 is much lower, at 0.35%.

Fund 2 has the smaller standard deviation, but the returns are clustered around −10.00%. Nevertheless, despite the smaller standard deviation, an investment in Fund 2 would have lost three quarters of its principal, while an investment in Fund 1 would have increased, though not steadily, over time. This example is an extreme case of where standard deviation, used in isolation, does not accord with our sense of risk. Standard deviation reports that a fund that is growing at a varying rate is more risky than a fund that is losing money at a steady rate. Downside measures of risk, such as the downside deviation, which is covered in this chapter, attempt to better measure risk in situations such as these. In this example, we can see the risk in Fund 2 better by noting the downside deviation statistic: 10.19% for Fund 2 and only 1.96% for Fund 1.

Downside risk measures focus on the returns that fall below a certain value. They address the criticisms of the standard deviation in that:

■ The reference point below what we consider a return to be risky is set according to the investment strategy of the fund rather than by using the mean return.

■ Only return deviations below this target return are weighted in the measurement of risk.

■ Downside risk measures represent risk better than standard deviation when the distribution of returns is not normal.

Semideviation

Downside risk statistics are based on the concept of partial, or semi-deviation. *Semideviation* is the standard deviation of the returns that fall below the mean return. Semideviation is the square root of *semivariance,* and *below mean semivariance* is the variance of the returns below the mean return. We calculate the semideviation in the same way as standard deviation, except that we modify the formula to use only those returns that fell below the mean return for the period.

$$\text{Semideviation} = \sqrt{\frac{\sum (RP_i - \overline{RP}) \text{ where } (RP_i < \overline{\overline{RP}})}{N}} \qquad (10.1)$$

To calculate the semideviation, we identify the returns that fall below the mean return. Then we take the difference between each of these returns and the mean return, square each difference, sum the squared differences, and divide the sum of the squared differences by the total number of returns. This gives the semivariance. Taking the square root of the semivariance converts the statistic into units of return, meaning that the statistic is directly comparable with returns.

Exhibit 10.2 illustrates the calculation of semideviation using the same return series that we have been working with from Exhibit 8.1. Fund semideviation is 3.16% and benchmark semideviation is equal to 2.76%.

Notice that in the calculation of semideviation the denominator is the total number of observations. We are calculating an average of the below average deviations from the mean, spread over the total number of observations. Here, we divide by thirteen months even though only six returns fell below the fund mean return. Our formula is equivalent to calculating the standard deviation with the replacement of above average deviations with zero.

The semideviation measures the volatility implied by returns that fall below the average return. Exhibit 10.3 shows that it is the portion of the return distribution to the left of the mean that counts as risky, using semideviation as a measure.

Statistics that measure a portion of the distribution are called *partial moments*, and downside risk statistics are *lower partial moments*. Using the lower partial moments addresses the criticism that standard deviation treats above-average deviations, which we may not consider to be risky, in the same way as below-mean deviations. Note that if a return series is normally distributed, funds will exhibit the same relative riskiness whether measured by standard or semideviation because investments with large downside deviations also have large upside deviations. If, however, the returns distribution is not normal, the semideviation and other downside risk statistics convey important information as to the downside risk of the investment. In the case of semideviation, the downside is measured relative to the mean return, but, in fact, we can measure the downside risk relative to any point in the return distribution.

EXHIBIT 10.2   Semideviation

	A	B	C	D	E
				Difference if	Squared
1	Month	Fund	Mean Return	Return < Mean	difference
2	1	7.00	2.35		
3	2	5.00	2.35		
4	3	-4.00	2.35	-6.35	40.37
5	4	4.50	2.35		
6	5	4.00	2.35		
7	6	-3.00	2.35	-5.35	28.66
8	7	8.00	2.35		
9	8	0.10	2.35	-2.25	5.08
10	9	1.00	2.35	-1.35	1.83
11	10	-5.00	2.35	-7.35	54.08
12	11	2.00	2.35	-0.35	0.13
13	12	4.00	2.35		=IF(B12<C12,B12-C12," ")
14	13	7.00	2.35		
15					
16		Count of Returns:	13.00	=COUNT(B2:B14)	
17	Sum Squared Difference:		130.15	=SUM(E2:E14)	
18		Semideviation:	3.16	=SQRT(C17/C16)	
19		Standard Deviation:	4.13	=STDEVP(B2:B14)	
20					
21		Benchmark:	2.76		

EXHIBIT 10.3   Risk Implied by Semideviation

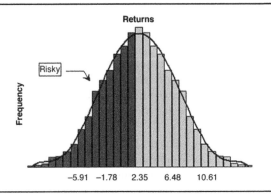

EXHIBIT 10.4   Risk Implied by Target Return Equal to 10%

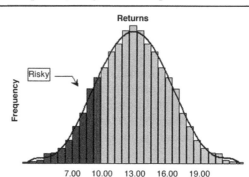

RETURN TARGETS

The second criticism of standard deviation is that it measures risk relative to the mean return, while investors instead may consider as risky returns that fall below some periodic assumed return objective. The objective can be considered a *Minimum Acceptable Return* or MAR. The MAR embodies the concepts that returns above the minimum are acceptable and the target return can be different than the mean return. MAR can be considered a *target return*. The target return replaces the mean return as the point on the return distribution where we identify risky returns. Exhibit 10.4 shows the area of the distribution considered risky if the target return equals 10%, where the mean of the return distribution equals 13%.

The target return can be considered a risk benchmark customized to the investor's tolerance for periodic losses. The target return is set based on the goals and objectives of the investor and can be a fixed percentage or a floating value that changes each period. Examples of target return values include:

- Zero, which is the return required to maintain nominal principal. Using a zero percent rate of return would assume that we consider any loss in market value to be undesirable.
- The actuarially assumed rate of return used to project portfolio values.
- The risk-free return, or yield on T-bills converted into a return.
- The return of a market benchmark.
- The return earned by competing money managers, such as the third quartile manager universe return.

EXHIBIT 10.5   Shortfall Risk

	A	B	C	D
1	Month	Fund	Target	RP - T
2	1	7.00	1.20	
3	2	5.00	1.20	
4	3	-4.00	1.20	5.20
5	4	4.50	1.20	
6	5	4.00	1.20	
7	6	-3.00	1.20	4.20
8	7	8.00	1.20	
9	8	0.10	1.20	1.10
10	9	1.00	1.20	0.20
11	10	-5.00	1.20	6.20
12	11	2.00	1.20	=IF(B11<C11,
13	12	4.00	1.20	C11-B11," ")
14	13	7.00	1.20	
15				
16		Count of Returns:	13.00	
17		Count of Returns Below Target:	5.00	=COUNT(D2:D14)
18		Shortfall Risk	38.46	=(C17/C16)*100
19				
20		Benchmark:	38.46	

We can use several statistics to measure risk relative to a target return: shortfall risk, expected downside value, downside deviation, and value at risk. Because the target rate of return will differ between investors, the semideviation and other downside risk statistics examined here are not found commonly in published summaries of ex-post portfolio risk and return.

SHORTFALL RISK

If the distribution of returns were normal and we defined risk as the semideviation, we would expect 50% of the returns to fall below the mean return. If we change the reference point from the historical mean to a target return, we can measure the past probability of returns falling below the target value. This *shortfall risk* is the percentage of periodic returns that fall below the target return.

$$\text{Shortfall risk} = \frac{\text{\# of returns} < \text{target return}}{\text{total \# of returns}} \times 100 \qquad (10.2)$$

Shortfall risk is the number of returns that fell below the target return over the period divided by the total number of returns and reported as a percentage. It represents the relative frequency of a fund earning a return below some target rate of return. Exhibit 10.5 illustrates the calculation of shortfall risk using a target monthly return of 1.20%. Given this target, the shortfall risk of our fund is 38.46%, and the corresponding shortfall risk for the benchmark is the same.

Shortfall risk shows that 38.46% of periodic monthly returns fell below our target return of 1.20% per month. We can compare the shortfall risk of different funds to see how well they met the needs of the investor for the target return. Shortfall risk also is used for determining asset allocation. We might set the asset allocation for a multimanager fund where the combined expected annual shortfall risk is equal to 5%. Here we would expect to see a return below the shortfall target only once out of every 20 years (5% of the time).

Shortfall risk is a simply calculated statistic with a powerful application: It can show as risky strategies that are not normally considered risky. For example, a fund of treasury bills would not usually be classified as a risky investment. Principal is protected and income is guaranteed. Using history as a guide, we know that T-bills are unlikely to return our target 1.2% per month. Therefore, our shortfall risk would be near 100% for a T-bill portfolio.

EXPECTED DOWNSIDE VALUE

Shortfall risk tells us the percentage of time that an investment fell below some target, but it says nothing about the magnitude of the deficit. Suppose we have a strategy that usually exceeds the target return, but when it fails to meet the target, it is a great deal short. The *Expected Downside Value* quantifies the amount by which a return falls below the target return. The amount of the shortfall is averaged over the total number of observations. We calculate the expected downside value using Equation (10.3).

$$\text{Expected downside value} = \frac{\sum RP_i - T \text{ where } RP_i < T}{N} \qquad (10.3)$$

where T = the target return. Here we identify the fund returns where the fund return is less than the target return, take the difference between each of these returns and the target return and add these differences. We then divide the sum by the total number of returns to yield an average deviation.

Exhibit 10.6 shows the calculation of expected downside value for the sample fund and benchmark. Given a monthly target return of 1.2%, the expected downside value is 1.30% for the fund and 1.37% for the benchmark.

Notice that we continue to divide by N, the total number of returns, in order to average the downside value across all of the observations. The expected downside value shows that when the return fell below the monthly target return of 1.20%, it fell below by an average of 1.30% per month.

EXHIBIT 10.6 Expected Downside Value

	A	B	C	D	E
1	Month	Fund	Target	RP - T	(RP - T)²
2	1	7.00	1.20		
3	2	5.00	1.20		
4	3	-4.00	1.20	5.20	27.04
5	4	4.50	1.20	↖	=IF(B4<C4,C4-B4," ")
6	5	4.00	1.20		
7	6	-3.00	1.20	4.20	17.64
8	7	8.00	1.20		
9	8	0.10	1.20	1.10	1.21
10	9	1.00	1.20	0.20	0.04
11	10	-5.00	1.20	6.20	38.44
12	11	2.00	1.20		
13	12	4.00	1.20		
14	13	7.00	1.20		
15					
16			Count of Returns: 13.00		
17		Sum of (RP - T) where RP < T: 16.90		=SUM(D2:D14)	
18		Expected Downside Value: 1.30		=(C17/C16)	
19					
20			Benchmark: 1.37		

DOWNSIDE DEVIATION

Downside deviation, like semideviation, eliminates from the calculation of risk the returns that contribute to positive volatility. We calculate the downside deviation in the same way as semideviation, except we replace the mean return with the target return.

$$\text{Downside deviation} = \sqrt{\frac{\sum (RP_i - T)^2 \text{ where } RP_i < T}{N}} \quad (10.4)$$

To calculate downside deviation, we identify the fund returns less than the target and take the differences of these returns to the target. We then square the differences, add the squared differences, and divide by the total number of returns. This gives the downside variance, or *below-target semivariance.* Taking the square root of the downside variance yields a statistic measured in rate of return units.

Exhibit 10.7 shows the calculation of downside deviation with the result of 2.55% for the fund and 2.29% for the benchmark. We can annualize the downside deviation in the same way we annualize standard deviation, by multiplying the downside deviation by the square root of the number of return observations per year.

$$\text{Annualized downside deviation}$$
$$= \sqrt{\frac{\sum (RP_i - T)^2 \text{ where } RP_i < T}{N}} \times \sqrt{P} \quad (10.5)$$

EXHIBIT 10.7 Downside Deviation

	A	B	C	D	E
1	Month	Fund	Target	RP - T	(RP - T)²
2	1	7.00	1.20		
3	2	5.00	1.20		
4	3	-4.00	1.20	5.20	27.04
5	4	4.50	1.20		=IF(B4<C4,C4-B4," ")
6	5	4.00	1.20		
7	6	-3.00	1.20	4.20	17.64
8	7	8.00	1.20		
9	8	0.10	1.20	1.10	1.21
10	9	1.00	1.20	0.20	0.04
11	10	-5.00	1.20	6.20	38.44
12	11	2.00	1.20		
13	12	4.00	1.20		
14	13	7.00	1.20		
15					
16		Count of Returns:	13.00		
17		Sum of (RP - T)2 where RP < T:	84.37	=SUM(E2:E14)	
18		Downside Devation:	2.55	=SQRT(C17/C16)	
19		Annualized Downside Deviation:	8.82	=C18 * SQRT(12)	
20					
21		Benchmark:	2.29		

where P is the periodicity, or number of return observations in a year. If we are using monthly returns, we multiply by the square root of 12.

Given the target monthly return equal to 1.20%, the annualized downside deviation for the fund is 8.82% and 7.94% for the benchmark. The fund has a higher propensity for downside returns than the benchmark, given the target return of 1.2% per month.

Like all of the statistics we calculate in the process of performance measurement, the downside deviation is calculated using the actual history of fund returns experienced over the period. This fact makes downside deviation very sensitive to the number of return observations and the time period selected. Basically, if market returns are generally positive during the period sampled, then the downside deviation will be understated, potentially to a great degree. To deal with this problem, analysts have developed ways of calculating downside risk via the simulation of the true distribution of returns. One method, called bootstrapping, involves the generation of a return distribution by repeated sampling of the actual periodic returns. Bootstrapping allows us to consider a number of possible scenarios in the calculation of downside risk rather than relying on one scenario, actual past history. Determination of downside risk using simulations may be more useful for the estimation of forward-looking risk than that calculated using the actual historical data. In this book we focus on the measurement of historical risk, and we have measured the downside risk inherent in the actual series of fund and benchmark returns.[1]

---

[1] For more on downside risk, see Frank Sortino and Stephen Satchell, *Managing Downside Risk in Financial Markets* (Oxford: Butterworth Heinemann, 2001).

CHAPTER 11

Relative Risk

One of the purposes of return measurement is to determine whether the manager added value over the benchmark. We quantify the portion of the returns that can be attributed to the actions of the portfolio manager by isolating the value added from the absolute returns to the fund over the period. Given the relationship between risk and return, we are also interested in whether the risk level of the portfolio differs from the benchmark. Many times the benchmark chosen guides the expected level of risk in the strategy. If the benchmark was set based on the investor's appetite for risk and the combination of the fund being evaluated with the other assets in the investor portfolio, it is the risk of the fund relative to that of the benchmark that we are interested in measuring. If the fund was riskier than the benchmark, then we would expect higher fund returns over time. For many situations, the manager will set an expected band of risk relative to the benchmark. We measure risk periodically to ensure that it is within acceptable limits. If the fund was less risky than the benchmark, the manager may be avoiding risks that are required to achieve the investor's long-term goal. Taking the perspective of the manager, it is the benchmark relative return, benchmark relative risk, and risk-adjusted return that our performance is being measured by. So both investors and investment managers are interested in measuring the degree of benchmark-relative risks taken, along with the benchmark-relative return.

Where absolute risk is proxied by the standard deviation of returns, relative risk is measured by looking at how the fund returns and the benchmark returns vary together. If the fund and benchmark move up and down together, there is a degree of absolute risk, as measured by standard deviation, but there would not be any relative risk. If the fund and benchmark returns vary in different ways, for example, if fund returns are generally more negative than the benchmark when the market

165

is down, then the fund has a greater degree of benchmark-relative risk than the risk implied by the benchmark. The volatility of the periodic return differences to the benchmark measures the risk specific to the strategy being evaluated. In this chapter we look at ways to measure these benchmark relative risks.

COVARIANCE

Measures of the association between the fund and the benchmark return series give us an understanding as to how much benchmark relative risk was exhibited by the portfolio. Benchmark-relative risk statistics are based on the concept of measuring how closely periodic fund returns vary from the returns of the comparison benchmark. We can get a sense of how funds vary together using a line graph that plots the sequence of monthly returns, such as Exhibit 11.1. Here we have a benchmark and two alternative portfolios. The benchmark and Fund 1 are the sample fund and benchmark that we have been working with from Exhibit 8.1. We have added a second fund, Fund 2, for comparison. We can see that the returns for Fund 1 generally move up and down with the benchmark. The returns of Fund 2 do not move close to the benchmark, as a matter of fact, Fund 2 sometimes moves in opposite directions than the benchmark returns.

We are interested in quantifying this degree of covariability, or covariance. *Covariance* is a statistical measure of the tendency for two data series to move together and is calculated using the series of fund and benchmark returns. It measures the direction and degree of association of the fund and benchmark returns, as well as the magnitude of the variability in the fund and benchmark returns.

EXHIBIT 11.1   Covariance

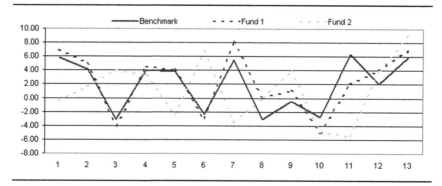

EXHIBIT 11.2 Covariance and Correlation

	A	B	C	D	E	F	G	H
1	Month	Fund	Average Fund	Fund Diff	Index	Avg Index	Index Diff	Fund Diff * Index Diff
2	1	7.00	2.35	4.65	5.76	1.98	3.78	17.548
3	2	5.00	2.35	2.65	4.18	1.98	2.20	5.813
4	3	-4.00	2.35	-6.35	-3.11	1.98	-5.09	32.361
5	4	4.50	2.35	2.15	4.00	1.98	2.02	4.329
6	5	4.00	2.35	1.65	3.87	1.98	1.89	3.106
7	6	-3.00	2.35	-5.35	-2.36	1.98	-4.34	23.252
8	7	8.00	2.35	5.65	5.55	1.98	3.57	20.139
9	8	0.10	2.35	-2.25	-3.12	1.98	-5.10	11.502
10	9	1.00	2.35	-1.35	-0.50	1.98	-2.48	3.362
11	10	-5.00	2.35	-7.35	-2.74	1.98	-4.72	34.733
12	11	2.00	2.35	-0.35	6.33	1.98	4.35	-1.538
13	12	4.00	2.35	1.65	2.03	1.98	0.05	0.077
14	13	7.00	2.35	4.65	5.89	1.98	3.91	18.152
15								
16	Standard Deviation Fund: 4.13				Covariance: 13.30		=SUM(H2:H14)/13	
17	Standard Deviation Index: 3.65				Correlation: 0.8817		=F16/(C16*C17)	

$$\text{Covariance} = \frac{\sum[(RP_i - \overline{RP}) \times (RM_j - \overline{RM})]}{N} \qquad (11.1)$$

We calculate covariance by first taking both the periodic differences between:

■ Returns of the fund and the average fund return, and the
■ Returns of the benchmark and the average benchmark return.

We then multiply the periodic differences from the two sets together and add the product of the differences. Finally, we take the average by dividing by the number of periodic observations. Exhibit 11.2 demonstrates the calculation of covariance for the sample fund and benchmark, 13.30.

Covariance is a powerful statistic measuring the size of the difference in variability between two return series. Along with the expected returns for a set of assets, we use the covariance between a set of assets to determine the optimal asset allocation. In fact, in a diversified portfolio, the degree of portfolio risk will approximate the average covariance between the assets held in the portfolio. We can use Exhibit 11.2 to see how the fund and benchmark returns influence the covariance:

1. Periods where both the fund and benchmark returns are *either* above or below their average returns contribute *positively* towards covariance. In month 10 the fund return falls the farthest from the average of the fund returns, a return deviation of −7.35%. And in the same month the benchmark return also fell well below its own average for

a deviation of –4.73%. The two deviations are multiplied together to form the contribution to covariance for the period. We can see in cell H11 the large contribution to covariance for that month equal to 34.73.

2. Periods where the fund and benchmark returns move in opposite directions, relative to their averages, contribute *negatively* towards covariance. In month 11 the fund return fell below its own average, but the benchmark return was above average. The product of the differences leads to a negative contribution to covariance equal to –1.54.

A total positive covariance indicates that the return series are associated, in that they move together. A negative covariance indicates that they move in opposite directions. This would be an interesting property for a fund to have because of its diversification benefits. When there is no relation between the fund and the benchmark returns, the products of the monthly differences will sometimes be positive and sometimes be negative. Averaging these over the entire period produces a low or zero covariance. Exhibit 11.3 summarizes the interpretation of covariance.

The fund has a covariance with the benchmark equal to 13.30, but what does this mean? Covariance is difficult to interpret as anything other than the average product of the differences between the fund and benchmark return deviations. Covariance is also difficult to use for portfolio comparisons because it is impacted by the absolute size of the returns.

CORRELATION

Given the difficulties in using covariance, we can standardize it by converting it into the correlation coefficient, which is more useful for direct comparisons. *Correlation* is a measure of the amount by which two investments vary together. It measures the direction and degree of association in the fund and benchmark returns.

EXHIBIT 11.3   Interpreting Covariance

Covariance	Fund and Benchmark
Large Positive	Move together.
Near Zero	Out of sync. Possibly the wrong benchmark for the fund.
Large Negative	Move in opposite directions.

To calculate the correlation we first calculate the covariance of the fund and benchmark returns. Then we divide the covariance by the product of the fund and benchmark standard deviations, which has the effect of scaling the covariance into a range between positive 1.0 and negative 1.0.

$$\text{Correlation} = \frac{\text{Covariance}}{\text{Stdevp(fund returns)} \times \text{Stdevp(index returns)}} \quad (11.2)$$

A correlation of +1.0 indicates that the returns are perfectly correlated, but does not indicate that the return series are the same. For example, a fund with returns in each period exactly twice those of the benchmark return for the period, would have a correlation equal to 1.0. A correlation coefficient of −1.0 indicates perfect negative correlation, which means that fund returns move in an exactly inverse and proportionate direction as the benchmark. A correlation above or below but near zero indicates a lack of correlation. Correlations can be used to examine relationships between a fund and its benchmark, between different funds, or between different benchmarks. Exhibit 11.2 also demonstrates the calculation of correlation for our fund and benchmark to be 0.88. This means there is a strong, positive relationship between the two series of returns, but there is some difference in how they vary and, therefore, some benchmark-relative risk. Exhibit 11.4 summarizes the interpretation of correlation.

COEFFICIENT OF DETERMINATION

While it is easy to interpret correlation coefficients that are near the extremes of 1 and −1, it is harder to get an intuitive understanding of correlations that lie in between. By squaring the correlation coefficient, we can derive a statistic that is easier to interpret. The square of the correlation coefficient is called the *coefficient of determination*, *R-squared*, or R^2.

$$\text{Coefficient of determination} = (\text{Correlation coefficient})^2 \quad (11.3)$$

EXHIBIT 11.4 Interpreting Correlation

Correlation	Fund and Benchmark
+1.0	Move together
Near Zero	Not related
−1.0	Move in opposite directions

EXHIBIT 11.5   Coefficient of Determination

	A	B	C	D
1	Correlation:	R	0.8818	
2	Coefficient of Determination:	R2	0.7775 ➤	=C1^2

EXHIBIT 11.6   Comparing R and R-Squared

R (+ or -)	1.00	0.90	0.80	0.70	0.60	0.50	0.40	0.30	0.20	0.10
R²	1.00	0.81	0.64	0.49	0.36	0.25	0.16	0.09	0.04	0.01

R-squared is the proportion of variability in fund returns that we can relate to the variability of the benchmark returns. It measures the degree of association in the fund and benchmark returns. We interpret R-squared as the ratio of the amount of portfolio market risk to total risk. R-squared can be used to determine the appropriateness of the benchmark used to evaluate and attribute fund performance. A high R-squared indicates that the portfolio and benchmark are probably exposed to similar risk factors that are driving returns.

Exhibit 11.5 demonstrates the calculation of R-squared for our example fund, which is equal to 0.78. An R-squared of 0.78 indicates that 78% of the variation in the fund returns is related to the variation in the benchmark returns and 22% is not. $(1 - R^2)$ is called the coefficient of nondetermination, i.e., the percentage of variation in fund returns not related to the variation in benchmark returns.

The values of R-squared can range from 0 to 1.0. A comparison of the values for correlation and R-squared illustrate the reason why R-squared is easier to interpret. Exhibit 11.6 shows the R-squared values for various levels of correlation. Notice how easily "high" values for correlation can give the wrong impression about the proportion of variability in fund returns that is really explained by benchmark returns.

It might seem that R-squared, correlation, and covariance duplicate each other as measures of benchmark relative variability. In fact each statistic offers more information than the last:

Measure	Interpretation
Coefficient of Determination (r^2)	The degree of association in the fund and benchmark returns.
Correlation Coefficient (r)	The direction and degree of association in the fund and benchmark returns.
Covariance	The direction and degree of association of the fund and benchmark returns, as well as the magnitude of the variability in the fund and benchmark returns.

EXHIBIT 11.7   Scatter Diagram Fund and Benchmark Returns

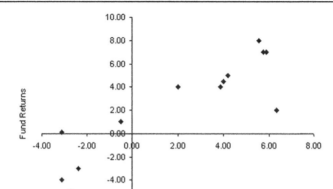

REGRESSION ANALYSIS

We can gain insight into the degree of association between two variables by plotting the observations. A graph plotting the periodic fund-benchmark return pairs allows us to visualize the relationship between the fund and benchmark returns. Exhibit 11.7 is a *scatter diagram* plotting the relationship between the fund and benchmark returns.

Each marker represents one monthly return. Its distance from the vertical or Y-axis, measured along the horizontal scale, represents the benchmark return. The distance of the marker from the horizontal or X-axis, measured on the vertical axis in the middle, represents the fund return. The arrangement of the plotted returns on the chart shows that there is a strong correlation between the two sets of returns. Most of the return pairs are located in the top right and bottom left quadrants of the chart. This dispersion occurred because when we had high benchmark returns, we also had high fund returns, and vice versa. The scatterplot is a visual indicator of the high degree of fund and benchmark return correlation. If the returns were less correlated, the scatterplot would show more returns in the other two quadrants.

Assuming that the fund is comprised of holdings selected from an underlying universe represented by the benchmark, we expect a high degree of correlation between the fund and benchmark returns. To identify the degree to which the fund returns vary given the variability in the benchmark returns we can calculate a statistic called *Beta*. Beta isolates the degree of benchmark, or market-related risk inherent in the fund, where risk is defined as the total variability in returns. A fund with a higher Beta than another indicates that it has taken on more benchmark relative risk than the other. We calculate the Beta through regression analysis.

If the returns are strongly correlated, we can imagine a clear line about which the fund-benchmark returns cluster. We can draw a straight, upward sloping line over the scatterplot from the bottom left to the top right quadrant that comes closest to representing the trend in the actual data. This *line of best fit* represents a linear relation between the return pairs. Exhibit 11.8 shows the line of best fit relating the fund and benchmark returns.

We can use the line of best fit to interpolate the fund return if we were given the benchmark return. For example, we do not have a benchmark return observation equal to approximately 1%. But we could extrapolate using the best-fit line and take a guess that the fund return for that period would be a little over 1%. We can see this in Exhibit 11.9.

EXHIBIT 11.8   Line of Best Fit

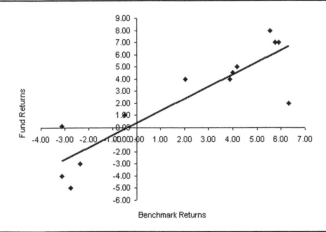

EXHIBIT 11.9   Extrapolating Returns Using the Line of Best Fit

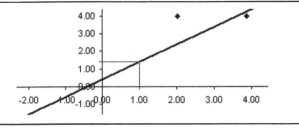

This, of course, is just a guess, and we can see from the differences between the points on the line and the actual observations that the line itself is the best line relating the benchmark and fund returns. However, it cannot be used to perfectly predict fund returns. The line instead is useful as a description of the relationship. We can quantify the relationship implied by the best-fit line mathematically using a *linear regression equation*:

Predicted fund return = Alpha + (Beta × Benchmark return)   (11.4)

The linear regression equation assumes that the value of one of the variables is at least partially dependent on the other. We know that a particular fund's return is more likely to be influenced by market returns represented by the benchmark than the reverse relationship. So, in performing a regression of fund versus market returns we make the fund return a *dependent variable* and the market return the *independent variable*. The market return is taken to be a random variable upon which the fund return at least partially depends.

There are two coefficients in the regression equation. The *Alpha* coefficient of the regression equation represents the value of the dependent variable when the independent variable equals zero. We can see in Exhibit 11.9 that the line passes through the fund return axis at a point between 0% and 1%. So Alpha is something between 0% and 1%.

The second coefficient, Beta, scales the value of the benchmark return up or down to derive the value of the fund return when added to the Alpha. Beta represents the slope of the regression equation. If beta equals one, then the slope of the line is at a 45-degree angle. In terms of our example, each percentage point of return on the X-axis is associated with the same percentage return on the Y-axis (after we add the Alpha).

The best values for Alpha and Beta are those that minimize the distance between the actual observed values and those derived using Equation (11.4). This procedure is equivalent to trying to draw a line that minimizes the sum of the individual distances from the line to the individual observations. Because the line represents forecasted values of Y for each actual value of X, we try to minimize the squared differences between the derived Y values and the actual Y values. The process for doing so is called *ordinary least squares regression* and the coefficient values that minimize the differences are calculated using formulas related to the formulas for variance and covariance.

REGRESSION BETA

To define the regression line, we first calculate the value of the slope, or Beta.

$$\text{Regression beta} = \frac{\sum_i [(RM_i - \overline{RM}) \times (RP_i - \overline{RP})]}{\sum_i (RM_i - \overline{RM})^2} \tag{11.5}$$

This can be simplified as the product of the correlation between the fund and benchmark returns multiplied by the ratio of the standard deviations of the fund and benchmark returns, or

$$\text{Regression beta} = \text{Correlation} \times \left[\frac{\text{Stdev}(RP_i)}{\text{Stdev}(RM_i)} \right] \tag{11.6}$$

Exhibit 11.11 shows the calculation of Beta for our sample fund. The Beta is equal to approximately 1.00, which indicates that the fund varies along with the benchmark. Beta measures how an asset fluctuates along with the market itself and is equivalent to the covariance of the fund and benchmark returns divided by the variance (square of the standard deviation) of the benchmark returns. The formulas are different from the covariance and variance only in that we have eliminated the count of the returns from each of the formulas. (We do this because they cancel each other out.) The Beta represents the proportion of the covariance in fund/benchmark returns that is related to the variance in benchmark returns. We can make several inferences about the values for Beta based on this formula:

- If the fund returns varied exactly in proportion to the benchmark returns, this would be equivalent to replacing the fund deviations in the numerator (right hand expression) with the benchmark deviations. Beta will be equal to 1 if the fund returns vary from the mean fund return in the same direction and degree as the benchmark returns vary from the mean benchmark return.
- If Beta is less than 1, then the numerator is smaller than the denominator. This indicates that the fund returns have been less variable than the benchmark returns over the period, in relation to their means.
- If Beta is greater than one, the numerator would be greater than the denominator so the fund returns have varied to a greater degree relative to the mean during the period, than the benchmark returns.
- Covariance close to zero indicates that there was little relationship between the fund and benchmark returns during the period. This will cause the numerator of the Beta calculation to be close to zero, which divided by the variance in index returns will yield a result close to zero. So a Beta close to zero indicates that there is little relation between the fund and benchmark returns.

■ If the covariance was negative, the Beta will be negative because we cannot have a negative variance. So the negative Beta indicates that there is an opposite relationship between the fund and benchmark returns for the period.

Exhibit 11.10 summarizes the interpretation of Beta.

REGRESSION ALPHA

Alpha equals the Y-axis intercept, or the value of the fund return when the benchmark return is equal to 0 as modeled by the regression equation. Alpha is calculated using the average fund and benchmark returns adjusted by the Beta:

$$\text{Alpha} = \overline{RP} - (\text{Beta} \times \overline{RM}) \tag{11.7}$$

EXHIBIT 11.10 Interpreting Beta

Beta	Fund Returns
Over 1	Vary to a greater degree proportion than the benchmark.
1	Vary to a degree equal to the benchmark.
Near Zero	Not related to the variability in the benchmark.
Negative	Vary to an opposite degree than the benchmark.

EXHIBIT 11.11 Regression Analysis

	A	B	C	D	E	F	G
1	Month	Fund Returns Y	Benchmark Returns X	X - avg(X)	Y - avg(Y)	(X - avg(X))2	(X - avg(X)) * (Y - avg(Y))
2	1	7.00	5.76	3.78	4.65	14.27	17.55
3	2	5.00	4.18	2.20	2.65	4.83	5.81
4	3	-4.00	-3.11	-5.09	-6.35	25.94	32.36
5	4	4.50	4.00	2.02	2.15	4.07	4.33
6	5	4.00	3.87	1.89	1.65	3.56	3.11
7	6	-3.00	-2.36	-4.34	-5.35	18.86	23.25
8	7	8.00	5.55	3.57	5.65	12.72	20.14
9	8	0.10	-3.12	-5.10	-2.25	26.04	11.50
10	9	1.00	-0.50	-2.48	-1.35	6.17	3.36
11	10	-5.00	-2.74	-4.72	-7.35	22.31	34.73
12	11	2.00	6.33	4.35	-0.35	18.90	-1.54
13	12	4.00	2.03	0.05	1.65	0.00	0.08
14	13	7.00	5.89	3.91	4.65	15.26	18.15
15	Average:	2.35	1.98			Sum: 172.92	172.84
16			=AVERAGE(B2:B14)		=SUM(G2:G14)		
17	Regression						
18	Beta:	0.9995		=G15/F15			
19	Alpha:	0.3717		=B15-(B18*C15)			
20							

Alpha is equal to the average of the fund returns less the Beta times the average benchmark return. Exhibit 11.11 illustrates the calculation of the regression coefficients using our sample fund data. The fund Beta is approximately 1.0 and the Alpha is approximately 0.37.

The Alpha and Beta coefficients yield the linear regression equation describing the line of best fit. The equation is a statistical description of the actual historical fund and benchmark return series. The equation suggests that fund returns equaled the benchmark return times one (Beta) plus 0.37% (Alpha).

$$RP_i \approx 0.37 + (1.00 \times RM_i)$$

The Alpha equal to 0.37% indicates that we could add 0.37% to each of the benchmark returns, adjusted by the Beta, to equal the fund return. We will return to the concept of Alpha in the discussion of risk-adjusted returns in Chapter 12. The Beta equal to 1 indicates that the degree of covariance in the fund and benchmark returns equals the amount of variance in the benchmark returns. Notice that even though Beta is 1, the fund and benchmark returns are different for each individual period. Beta indicates the degree to which the *variability* in fund returns is related to the variability in the benchmark returns.

The Beta equal to 1 indicates that the degree of benchmark-related risk exhibited by our fund equals that of the benchmark. Although the fund returns vary to the same degree as the benchmark returns, the fund's returns are different than the benchmark, and we are interested in the proportion of the fund's returns that are explained by the benchmark return. We determine this proportion by calculating the coefficient of determination, or R-squared, between the fund and benchmark returns.

Degree of Fit

The regression coefficients Alpha and Beta are used to build a linear formula that turns out to be the best one for minimizing the differences between the fund returns calculated using the regression equation and the actual fund returns. If all of the observed data points lie on the line of best fit, then the formula can be used to precisely calculate the fund returns given the benchmark returns, and the Alpha and Beta coefficients will have a high degree of reliability. Given that the observed returns do not all lie on the best fit line, we are interested in the degree of error present in the regression coefficients. The degree of error depends on the degree of scatter around the regression line. The more scattered the return pairs the worse the regression formula will perform in describing the relationship between the returns.

The coefficient of determination, or R-squared, can be used to gauge the significance of the regression coefficients. The R-squared for our sample fund, calculated in Exhibit 11.5, is 78%. This indicates that 78% of the changes in fund returns can be related to changes in the benchmark returns. This is a moderately high R-squared and merits a higher degree of confidence in the Alpha and Beta statistics than if the R-squared was lower. It does indicate that 22% of the fund returns are not explained by variation in the benchmark return. This variability is instead specific to the fund.

TRACKING RISK

The Beta equal to 1 indicates that the degree of covariance in the fund and benchmark returns equals the amount of variance in the benchmark returns. Notice that even though Beta is 1, the fund and benchmark returns are different for each individual period. The tracking risk statistic quantifies the amount of this fund-specific difference between the fund and benchmark returns, if we assume that the benchmark is a meaningful benchmark for the portfolio. That is, tracking risk is most useful when the Beta of the portfolio is close to 1. If it is not, the tracking risk statistics will lose their meaning.

Many investment strategies are designed to minimize return differences to the market benchmark. A fund or strategy that perfectly tracked its benchmark would have a correlation equal to one. This fund would have a zero tracking risk. Other strategies are managed to a particular expected tracking risk target. *Tracking risk*, also called *tracking error*, or *active risk*, is a measure of the magnitude of departures in fund returns from benchmark returns over time. The term tracking error has its roots in the management of index funds. The minimization of expected tracking error at an acceptable cost is a key factor in the management of index funds. But the estimation of expected tracking risk is also a key consideration in the construction of many types of portfolios. Some investment policies include a particular fixed boundary around the allocation of assets to particular asset classes or other portfolio segments in order to minimize the expected tracking error to benchmarks. Risk budgeting and other portfolio management techniques also serve to minimize tracking error. There are tools for estimating future tracking error, for example, by using a multifactor risk model. Here we are concerned with measuring historical tracking error, which provides information both as to the success of the manager in meeting the tracking error targets and the benchmark relative risk taken by the manager.

The historical tracking risk of a fund or strategy equals the standard deviation of the difference between the periodic fund and benchmark returns:

$$\text{Tracking risk} = \sqrt{\frac{\sum (D_i - \bar{D})^2}{N}} \qquad (11.8)$$

Where D_i are the periodic differences between the fund and benchmark returns and $\bar{D}$ is the mean of the return differences. To calculate tracking risk, take the periodic differences between the returns of the fund and the returns of the benchmark. Then take the standard deviation of these differences. This will yield a tracking risk with the same periodicity as the underlying returns. The tracking error statistic is useful because it is expressed in units of return. Exhibit 11.12 illustrates the calculation of the tracking risk, 1.95% per month, for our sample fund.

The tracking risk is a function of the standard deviation of the fund returns and the correlation of the fund and benchmark returns. In fact, we also can calculate tracking error with the following calculation:

$$\text{Tracking risk} = \text{Stdevp}(\overline{RP_i}) \times \sqrt{1 - (\text{correlation})^2} \qquad (11.9)$$

EXHIBIT 11.12   Tracking Risk

	A	B	C	D	E
1	**Month**	**Fund**	**Benchmark**	**Difference**	
2	1	7.00	5.76	1.24	
3	2	5.00	4.18	0.82	
4	3	-4.00	-3.11	-0.89	
5	4	4.50	4.00	0.50	
6	5	4.00	3.87	0.13	
7	6	-3.00	-2.36	-0.64	
8	7	8.00	5.55	2.45	
9	8	0.10	-3.12	3.22	
10	9	1.00	-0.50	1.50	
11	10	-5.00	-2.74	-2.26	
12	11	2.00	6.33	-4.33	
13	12	4.00	2.03	1.97	
14	13	7.00	5.89	1.11	
15					
16			Tracking Risk:	1.95	=STDEVP(D2:D14)
17			Annualized Tracking Risk:	6.76	=D16* SQRT(12)

We annualize tracking risk by multiplying it by the square root of the number of periodic return observations in a year.

$$\text{Annualized tracking risk} = \sqrt{\frac{\sum(D_i - \bar{D})^2}{N}} \times \sqrt{P} \qquad (11.10)$$

Where D_i are the periodic differences between the fund and benchmark returns, $\bar{D}$ is the mean of the return differences, and P is the frequency of the return observations. Exhibit 11.12 illustrates the calculation of the annualized tracking risk for our sample fund equal to 6.76%. Passive funds have a very low tracking risk. For an actively managed strategy, tracking risk provides a measure of active, rather than total, risk. When the fund and the benchmark are equally risky and returns are highly correlated, there will be a low tracking risk. It is possible for a fund and benchmark to have similar average returns and standard deviations of return, but imperfect correlation of returns. The tracking risk statistic can identify this situation. The lower the tracking risk, the closer you should be to the benchmark return. One issue with tracking error is the same problem exhibited by standard deviation: It provides no information as to the direction of the deviation. A manager who consistently outperformed the benchmark could exhibit the same tracking risk as the manager who trailed his benchmark.

The risk statistics we have calculated here are only some of the possibilities at our disposal for evaluating a particular situation. For example, one of the problems with using tracking risk as a measure of benchmark relative risk is that it is based on the standard deviation, so it weights upside deviations equally with downside deviations. If the benchmark deviations are normally distributed, this is not a problem. But if the manager can produce returns with more upside risk than downside, tracking risk will not capture this fact. We can measure this instead by calculating the *downside tracking risk*, which is the standard deviation of the returns below some target difference. For example, we can calculate a downside tracking risk with a target value added equal to zero. There are many other possible adaptations of the basic calculations.

We could also calculate tracking risk as the relative difference between the fund and benchmark returns, or

$$\text{Relative tracking risk} = \text{Standard deviation}\left(\frac{RP_i}{RM_i}\right) \qquad (11.11)$$

EXHIBIT 11.13   Risk Statistics Using Different Benchmarks

	Regression Alpha	Regression Beta	R^2
Russell Value	0.90	0.90	0.90
Wilshire Mid Value	0.15	0.79	0.92
Russell 2000	0.88	0.88	0.88
S&P500	0.90	0.84	0.79
Wilshire 5000	0.91	0.69	0.58

Benchmark Selection

Tracking risk and other relative risk statistics are very sensitive to the benchmark selected for the comparison. We need to keep this in mind when ranking portfolios based on benchmark relative or risk adjusted return statistics. We demonstrate the reason for this in Exhibit 11.13. Here we calculated the Alpha, Beta, and R-squared for the same fund versus several different benchmarks to show how much the results can differ depending on the benchmark used.

Absolute, downside, and relative risk statistics are valuable tools for measuring risk. But these statistics still leave some of our performance measurement questions unanswered. These questions include the question as to whether the return earned is high enough to justify the risks quantified given the standard deviation, downside deviation, or tracking error exhibited by the strategy. In the Part III of the book we address the issue of relating risk to return.

Measuring Risk-Adjusted Performance

Absolute Risk-Adjusted Return

The standard deviation and downside risk measures quantify the dispersion of returns earned over time, which is our primary proxy for absolute risk. The Beta and tracking error provide us with measures of the benchmark relative risk of a portfolio. Given a measure of risk, our next task is to address the question of whether the return was sufficient given the risks taken. One way to do this is to compare the combined risk and return earned by several peer group portfolios and our portfolio to a benchmark. We can make a visual comparison by creating a chart plotting the combination risk/return observations for each portfolio. Exhibit 12.1 plots the 3-year annualized return and 3-year annualized standard deviations for ten large company stock funds.

EXHIBIT 12.1   Risk versus Return

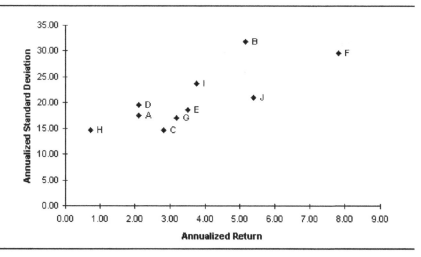

The Y-axis represents the standard deviation of returns over the period and the X-axis represents the measure of return, here the arithmetic average return, for the period. We can see that there is a general relationship between the risks taken and the returns earned. But there are some exceptions. For example, Fund B exhibited the highest standard deviation, but earned a lower return than funds F and J. Funds C and H had approximately the same risk, but Fund C had a higher return. So it is important to relate risk and return in order to evaluate the performance of a fund.

In addition to the graphical representation, it would be worthwhile to have numerical measures of the combined risk and return exhibited by a portfolio. We can adjust the returns earned over time by the standard deviation of return and other statistical descriptions of risks taken in order to derive measures of risk-adjusted return. *Risk-adjusted returns* are composite risk-return measures that are used to help determine whether or not the returns earned were sufficient compared to those earned by similar portfolios and benchmarks exhibiting a similar level of risk. There are several ways to determine the risk-adjusted returns to a portfolio. In this chapter, we consider measures of risk-adjusted return calculated in the context of Modern Portfolio Theory (MPT). MPT-based statistics evaluate risk using the Capital Asset Pricing Model, a theoretical model of risk and return. In Chapter 13 we look at some measures of risk-adjusted return useful, where risk is measured as the downside or benchmark relative risk taken by the manager. Chapter 14 reviews how we can use the return history, along with the composite risk and return statistics, to quantify the consistency, or skill, of an investment manager.

COEFFICIENT OF VARIATION

Given standard deviation as a measure of return variability, it is natural to want to compare two investments to determine whether one is more volatile than the other. We can see from previous examples our sample fund has a higher standard deviation of return over the period than the benchmark, 4.13% to 3.65%. However, the arithmetic mean fund return was also higher than the arithmetic mean benchmark return for the period. Because standard deviation is calculated in the same units of return as the underlying mean return, the standard deviation of returns for different investments are not directly comparable, unless the means are quite similar. To compare two investments for relative variability, we need to normalize the standard deviation. The *coefficient of variation* is a measure of risk-adjusted return. It is equal to the standard deviation scaled by the mean of the return series.

EXHIBIT 12.2   Coefficient of Variation

	A	B	C
1		Fund	Benchmark
2	**Standard deviation:**	4.13	3.65
3	**Arithmetic Average:**	2.35	1.98
4	**Coefficient of Variation:**	1.76	1.84
5		=(C2/C3)	
6			

$$\text{Coefficient of variation} = \frac{\text{Standard deviation}(RP_i)}{\overline{RP}_i} \tag{12.1}$$

Here the coefficient of variation is expressed as a ratio. It can be used to compare the relative variability of two data sets. We can use the coefficient of variation to compare the variability of fund returns. Exhibit 12.2 shows the calculation of the coefficients of variation for our sample fund and benchmark.

The standard deviations are approximately 1.76 times the mean fund return and 1.81 times that of the benchmark mean. We conclude that the variability of the benchmark returns, as expressed as a percentage of the mean return, is higher than the variability in the fund returns. This is the opposite conclusion that we come to by comparing the absolute standard deviations.

SHARPE RATIO

We use ratios to make comparisons between two things. A ratio itself is a yardstick for comparisons in situations where there are differences in the absolute measures being compared. For example, I can go on a short trip and you can go on a long trip, but if we are interested in who drove faster along the way, we can normalize both the different distances and times by comparing the average speed taken as measured in miles per hour. Similarly, if we are interested in comparing the risk to return efficiency of two strategies, we can take the inverse of the coefficient of determination by dividing the average return over a period by the risk taken during the period to derive the return per unit of risk. This measure is sometimes called the *risk-adjusted return*.

$$\text{Risk-adjusted return} = \frac{\overline{RP}}{\text{Standard deviation}(RP_i)} \tag{12.2}$$

Where RP_i are the periodic fund returns. The risk-adjusted return is equivalent to the inverse of the coefficient of variation. It can be used to rank the risk and return efficiency of portfolios, but it is not often reported.

Dr. William Sharpe, Nobel Prize winner and one of the originators of the Capital Asset Pricing Model, is credited with developing the *Sharpe ratio* for risk-adjusted performance measurement. The Sharpe ratio is a modification to the risk-adjusted return. The modification is based on the idea that we should not be able to earn returns over and above a risk free return without taking on risk. The *risk-free return* is the return that we can earn on an investment with little or no market or credit risk, like a U.S. Treasury Bill. It is the return over the risk-free return that we expect to earn for bearing the market and credit risk that accompanies most investments. This return is called the *excess return*, equal to the difference between the periodic return earned on the investment and the risk-free rate for the period.

$$\text{Excess return} = RP_i - RF_i \qquad (12.3)$$

where RF_i are the periodic returns for the risk-free investment.

Given standard deviation as a proxy for risk, theoretically there should be no standard deviation of returns for the risk-free investment. So it is the excess return that we earn in exchange for taking on risk, or standard deviation of return. The Sharpe ratio takes these theoretical constructs into account by relating the excess fund return to risk, instead of using the absolute fund return. The Sharpe ratio can be visualized as the slope of a line relating theoretical models of risk and return, such as the Capital Market Line in Exhibit 12.3. The *Capital Market Line* relates the risk and return properties of various investments. The return axis intercept of the CML equals the average risk-free rate.

EXHIBIT 12.3   Capital Market Line

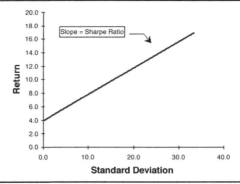

The Sharpe ratio is the difference between the annual arithmetic mean fund return and annual arithmetic mean risk-free return divided by the annualized standard deviation of the fund returns.

$$\text{Sharpe ratio} = \frac{\overline{RP} - \overline{RF}}{\text{Standard deviation}(RP_i) \times \sqrt{P}} \qquad (12.4)$$

Dr. Sharpe calls this ratio the *reward to variability ratio*. We calculate Sharpe ratios by taking the annual mean of the periodic fund returns and subtracting the annual mean of the periodic risk free returns to form the numerator. We then take the difference between the averages and divide the difference by the annualized standard deviation of the fund returns to yield the risk/reward ratio.[1] The difference between the Sharpe ratio and the risk-adjusted return is that we subtract the risk free rate from the gross return when calculating a Sharpe ratio. This has the effect of removing the portion of return yielded by the risk free rate, for which we do not expect to suffer any risk. The Sharpe ratio for our sample fund, calculated in Exhibit 12.4, equals 1.62.

The Sharpe ratio reveals the risk/return efficiency of a portfolio. We can compare investments with similar risk characteristics by Sharpe ratio to identify the most efficient portfolios. By using the Sharpe ratio, we can put into practice the idea that we shouldn't compare only the absolute returns earned on an investment, but also keep in mind the attending risk, as long as we are comfortable using standard deviation as a proxy for risk. Two managers with similar returns can be differentiated on a risk-adjusted basis using the Sharpe ratio. The higher the Sharpe ratio, the more return the fund has provided per unit of risk. Average Sharpe ratios will differ depending on the type of portfolio and time period used, so it is difficult to offer an idea of what a "good" Sharpe ratio is without looking at it relative to other funds. A negative Sharpe ratio indicates that the fund performed worse than the risk-free investment. We still cannot however use Sharpe ratios alone to select investments; for example, a fund with both low returns and low standard deviations could exhibit a higher Sharpe ratio than the fund with the higher absolute returns required for the investment situation.

---

[1] We can also calculate Sharpe ratios and the other risk-adjusted returns using geometric returns. To do this we take the difference between the geometric fund return and geometric risk-free return, and divide it by the standard deviation of the natural log of the single period growth rates. In practice, some analysts mix the arithmetic and geometric approaches, by using the *geometric* average return in the numerator but the standard deviation of the periodic returns around the *arithmetic* mean return in the denominator.

EXHIBIT 12.4   Sharpe Ratio

	A	B	C	D
1	Month	Fund Returns	Risk Free Return	Excess Return
2	1	7.00	0.43	6.57
3	2	5.00	0.46	4.54
4	3	-4.00	0.47	-4.47
5	4	4.50	0.44	4.06
6	5	4.00	0.41	3.59
7	6	-3.00	0.36	-3.36
8	7	8.00	0.39	7.61
9	8	0.10	0.36	-0.26
10	9	1.00	0.38	0.62
11	10	-5.00	0.41	-5.41
12	11	2.00	0.48	1.52
13	12	4.00	0.44	3.56
14	13	7.00	0.46	6.54
15				
16	Arithmetic Average Return: 2.35		0.42	=AVERAGE(C2:C14)
17	Annual Average Return: 28.25		5.07	=C16*12
18	Standard Deviation: 4.13		0.04 →	=STDEVP(C2:C14)
19	Annualized Standard Deviation: 14.32		0.14	=C18* SQRT(12)
20	Sharpe Ratio: 1.62			=(B17-C17)/B19
21				
22	Benchmark: 1.48			

Risk-Free Returns

We use the return on a risk-free investment in the calculation of the Sharpe ratio and other Capital Asset Pricing Model (CAPM) statistics. The risk-free rate is a hurdle rate, or benchmark for risk, in that we can earn this rate without taking on risk. A risk-free investment is one where the actual return equals the expected return, i.e., there is no variance around the expected return. In practice, we use the rates on short-term government securities to represent the risk-free investment because they do not suffer from credit risk. The return on a risk-free investment represents the pure time value of money. All other investments that incur other risks, such as the risk of default or risk of losing principal, should return a premium to the risk-free rate. To select the risk-free rate, we choose an instrument with a time to maturity that has no reinvestment risk, i.e., we use the return on a 30-day T-bill for comparison to one-month returns on risky securities or funds. Because we frequently measure risk using quarterly rather than monthly observations, we would use a 90-day T-bill return if the periodic returns were quarterly instead of monthly. The risk-free rate should also be selected based on the currency of the portfolio, i.e., the euro rate for euro-denominated funds and so on.

M-SQUARED RETURN

Most investors are intuitively comfortable interpreting the economic meaning conveyed by a rate of return. Some are comfortable interpreting the various measures of risk based on the idea of return deviations. Professional investors understand the information conveyed by the Sharpe ratio. But many consumers of performance measurement statistics, not working day to day with these tools, find Sharpe ratios confusing because they do not know its inputs and meaning. If an investor does not know what goes into it, it is hard to know whether a fund is better because it has a higher or lower ratio, etc. Because the risk and return tradeoff is the focus of investment decision making, the development of an unambiguous measure of risk-adjusted performance that is understandable by a wide audience is of critical importance. Without such a measure, many investors may be making decisions based on absolute returns or with only a rough consideration of the risks taken to earn these returns. Regulators and industry are still searching for this measure. There is no standard risk-adjusted performance statistic that has the broad based support that the time weighted return has on the return side of the performance measurement coin, but one candidate is the *Modigliani and Modigliani*, or M^2, return. Dr. Franco Modigliani, a Nobel economic laureate at MIT, and Leah Modigliani, analyst at Morgan Stanley, are credited with developing the M-squared return to help investors compare returns that have been adjusted for risk.[2] With M-squared we lever the return of the fund up or down depending on the risk taken. We do this to put the fund and benchmark on the same risk basis before we compare returns. Because it is a return, it has the benefit of being easily understood. To compare the risk and return efficiency of funds, we can rank them by M-squared in the same way as we can rank by Sharpe ratio.

M-squared is the Sharpe ratio scaled by the standard deviation of the benchmark return. To calculate it we calculate the Sharpe ratio for the period and calculate the annualized standard deviation of the benchmark returns for the period. Multiply the Sharpe ratio by the annualized standard deviation of the benchmark returns and add the annual average risk free return to calculate the M^2 return.

$$M^2 \text{ return} = \left[\left(\frac{\overline{RP} - \overline{RF}}{\text{Standard deviation}(RP_i) \times \sqrt{P}} \right) \right. \tag{12.5}$$
$$\left. \times (\text{Standard deviation}(RM_i) \times \sqrt{P}) \right] + \overline{RF}$$

---

[2] Franco Modigliani and Leah Modigliani, "Risk Adjusted Performance," *Journal of Portfolio Management* (Winter 1997).

EXHIBIT 12.5   M-Squared Ratio

	A	B	C	D	E
1	Month	Fund	Benchmark	Risk Free	Excess Return
2	1	7.00	5.76	0.43	6.57
3	2	5.00	4.18	0.46	4.54
4	3	-4.00	-3.11	0.47	-4.47
5	4	4.50	4.00	0.44	4.06
6	5	4.00	3.87	0.41	3.59
7	6	-3.00	-2.36	0.36	-3.36
8	7	8.00	5.55	0.39	7.61
9	8	0.10	-3.12	0.36	-0.26
10	9	1.00	-0.50	0.38	0.62
11	10	-5.00	-2.74	0.41	-5.41
12	11	2.00	6.33	0.48	1.52
13	12	4.00	2.03	0.44	3.56
14	13	7.00	5.89	0.46	6.54
15					
16	Arithmetic Average Return:	2.35	1.98	0.42	=AVERAGE(D2:D14)
17	Annual Average Return:	28.25	23.80	5.07	=D16*12
18	Standard Deviation:	4.13	3.65	0.04	=STDEVP(D2:D14)
19	Annualized Standard Deviation:	14.32	12.63	0.14	=D18* SQRT(12)
20					
21	Sharpe Ratio:	1.62			=(B17-D17)/B19
22	M2 Return	25.51			= D17+(B21*C19)
23					
24	Benchmark:	23.81			

where RM_i is the individual benchmark returns. Note that the fund and risk-free rates are the annual average and that the standard deviations are the annualized standard deviations. Exhibit 12.5 illustrates the calculation of M-squared for our sample fund, which equals 25.51%. We also calculate M-squared for the benchmark, which equals the benchmark return of 23.81%. Using M-squared we can say that the fund had a higher return than the benchmark, even on a risk-adjusted basis.

We can compare the fund M-squared return to the benchmark return. If M-squared is higher than the benchmark, the fund has a positive risk-adjusted return. We also can compare and rank funds using the M-squared return as each of the fund returns has been adjusted to have the same volatility as the benchmark return. The relative ranking will be the same as a ranking of funds by the Sharpe ratio, but the results should be easier to interpret.

CAPITAL ASSET PRICING MODEL

Linear regression analysis is used in one of the most frequently encountered models of the relationship between investment risk and return, the *Capital Asset Pricing Model*, or *CAPM*. Originally developed to explain the difference in returns produced by investments in individual common stocks, CAPM has been put into service to carry out the risk-adjusted performance assessment of investment funds. The CAPM is one of the fundamental building blocks of *Modern Portfolio Theory*, or MPT. The regression coefficients we derive using CAPM are sometimes called MPT statistics.

The CAPM is concerned with explaining the differences in returns earned on different investments. An investment can be a single asset like a stock or a collection of assets in a fund. Using an investment fund as our example, the CAPM equation rests on several principles:

- An investment that has no risk will earn the risk-free return, where risk is measured by the volatility of returns.
- Two different types of risk cause the volatility in investment returns. The first is the *market risk* of the investment, which reflects the degree to which investment values vary when the level of prices in the underlying market changes. Volatility that affects the market as a whole is assumed to correspond to changes in the underlying factors that influence market prices in general. For example, if we can assume that stock market valuations respond positively to increases in the growth rate of the economy as a whole, we can say that the economic growth factor is to some degree common to all stocks. Economic growth, and other factors which influence the value of market prices as a whole, are *systematic* risk factors.
- Systematic risk factors are reflected in the market returns, therefore, we can isolate the influence of systematic factors on an individual asset by observing market returns.
- All investments within the market are influenced by systematic risk, but the degree of exposure to systematic risks varies from asset to asset.
- Factors specific to the asset can generate volatility, for example, a change of management within a company. This type of volatility is unique to the asset, or *unsystematic*.
- Of the two components of risk, those risks specific to particular assets can be eliminated via portfolio diversification. We assume that the particular risks of different assets will offset each other in a diversified investment fund.
- Because the unique risk is diversifiable, the market *does not* reward the asset with a risk premium for this risk. The market rewards only the exposure to systematic risk. This is because systematic risk cannot be diversified away and is thus borne by every investor in the market.
- Investors expect a risk premium in exchange for bearing this risk.
- Investments are awarded a degree of return over the risk free rate, or a *risk premium*, based on the degree of market risk. The reward to

risk ratio is a linear function: For each unit of systematic risk the asset is exposed to the market, the market will reward the asset with one unit of excess return.

- An investment that has risk exposures similar to the market taken as a whole will have returns that vary in line with the market. If an asset is less exposed to market factors, its returns will vary to a lesser degree as the market as a whole. If the investment has greater exposure to systematic factors, returns will vary to a greater degree than the market returns.[3]

Assuming that these views are true, the relative performance of one asset to another is determined by the degree of market risk inherent in the two instruments. We can formulate a regression equation representing the principles of the CAPM to derive the return we should theoretically observe for a fund given the returns of the market, as represented by a market index or other benchmark. First, assume that we have an asset with no market risk. CAPM proposes that an asset that has no market risk will earn a return equal to the risk free return, or:

$$RP_i = RF_i$$

If an asset does have an element of market risk, CAPM states that we should earn a risk premium proportionate to the amount of market risk reflected in the asset. If the underlying market itself has a degree of return uncertainty, we assume that the market return will be higher than the risk free return. This is the excess market return. To derive the incremental excess return we expect for the fund, we lever the excess market return up or down by the degree of market risk exposure inherent in the asset. The *CAPM Beta* represents the degree of market risk exposure.

$$\text{CAPM beta} = \frac{\sum (ERM_i - \overline{ERM}) \times (ERP_i - \overline{ERP})}{\sum (ERM_i - \overline{ERM})} \qquad (12.6)$$

where *ERM* is the market excess return values, and *ERP* is the fund excess return values. The CAPM Beta is equal to the covariance of the fund and benchmark excess returns divided by the variance of the benchmark excess returns. CAPM Beta measures the degree of variabil-

---

[3] For a history of modern finance including the development of the CAPM, see Peter Bernstein, *Capital Ideas: The Improbable Origins of Modern Wall Street* (New York: The Free Press, 1992).

ity in fund returns around the mean fund return that is correlated with the degree of market return differences to the mean market return. This Beta coefficient is calculated in the same way as the regression Beta, but we distinguish CAPM Beta from the regression Beta in that we are relating excess fund returns to excess market returns, instead of using the full fund and market returns.

Finally, by adding the excess market return levered by the CAPM Beta to the risk-free return we can derive the expected fund return:

$$RP_i = RF_i + [CAPM \text{ beta} \times (RM_i - RF_i)] \tag{12.7}$$

Equation (12.7) is the CAPM equation. It can be interpreted as saying that fund returns should be equal to the risk-free rate plus a risk premium, where the risk premium is calculated by looking at the amount by which fund returns vary in proportion to the variability in the underlying market return.

Exhibit 12.6 illustrates use of the CAPM with several scenarios. In these examples, the risk-free rate equals 5.00% and the market return equals 8.00%. In the first case, the Beta of the fund to the market equals zero, which indicates that the returns of this asset are not related to the variability in returns of the market portfolio. Using CAPM, if Beta equals zero, the fund return should equal the risk-free rate, or 5.00%.

In Case 2, the Beta of the fund is 0.80. A Beta of less than one indicates that the fund return had less than market risk, but the fund returns did move substantially in line with the market returns. Where the fund returns varied to a lesser degree than the market return, CAPM proposes a smaller return than the market return, yet the asset does exhibit market related volatility, so the return should be higher than the risk free rate. In our example the return is 7.40%.

Case 3 represents a fund with a Beta equal to one. If the fund has returns that vary to the same degree as the benchmark returns, Beta equals one. The CAPM return where Beta equals one should equal the market return, or 8.00%.

EXHIBIT 12.6 CAPM Returns

	A	B	C	D	E
1	Case:	1	2	3	4
2	Risk free rate:	5.00	5.00	5.00	5.00
3	Market return:	8.00	8.00	8.00	8.00
4	Beta:	0.00	0.80	1.00	1.20
5					
6	CAPM return:	5.00	7.40	8.00	8.60
7		=D2 + D4*(D3-D2)			
8					

EXHIBIT 12.7   CAPM Beta and Alpha

	A	B	C	D	E	F	G	H	I ERP - AVG(ERP) * ERM - AVG(ERM)	J
1	Month	Fund	Benchmark	Risk Free	ERP = RP - RF	ERM = RM - RF	ERP - AVG(ERP)	ERM - AVG(ERM)		(ERM - AVG(ERM))²
2	1	7.00	5.76	0.43	6.57	5.33	4.64	3.77	17.48	14.21
3	2	5.00	4.18	0.46	4.54	3.72	2.61	2.16	5.63	4.66
4	3	-4.00	-3.11	0.47	-4.47	-3.58	-6.40	-5.14	32.91	26.43
5	4	4.50	4.00	0.44	4.06	3.56	2.13	2.00	4.26	4.00
6	5	4.00	3.87	0.41	3.59	3.46	1.66	1.90	3.15	3.61
7	6	-3.00	-2.36	0.36	-3.36	-2.72	-5.29	-4.28	22.65	18.32
8	7	8.00	5.55	0.39	7.61	5.16	5.68	3.60	20.44	12.95
9	8	0.10	-3.12	0.36	-0.26	-3.48	-2.19	-5.04	11.05	25.41
10	9	1.00	-0.50	0.38	0.62	-0.88	-1.31	-2.44	3.20	5.96
11	10	-5.00	-2.74	0.41	-5.41	-3.15	-7.34	-4.71	34.58	22.19
12	11	2.00	6.33	0.48	1.52	5.85	-0.41	4.29	-1.77	18.40
13	12	4.00	2.03	0.44	3.56	1.59	1.63	0.03	0.05	0.00
14	13	7.00	5.89	0.46	6.54	5.43	4.61	3.87	17.83	14.97
15	Avg:	2.35	1.98	0.42	1.93	1.56		Sum:	171.47	171.11
16										
17			Beta:	1.0021	→=I15/J15		Alpha:	0.3675	→=E15-(E17*F15)	
18						Annual Average Alpha:	4.41	=H17*12		

The Beta for the fund in Case 4 is equal to 1.2. A Beta higher than one indicates that market volatility has been magnified when reflected in the fund. With CAPM, higher volatility than the market deserves higher returns, and the return for this fund equals 8.60%. Using CAPM, Beta also amplifies downside returns, so a fund with a Beta higher than one suffers greater losses than the market when the market is down.

Exhibit 12.7 illustrates the calculation of Beta for our sample fund. The fund has a Beta of 1.00, which indicates that the fund has no additional market risk than that implied by the benchmark. Given a Beta of 1.00, CAPM anticipates an average monthly fund return equal to the benchmark return, or 1.98% (0.42 + 1.00 × (1.98 − 0.42)).

The CAPM was originally developed by William Sharpe building on the work on portfolio theory by Harry Markowitz and James Tobin. The model has been the subject of extensive testing to determine its validity versus real world data and there have been many extensions and variations proposed. Multifactor models extend the market index model to determine the influences of the manager's returns over and above that predicted by the CAPM. Even given this experimentation and subsequent evolution, the original single-factor linear regression model reviewed here continues to be the most widely used risk-adjusted performance evaluation tool.

Treynor Ratio

One application of the CAPM Beta is in the calculation of the Treynor Ratio. The *Treynor Ratio* is the return in excess of the risk-free rate divided by the Beta. The Treynor ratio can be used to rank the desirability of a particular asset in combination with other assets, where part of the total risk inherent in the standard deviation will be diversified. It is calculated in the same way as the Sharpe ratio, except that the Beta replaces the standard deviation in the denominator. By replacing the standard deviation with Beta, we are substituting a measure of total risk with a measure of market, or benchmark risk.

$$\text{Treynor ratio} = \frac{(\overline{RP} - \overline{RF})}{\text{Beta}} \tag{12.8}$$

JENSEN'S ALPHA

Our sample fund's average return (2.35%) is higher than that generated by the CAPM equation (1.98%), showing that our fund has better risk and return efficiency than the CAPM indicates. We could hypothesize that this difference is due to the active management of the fund by the portfolio manager, for example, by selecting assets that are underpriced by the market. We would then take the magnitude of this outperformance as valuable information, as this represents value added over the benchmark, but on a risk-adjusted basis. We can use CAPM to isolate this outperformance by adding an additional coefficient, CAPM Alpha, to the right hand side of the CAPM equation.

$$RP_i = \text{CAPM Alpha} + RF_i + [\text{CAPM beta} \times (RM_i - RF_i)] \tag{12.9}$$

Here, the fund return equals the risk free rate, plus the risk premium, plus the CAPM Alpha. The *CAPM Alpha*, or *Jensen's Alpha*, is the factor of return that reconciles actual returns to those predicted by the CAPM. Jensen's Alpha is frequently used as a measure of the risk-adjusted return earned by a portfolio. Michael Jensen developed this extension to the CAPM as a tool for evaluating fund managers. The adjusted CAPM equation can be manipulated algebraically in order to put it into linear regression form.

$$RP_i - RF_i = \text{CAPM Alpha} + [\text{CAPM beta} \times (RM_i - RF_i)] \tag{12.10}$$

This regression equation is the same as the regression Equation (11.4) in the previous chapter, except we made the independent variable the excess market returns and the dependent variable the excess fund returns. Subtracting the levered excess market return from the left side gives us the formula for calculating Jensen's Alpha

$$\text{Jensen's Alpha} = (RP_i - RF_i) - [\text{CAPM beta} \times (RM_i - RF_i)] \tag{12.11}$$

Our sample fund's Jensen's Alpha is 0.3675, calculated in Exhibit 12.7. We interpret this as performance of 0.37% of positive average return per month in excess of that explained by the amount of market risk taken over the period.

Alpha is a measure of the risk-adjusted performance of a fund. Alpha can be interpreted as the risk-adjusted value added by active fund management. If Alpha is greater than zero, the fund had a return higher than expected by the CAPM. Portfolios with a positive Jensen's Alpha lie above the capital market line. A large Jensen's Alpha indicates excess returns after controlling for the market sensitivity (Beta) of the portfolio. The higher the Alpha, the better the fund or manager performed on a risk-adjusted basis, given the CAPM assumptions. A negative Alpha indicates that the fund performed worse than predicted given the market risk taken.

We calculate Alpha with the same periodicity as the underlying returns. It is common to express Alpha in annual equivalents. *Annual Average Alpha* is the average monthly Alpha times the number of periods per year.

$$\text{Alpha} = [\overline{ERP} - (\text{Beta} \times \overline{ERM})] \times P \tag{12.12}$$

The Annual Average Alpha for our fund is $0.3675\% \times 12 = 4.41\%$.

Defining Alpha

Investment managers are frequently judged on their ability to add "Alpha." But one problem with the term Alpha is that it has several different meanings. Sometimes Alpha is used in the way we have been describing Value Added, or the difference between the fund return and the benchmark return. Used in this way, Alpha measures outperformance unadjusted for the risk taken. Both the regression Alpha and Jensen's Alpha adjust for the risk taken by levering the market return up or down by the Beta. But sometimes a fund's Alpha or Beta will be reported without reference to whether the Alpha or Beta was calculated using a regression analysis of the returns or using a CAPM equation with excess return inputs. As the regression and CAPM coefficients have different values and interpretation, it is important to differentiate between them when calculating and reporting risk statistics. The regression coefficients are a statistical description of a portfolios expected return given the market return as represented by the benchmark. The CAPM return and Alpha coefficient are theoretical estimates of expected return and excess return due to fund management. Exhibit 12.8 summarizes different definitions of Alpha.

EXHIBIT 12.8   Definitions of Alpha

Alpha Definition	Calculation As	Term Used Here	Not Measured
Difference of fund and benchmark return	$A = RP - RM$	Value Added	Adjustment for risk taken
Difference of fund and risk free return	$A = RP - RF$	Excess Return	Adjustment for market risk
Intercept of the linear regression equation	$A = RP - (B \times RM)$	Regression Alpha	Adjustment for the risk free return
Excess return not predicted by the CAPM equation	$A = (RP - RF) - B \times (RM - RF)$	Jensen's Alpha	

Where A = Alpha, RP = Portfolio Return, RF = Risk Free Return, and RM = Market Return.

CHAPTER 13

Downside and Relative Risk-Adjusted Return

When we are interested in comparing the total risk and return, the Sharpe ratio and related statistics are appropriate measures of risk-adjusted return. We saw in Chapters 10 and 11 that we can adjust the measurement of risk based on the total variability of return to measure risk in a downside and relative framework. We calculate these risk measures, such as the downside deviation and tracking error, in part to evaluate whether the risk-adjusted returns were sufficient given the risks taken. In this chapter, we cover measures of risk related to the Sharpe ratio, but we will replace standard deviation as the measure of risk with measures of downside and relative risk.

SORTINO RATIO

The Sharpe ratio is the most commonly used measure of reward to variability. But the Sharpe ratio uses the standard deviation of returns as a proxy for risk, so it could be relating excess return to a measure of risk that is not meaningful to the investor. If risk is instead defined relative to a target return, we can use the downside risk measures in the denominator of the risk to reward ratio to make rankings of the ratios consistent with the investor's definition. The Sortino ratio is a modification to the Sharpe ratio that uses downside risk as a denominator and the target return as the hurdle rate in the numerator. The measure is associated with Dr. Frank Sortino of the Pension Research Institute.

EXHIBIT 13.1   Sortino Ratio

	A	B	C	D	E	F	G
1	Month	Fund	Target Return	RP - T	Target Return	RP - T	(RP - T)^2
2	1	7.00	1.20	5.80	1.20		
3	2	5.00	1.20	3.80	1.20		
4	3	-4.00	1.20	-5.20	1.20	5.20	27.04
5	4	4.50	1.20	3.30	1.20		
6	5	4.00	1.20	2.80	1.20		
7	6	-3.00	1.20	-4.20	1.20	4.20	17.64
8	7	8.00	1.20	6.80	1.20		
9	8	0.10	1.20	-1.10	1.20	1.10	1.21
10	9	1.00	1.20	-0.20	1.20	0.20	0.04
11	10	-5.00	1.20	-6.20	1.20	6.20	38.44
12	11	2.00	1.20	0.80	1.20		
13	12	4.00	1.20	2.80	1.20		
14	13	7.00	1.20	5.80	1.20		
15							
16	Arithmetic Average:	2.35	1.20	1.15			
17							
18	Annual Average Excess Return:	13.85	=(B16-C16) * 12				
19	Count of Returns:	13.00		Sortino Ratio:	1.57	→=B18/B22	
20	Sum of (RP - T)2 where RP < T:	84.37	→=SUM(G2:G14)	Benchmark:	1.18		
21	Downside Deviation:	2.55	=SQRT(B20/B19)				
22	Annualized Downside Deviation:	8.82	=B21 * SQRT(12)				

$$\text{Sortino ratio} = \frac{(\overline{RP} - T) \times P}{\sqrt{\dfrac{\sum (RP_i - T)^2 \text{ where } RP_i < T}{N}} \times \sqrt{P}} \tag{13.1}$$

We calculate the Sortino ratio by taking the annual average difference of the fund and the target returns and dividing it by the annualized downside deviation. The calculation of the Sortino ratio is demonstrated in Exhibit 13.1. The Sortino ratio for our sample fund is 1.57, using a target return of 1.20% per month. The use of the downside deviation makes the Sortino ratio a measure of excess return to downside risk taken, where excess return is defined as the return over a target return. By ranking portfolios by the Sortino rather than the Sharpe ratio, we might find that portfolios appearing to be the most efficient users of risk are not as appropriate investments for a particular situation as others.

INFORMATION RATIO

Tracking error is useful in measuring the degree of historical return deviation from the benchmark. But what if we have an active strategy designed to divert from the benchmark in order to exceed the benchmark return? We would be interested in measuring the gains over and above the benchmark return relative to the benchmark risk taken, as measured by the tracking error. We do this because in many situations we can earn the benchmark return itself with little tracking error and at low cost by implementing a passive strategy. The *Information ratio* is a measure of the benchmark relative return gained for taking on benchmark relative risk. It is analogous to the role that the Sharpe ratio takes in measuring absolute returns, but adjusted to support a benchmark relative reward to risk analysis. The ratio described here is sometimes called the *excess return Sharpe ratio*.

The measure of differential return over the benchmark that we use in the Information ratio is the average periodic *value added*, which is the average differential return over the measurement period.

$$\text{Value added} = \frac{\sum (RP_i - RM_i)}{N} \tag{13.2}$$

To calculate value added, we take the periodic differences between the fund and benchmark returns, add the differences, and divide the sum by the total number of returns. To convert value added to an annualized equivalent, multiply it by the number of periodic observations in a year.

$$\text{Annualized value added} = \frac{\sum (RP_i - RM_i)}{N} \times P \tag{13.3}$$

Annualized value added is the annual equivalent of the average monthly arithmetic difference between the fund and the benchmark returns. Cell F4 in Exhibit 13.2 shows the calculation of value added for our sample fund equal to 4.45%.

EXHIBIT 13.2   Information Ratio

	A	B	C	D	E	F	G
1	**Month**	**Fund**	**Benchmark**	**Difference**			
2	1	7.00	5.76	1.24	Count of Returns:	13.00	
3	2	5.00	4.18	0.82			
4	3	-4.00	-3.11	-0.89	Value Added:	0.37	=SUM(D2:D14)/D19
5	4	4.50	4.00	0.50	Annualized Value Added:	4.45	=F4 * 12
6	5	4.00	3.87	0.13			
7	6	-3.00	-2.36	-0.64	Tracking Risk:	1.95	=STDEVP(D2:D14)
8	7	8.00	5.55	2.45	Annualized Tracking Risk:	6.76	=F7* SQRT(12)
9	8	0.10	-3.12	3.22			
10	9	1.00	-0.50	1.50	Information Ratio:	0.19	=F4/F7
11	10	-5.00	-2.74	-2.26	Annualized Information Ratio:	0.66	=F5/F8
12	11	2.00	6.33	-4.33			
13	12	4.00	2.03	1.97			
14	13	7.00	5.89	1.11			

The Information ratio presents in a single statistic the units of incremental return given the amount of benchmark relative risk taken to earn it.

$$\text{Information ratio} = \frac{\left(\dfrac{\sum(RP_i - RM_i)}{N}\right)}{\text{stdevp}(RP_i - RM_i)} \quad (13.4)$$

We calculate Information ratio by calculating the value added and dividing it by the tracking risk. The monthly Information ratio for our sample fund is 0.19. We are interested in stating the ratio in annual equivalents, so we will multiply by the square root of the number of periods in a year.

Annualized information ratio

$$= \frac{\left(\dfrac{\sum(RP_i - RM_i)}{N}\right) \times \sqrt{P}}{\text{Standard deviation}(RP_i - RM_i) \times \sqrt{P}} \quad (13.5)$$

Taking the annualized value added and dividing it by the annual equivalent tracking risk gives the annual Information ratio. Exhibit 13.2 illustrates the calculation of the Information ratio for our sample fund as 0.66.

Sometimes the Information ratio is used as a measurement of the active investment manager's skill. The term Information ratio refers to the idea that the manager would depart from the benchmark only if he had some special information not already priced into the market, which presumably will lead to value added over the benchmark return. The manager with the higher Information ratio has earned more value added per unit of departure from the benchmark. An annualized Information ratio above one, using a long enough series of observations, is commonly interpreted as an indication of skill on behalf of the investment manager. A ratio of 0.50 is considered an adequate measure; a negative Information ratio indicates that a fund underperformed its benchmark.

The Sharpe ratio, Sortino ratio, and Information ratio are the most often used, but by no means only, measures of risk adjusted return. They all derive from the Sharpe ratio and the concept of determining the units of return gained for risks taken. We can replace both the numerator and denominator with components that reflect the returns and risks that we are concerned with in a particular situation.

CHAPTER 14

Assessing Skill

One of the main reasons to measure return, risk, and risk-adjusted return is to use these performance statistics to differentiate fund managers by evidence of relative skill in the management of portfolios in the past. *Skill* can be defined as the ability to deliver value added above the benchmark over time in a statistically significant manner. That is, we seek to differentiate skill from luck. In this chapter, we look at how we can use the measures of return, risk, and risk adjusted returns developed in previous chapters to add quantitative input to the process of the evaluating portfolio managers.

USING RISK AND RETURN TO ASSESS SKILL

Unfortunately historical performance measurement data does not provide us with a direct measure of skill. Over a single period, 50% of managers will achieve more than the median return and 50% will achieve less. We couldn't say much about the fact that a manager achieved superior performance in a single period, because it is only one observation. So we look to observe performance over many time periods, and if the manager consistently outperformed, maybe we could say that there is some evidence of managerial talent, or skill. Even here we face the problem that, completely due to chance, there will be, say, one manager in 20 who delivers consistent value added over the benchmark over a number of years. So, it is hard to differentiate between skill and luck.

Even if we are willing to accept the fact that it is possible to infer skill when in fact there is none, we have the problem that we seldom have the desired amount of historical observations necessary to assess performance. If we consider a year the shortest single period over which we wish to evaluate the performance of a manager, we would need many yearly returns to statistically isolate skill from luck. If we shorten the measurement period to quarters or months, we artificially introduce a short-term horizon into a situation where it is probably the long-term results that matter. In fact, it is both the combined average size of the periodic value added and the number of periods over which we have return observations that determine whether or not we can statistically isolate skill from luck.

Accepting these challenges, along with the usual warning that superior past performance is no guarantee of skill in the future, we can use historical performance measures to try to infer investment management skill. *Skill measurement* refers to the quantitative evaluation of past performance to determine statistical evidence of past skill, given the limits of the historical data. Together with more qualitative information and forward-looking information such as information about manager changes, changes in style, and the like, performance measurement is used in the assessment and selection of investment managers. There are several ways to use risk, return, and risk-adjusted returns in the estimation of past skill. Here we look at measurement of the statistical significance of the value added, along with other ways to examine the consistency of the added value delivered by the manager.

STATISTICAL SIGNIFICANCE OF VALUE ADDED

We isolate the value added to active management by subtracting the periodic benchmark return from the fund returns. Averaging the value added over a period of time gives us an indication as to the direction and magnitude of the value added. If value added was both positive and large over time, we might take that as an indication of the manager's skill. We can quantify whether or not the value added was significant (or not) by calculating the *t-statistic* for the value added. The t-statistic is a tool used in the branch of statistics known as inferential statistics. *Inferential statistical tests* calculate a statistic based on the data that have been collected, where the statistic can be used to infer the strength in the relationship between variables. For example, we are interested in knowing whether or not the value added by a manager is statistically different than zero. To determine this we set up the null hypothesis that the manager has added no value over the period; the alternative hypothesis is that the manager did add value, and we then use the t-statistic to try to prove the null hypothesis false.

EXHIBIT 14.1   T-Statistic for Value Added

	A	B	C	D
1	**Month**	**Fund**	**Benchmark**	**Difference**
2	1	7.00	5.76	1.24
3	2	5.00	4.18	0.82
4	3	-4.00	-3.11	-0.89
5	4	4.50	4.00	0.50
6	5	4.00	3.87	0.13
7	6	-3.00	-2.36	-0.64
8	7	8.00	5.55	2.45
9	8	0.10	-3.12	3.22
10	9	1.00	-0.50	1.50
11	10	-5.00	-2.74	-2.26
12	11	2.00	6.33	-4.33
13	12	4.00	2.03	1.97
14	13	7.00	5.89	1.11
15				
16	Count of Returns:	13	13	13
17	Monthly Average:	2.35	1.98	0.37
18	Standard Deviation:	4.13	3.65	1.95
19	T-Statistic:			0.69
20		=(D17/(D18/SQRT(D16)))		
21				

The t-statistic is calculated by Equation (14.1). We take the average value added and divide it by the standard deviation of the value added, which is divided by the square root of the number of observations.

$$\text{t-statistic for value added} = \frac{\text{Average}(RP_i - RM_i) - 0}{\text{Standard deviation}(RP_i - RM_i)/\sqrt{N}} \quad (14.1)$$

Exhibit 14.1 is an example of the calculation of the t-statistic for the value added for our sample fund, which equals 0.69.

The interpretation of the t-statistic depends on the number of observations used and the significance level selected. The significance level is the tolerance level for accepting that the manager has skill, when in fact he might not. In practice, a significance level of 5% is usually selected and the associated t-statistic required to reject the null hypothesis (that the value added is statistically undifferentiated from zero) is approximately two, depending on the number of observations. With 13 observations we would reject the null hypothesis if the t-statistic were greater than 1.782.[1] Because it is not, we cannot reject the null hypothesis that the value added is statistically different from 0. The t-statistic works by comparing the value added to that which we might expect to observe given the standard deviation of the value added. If the t-statistic is high

---

[1] Using the t-table, here with 12 degrees of freedom and a significance level = 0.05. See a statistics text for other t-table values.

enough that it is improbable that we would observe it by chance, we reject the null hypothesis and accept that the manager has added value over the period.

If either the fund had outperformed the benchmark to a greater degree over a few short periods of time or we had many more observations of the same relative value added, we might have reached a t-statistic that allowed us to reject the null hypothesis. The t-statistic is closely related to the Information ratio. We could take the Information ratio, multiply it by the square root of the number of observations and look up the result in the t-table in order to determine whether value added was statistically significant.

CONSISTENCY OF VALUE ADDED

There are several problems with the evaluation of performance presented so far. First, we have been looking at the value added produced over a period of time, without regard to the consistency of the average value added. For example, suppose we reanalyzed manager performance after several additional months where the manager dramatically beat the benchmark. This would increase the value added statistic and possibly push the t-statistic into significance. Then, in the next quarter, the manager might produce terrible performance and the conclusions drawn from the statistics will change. This pattern is referred to as *nonstationarity*. The statistics we calculate are *stationary* if they remain stable over time. In addition, we might be interested in the performance of the manager over single periods longer than a month or quarter. For example, suppose we are evaluating the performance of three alternative managers, each with a 5-year track record, so we have access to 20 quarterly returns for each manager. Exhibit 14.2 shows the quarterly returns for three funds along with an appropriate market index over 5-years. We will use this data to produce the examples in this section.

One way to get a sense of the stability of performance is to look at how consistently the fund delivers value added over the benchmark. An easy way to do this is to perform a *runs test,* which is used to decide whether the value added over the benchmark, or some other statistic, is the result of a random process or evidence of consistency. One way to perform a runs test is to first calculate the value added over the benchmark for each period. Then we mark each period according to whether there was value added over the period or not. In Columns K through M in Exhibit 14.3 we do this for each fund by assigning a "1" to periods where there was value added over the benchmark, and a "0" where there is not.

EXHIBIT 14.2   Sample Track Records

	Return			
	Fund A	Fund B	Fund C	Index
2000 Q4	(11.25)	7.83	2.23	6.43
2000 Q3	7.63	13.59	(0.84)	5.89
2000 Q2	(5.71)	0.55	(2.89)	0.24
2000 Q1	7.75	(0.55)	2.23	(0.96)
1999 Q4	10.36	(3.90)	4.85	2.89
1999 Q3	(8.77)	(5.50)	(6.28)	(9.01)
1999 Q2	11.07	16.70	6.96	10.26
1999 Q1	(3.61)	(7.07)	4.85	(0.44)
1998 Q4	12.10	7.64	13.92	13.02
1998 Q3	(12.34)	8.00	(9.93)	(10.41)
1998 Q2	(6.01)	(2.55)	3.29	0.70
1998 Q1	11.91	11.00	13.92	9.52
1997 Q4	0.85	13.00	2.63	2.02
1997 Q3	9.56	5.83	7.50	10.61
1997 Q2	12.72	7.39	17.37	12.14
1997 Q1	1.13	(2.34)	2.63	0.00
1996 Q4	8.07	6.33	5.32	9.51
1996 Q3	3.15	0.40	3.03	1.59
1996 Q2	3.03	2.24	4.41	2.62
1996 Q1	6.21	(1.13)	5.32	5.71

EXHIBIT 14.3   Runs Test for Consistency of Value Added

A	B	C	D	E	F	G	H	I	J	K	L	M	N	O	P	Q	R
	Return					Value Added								Reversal			
							Absolute			1=Yes 0 = Ho				Y = Yes N = Ho			
	Fund A	Fund B	Fund C	Index		Fund A	Fund B	Fund C		A	B	C		A	B	C	
2000 Q4	(11.25)	7.83	2.23	6.43	2000 Q4	(17.68)	1.40	(4.20)		0	1	0					
2000 Q3	7.63	13.59	(0.84)	5.89	2000 Q3	1.74	7.70	(6.73)		1	1	0		Y	N	N	
2000 Q2	(5.71)	0.55	(2.89)	0.24	2000 Q2	(5.95)	0.31	(3.13)		0	1	0		Y	N	N	
2000 Q1	7.75	(0.55)	2.23	(0.96)	2000 Q1	8.71	0.41	3.19		1	1	1		Y	N	Y	
1999 Q4	10.36	(3.90)	4.85	2.89	1999 Q4	7.47	(6.79)	1.96		1	0	1		N	Y	N	
1999 Q3	(8.77)	(5.50)	(6.28)	(9.01)	1999 Q3	0.24	3.51	2.73		1	1	1		N	N	N	
1999 Q2	11.07	16.70	6.96	10.26	1999 Q2	0.81	6.44	(3.30)		1	1	0		N	N	Y	
1999 Q1	(3.61)	(7.07)	4.85	(0.44)	1999 Q1	(3.17)	(6.63)	5.29		0	0	1		Y	Y	Y	
1998 Q4	12.10	7.64	13.92	13.02	1998 Q4	(0.92)	(5.38)	0.90		0	0	1		N	N	N	
1998 Q3	(12.34)	8.00	(9.93)	(10.41)	1998 Q3	(1.93)	18.41	0.48		0	1	1		N	Y	N	
1998 Q2	(6.01)	(2.55)	3.29	0.70	1998 Q2	(6.71)	(3.25)	2.59		0	0	1		N	Y	N	
1998 Q1	11.91	11.00	13.92	9.52	1998 Q1	2.39	1.48	4.40		1	1	1		Y	Y	N	
1997 Q4	0.85	13.00	2.63	2.02	1997 Q4	(1.17)	10.98	0.61		0	1	1		Y	N	N	
1997 Q3	9.56	5.83	7.50	10.61	1997 Q3	(1.05)	(4.78)	(3.11)		0	0	0		N	Y	Y	
1997 Q2	12.72	7.39	17.37	12.14	1997 Q2	0.58	(4.75)	5.23		1	0	1		Y	N	Y	
1997 Q1	1.13	(2.34)	2.63	0.00	1997 Q1	1.13	(2.34)	2.63		1	0	1		N	N	N	
1996 Q4	8.07	6.33	5.32	9.51	1996 Q4	(1.44)	(3.18)	(4.19)		0	0	0		Y	N	Y	
1996 Q3	3.15	0.40	3.03	1.59	1996 Q3	1.56	(1.19)	1.44		1	0	1		Y	Y	N	
1996 Q2	3.03	2.24	4.41	2.62	1996 Q2	0.41	(0.38)	1.79		1	0	1		N	N	N	
1996 Q1	6.21	(1.13)	5.32	5.71	1996 Q1	0.50	(6.84)	(0.39)		1	0	0		N	N	Y	=IF(M23<>M22,"Y","N")
							=IF(I23>0,1,0)										
										Count: 9	7	8					=COUNTIF(Q5:Q23,"Y")
										Possible: 18	18	18					=COUNT(I4:I23)-2
										R: 0.50	0.39	0.44					=Q25/Q26

This is like flipping a coin and noting whether it lands on heads or tails in each flip. Next, we look for evidence that the fund performed consistently over the benchmark. We can do this by looking for runs in the data, that is, periods where there was a trend of value added. This is analogous to looking for periods where a series of coin flips landed consistently on heads or tails. If the values in Column K are the same from one quarter to the next, there is a run. When the results change from one quarter to the next, then there is a break in the run. Columns O through Q indicate runs with an "N" and breaks in the run with a "Y." Next, we count the number of breaks in the run. If the pattern of value added were random, we would expect half of the months to reverse. If there were periods of consistent value added, we would expect a smaller number of reversals. We can divide the number of runs by the possible number of runs to derive a run ratio. A random process would exhibit a ratio of runs to expected runs of 0.5. A ratio near 0 would indicate that there was a pattern of trending value added. Although a ratio near 1 would indicate that there were no trends, the process wasn't entirely random either. We are interested in funds with a ratio closer to 0. Here Fund B had the best runs ratio.

ROLLING PERIOD ANALYSIS

One problem with the runs test as a measure of performance consistency is that the runs test accounts for whether or not there was value added, but not for the size of the value added. We can use the risk-adjusted return measures to look for both evidence of and magnitude of consistent performance. First we calculate the major risk, return, and relative risk-adjusted return statistics for the period in the spreadsheet below. We can see that Funds B and C dominate Fund A in all respects, with higher return, value added, and Information ratios as well as lower standard deviation and downside deviations.

	Fund A	Fund B	Fund C	Index
	Annualized 5-Year			
Return:	10.68	15.47	16.25	14.42
Standard Deviation:	16.03	13.27	12.52	12.46
Downside Deviation, T=0:	8.05	4.06	5.04	5.81
Value Added:	0.67	0.79	2.61	
Tracking Error:	10.46	12.76	6.70	
Information Ratio:	0.06	0.06	0.39	

So we are left to choose from Funds B and C. These funds both outperformed the benchmark, with similar standard deviations. Fund C has a higher return, lower standard deviation, and higher Information ratio. But the choice is not totally clear-cut, because Fund B exhibited a lower downside deviation, if this was an important criterion in our manager selection. Before making a decision, we might be interested in evaluating the consistency of the managers with regard to these statistics. With a one-year evaluation horizon in mind, and with five years of data, we could calculate five yearly calendar cumulative returns, standard deviations, and derived risk adjusted returns. Exhibit 14.4 shows the yearly risk and return statistics for each of the managers.

By looking at the statistics over finer periods, we can get a sense of the variability in the relative ranking of the funds over time. Exhibit

14.5 shows that Fund C has had a higher Information ratio for three out of the last five years, and that Fund B has had better relative risk adjusted performance for the most recent year.

We can also see that the relative ranking of the second and third portfolios has changed several times, in fact each portfolio has been the best performing or second-best performing fund for three out of the five periods. If we had more funds to select from, we could perform this analysis using rank and order statistics to see how consistently each manager ranked in the first quartile of managers, and so on.

When we measure the performance of a manager, we frequently do so over long periods of time, but not a long enough period of time to determine whether or not he has added statistically sufficient value over the benchmark. We can add to the number of observations and construct a more robust consistency analysis by performing a rolling period analysis. In a *rolling period analysis,* we calculate statistics for a fixed window of time, where with each new observation we add a new period and drop an earlier period. For example, instead of calculating annual Information ratios based on the five calendar years for which we have data, we can in fact calculate 17 yearly Information ratios with 20 quarters of data. We start with the first quarter where we have four prior quarters of data, and calculate an Information ratio for each quarter subsequent to that, adding the most recent and dropping the oldest quarter each time. Exhibit 14.6 shows how we can analyze performance on a rolling basis.

EXHIBIT 14.4   Yearly Statistics

	Fund A	Fund B	Fund C	Index		Fund A	Fund B	Fund C		Fund A	Fund B	Fund C
	Annual Average Return					Annual Value Added				Downside Deviation, T=0		
Year 2000:	(1.58)	21.42	0.73	11.60	Year 2000:	(13.18)	9.82	(10.87)	Year 2000:	9.34	0.48	2.36
Year 1999:	9.05	0.23	10.38	3.70	Year 1999:	5.35	(3.47)	6.68	Year 1999:	7.19	5.26	5.44
Year 1998:	5.66	24.09	21.20	12.83	Year 1998:	(7.17)	11.26	8.37	Year 1998:	10.21	2.21	8.60
Year 1997:	24.26	23.88	30.13	24.77	Year 1997:	(0.51)	(0.89)	5.36	Year 1997:	0.00	2.03	0.00
Year 1996:	20.46	7.84	18.08	19.43	Year 1996:	1.03	(11.59)	(1.35)	Year 1996:	0.00	0.98	0.00
	Annualized Standard Deviation					Tracking Error				Information Ratio		
Year 2000:	16.64	11.48	4.34	6.59	Year 2000:	19.58	6.12	7.31	Year 2000:	(0.67)	1.61	(1.49)
Year 1999:	17.30	19.35	10.39	13.84	Year 1999:	7.71	11.87	6.25	Year 1999:	0.69	(0.29)	1.07
Year 1998:	21.65	10.24	19.61	18.11	Year 1998:	6.52	18.68	3.10	Year 1998:	(1.10)	0.60	2.70
Year 1997:	10.39	10.98	12.04	10.52	Year 1997:	2.00	13.09	6.09	Year 1997:	(0.25)	(0.07)	0.88
Year 1996:	4.26	5.58	1.87	6.17	Year 1996:	2.16	4.99	4.75	Year 1996:	0.48	(2.32)	(0.28)

EXHIBIT 14.5   Annual Ranking by Information Ratio

	Fund A	Fund B	Fund C	Rank
Year 2000:	(0.67)	1.61	(1.49)	B-A-C
Year 1999:	0.69	(0.29)	1.07	C-A-B
Year 1998:	(1.10)	0.60	2.70	C-B-A
Year 1997:	(0.25)	(0.07)	0.88	C-B-A
Year 1996:	0.48	(2.32)	(0.28)	A-C-B

EXHIBIT 14.6   Rolling Period Analysis

Rolling Annual Information Ratio			
	Fund A	Fund B	Fund C	Rank
2000 Q4	(0.67)	1.61	(1.49)	B-A-C
2000 Q3	1.03	0.16	(0.59)	A-B-C
2000 Q2	0.89	(0.34)	0.94	C-A-B
2000 Q1	2.26	0.36	0.88	A-C-B
1999 Q4	0.69	(0.29)	1.07	C-A-B
1999 Q3	(1.00)	(0.18)	0.90	C-B-A
1999 Q2	(1.79)	0.63	0.55	B-C-A
1999 Q1	(2.91)	0.15	2.45	C-B-A
1998 Q4	(1.10)	0.60	2.70	C-B-A
1998 Q3	(1.14)	1.65	2.51	C-B-A
1998 Q2	(1.00)	0.36	0.81	C-B-A
1998 Q1	0.26	0.23	1.07	C-A-B
1997 Q4	(0.25)	(0.07)	0.88	C-B-A
1997 Q3	(0.36)	(7.20)	0.07	C-A-B
1997 Q2	0.80	(4.42)	0.74	A-C-B
1997 Q1	0.72	(3.31)	0.31	A-C-B
1996 Q4	0.48	(2.32)	(0.28)	A-C-B

Here we have calculated an Information ratio for each quarter starting in the fourth quarter of 1996. This quarter is the first for which we have four prior quarters of data including the current quarter and the three prior, which are not shown. Then, in the first quarter of 1997, we calculated a new Information ratio including the returns from the first quarter of 1997 and dropping the returns from the first quarter of 1996. We did this for each period up to the current period in order to derive the rolling time series of Information ratios. We can use this data in several ways. First, we can look at the rank consistency of the three funds over time. We can see that there was a definite pattern at the start and middle of the period under analysis, with Funds A and C dominating early on, and then a switch where Funds C and B dominated for a period. More recently there has been no clear pattern, as the ranking has switched several times. Exhibit 14.7 shows how we can get a better sense of the relative performance of the manager using a line graph.

In addition to giving us some information as to the relative performance of the managers, the rolling analysis gives us some information that we can use to put the performance into perspective. For example, the yearly Information ratio for Fund B in the third quarter 1997 (14 periods ago) is an outlier. We might discuss the situation with the manager and decide to exclude that period from the analysis when we better understand the reasons for the performance during that period. Or alternatively, we could decide that that period is more representative of the manager's expected performance over a particular market cycle and overweight that period in our analysis of performance. It also might be interesting to look more closely at the recent performance of Fund C.

Even though this fund had the best 5-year track record, it has not been as attractive in the most recent periods.

We can gain some additional insight into performance by creating a chart that graphs the movement over time of the 1-year tracking error versus the rolling 1-year value added. These are the two variables that make up the Information ratio. This kind of a chart is sometimes called a "snail trail" (see Exhibit 14.8).

Including the time period over which the observation occurred adds value over simply plotting the risk and return statistics. For example, here we can see that the rolling value added has been falling and the tracking error increasing over the past few periods.

EXHIBIT 14.7   Rolling Information Ratio Graph

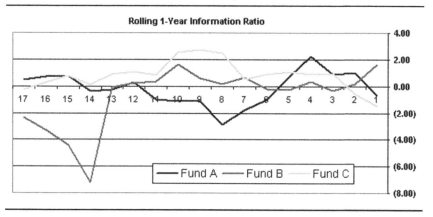

EXHIBIT 14.8   Information Ratio Snail Trail

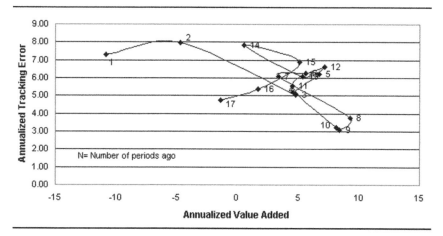

We have presented here one of many possible methods to use the return, risk, and risk-adjusted return statistics to analyze and rank the performance of portfolios. You can adapt the tools presented here, including consistency tests and rolling period analysis, to perform a more comprehensive analysis of performance.

Performance Attribution

Security and Segment Returns

The subjects of this book so far have been the calculation of portfolio level returns, the risk taken to achieve these returns and the analysis of risk-adjusted return. With this information we have some quantitative input for analysis of historical fund performance. We can answer questions as to whether the fund did well compared to our goals for the fund, the fund's benchmark, and other funds managed according to a similar strategy. There are, however, some additional questions we can consider related to not just *what* performance was achieved, but *how* it was achieved.

Performing calculations at the total fund level tells us *how* a fund performed in the aggregate. But we are also interested in quantifying *why* the fund performed as it did. To provide insight to this question, we need to open up the fund and examine the performance of the individual components. The smallest building block of portfolio performance is the individual security position. If we have a portfolio of one security, and no transactions or expenses, the total fund return will equal the return earned on that security.

When we hold many positions in a portfolio, the performance of various groupings of securities is also of interest. We can partition the portfolio into *segments*, where each security in a segment has some factor in common and this factor is of interest to the analyst. For example, we could be interested in segmenting the stocks in a global fund by country and a domestic equity fund by economic sector. Once we have segmented the securities, we can sum the market value and transactions and strike returns at the segment level, almost as if each segment were a portfolio on its own. We often analyze portfolios in a hierarchical, top down fashion. While we *drill down* into the portfolio to analyze performance by, for example, country, then industry within country, and then security within industry, the returns to the nested segments are calculated using a *bottom up* process that uses security values. Segment and security returns and their relative weightings explain how the total return of the fund was achieved by giving us a measure as to how the individual assets and combinations of assets within the portfolio appreciated over the period.

The market exposures and resulting returns earned by these segments can be modified via the use of derivatives. For example, we could enter into a long equity futures contract that has the effect of exchanging the return earned on cash for the return earned by equity. So when we are analyzing segment level returns, we need to account for the economic effect, or effective exposures, created by these transactions. We discuss the calculation of performance on an effective exposure basis in Chapter 16.

The performance of diversified portfolios is driven by individual holdings. We might hold one stock that performs extremely well, but if it was a negligible share of our total investment, it won't have much of a total fund impact. The weighted returns can be thought of as *contributions* to total fund return. In Chapter 17 we explore the methods for analyzing contribution to return for single and multiple periods. If the fund and its benchmark held exactly the same securities in the same proportion, the individual component contributions to return would be the same for both entities. But, depending on the type of portfolio, the manager might diverge from the index by overweighting attractive securities and segments and underweighting unattractive securities and segments. For example, a pension plan sponsor might make periodic tactical asset allocation shifts away from the fund's long-term strategic weightings to take advantage of opportunities presented by (what he feels are) temporarily undervalued asset classes. In a similar way a domestic equity manager might overweight particular industries and so on. These shifts in asset allocation are the sources of value added over the benchmark return. We can use various *value-added decomposition* techniques to "reverse-engineer" the value added and determine their sources. We can, for instance, determine the value added by a decision made by a global fund manager to overweight Japan in a period where the Japanese market did well. Chapter 18 deals with the general techniques for decomposing the value added earned by a manager over the benchmark and in Chapter 19 we extend these methods to the analysis of particular asset classes.

The term "performance attribution" represents different things to different people. Here we use the term in its broadest sense, as the:

> Quantification of the sources of fund, benchmark, and benchmark relative value added.

Our definition includes the calculation of portfolio security and segment returns, contribution analysis, and decomposition of benchmark relative value added into various management effects. Many times the term "attribution" is used to refer only to the process of value-added decomposition, but here we aim to be inclusive by defining it more broadly.

SECURITY RETURNS

Let's briefly review how we calculated the returns achieved by a portfolio. We calculate the single period total fund return by periodically summing up the market values of the securities held by the fund and comparing the change in total value from one period to the next. If there were additional contributions into or withdrawals out of the portfolio, we adjust the value added by these cash flows. We take the single period returns calculated in this way and compound them over time to derive the return over multiple periods. If the fund were unitized we calculate the return by observing the change in Net Asset Value per share adjusted by any dividend distributions.

We use largely the same methodology to calculate returns for the securities and segments held by the portfolio. At its core, the calculation of return involves the comparison of current market value with prior market value, so we can use the calculation to determine the return for any asset. But while the concept is the same, there are some issues specific to the calculation of returns within the fund.

- Security returns versus returns that reflect actual transactions made.
- Dollar- versus time-weighted returns.
- Assumptions as to the intraday timing of transactions
- Treatment of security level transactions, income accrued, and income paid.
- Multiperiod security and segment level returns

Returns that Reflect Transactions

The market value of an equity security held within a fund equals the number of shares held, multiplied by the current price for that security at the end of the day. Why do we use the *market value* of a security holding instead of simply using the *price* of the stock when calculating the return? After all, when we see stock returns that are quoted in the newspaper and other sources, they are calculated by observing the change in stock price. For example, if yesterday a stock closed at $10.00 and today at $11.00, the daily return is equal to 10.00% ((11/10) − 1). But we don't calculate returns this way; instead we multiply the shares held by the price for each day and then calculate the return. If we held ten shares we would calculate the return as ((110/100) − 1), and if we held a thousand shares as ((11,000/10,000) − 1), and so on. No matter the amount held, we would always calculate a return equal to 10%.

EXHIBIT 15.1   Buy and Hold Return versus Return that Includes Trading Effects

	A	B	C	D	E	F
1		Shares	Price			Market Value
2	Prior Night Close	0.00	8.00			-
3					=D5+E5	
4	Purchases	Shares	Price	Principal	Commission	Net Amount
5	1	300.00	8.25	2,475.00	15.00	2,490.00
6	2	200.00	9.00	1,800.00	10.00	1,810.00
7	3	250.00	10.00	2,500.00	12.50	2,512.50
8	Total	750.00	=B7*C7			6,812.50
9						
10		Shares	Price			Market Value
11	Current Day Close	750.00	10.25			7,687.50
12						
13	Price to Price Return: 28.13		=((C11/C2)-1)*100			
14	Fund Specific Return: 12.84		=((F11/(F2+F8))-1)*100			

So we *could* refer to the change in market prices to calculate the returns to securities held in the portfolio, in some cases. However, returns calculated in this manner have a built-in assumption that there was no trading of the security or income earned by the security for the day. We can see this assumption by way of an example. Say that the price of our stock increased steadily through the day, from 10 to 11. And instead of holding the stock at the beginning of the day, we purchased the stock during the day. If we bought the stock at mid-day for 10.50, our dollar gain would have been only 50 cents per share, not $1.00. So our return would only be 4.76% ((11.00/10.50) − 1). If we had used the daily price change to calculate the return, the reported return to the fund would be misleadingly high. If we bought the security in multiple lots through the day, all at different prices, we would find it easiest to calculate our return by taking the market value of the position at the end of the day (shares × end of day price) and dividing it by the sum of the net amounts of the individual stock trades. The difference between our two returns, 10% and 4.76%, reflects the trading done in the portfolio. Sometimes the return calculated without the effect of trading, in this case the 10% return, is called a *price-to-price* return or a *buy-and-hold* return. Buy-and-hold returns might approximate the actual return earned to the security by the fund, but depending on the type of portfolio, amount of turnover and volatility experienced, the differences can be large. The implication of portfolio trading is that if we want to calculate the true fund-specific return earned on a security, we have to calculate the security level returns for each fund independently. Thus, performance measurement at the security level requires more work to implement than many portfolio management functions, for example, calculating the duration or the P/E ratio for each security held within a fund (since these values are the same for every portfolio holding that security). Exhibit 15.1 shows the difference between the single period price-to-price return and the actual total return, which includes the effect of trading.

EXHIBIT 15.2 Modified Dietz Return for a Security

	A	B	C	D	E	F
1		Shares	Price			Market Value
2	Prior Month Close	0.00	8.00			-
3						
4	Trades	Shares	Price	Principal	Commission	Net Amount
5	1-Oct	300.00	8.25	2,475.00	15.00	2,490.00
6	15-Oct	200.00	9.00	1,800.00	10.00	1,810.00
7	28-Oct	250.00	10.00	2,500.00	12.50	2,512.50
8	Total	750.00				6,812.50
9						
10		Shares	Price			Market Value
11	Current Month Close	750.00	10.25			7,687.50
12						
13		Days Held	Day Weighting	Wtd Flow		
14	1-Oct	31	1.00	2,490.00		31
15	15-Oct	17	0.55	992.58		17
16	28-Oct	4	0.13	324.19		4
17	31-Oct		=B16/31 ↗	=C16*F7 ↗		
18						
19						
20	Price to Price Return:	28.13	=((C11/C2)-1)*100			
21	Return on Investment:	12.84	=((F11/F8)-1)*100			
22						
23	Dollar Value Added:	875.00	=(F11-F2-F8)			
24	Average Invested Balance:	3806.77	=F2+D14+D15+D16			
25						
26	Modified Dietz Return:	22.99	=(B23/B24)*100			

Here the price-to-price return is 28.13%, but we earned only a 12.84% return in this security. We earned less than the price-to-price return because we purchased the security three times at successively higher prices through the day. If instead of holding the position until end of day, we had sold the security at a higher price than the market close, we would have earned a higher return than the price-to-price return. Notice that the net amount of the transaction also includes a commission and fees like the SEC fee. When we trade securities, our returns differ from the quoted market return by not only the difference between closing and actual trade prices, but also by the trading costs.

Money-Weighted Return versus Time-Weighted Return

Having established the need to refer to the portfolio's actual security transactions to calculate a security level return, the next issue we face is the timing of these transactions. At the highest level, we need to decide whether we want to calculate a Money-Weighted Return (MWR) or a Time-Weighted Return (TWR). We can calculate segment and security level returns using either an MWR or TWR.

Let's look at the security level MWR first. Security level returns that are calculated using MWR are very sensitive to the amount and timing of cash flows. Consider Exhibit 15.2, where we calculate the Modified Dietz return for a security in a month when we purchased the security over the course of the month, and the security price has also appreciated steadily through the month.

Notice first that we calculated three different returns for the same security, in the same account, for the same period and they are all the "correct" return! First, the price-to-price return is 28.13%. This is the return we would see quoted in the newspaper as the security return for the month. It does not reflect any fund specific cash flows. Next, we calculate the Return on Investment, which takes into account the amount, but not the timing, of the fund-specific cash flows. Next, we calculate the Modified Dietz return. The Modified Dietz return is an MWR; it incorporates the effect of the amount and timing of cash flows that occurred during the period. To calculate the Modified Dietz return, we treat the purchases and sales in the same way that we treated contributions and withdrawals when calculating total portfolio level Modified Dietz returns. The purchases and sales are the cash flows required to reconcile the beginning and ending market values and appreciation over the period. The monthly MWR for this security is 22.99%. It is higher than the ROI; because we weight the cash flows by the time they were invested in the security. If the cash flows occurred later in the month and we earned a gain, the effect is an increase to the return credited to this security. This cash flow treatment is contrasted with the ROI, which assumes that the cash flows were all invested at the start of the period. The Modified Dietz return is, however, still lower than the price-to-price return because we traded at a higher price than the beginning of month price, with the effect of lowering the return.

Now consider the same case, except that we have valuations available for the end of day for each day that we traded the security. With valuations available, we can calculate a true time-weighted return. Exhibit 15.3 illustrates the calculation of the security level time-weighted return.

The TWR is calculated by compounding the subperiod growth rates in between valuation dates. While we might expect the time-weighted return to equal the price-to-price return, it does not. The time-weighted return is lower than the price-to-price return for two reasons:

1. The trade prices are different from the prior night closing price. In our case, with a rising market, the higher trade prices serve to lower the return.
2. The commissions and other trading costs reduce the return. They are incorporated into the TWR calculation when we add the cash flow to the prior night's market value in the denominator of the subperiod return formula.

EXHIBIT 15.3 Security Level Time-Weighted Return

	A	B	C	D	E	F
1		Shares	Price			Market Value
2	Prior Month Close	0.00	8.00			-
3						
4	Trades	Shares	Price	Principal	Commission	Net Amount
5	1-Oct	300.00	8.25	2,475.00	15.00	2,490.00
6	15-Oct	200.00	9.00	1,800.00	10.00	1,810.00
7	28-Oct	250.00	10.00	2,500.00	12.50	2,512.50
8	Total	750.00				6,812.50
9						
10		Shares	Price			Market Value
11	Current Month Close	750.00	10.25			7,687.50
12		=((C14/(0+F5))-1)*100				
13	Subperiod	End Price	EMV	Subperiod Return	Growth Rate	
14	1-Oct to 14-Oct: 8.75		2,625.00	5.42	1.054	
15	15-Oct to 27-Oct:: 9.75		4,875.00	9.92	1.099	
16	28-Oct to 31-Oct: 10.25		7,687.50	4.06	1.041	
17				=((C16/(C15+F7))-1)*100		
18	Price to Price Return: 28.13	=((C11/C2)-1)*100				
19	Return on Investment: 12.84	=((F11/(F2+F8))-1)*100				
20	Modified Dietz Return: 22.99					
21	Time Weighted Return: 20.59	=(PRODUCT(E14:E16)-1)*100				

The TWR in our example is still lower than the MWR because the MWR assumes that the rate of return is constant during the measurement period. The MWR return can provide a good estimate of total portfolio TWR, and many times of segment-level TWR. However, the security level MWR is very sensitive to large cash flows, which, because of trading, occur more frequently at the segment and security level than the total portfolio level. So here we can see that there are four different returns to the security, for a single period, each with a different interpretation.

Timing of Transactions

Let's take a closer look at the calculation of the return for the subperiod between Oct. 28 and Oct. 31 in Exhibit 15.3. The return we calculated for the period was 4.06% with a BMV equal to 4875, a purchase trade on the 28th for 2512.50 and an EMV equal to 7687.50.

$$\frac{7687.50 - 4875 - 2512.50}{4875 + 2512.50} \times 100 = 4.06\%$$

Clearly we need to exclude the amount of the buy when we calculate the gain in the numerator of the return. The addition of the trade net amount to the invested balance in the denominator might not be as clear.

We need to take any purchases or sales of securities into account when we calculate security level single period returns. The methods for doing so are analogous to those for allowing for contributions to or withdrawals out of the portfolio when we calculate total portfolio level returns. When calculating a total portfolio return, we adjust the market value balances by the amount of these contributions or withdrawals. For example, if we had a portfolio worth 1000 at the begin of the day, 1200 at the end of the day, and a 100 contribution, or inflow, we could calculate a 10.00% return:

$$\frac{1200 - 1000 - 100}{1000} \times 100 = 10.00\%$$

Or, alternatively, we could calculate a 9.09% return:

$$\frac{1200 - 1000 - 100}{1000 + 100} \times 100 = 9.09\%$$

The return that we attribute to the fund depends on whether or not we adjust the denominator for the amount of the cash flow. We can think of this decision as the *cash flow time of day assumption*. The 10.00% return assumes that the cash flow occurred at the *end of the day*, so it should not be included in the denominator, which is the invested balance. The 9.09% return assumes that the cash flow occurred at the *beginning of the day*. To determine the actual return to the fund we could either track the time of day that each cash flow is made or make an assumption as to the time of day each type of cash flow is made. Neither solution will be acceptable for every situation. For example, we could generally assume that contributions occur at the beginning of the day. But if the manager receives a large contribution at the end of the day on a day with a large market move, he may want to reflect this fact in the return and not include the cash flow in the denominator. This decision reflects the reality that the cash flow was not actually invested in the market during the day when the market went up, but if the cash flow is included in the denominator, the manager's return will be penalized.

Purchases and sales of securities can be thought of as *security level cash flows*. We adjust the market value balances by the security level cash flows in order to calculate security level returns. In the same way that we need to make an allowance for a time of day assumption when we calculate the portfolio return, we need to make the same allowance for transactions at the security level when we calculate the security returns. Perhaps the ideal situation would be to make no assumptions, but instead link *intraday,* subperiod returns reflecting the values at the time of each cash flow, like a TWR for each day. If we did this we would not need to make a time of day assumption for transactions. Most practitioners, however, make an assumption as to when during the day cash flows occur.

We've seen the effect that the different time of day assumptions have on the security level return calculation. What time of day should we assume that transactions occur? Lets look at the effect of making different assumptions.

Exhibit 15.4 illustrates the single period security return calculation for various trading scenarios where we make an assumption that cash flows occur at the end of the day. Notice that when the security is a new purchase for the day, there is no return calculated because we would be dividing by a beginning market value of zero, which results in an undefined return.

In Exhibit 15.5 we calculate the returns for the same trading scenarios, but with a beginning of day cash flow assumption. Notice that we have the reverse of the new buy problem; here we do not calculate a return when there is a full sell of the security.

Our instinct tells us we *should* be able to calculate a return for these two scenarios. In the example with a new purchase, we purchased the security at 100 and it was worth 110 at the end of the day. Certainly that counts as a return, in fact, for many initial public offerings, much of the return may be realized on the first trading day. And, for our full sale example, we sold a security for 110 that was worth 100 at the beginning of the day. This too should count towards the return. There are several methods of accounting for the gains in these situations.

EXHIBIT 15.4   Security Level Returns—End of Day Assumption

	A	B	C	D	E	F	G	H	I
1	End of Day	MVE	MVB	Inflows	Outflows	Net Flows	Numerator	Denominator	Return
2	Purchase	120	100	10	0	10	110	100	10.00
3	Sale	100	100	0	10	-10	110	100	10.00
4	New Purchase	100	0	90	0	90	10	0	N/A
5	Full Sell	0	100	0	110	-110	110	100	10.00

EXHIBIT 15.5   Security Level Returns—Begin of Day Assumption

	A	B	C	D	E	F	G	H	I
1	Begin of Day	MVE	MVB	Inflows	Outflows	Net Flows	Numerator	Denominator	Return
2	Purchase	120	100	10	0	10	120	110	9.09
3	Sale	100	100	0	10	-10	100	90	11.11
4	New Purchase	100	0	90	0	90	100	90	11.11
5	Full Sell	0	100	0	110	-110	0	-10	N/A

EXHIBIT 15.6 Security Level Returns—Begin of Day for Buys/End of Day for Sales Assumption

	A	B	C	D	E	F	G	H	I
1		MVE	MVB	Inflows	Outflows	Net Flows	Numerator	Denominator	Return
2	Purchase	120	100	10	0	10	120	110	9.09
3	Sale	100	100	0	10	-10	110	100	10.00
4	New Purchase	100	0	90	0	90	100	90	11.11
5	Full Sell	0	100	0	110	-110	110	100	10.00

One acceptable approach to the problem is to modify the return calculation to incorporate a timing assumption that depends on the type of transaction. Rather than assuming that all transactions occur at the same time of day, we could assume that purchases take place at the beginning of the day and sales at the end of the day. Income receipts, as we will see in the next section, are treated like sales. Equations (15.1) and (15.2) are equivalent forms of the security level return formula for incorporating the sales at end, buys at beginning of day timing assumption.

Security and segment level single period return

$$= \left(\frac{(\text{Ending market value} + \text{Income accrued}) + \text{Income paid} + \text{Sales}}{(\text{Beginning market value} + \text{Income accrued}) + \text{Purchases}} - 1 \right) \quad (15.1)$$
$$\times 100$$

Or alternatively:

$$\left(\frac{(\text{EMV} + \text{AI}) - (\text{BMV} + \text{AI}) - \text{Purchases} + \text{Sales} + \text{Income paid}}{(\text{BMV} + \text{AI}) + \text{Purchases}} \right) \times 100 \quad (15.2)$$

Exhibit 15.6 shows how we can use these formulas to calculate returns that accord to our intuition for each scenario.

Transactions like Purchases and Sales

If we treat purchases as inflows to a security balance and sales as outflows, what about other security transactions, such as the maturity of a bond? In fact every transaction type that affects a security can be reduced to either an inflow or an outflow for the purposes of calculating a return. The maturity of a bond is much like a sale of the bond back to its issuer. A bond that is called by the issuer is also like a sale. The basic procedure is to map each transaction that affects a security balance to either "Transactions that are like Purchases" or "Transactions that are like Sales." The former group will be treated as inflows and the latter group as outflows to the security.

There are some events that impact a security price but are not explicitly recognized in the calculation of returns. S*tock splits, reverse splits,* and *stock dividends* affect security prices and shares outstanding, but they have no effect on the market value of the security holding. For example, if we own a stock that has a two-for-one stock split, the share price will drop in half, and the number of shares that we own will double on the ex-dividend date of the split. The total market value of our holding does not change. Reverse splits are treated the same way, except the share price increases and the number of shares decreases.

Income Accrued and Received

In Equation (15.1) we added the income received to the numerator of the return calculation. The treatment of income accrued and received in the calculation of security returns also deserves a closer look. The dividend and interest income earned by a portfolio is counted in the calculation of return along with the change in market value over the period. Here we develop the treatment of income in the daily security level return calculation using some examples. Starting with the base case, assume that the fund owns a security that was held from the beginning to the end of the day; there was no income earned, and there were no trades or other transactions affecting the security balance. If the BMV was 100 and the EMV 120, then the return is 20.00%:

$$\left(\frac{120}{100} - 1\right) \times 100 = 20.00\%$$

Assuming it is an equity security, the market value is calculated as the number of shares times the price per share at the beginning and end of the day. Next, consider the same scenario except there was $2 of income earned but not yet paid during the period. The income here is a dividend declared on a stock. We add the accrued income to the market value in the numerator and then calculate the return equal to 22.00%:

$$\left(\frac{120 + 2}{100} - 1\right) \times 100 = 22.00\%$$

Just as the market value at the end of one day becomes the starting market value for the next day, the accumulated accrued income becomes the starting accrued income for the next day. We include the accrued income in both the numerator and the denominator when the income is still in a receivable status. Continuing our example, assuming no change in market value the next day, the return is 0.00%:

$$\left(\frac{120 + 2}{120 + 2} - 1 \right) \times 100 = 0.00\%$$

Here we had a market value of 120 at the beginning and end of the day, and two dollars of income receivable at the beginning and end of the day. There is no return on the security on this day.

Assume that at the end of the next day the income is paid to the fund. We will no longer have an accrued income receivable balance, but we need to take the income paid into account when we calculate the return on the day when it is received. If we did not, we would calculate the incorrect return:

$$\left(\frac{120 + 0}{120 + 2} - 1 \right) \times 100 = -1.64\%$$

Here we calculated the return, including the income accrual in the denominator, but not in the numerator, because it was paid during the day. This was correct. But, assuming no change in market value, we should have calculated a 0.00% return for the day. To account for the drop in accrued income, we need to add the income paid to the numerator when we calculate the return for the day that the income is paid.

$$\left(\frac{120 + 0 + 2}{120 + 2} - 1 \right) \times 100 = 0.00\%$$

On the next day, again assuming no change in market value, we would calculate the return equal to

$$\left(\frac{120 + 0 + 0}{120 + 0} - 1 \right) \times 100 = 0.00\%$$

Here the accrued income in the denominator is equal to zero, which is the ending accrued income from the day before. So we should treat income receipts the same way we treat sales in the calculation of the return, as additions to the numerator.

EXHIBIT 15.7 Return Calculation for Bond Interest Accrual

	A	B	C	D	E	F	G	H
1	5% coupon bond payable semi-annually							
2	Day	Par Held	Price	MV	Accrual	Accrued Income	MV + AI	Return
3	1	100,000	99.0000	99,000.00	13.89	13.89	99,013.89	-
4	2	100,000	99.0297	99,029.70	13.89	27.78	99,057.48	0.0440
5	3	100,000	99.0594	99,059.41	13.89	41.67	99,101.08	0.0440
6	4	100,000	99.0891	99,089.13	13.89	55.56	99,144.68	0.0440
7	5	100,000	99.1189	99,118.85	13.89	69.44	99,188.30	0.0440
8	6	100,000	99.1486	99,148.59	13.89	83.33	99,231.92	0.0440
9	7	100,000	99.1783	99,178.33	13.89	97.22	99,275.56	0.0440
10						↓		
11				=B9*(C9/100)	=B9*(0.05/360)	=E9+F8	=D9+F9	=((G9/G8)-1)*100

Income accrued but not yet paid represents a major component of the value of a bond. The accrued income value will increase each day between coupon payment dates. Each market has a different convention regarding the payment frequency and day count convention for accruals. Payments on corporate bonds issued in the U.S. are generally made semi-annually, but there are bonds that pay out income on a monthly, quarterly, and an annual basis. For example, corporate bonds typically pay interest twice a year and the accrued income is calculated with a *day count convention* of 30/360. This means that we assume that there are 360 days in a year and 30 days in each month. For these bonds we accrue income up through the 30th day of each month, i.e., on August 31 we do not credit the fund with an accrual factor for the day. On February 28 of a non-leap year, we accrue three days of income. Funds also need to establish a convention for accruing bonds to the end of the month when the month ends on a weekend. For example, if the 30th of a 30-day month falls on a Saturday, the fund might accrue two day's of income on Friday the 29th, so that the return of the 29th reflects the month-end accrual.

The treatment of income earned between bond payment dates is the same as that for a stock dividend. Exhibit 15.7 shows the return calculation for a bond held between coupon dates.

Notice that we include income in both the numerator and the denominator of the return calculation. The accrued income is included in the denominator because it is, along with the principal, part of the capital that is put at risk in the next period. If we did not include accrued income in the denominator, we would overstate the return earned in the period.

Another issue related to income is the treatment of income accrued in prior periods, and due, but not yet paid. The treatment of this past due income depends on the basis upon which income is paid for the portfolio: actual or contractual income. In some situations, income is not credited to the portfolio until it is actually received. In this case the accrued income balance should include this past due income until it is received. When income is credited on a contractual basis, then the receivable is relieved and the payment credited on the contractual payment date.

EXHIBIT 15.8 Security Level Return Calculation

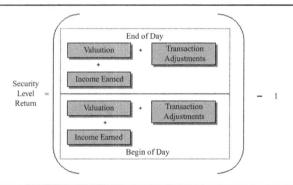

To summarize the calculation of a daily return for a security held within a portfolio:

- When there are no trades or income earned, the return is equal to the change in the market value of the position.
- When there is income earned, the return is equal to the change in market value, plus the increase in income accrued.
- When there is a transaction, the return is equal to the change in market value, plus the increase in income accrued. Before calculating the return the beginning or ending market values are adjusted to reflect the change in value caused by the transaction.

The security return formula can be adjusted to fit the needs of different situations. Exhibit 15.8 shows how we can visualize the calculation of security returns.

ISOLATING THE COMPONENTS OF THE SECURITY RETURN

Many times we are interested in not only knowing the total return to a security, but also understanding the sources of the security return over the period. For example, a bond return is comprised of both the accrued income recognized each day and the change in value due to price fluctuations. It is useful to analyze the separate contributions to the security return due to income accruals and price changes. In a similar way, the return that we earn by holding a foreign security is influenced by both the change in the value of the security and the fluctuation in the exchange rate between the foreign currency and the investor's home currency. So we can break the total base currency return into a local return and a currency return to facilitate analysis of the sources of return. There are other breakdowns of the security level return, appropriate for particular security types. But the principles of isolating components of return are based on the two examples we look at in this section.

Principal and Income Returns

It is useful to dissect the return to a fixed income security into price return and income components. *Principal return,* or *capital return*, is the percentage change in the value of the assets over the period. *Income return* is the income yielded over the period given the capital invested, where the income is comprised of interest earned on the fixed income security. The *total return* of the bond for the period equals the sum of the price and the income returns. The first step to isolate the components is to distinguish between the dollar sources of return used in the numerator of the return calculation. In this case we need to separate the daily income accrual from the gain resulting from the change in the bond's price. We then calculate the component returns by dividing the individual dollar components by the same denominator used in the calculation of the bond's total return. Exhibit 15.9 shows the calculation of income and price return for a bond.

By taking the daily accrual factor and dividing it by the prior days market value plus accrued income ($0.014\% = 13.89/99,013.89$), we calculated the income return. Price return was calculated by taking the dollar change in market value due to the price increase from 99.00 to 99.03 and also dividing it by the prior day's market value plus accrued income ($0.03\% = 29.70/99,013.89$). In both cases we use the market value plus accrued income as the denominator because the amount put at risk from one day to the next includes *both* components. We calculate income returns using Equation (15.3).

$$\text{Income return} = \frac{\text{Income earned}}{\text{Begin market value} + \text{Income}} \times 100 \qquad (15.3)$$

EXHIBIT 15.9   Fixed Income Price and Income Returns

	A	B	C	D	E	F	G	H
1	Day	Par Held	Price	MV	Accrual	Accrued Income	MV + AI	Total Return
2	1	100,000	99.0000	99,000.00	13.89	13.89	99,013.89	-
3	2	100,000	99.0297	99,029.70	13.89	27.78	99,057.48	0.04402300
4						↓		
5				=B3*(C3/100)	=B3*(0.05/360)	=E3+F2	=D3+F3	=((G3/G2)-1)*100
6								
7						Return Components		
8						Income Return	Price Return	Total Return
9	2					0.01402721	0.02999579	0.04402300
10							↓	
11						=(E3/G2)*100	=((D3-D2)/G2)*	=G9+F9

The component return is calculated in the same way as the total return to a security, where the numerator is the amount gained and the denominator the amount put at risk to earn the gain. The income earned on the bond is equal to the difference between the beginning accrued interest and the ending accrued interest. If there were a trade for the day, we would need to adjust the calculation for the interest purchased or sold. If there is a purchase, we subtract the interest purchased from the numerator in the calculation of income earned. If there is a sale, we would add the interest sold into the numerator of the calculation. Using this method, all of the income to be accrued between the trade date and settlement date of the sale is recognized on the day that the bond is sold. There are also other methods of recognizing the income earned between trade date and settlement date for a bond.

$$\text{Price return} = \frac{\text{End market value} - \text{Begin market value}}{\text{Begin market value} + \text{Income}} \times 100 \qquad (15.4)$$

When we break down security level returns into component factors, we can sum them to equal the total return. We can do this because we can add fractions that have the same denominator.

$$\frac{A}{C} + \frac{B}{C} = \frac{A + B}{C}$$

Local, Base, and Currency Returns

Foreign securities introduce the need to value the security in multiple currencies, and to break down the return into local price change and currency fluctuation components. There are some extra steps to take when we calculate returns for securities that are quoted in a currency different than the base currency of the fund. The *base currency* is the home currency of the investor or fund. Consider a fund managed on behalf of investors located in the U.S., which invests in the Unites States, Japan, and Germany. This fund holds securities that trade in dollars, yen, and euro. The currency used to trade these securities is called the *local currency*. The local currency of securities that trade in Japan is yen, and so on. If the manager and client are based in the U.S., the fund's base currency will be the dollar, so we will want to calculate performance in dollars. The return in dollars will be influenced by both price changes measured in local currency and the change in the local to base currency exchange rate. Exhibit 15.10 illustrates the calculation of returns for a fund holding a portfolio of cash and foreign securities.

EXHIBIT 15.10   Multicurrency Portfolio Performance

	A	B	C	D	E	F	G	H	I
1	Day 1				Local			Base	
2	Position	Local	Shares	Price	MV	X-rate	MV		
3	1	USD Cash	USD	200	1.00	200.00	1.00	200.00	
4	2	Apple	USD	240	21.36	5,126.40	1.00	5126.40	=F5*G5
5	3	JPY Cash	JPY	10,000	1.00	10,000.00	0.0076	76.00	
6	4	Sony	JPY	120	5,600.00	672,000.00	0.0076	5107.20	
7	5	AXA	EUR	250	22.80	5,700.00	0.8784	5006.88	
8	6	Bayer	EUR	170	34.42	5,851.40	0.8784	5139.87	
9		Total						20,656.35	
10						=D8*E8			
11									
12	Day 2				Local			Base	Return
13	Position	Local	Shares	Price	MV	X-rate	MV		Base
14	1	USD Cash	USD	200	1.00	200.00	1.00	200.00	0.00
15	2	Apple	USD	240	22.00	5,280.00	1.00	5280.00	3.00
16	3	JPY Cash	JPY	10,000	1.00	10,000.00	0.0080	80.00	5.26
17	4	Sony	JPY	120	5,700.00	684,000.00	0.0080	5472.00	7.14
18	5	AXA	EUR	250	25.00	6,250.00	0.8350	5218.75	4.23
19	6	Bayer	EUR	170	34.42	5,851.40	0.8350	4885.92	-4.94
20		Total						21,136.67	2.33
21						=((H20/H9)-1)*100			

EXHIBIT 15.11   Local and Base Return

	A	B	C	D	E	F	G	H
1								Return
2	Day	Shares	Price	MV Local	X-rate	MV Base	Local	Base
3	1	120	5,600.00	672,000.00	0.0076	5107.20		
4	2	120	5,700.00	684,000.00	0.0080	5472.00	1.79	7.14
5								
6				=B4*C4		=D4*E4	=((D4/D3)-1)*100	=((F4/F3)-1)*100

Here we calculate base currency returns for each security in the fund. Notice that the price for Bayer remained the same in euros, but when restated in dollars we had a loss as the euro/dollar exchange rate fell −4.94% [(0.8350/0.8784) − 1]. The yen strengthened against the dollar, so we had a gain on the cash held in Japan equal to 5.26%. The increase in the yen price for Sony and the improved yen/dollar exchange rate compounded to deliver a 7.14% return for holding Sony, as measured in dollars.

We can analyze the performance of a foreign investment by breaking down the components of the total return into local price and exchange rate change components. Suppose we have a foreign stock whose local price goes up in value, and the local currency strengthens so that the holding is worth more when restated in base terms. We expect that the base return will be higher than the local return, because of the compounding of the price and exchange rate effects. Exhibit 15.11 shows the calculation of return for this security.

EXHIBIT 15.12 Currency Return

	G	H	I	J	K
1		Return			
2	Local	Base	Currency	Curr + Local	Difference
3					
4	1.79	7.14	5.26	7.05	-0.09
5			↓		
6	=((D4/D3)-1)*100	=((F4/F3)-1)*100	=((E4/E3)-1)*100	=I4+G4	=J4-H4

The local return equals 1.79% (684,000/672,000 − 1) and the base return equals 7.14% (5472.00/5107.20 − 1). The difference between the two returns is attributable to the change in exchange rates during the day. Now, suppose we try to calculate the exchange rate return independently. The begin day rate equals 0.0076 and the end day rate equals 0.0080. Cell I4 in Exhibit 15.12 shows the calculation of the exchange rate return.

The currency return, calculated using the change in exchange rates, equals 5.26% [(0.0080/0.0076) − 1]. Notice that when we add the currency return to the local return in cell J4, it does not equal the base return in cell H4 that we calculated earlier using the base market values. This introduces a fundamental problem of working with currency returns:

$$\text{Base return} \neq \text{Local return} + \text{Currency return}$$

The reason is that, when both the local price and the exchange rates change, there is an *interaction* between the two effects. We earn a local return, an exchange rate return, and an incremental exchange return on the local return:

$$\text{Base return} = \text{Local return} + \text{Currency return} + \text{Interaction return}$$

Notice that this is different than when we were working with price and income returns in Exhibit 15.9, which we *can* add together. This is because the price and income returns components of a security are independent of each other. The interaction term is equal to the local return times the currency return, so that:

$$\begin{aligned} \text{Base return} = {} & \text{Local return} + \text{Currency return} \\ & + (\text{Local return} \times \text{Currency return}) \end{aligned} \tag{15.5}$$

Exhibit 15.13 shows the reconciliation of the base return using the additional interaction effect, equal to 0.09% (0.0179 × 0.0526 × 100).

EXHIBIT 15.13   Currency Return with Interaction Effect

	G	H	I	J	K	L
1			Return			
2	Local	Base	Currency	Interaction	Curr + Local + Int	Difference
3						
4	1.79	7.14	5.26	0.09	7.14	0.00
5			↓			
6	=((D4/D3)-1)*100	=((F4/F3)-1)*100	=((E4/E3)-1)*100	=(G4/100)*(I4/100)*100	=I4+G4+J4	=K4-H4

The interaction effect will be small unless there are large changes in both local prices and exchange rates. Because of this, analysts sometimes work with an approximation of the relationship by just adding the currency return to the local return to derive the base returns.

$$\text{Base return} \approx \text{Local return} + \text{Currency return}$$

The exact currency return can also be derived geometrically by Equation (15.6).

$$\text{Currency return} = \left[\frac{(1 + \text{Base return})}{(1 + \text{Local return})}\right] - 1 \tag{15.6}$$

PORTFOLIO SEGMENT RETURNS

In addition to calculating the returns to the securities held by the portfolio, we are interested in calculating returns for various groupings of securities, or *segments* of the portfolio. We can segment the securities held by a portfolio in any way that is relevant for the type of portfolio and style of management. Securities could be grouped by security characteristics such as asset class, country, or industrial sector. Index vendors, stock exchanges, and market data services maintain industry sector classification schemes. Some managers have proprietary security schemes that they use to analyze portfolio structures in particular ways. Securities can also be grouped into *ranges* based on some characteristic, for example, by duration and credit quality range for a fixed income portfolio or P/E and market capitalization for a stock fund. Ranges can be set using fixed values or defined using rank and order statistics. For example, we could group stocks by P/E deciles, and then calculate the returns to each decile. We could track performance by analyst if analysts were assigned different segments of the portfolio to track. We can also nest segments. For example, we could measure returns by industrial sector within each country. We can reverse the order of the segment groupings, for example, by calculating returns by country within industrial sector.

One way to think of the way we calculate segment returns is to think of each segment as a security. To calculate a segment return we sum the market values, transactions, and income flows for each security within a segment and then calculate a return using the same methodology covered in the previous sections. Exhibit 15.14 shows the calculation of returns for a portfolio segmented by industries.

The return for this fund is 2.39% and the segment returns are Technology at 2.33% and Utilities at 2.17%. To calculate the industry segment returns in Exhibit 15.14, we

1. Grouped each individual security into a segment. Here HP, IBM, and Intel are classified as Technology stocks, and Conoco, Exxon, and Unocal as Energy stocks.
2. Summed each of the components of the return calculation for each security. This is a simplified example where we calculated a daily return on a day when there are no cash flows, so we used the formula (MVE/ MVB) − 1. If there were transactions we could use the same security return calculation formulas covered in the previous section. To calculate the Energy return, the sum of the market values for the three component stocks at the beginning of the period is 30, and the end of the period 30.65, so the return is (30.65/30.00) − 1 = 2.17%.

EXHIBIT 15.14   Segment Level Returns

	A	B	C	D	E	F
1			**MVB**	**MVE**	**Percent Return**	
2			Fund	Fund	Fund	
3		Cash	3.00	3.11	3.50	
4		Energy	22.00	21.78	-1.00	
5		Financials	30.00	31.50	5.00	
6		Healthcare	0.00	0.00	0.00	
7		Technology	15.00	15.35	2.33	=E14
8		Energy	30.00	30.65	2.17	=E19
9		**Total Fund**	100.00	102.39	2.39	
10						
11		HP	5.00	5.15	3.00	
12		IBM	5.00	4.95	-1.00	
13		Intel	5.00	5.25	5.00	
14		**Technology**	15.00	15.35	2.33	=((D14/C14)-1)*100
15						
16		Conoco	10.00	10.50	5.00	
17		Exxon	15.00	14.85	-1.00	
18		Unocal	5.00	5.30	6.00	
19		**Energy**	30.00	30.65	2.17	=((D19/C19)-1)*100
20						
21			=SUM(C16:C18)	=SUM(D16:D18)		

To calculate segment returns, each security held in a portfolio must be accounted for, or *classified*, in one segment grouping. Many times, we calculate segment level returns using the same segment scheme used to classify securities within the fund's benchmark. Each of the major benchmark index vendors has a scheme for classifying the securities within the index. To facilitate fund-to-benchmark comparisons, we classify each of the securities held by the fund using the same scheme. While this process is usually straightforward, there is a problem to consider when calculating segment level returns, which are securities whose classification changed during the period.

Security Segment Classification Changes

Some reasons a security classification might change include:

- The segment scheme may be based on a factor that changes over time, such as time-to-maturity, duration, or credit quality. In a scheme based on time-to-maturity, the bond will change segments as it rolls down the yield curve, or approaches maturity.
- The fund is segmented by industry and a company changes industrial segments because of a merger.
- The analyst assigned to a security changes, and we are calculating performance by analyst.

For these and other reasons, we need a method for dealing with segment changes. The reason we need to handle this explicitly is that on the day of the change we will see the market value of the stock leave one segment and join another. If we don't account for it we would see the return for the old segment fall and the new one rise. One way to eliminate the distortion is to create a notional cash flow for the security out of one segment and into the next on the day of the change. A *notional cash flow* is a cash flow that is not an actual transaction, but instead is only required for the purpose of return calculation. Exhibit 15.15 illustrates a segment change handled via a notional cash flow.

In this example:

- The fund holds one security. It is classified as a Software stock on Day 0 and Day 1, but its classification changes to Hardware at the beginning of the day on Day 2.
- On Day 2 we created a notional cash flow, out of Software and into Hardware, to compensate for the change. If we did not, we would have an incorrect return for both segments: In Software the market value would drop from 10.50 to 0 with no offsetting cash flow, and

Hardware value would go from zero to 11.03 with no flow. The use of notional cash flows requires making an assumption as to the timing of classification changes, i.e., do they occur at the start or end of the day. Here we make a start of day assumption; so the notional cash flows are created using the prior days ending market value.

■ The notional cash flows offset each other at the total fund level. The notional cash flows are only used in the return calculation at the security and segment levels.

There are other ways of handling segment changes, but the concept is the same: We need to make sure we do not distort the return to the segment when a security moves from one segment to another, in either the current or prior periods.

The Cash Segment

When we calculated total portfolio level returns in Part I, we adjusted the total fund market value by the external cash flows, i.e. contributions and withdrawals, before calculating returns. When we calculated security and segment level returns, we adjusted the market value by the purchases and sales of the security itself. In this section we look at how the two types of transactions come together via cash balances enabling the calculation of returns for the complete portfolio. We start with an example using a newly established portfolio.

EXHIBIT 15.15 Security Changes Segments

	A	B	C	D	E
		Day 0	Day 1	Day 2	Day 3
1		Day 0	Day 1	Day 2	Day 3
2	Security Value	10.00	10.50	11.03	11.58
3					
4	Segment Value				
5	Software	10.00	10.50		
6	Hardware			11.03	11.58
7	Total Fund	10.00	10.50	11.03	11.58
8					
9	Notional Cash Flow				=C2*-1
10	Software		=C2	-10.50	
11	Hardware			10.50	
12	Total Fund Net Flows			0.00	
13					=(((D5-D10)/(C5))-1)*100
14	Return				
15	Software		5.00	0.00	-
16	Hardware		-	5.05	4.99
17	Total Fund		5.00	5.05	4.99
18		=(((D6)/(C6+D11))-1)*100			

A new fund starts as an empty shell, a legal entity or account that exists, but has no holdings. The spreadsheet below shows the accounts of the fund on Day 1. The portfolio starts with nothing except for a bank account at a custodian bank:

	A	B	C	D
1			Market Value	
2	Country	Day 1		
3	Bank Cash	0.00		
4				
5	Total	0.00		

On Day 2 we receive an investor contribution of 1000. Here we show the fund at the end of Day 2, the contribution is recorded as Cash worth 1000.

	A	B	C	D
1			Market Value	
2	Country	Day 1	Day 2	
3	Bank Cash	0.00	1000.00	
4				
5	Total	0.00	1000.00	

On Day 3 the portfolio manager decides to buy shares of AOL for a net amount of 1000. The fund begins pricing the position at the end of Day 3, and assuming AOL does not change in value, the fund now has a position in AOL worth 1000. Because trades in many markets, including the U.S. equity markets, do not clear or settle on the day of the trade, the fund still has the 1000 cash position. So we have cash worth 1000 and the AOL stock worth 1000. Unfortunately, we do not all of a sudden have a fund that is worth 2000. The value of the fund is still 1000. What we need is an offsetting position to the cash in the bank to reflect the commitment to pay for the AOL shares on settlement date. In the financial statements for the fund at the end of Day 3, we will see an additional entry, a *payable*, for the amount of the trade. Notice that we now have three "holdings" for the day: a position in cash, the payable for the AOL shares, and the AOL shares themselves. The total fund value is still 1000.

	A	B	C	D	E	F	G
1			Market Value				
2	Country	Day 1	Day 2	Day 3			
3	Bank Cash	0.00	1000.00	1000.00			
4	Payable for AOL			-1000.00			
5	Net Cash			0.00		=SUM(D3:D4)	
6				——▶			
7	AOL			1000.00			
8							
9	Total	0.00	1000.00	1000.00		=SUM(D5:D8)	

We include the AOL shares in the fund's accounts on Day 3 because we take ownership of a stock on Trade Date rather than Settlement Date. *Settlement Date* is the date on which we need to deliver cash to the broker for the purchase. The *Trade Date Accounting* used in the investments' industry is consistent with the Accrual basis accounting upon which corporate financial accounts are prepared. Investment performance is also based on the principal of trade date accounting: We start calculating performance on the day that we take ownership of the shares.

Notice that in the spreadsheet above we sum the Bank Cash and Payable for AOL holdings into a subtotal category called Net Cash. *Net Cash*, sometimes called *Trade Date Cash*, or *Traded Cash*, or simply *Cash*, is equal to the value of cash in the bank net of the open payables and receivables. Payables or receivables included in Net Cash include not only trade payables and receivables, but also payables and receivables for any accrued payable or receivable owed or owed to the portfolio. For example, if management fees are paid out of the fund to the advisory firm we might accrue a daily Payable for Management Fees accrued but not yet paid.

Continuing with our example, on Day 4, the value of the AOL shares goes up to 1200 and we calculate a return = (1200/1000) − 1 = 20%. In addition, the AOL trade settles, which relieves the payable. The cash balance is reduced by 1000 to reflect the payment to the broker.

	A	B	C	D	E
1			Market Value		
2	Country	Day 1	Day 2	Day 3	Day 4
3	Bank Cash	0.00	1000.00	1000.00	0.00
4	Payable for AOL			-1000.00	0.00
5	**Net Cash**			**0.00**	**0.00**
6					
7	AOL			1000.00	1200.00
8					
9	Total	0.00	1000.00	1000.00	1200.00
10	Return				20.00

There were two sides to the purchase of AOL stock: the actual purchase of AOL stock and the liability for payment for the AOL stock. Most security transactions have two sides. We can think of the two sides as a security trade and a cash trade. In the case of a security buy, the first side is a security purchase, and the second is a *Cash Sell*. We might call the cash offset a *Reflexive Cash Transaction*, because it is an automatic offset to the security transaction, required to keep the fund's value in balance. Reflexive cash transactions are different than the settlement of cash with the broker, which is a real cash transaction. Exhibit 15.16 illustrates the way different transactions affect fund cash and security balances for a portfolio where the fees and expenses are being paid out of the investment account.

EXHIBIT 15.16   Portfolio Transactions

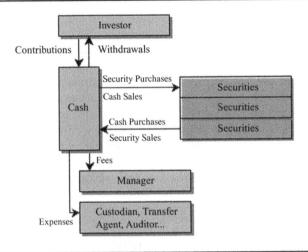

EXHIBIT 15.17   Transaction Return Effects

	Level Security and Segment	Traded Cash	Total Portfolio
Transaction			
Cash Contribution	None	Inflow	Inflow
Cash Withdrawal	None	Outflow	Outflow
Security Purchase	Inflow	Outflow	None
Security Sale	Outflow	Inflow	None
Interest Income	Outflow	Inflow	None
Cash Dividend	Outflow	Inflow	None

External transactions have a one-sided effect on the net cash balance. A contribution into the portfolio is equal to a cash purchase, or inflow to traded cash. A withdrawal is equivalent to a sale, or outflow, of traded cash. Exhibit 15.17 shows how transactions affect the security/segment, traded cash and total portfolio levels of a portfolio.

The treatment of income received as an outflow to the security/segment and inflow to cash might be confusing. One way to think of this is that the inflow to cash did not come from an external cash contribution into the portfolio. Therefore the cash had to come from within the portfolio. In order for the transactions to balance, there must be an outflow to some other security/segment. The receipt of income reduces the invested balance of the segment where the income originated. If the income payment were reinvested into the security/segment, then this will be recorded as a separate security purchase cash flow, having the inverse effect of the income receipt.

As we have seen, transactions have an effect on not only security balances but also the net cash balance. The last piece that we need to put in place to finish the within-the-fund return calculation puzzle is the calculation of a return on the cash balance. We calculate a return on traded cash just as we do any other segment. Assuming daily returns, we take the value at the end of the day plus any income earned and divide by the value at the beginning of the day. We adjust for inflows and outflows to the cash balances just as we would a security return. Where income is earned on cash, it is included in the cash return. If excess cash in the bank is used to purchase a short-term security such as a repurchase agreement or commercial paper, we calculate a return on the short-term security just as we would any other security, and record the reflexive cash transactions to the net cash account upon purchase and sale.

MULTIPERIOD SECURITY AND SEGMENT RETURNS

Once we have calculated the single period security and segment returns, we can compound them over multiple time periods in the same way that we calculate multiperiod fund level returns. We chain link the $(1 + R)$ single period growth rates, and we can annualize security and segments returns in the same way we do the total returns. There is, however, one unique issue to the calculation of multiperiod security and segment level returns.

When we were calculating multiple period cumulative and annualized total portfolio level returns, one unstated assumption was that there was a return for every period between the beginning and the end date. For example, when we calculate a 3-year cumulative return using monthly periodic returns, we compound the 36 monthly returns.

We cannot make this assumption with security and segment level returns. This is because we introduce new and sell out of existing securities and segments by trading. For example, a global portfolio might start investing in a new country in the middle of a year creating the question how to calculate, for example, a 1-year return for this country. There are two ways of dealing with this situation:

1. Compound the periods that the fund has invested in the segment or security.
2. Compound only those securities or segments with a position for the full time period.

EXHIBIT 15.18   Partial Period Returns

	A	B	C	D	E	F	G
1			Single Period Returns			Cumulative Returns	
2		Month 1	Month 2	Month 3		Link All	Link Complete
3	United States	-	1.00	1.00		2.01	-
4	Canada	2.00	0.00	-1.00		0.98	0.98
5	Japan	4.00	6.00	-2.00		8.04	8.04
6	Total	2.14	2.19	2.24		6.71	6.71
7			=(PRODUCT(B11:D11)-1)*100				
8			Growth Rates				
9	United States	-	1.0100	1.0100			
10	Canada	1.0200	1.0000	0.9900			
11	Japan	1.0400	1.0600	0.9800			
12	Total	1.0214	1.0219	1.0224			

Exhibit 15.18 demonstrates the two alternatives. We have three months of single period returns for a fund, and the securities in the fund are partitioned for analysis by country.

The United States segment has a return for months two and three, but the fund was not invested in the United States in the first month, so there is a partial period United States return for the quarter. In Column F, we calculate a segment return using the month two and three returns only. Using the alternative approach in Column G, we show a dash instead of calculating a return for this segment. The choice of approach depends on analyst preference; they are both valid ways of dealing with the problem. The presentation of a cumulative return earned over a shorter period of time, in this case two out of three months, along with returns earned over a longer period of time, might be misleading. For example, when we compare this fund to its benchmark, the benchmark returns will have been calculated using a full quarter of returns for each country. But in any case the raw returns do not tell us the complete story. We need to know the relative weights of the different country segments in order to infer their contribution to total fund return.

CHAPTER 16

Effective Exposure Basis Returns

The extension of the security level return calculation to the segment level is straightforward when the portfolio holds cash market instruments such as stocks and bonds. The term *cash market* is used to differentiate these assets from derivatives. When we calculate segment level returns for cash market instruments, we first group each of the assets into segments and then sum up the security level market value, income earned, and transaction adjustments to the segment level. We then calculate segment level returns using the combined values in the same way we calculate the security level returns for these assets. This methodology is used to calculate asset class returns for a balanced fund, returns by industry for a stock fund, returns by duration band for a bond fund, country level returns for a fund that invests globally, and so on. We can calculate performance in this way for any portfolio segmenting scheme of interest to the analyst.

INSTRUMENTS THAT ALTER SEGMENT EXPOSURES

In addition to cash market instruments, portfolio managers use derivatives to modify the segment exposures that result from investment in these instruments. *Derivatives* such as futures, options, and swaps derive their value from the price of an underlying security or index representing the asset class. We can use derivatives to modify our asset allocation either to increase or reduce exposure to an asset class. When we reduce exposure to the asset class, we are using the derivatives to *hedge* our exposure to the risks of investing in the asset class. Derivatives are also used in executing tactical asset allocation changes, equitization of cash balances, and other strategies.[1]

---

[1] For background on derivatives and their use see Don Chance, *Essays in Derivatives* (New Hope, PA: Frank J. Fabozzi Associates, 1998).

The asset class segment returns that we calculate for performance analysis should reflect this hedging and asset allocation activity. For example, if we have a balanced fund with cash and equity segments, we can reduce our exposure to the equity segment by selling equities in exchange for cash. As an alternative, we can enter into a futures contract to sell equity futures short. Either method will have the desired result: In subsequent periods the performance of the fund will be more like a cash fund than an equity fund. The futures effectively reduce our market exposure to the equity segment, even though we still own stocks in the fund.

When we sell futures in an amount equal to 100% of the equity segment exposure, the gains on the futures contract will approximately offset losses on the underlying equities when the market falls and the reverse when it rises, because futures provide symmetric exposure to the underlying asset class. That is, we are exposed to both the ups and downs. In this case, our effective exposure to equities becomes 0%. We can measure *effective exposure* to an asset class as the sum of the value of our cash market instruments plus the market exposure provided by our derivatives positions. The exposure provided by the derivatives is sometimes called a *notional market value*. The notional market value represents the market risk inherent in the derivative contract. The income earned on a derivatives position divided by the notional market value provides a return that has been adjusted for the leverage embedded in the derivatives position. This return over the period is the same as the return on an investment in the cash market asset that is underlying the derivatives position.

We can adjust the effective exposures of a portfolio using futures, swaps, currency forward contracts, options, and by other means. The general principle for segment level performance calculation for funds holding these instruments is to reclassify the market value, income, and transactions from one segment to another so that we can calculate returns that reflect the economic adjustment intended by the use of the contract. For example, we want to calculate an equity segment return reflecting the performance of both equity futures contracts and individual stocks held by the portfolio. In this chapter, we show how to do this for futures contracts and currency forward contracts; the principles illustrated here can be modified to handle other instruments.

FUTURES

Consider the portfolio in Exhibit 16.1. The securities in the fund are grouped into segments by asset class, and at the beginning of the period it was invested with 20% in cash and cash equivalents and 80% in equities. During the period the equity market went up 6% and the fund earned a 3% return on cash and, given the asset allocation, the fund earned a 5.40% return.

Now suppose that in addition to these holdings we had decided to equitize the majority of the cash balance by entering into a long futures contract covering 90% of the cash and cash equivalent balance. We determine that we need $90 in exposure to equities, and we buy contracts with an exposure equal to $90 ($90 = number of contracts × contract multiplier × price per contract).

$$\begin{aligned}\text{Notional value of futures} \\ = \text{Futures price} \times \text{Multiplier} \times \text{Number of contracts}\end{aligned} \quad (16.1)$$

For example, the S&P futures contract has a multiplier of 250. So if we wanted to buy exposure to $90 million of the S&P 500, and the current futures price was 1,000, we would need to buy 360 (90,000,000/ (1000 × 250)) contracts.

Exhibit 16.2 shows the change in beginning of period asset class exposures and the new exposures that include the futures contract.

EXHIBIT 16.1 Performance without Futures

	A	B	C	D	E	F
1	**Before Futures**	**MVB**	**Income**	**MVE**	**MVE+AI**	**Return**
2	Cash	100.00	3.00	100.00	103.00	3.00
3	Equities	400.00	2.00	422.00	424.00	6.00
4	**Total Fund**	500.00	5.00	522.00	527.00	5.40

EXHIBIT 16.2 Exposure Adjustment from Futures

	A	B	C	D
1	**Before Adjustment**	**MVB**		**Cash Market Weights**
2	Cash	100.00		0.20
3	Equities	400.00		0.80
4	**Total Fund**	500.00		1.00
5				
6	**Exposure Change from Futures**			
7	Cash	-90.00		
8	Equity Futures	90.00		
9	**Total Fund**	-		
10				**Exposure Weights**
11	**After Adjustment**		=B2+B7	
12	Cash	10.00		0.02
13	Equities	490.00		0.98
14	**Total Fund**	500.00		1.00

EXHIBIT 16.3 Futures Returns without Exposure Adjustments

	A	B	C	D	E	F
17	**After Futures**	**MVB**	**Income**	**MVE**	**MVE+AI**	**Return**
18	Cash	100.00	3.00	100.00	103.00	3.00
19	Equities	400.00	2.00	422.00	424.00	6.00
20	Futures	-	-	3.60	3.60	-
21	**Total Fund**	500.00	5.00	525.60	530.60	6.12
22						
23					=SUM(E18:E20)	=((E21/B21)-1)*100

After the adjustment, the fund is positioned so we should experience a return approximately the same as a fund that is 98% invested in equities, even though our fund is only 80% invested. The rest of the exposure is expected to come from variation margin payments and receipts on the futures contract. *Variation margin* is the daily gain or loss calculated when marking the future to market. Because the future is priced relative to the underlying equity market, the pattern of variation margin payments and receipts will closely follow the pattern in underlying cash market gains and losses.

In addition to the variation margin, interest on the cash balance represents another source of earnings during the period. Assuming that the fund is not using the futures to leverage the portfolio, the fund will hold a *cash backing* equivalent to the market exposure of the futures contract. Some of the cash backing will be held by the broker as the *initial margin*, and the cash backing will continue to earn income during the period.

Suppose that the market does go up and the fund earns the same 3.00% cash return, 6.00% return on the underlying equities and an incremental $3.60 in futures variation margin. Exhibit 16.3 shows the calculation of the fund return equal to 6.12% for the period.

We now have a higher return than we did in Exhibit 16.1 because of the increased exposure to the equity market underlying the futures contract. Although the fund level return is correct, and we have not distorted the cash return by including the variation margin payments, the presentation in Exhibit 16.3 is unsatisfactory for two reasons. The segment level valuations and returns do not reflect the altered effective exposure. We did add an asset class called "futures," but this provides no information as to how the futures were used to alter exposures toward the equity segment. We could improve the information content of the presentation by making notional exposure valuation, income, and transaction adjustments similar to what we did in Exhibit 16.2, and then calculate the returns using the adjusted exposures.

To do this we create exposure adjustments that reclassify the income earned on the cash backing, the gains earned on the contract and the effective exposure to the asset class underlying the futures contract. The first step is to calculate the net amount of these adjustments. Exhibit 16.4 shows these adjustments for our example fund.

We made two adjustments. First, we attributed 2.70 in income to the futures contract. We reclassify this *notional income* because futures are priced with the assumption that we are going to earn the income on the cash backing. Absent arbitrage opportunities, the current price of an equity index future equals the price of the underlying spot market index multiplied by (1 + short term interest cost – dividend income), where the interest cost and dividend income are calculated with reference to the time to delivery for the contract. The short-term interest cost represents the cost of financing the futures position. Where possible, we use the actual interest rate used to credit the income to the cash balance to calculate the amount of interest to be reclassified. In practice, this may be difficult to do and the rate can be approximated. If we do not reclassify the interest to the equity segment, we will understate the equity asset class return due to the decision to increase equity exposure via index futures. We credit the equity segment with the interest income regardless of whether or not the cash position actually exists. If the cash position does not exist because, for example, the fund is using the futures contract for leverage, then the decrease to cash represents the cost of financing the leveraged position.

Next, we calculated the effective exposure of the futures (90.00), added in the variation margin (3.60) and attributed the total to the equity futures. Given the adjustments, we can calculate a notional return on the cash and futures segments. We add the cash market values to the exposure adjustments, and in the bottom section of Exhibit 16.5 calculate effective asset class exposures and returns that reflect the effective exposures.

In both Exhibits 16.3 and 16.5, we calculate the same total fund return, 6.12%. The increase in equity exposure from futures led to an incremental return on futures equal to 72 basis points (6.12% – 5.40%). But notice that in Exhibit 16.5 we calculated an equity segment return equal to 6.18%, which is an increase on the 6.00% equity return calculated without the futures. The difference reflects the margin variation, the interest income earned on the cash backing (3.00%), and the dividend income earned on the underlying equities.

EXHIBIT 16.4 Exposure Adjustments for Futures

	A	B	C	D	E	F
		MVB	Income	MVE	MVE+AI	Return
6	Exposure Change	MVB	Income	MVE	MVE+AI	Return
7	Cash	-90.00	-2.70	-90.00	-92.70	3.00
8	Equity Futures	90.00	2.70	93.60	96.30	7.00
9	Total Fund			3.60	3.60	

EXHIBIT 16.5   Performance with Futures

	A	B	C	D	E	F
1	**Before Futures**	**MVB**	**Income**	**MVE**	**MVE+AI**	**Return**
2	Cash	100.00	3.00	100.00	103.00	3.00
3	Equities	400.00	2.00	422.00	424.00	6.00
4	**Total Fund**	500.00	5.00	522.00	527.00	5.40
5						
6	**Exposure Change**	**MVB**	**Income**	**MVE**	**MVE+AI**	**Return**
7	Cash	-90.00	-2.70	-90.00	-92.70	3.00
8	Equity Futures	90.00	2.70	93.60	96.30	7.00
9	Total Fund			3.60	3.60	
10						
11	**After Futures**		=D3+D8	=((E13/B13)-1)*100		
12	Cash	10.00	0.30	10.00	10.30	3.00
13	Equities	490.00	4.70	515.60	520.30	6.18
14	**Total Fund**	500.00	5.00	525.60	530.60	6.12

To recap, in order to present segment level performance on an effective exposure basis when the fund uses futures for asset allocation adjustments, we

1. Classify each of the cash market securities into an asset class segment.
2. Sum the valuations, income, and transactions for each of the securities by segment.
3. Calculate adjusting entries to move exposures, income, and variation margin into the segment reflecting the underlying economic exposure.
4. Add the adjustments to the cash market segment balances.
5. Calculate the returns on an effective exposure basis.

CURRENCY FORWARD CONTRACTS

When a fund holds foreign securities, the returns in base currency will be affected both by the change in security value measured in local terms and by the fluctuation in exchange rates. We can use *currency forward contracts* to mitigate the effects of these exchange rate changes. *Forward contracts* are agreements to purchase or sell a set amount of foreign currency at a specified price for settlement on some future date. A forward contract to purchase currency gives the fund exposure to that currency, and the exposure to the currency sold is reduced. When we enter into a forward contract, the local market exposures remain the same but the currency exposures change, for example, by protecting the portfolio from the risk of exchange rate fluctuations if the foreign currencies were sold forward in exchange for the base currency.

EXHIBIT 16.6 Foreign Portfolio Holdings

	A	B	C	D	E	F
1	Security	Country	Currency	Local MV+AI	X-rate	Base MV+AI
2	1	DE	EUR	60,000.00	0.8350	50,100.00
3	2	FR	EUR	30,000.00	0.8350	25,050.00
4	3	US	USD	100,000.00	1.0000	100,000.00
5	4	JP	JPY	10,000,000.00	0.0080	80,000.00
6	Total:				=D5*E5	255,150.00

EXHIBIT 16.7 Determining Currency Exposures

	A	B	C	D	E	F
1	Security	Country	Currency	Local MV+AI	X-rate	Base MV+AI
2	1	DE	EUR	60,000.00	0.8350	50,100.00
3	2	FR	EUR	30,000.00	0.8350	25,050.00
4			EUR exposure:	90,000.00		75,150.00
5	3	US	USD	100,000.00	1.0000	100,000.00
6			USD exposure:	100,000.00		100,000.00
7	4	JP	JPY	10,000,000.00	0.0080	80,000.00
8			JPY exposure:	10,000,000.00		80,000.00
9						
10	Total:					255,150.00

Exhibit 16.6 shows the holdings for a fund with a base currency of dollars. The fund holds four positions with a combined exposure to three different currencies, including the dollar. The fund returns will be affected by changes in the USD/Euro and USD/Yen exchange rates.

Now suppose that we are interested in eliminating our exposure to the euro for a period in time. Exhibit 16.7 shows the first two securities have euro exposure totaling EUR 90,000. Notice that because euro is the trading currency for several of the countries that we are investing in, we calculate currency exposure by currency instead of by country.

To reduce the effect of fluctuations in the EUR/USD exchange rate, we need to sell 90,000 euro forward for dollars. Suppose that the forward rate available for this trade is 0.8230, which is a discount to the current spot rate equal to 0.8350. The effect of this contract is to add a short position to the portfolio equal to 90,000 euro and a long position in dollars equal to 74,070 (90,000 × 0.823). Exhibit 16.8 shows the position statement including the hedge payable and receivable.

When we calculate performance for a portfolio that includes forward contracts, we break the forward contracts into two legs, a forward purchase, or payable, and a forward sale, or receivable. We separately mark to market the receivable and payable sides of the contract using the current forward exchange rate. Because the contract is to sell euro in exchange for dollars, the receivable side of the contract will be priced at an exchange rate of 1.0, but if the contract was a cross deal, where two nonbase currencies are exchanged, both sides of the contract would fluctuate in value. Exhibit 16.9 shows the mark to market of the portfolio and return calculation for Day 2.

On Day 2 the euro depreciates relative to the dollar. This affects both the spot and forward rates. For clarity we have left the yen exchange rate unchanged. After we mark to market the first two securities using the current spot rate, 0.8100, these holdings experience an unrealized loss due to the euro exchange rate change equal to 2250 dollars (72,900 − 75,150). This completely accounts for the dollar loss in the portfolio, (252,900 − 255,150) before consideration of the hedge. The unhedged portfolio return is −0.882% (252,900/255,150 − 1). Notice that we still mark to market the forward currency contracts even though the gain or loss, unlike with futures, does not actually change hands each day.

EXHIBIT 16.8   Portfolio Holdings Including Hedge

	A	B	C	D	E	F
9	Security	Country	Currency	Local MV+AI	X-rate	Base MV+AI
10	1	DE	EUR	60,000.00	0.8350	50,100.00
11	2	FR	EUR	30,000.00	0.8350	25,050.00
12	3	US	USD	100,000.00	1.0000	100,000.00
13	4	JP	JPY	10,000,000.00	0.0080	80,000.00
14	Total MV:					255,150.00
15						
16	EUR Currency Payable		EUR	(90,000.00)	0.8230	(74,070.00)
17	USD Currency Receivable		USD	74,070.00	1.0000	74,070.00
18	Total MV w/ Hedge:					255,150.00

EXHIBIT 16.9   Currency Returns Including Hedges

	A	B	C	D	E	F
21	Day 2					
22	Security	Country	Currency	Local MV+AI	xrate	Base MV+AI
23	1	DE	EUR	60,000.00	0.8100	48,600.00
24	2	FR	EUR	30,000.00	0.8100	24,300.00
25	3	US	USD	100,000.00	1.0000	100,000.00
26	4	JP	JPY	10,000,000.00	0.0080	80,000.00
27	Total MV					252,900.00
28						
29	EUR Currency Payable		EUR	(90,000.00)	0.7980	(71,820.00)
30	USD Currency Receivable		USD	74,070.00	1.0000	74,070.00
31	Total MV					255,150.00
32						
33				Base Return Unhedged:	-0.882	=((F27/F14)-1)*100
34				Base Return Hedged:	0.000	=((F31/F18)-1)*100

Next, we mark to market the hedge using the current forward rate available for the forward contract's delivery date. In our case the rate depreciates to 0.7980. Because we are short euro, a drop in the forward rate has the effect of increasing the value of the contract in dollar terms. The unrealized gain in the forward contract (2250 = 74,070 − 71,820) offsets the loss on the security positions. Given the gain on the contract, the fund hedged return is 0.00% (255,150 /255,150 − 1).

OPTIONS

The use of options in portfolio management is a subject all to its own. There are many types of options, and portfolio managers use options and combinations of option positions to execute many different strategies. Some of these strategies include the purchase of protective puts, the writing of covered calls, and the use of multiple options to create various spread, straddle, and strangle positions. The performance measurement and evaluation of portfolios with options should take into account the particular strategy at work.

We can also use options to change portfolio segment exposures. While the performance of a long futures position will mimic the performance of the underlying asset in both up and down directions, options returns are asymmetric. Purchased call options, which are agreements made to buy the underlying at a price locked in at the start of the contract, will reflect upside gains without any of the downside losses. A purchased put option has the opposite effect, we lock in the price at which we can sell the underlying asset, therefore the contract will move up in value as the underlying asset moves down in price.

Unlike futures, options do have a value at inception. The purchase price, or *option premium*, is paid to the seller in exchange for the rights to put or call. The daily change in the value of the premium reflects the asymmetric nature of the contracts. A call option will go up in value as the price of the underlying asset rises, to the point where the price of the option will go up dollar for dollar with the rise in price of the underlying asset. The price relationship between the option and the underlying is called the *delta*. Delta is the change in the market value of an option as a multiple of the change in the market value of the underlying. For example, suppose we purchase a call option on a stock with a current price equal to 50. We buy the option to purchase the stock at 55, and the option costs us 2 in premium. If the underlying stock starts to fall in value from 50 to 48 to 46, and so on, the value of the option contract will approach 0 and drop no further as the stock continues to fall. As this happens the delta will approach 0. If on the other hand the stock goes up in value to 52 to 54 to 58 and so on, at some point the value of the premium will go up 1 for every 1 rise in the underlying stock. As this happens the value of delta will approach 1.

The performance measurement of portfolios that contain options can proceed along two lines: first, we can simply use the change in option premium value from day to day as the basis for calculating the return. If, as in our example we paid 2 for the option and its price rises to 3, and we have purchased 20 contracts, we would have a 50% gain on the contract (60/40 − 1). Exhibit 16.10 shows the return calculation for a fund holding this option.

In the first section of the exhibit, we show the options in a distinct segment. As an alternative, we could classify the options together with the category representing the underlying. In the middle section we show the reclassification of the gains and losses to the equities segment. In the third section we recalculate the returns including the option in the equity segment.

While this approach is common, and acceptable for some purposes, one drawback to the approach is that it does not completely reflect the underlying economic exposure to equities. In the same way as we did for futures, we can adjust the segment exposures to reflect the economic exposure to the contract. The effective exposure of an options contract is equal to

$$\text{Options effective exposure} = \text{Contracts} \times \text{Price} \times \text{Delta} \qquad (16.2)$$

EXHIBIT 16.10 Option Performance without Exposure Adjustment

	A	B	C	D	E	F
1		MVB	Income	Gain/Loss	MVE	Return
2	Cash	4,000.00	120.00	-	4,120.00	3.00
3	Equities	16,000.00	160.00	800.00	16,960.00	6.00
4	Options	40.00	-	20.00	60.00	50.00
5	Total Fund	20,040.00	280.00	820.00	21,140.00	5.49
6						
7	Adjusts					
8	Cash	-	-	-	-	-
9	Equities	40.00	-	20.00	60.00	50.00
10	Options	(40.00)	-	(20.00)	(60.00)	-
11	Total Fund	-	-	-	-	-
12						
13	Cash	4,000.00	120.00	-	4,120.00	3.00
14	Equities	16,040.00	160.00	820.00	17,020.00	6.11
15	Total Fund	20,040.00	280.00	820.00	21,140.00	5.49

We can adjust the segment market value for the options effective exposure. The offsetting adjustment to the cash segment is different than for futures. Because option contracts have a value equal to the current value of the option premium, we subtract the premium value from the options effective exposure when we are calculating the cash offset. The result in our case is an adjustment in the presentation in Exhibit 16.10 to:

1. Increase the equity segment equal to the amount of the options effective exposure.
2. Decrease in the options segment equal to the value of the option premium.
3. Decrease in the cash segment reflecting the difference between the first two adjustments.
4. Reclassify the income earned on the cash backing to the equity segment.

CHAPTER 17

Contribution Analysis

One reason we calculate security level returns is to gain an understanding as to how the different securities held by the fund combined over time to deliver the fund return. The total return earned on a security, however, is only a part of the story; we also need to know how securities were allocated, or weighted, within the portfolio, in order to understand the securities' contribution to the fund's total return. The *contribution to return* of a security within a portfolio for a single period is equal to the weighted return for that security. For multiple periods, we employ a compounding methodology to determine the contribution made by a particular security holding to the total fund return. Contributions to fund return help explain why a particular fund or index performed as it did over a period, but we can also look at the relative contributions made by different securities to determine which securities contributed to and detracted from the benchmark relative value added. Contribution analysis is a very powerful tool for analyzing portfolio performance.

CONTRIBUTION TO RETURN

Suppose we had a portfolio comprised of four stocks, each held with an equal 25% weight, and each earned 10% during the period. We can see in Exhibit 17.1 that the contribution to return made by each security to the total fund return is 2.50%.

The 2.5% contribution for each security was calculated by multiplying the beginning of period weight by the return during the period.

$$\text{Contribution to return} = \text{Security begin weight} \times \text{Security return} \quad (17.1)$$

EXHIBIT 17.1   Contribution to Return

	A	B	C	D	E	F
1	Security	BMV	Weight	Return	Contribution	
2	A	200.00	25.00	10.00	2.500	=(C2/100)*(D2/100)*100
3	B	200.00	25.00	10.00	2.500	
4	C	200.00	25.00	10.00	2.500	
5	D	200.00	25.00	10.00	2.500	
6	Total:	800.00	100.00	10.00	10.000	=SUM(E2:E5)
7				=(B5/$B$6)*100		

EXHIBIT 17.2   Single Period Contribution

	A	B	C	D	E
1	Security	Weight	Return	Contribution	
2	A	50.000	20.000	10.000	=(B2/100)*(C2/100)*100
3	B	20.000	10.000	2.000	
4	C	20.000	10.000	2.000	
5	D	10.000	10.000	1.000	
6	Total:	100.000	15.000	15.000	=SUM(D2:D5)

It is the *beginning weight* that we use to calculate contribution to return, rather than use the ending weight. If we used the ending weight, we would overstate the contribution of securities that had a higher than average return and understate the contribution of securities with a lower than average return. This is because the end of period weighting of a security held in a portfolio is impacted by the return earned by that security over the period.

The sum of the security contributions equals the fund return, 10.00%, assuming that there was no management fee or other adjustment to the total fund return. For the total of the security contributions to equal the fund return, it is important that the weights of the individual securities add to 100% and that any transactions affecting the return are properly reflected in the weights. It is, of course, more interesting to analyze the contribution to return when the securities are held in different proportions. Exhibit 17.2 shows a fund with a bigger holding in Security A than the other securities, and Security A performed better over the period than the other securities. Exhibit 17.2 shows the contribution of security A to the fund return was 10%.

For diversified portfolios with many security holdings, we can summarize the major impacts to the fund by calculating, for example, the top contributors to and worst detractors from the fund's return. Exhibit 17.3 shows a contribution analysis displaying the top and bottom five contributions to return for a period where the fund return was 4.25%.

Contribution analysis shows us how both the asset allocation decision and the market return earned on the security combine to produce an impact on fund return. For example, securities D and E have different weights and returns, but a similar contribution to fund return.

EXHIBIT 17.3   Contribution Analysis

Top 5	Weight	Return	Contribution
Security A	12.00	18.00	2.16
Security B	6.00	25.00	1.50
Security C	9.00	15.00	1.35
Security D	2.50	25.00	0.63
Security E	4.50	14.00	0.63
Bottom 5			
Security F	6.00	(35.00)	(2.10)
Security G	12.00	(5.00)	(0.60)
Security H	5.00	(5.00)	(0.25)
Security I	7.00	(3.25)	(0.23)
Security J	4.25	(5.00)	(0.21)
Net Other	31.75		1.38
Total	100.00	4.250	4.250

MULTIPERIOD CONTRIBUTION TO RETURN

So far we have been looking at the contribution to return over a single period, which might be a day or a month. But we are usually interested in evaluating performance over many periods. Just as we cannot add single period returns to determine the multiperiod return, we cannot add contributions across days to calculate the multiperiod contribution to return. We need some way of compounding the contributions. One might be tempted to calculate the multiperiod contribution to return for a particular security by multiplying the compound security return and the beginning of the first period weight. This approach works if the weight of the security did not change over time. If the security weights change, however, this approach results in a distortion of the contributions that increases each time that the weights change. For example, suppose at the beginning of the next day the manager of the fund in Exhibit 17.2 sold out of Security A, which had the large gain the prior day. Cell I3 in Exhibit 17.4 shows how Security A makes no contribution to return on Day 2. But if we calculate the multiperiod contribution to fund return using the weight at the start of Day 1, we will not properly account for the impact of the decision to sell out of Security A. So the sum of the contributions calculated in this way does not equal the compound fund return for the two days.

To determine the multiperiod contribution to return earned by a fund over multiple days, we can employ an algorithm where we

1. take the security contributions earned on one day,
2. compound them by the fund return on subsequent days, and
3. sum the compounded single period contributions to return.

EXHIBIT 17.4   Multiperiod Contribution Using Begin Weight

	A	B	C	D	E	F	G	H	I	J	K	L
1		Day 1					Day 2				Day 1-2	Day 1-2
2	Security	Weight	Return	Contribution		Security	Weight	Return	Contribution		Return	Contribution
3	A	50.00	20.00	10.000		A	0.00	0.00	0.000		20.00	10.000
4	B	20.00	10.00	2.000		B	50.00	10.00	5.000		21.00	4.200
5	C	20.00	10.00	2.000		C	25.00	10.00	2.500		21.00	4.200
6	D	10.00	10.00	1.000		D	25.00	10.00	2.500		21.00	2.100
7	Total:	100.00	15.00	15.000		Total:	100.00	10.00	10.000		26.50	20.500
8								Does not equal 26.50				

EXHIBIT 17.5   Multiperiod Contribution Using Daily Weights

	A	B	C	D	E	F	G	H	I	J	K	L
1		Day 1					Day 2				Day 1-2	
2	Security	Weight	Return	Contribution		Security	Weight	Return	Contribution		Return	
3	A	50.00	20.00	10.000		A	0.00	0.00	0.000		20.00	
4	B	20.00	10.00	2.000		B	50.00	10.00	5.000		21.00	
5	C	20.00	10.00	2.000		C	25.00	10.00	2.500		21.00	
6	D	10.00	10.00	1.000		D	25.00	10.00	2.500		21.00	
7	Total:	100.00	15.00	15.000		Total:	100.00	10.00	10.000		26.50	
8											Day 1-2	
9	Day 1 Contribution to Day 1-2 Return					Day 2 Contribution to Day 1-2 Return					Contribution	
10		11.000	=D3*(1+H7/100)				0.000	=I3			11.00	=D10+G10
11		2.200	=D4*(1+H7/100)				5.000	=I4			7.20	=D11+G11
12		2.200	=D5*(1+H7/100)				2.500	=I5			4.70	=D12+G12
13		1.100	=D6*(1+H7/100)				2.500	=I6			3.60	=D13+G13
14		16.500					10.000				26.50	

Multiperiod contribution to return
$$= \text{[Prior cumulative contribution} \times (1 + \text{Fund total return)]} \qquad (17.2)$$
$$+ \text{ Current day contribution}$$

Exhibit 17.5 shows how we can analyze multiperiod contribution to return using this algorithm. Let's look at Security A. In Cell D10 we can see how we take the Security A contribution of 10% on Day 1 and compound it using the Day 2 *total fund return*. One way to think about this is that we take the contributions earned each day and invest them back into the fund on subsequent days. Taking the 10% contribution and growing it by 10% on Day 2 gives the Day 1 Security A contribution to the multiperiod return 11%.

To calculate the multiperiod contribution, we then take the Day 2 contribution and add it to the Day 1 compounded contribution, giving an 11% contribution to the two-day return for Security A. If we calculate and then sum the contributions for each security in this way, and then add the contributions, we can reconcile the two-day return equal to 26.50%.

We can extend this methodology to any number of days. If this were a three-day example, we would derive the contribution to return by taking the cumulative contribution to return on Day 2, compounding it at the Day 3 total return, and adding the Day 3 contribution.

It is important to note that this is not the only way to extend the contribution analysis to multiple periods, but the method presented here is a common approach to this problem.

CONTRIBUTION TO VALUE ADDED

The contribution to return gives us a way to understand the impact that the various components of the portfolio had on the multiperiod total return. We can use it to analyze which holdings helped and which ones detracted from fund performance. We can also determine the contribution to total return for the different constituents of the fund's benchmark. Now suppose we have an active portfolio, where the manager is overweighting certain attractive securities and underweighting others. He does this in the hope of earning value added, or excess return, over the benchmark. We can also use contribution analysis to analyze how these weighting decisions contributed to the relative returns of the fund and the benchmark.

To determine the impact of decisions to weight securities in a different proportion than the benchmark, we calculate a *contribution to value added* for each security held by the fund. The contribution to value added equals the difference in fund and benchmark security weights multiplied by the difference in the security or segment return and the benchmark total return.

> Contribution to value added
> = (Fund security weight − Benchmark security weight)   (17.3)
> × (Benchmark security return − Benchmark total return)

It may not be obvious why we calculate relative contributions in this way. Let's take an example, Exhibit 17.6, where we have a portfolio and its benchmark, which is equally weighted in four securities, and three of the four returns are the same for the period except one security, Security A, which had a higher return. Also assume that the manager overweighted this security at the beginning of the period, resulting in the fund enjoying a higher return than the benchmark for the period.

In this period the fund return was 14% and the benchmark return 12.5%, so the manager delivered 1.5% of value added during the period. Because of the overweight in Security A, which did better than the average stock during the period, we can see that Security A contributed 3% more to the fund return than it did to the benchmark return. The total benchmark return equal to 12.50% represents the weighted average stock return. We can think of the 3% as an absolute contribution to relative return. But by overweighting Security A, we also had to underweight some other securities as compared to the benchmark. For example, the Security B contribution to fund return was 2%. The higher weight in Security B leads to a contribution to benchmark total return of 2.5%. The difference is reflected in Column C as a negative adjustment to the total contribution to absolute return.

The negative contribution for Security B might not sit right with us, because just as we overweighted something that performed well, we have underweighted three securities that did not perform as well as the average during the period, and underweighting something that performed poorly creates as much value as overweighting something that performed well. So instead of analyzing absolute contributions, we instead look at the relative contributions to value added, calculated in Column D. The contribution of Security A to the value added equals the 15% overweight (40% − 25%) multiplied by the 7.5% (20% − 12.5%) difference between the Security A fund return and the weighted average security return, which equals 1.125%. Calculating contributions in this way also allows us to recognize the positive contribution made by underweighting securities that did poorly relative to the average during the period. For example, we underweighted Security B by 5% (−5% = 20% − 25%). Security B performed worse than the average security return (−2.5% = 10% − 12.50%). By multiplying the two differences we derive the 0.125% contribution to value added from the decision to underweight Security B. We can sum the contributions to value added for each security to derive the arithmetic difference between the fund and benchmark return for the period.

EXHIBIT 17.6 Contribution to Value Added

	A	B	C	D	E	F	G	H
1			Fund				Benchmark	
2	Security	Weight	Return	Contribution		Weight	Return	Contribution
3	A	40.00	20.00	8.000		25.00	20.00	5.000
4	B	20.00	10.00	2.000		25.00	10.00	2.500
5	C	20.00	10.00	2.000		25.00	10.00	2.500
6	D	20.00	10.00	2.000		25.00	10.00	2.500
7	Total:	100.00	14.00	14.000		100.00	12.50	12.500
8		Contribution to Value Added						
9	=D3-H3		Absolute	Relative				
10			3.000	1.125		=(B3/100-F3/100)*(G3/100-G7/100)*100		
11			(0.500)	0.125		=(B4/100-F4/100)*(G4/100-G7/100)*100		
12			(0.500)	0.125		=(B5/100-F5/100)*(G5/100-G7/100)*100		
13			(0.500)	0.125		=(B6/100-F6/100)*(G6/100-G7/100)*100		
14			1.500	1.500		=SUM(D10:D13)		

EXHIBIT 17.7   Value Added from Securities Not Held

	A	B	C	D	E	F	G	H	I	J
1			Fund				Benchmark			
2	Security	Weight	Return	Contribution		Weight	Return	Contribution		Value Added
3	A	0.00	0.00	0.000		25.00	(10.00)	(2.500)		2.438
4	B	40.00	8.00	3.200		25.00	8.00	2.000		1.238
5	C	40.00	5.00	2.000		25.00	5.00	1.250		0.788
6	D	20.00	(4.00)	(0.800)		25.00	(4.00)	(1.000)		0.188
7	Total:	100.00	4.40	4.400		100.00	(0.25)	(0.250)		4.650
8				=(B3/100-F3/100)*(G3/100-G7/100)*100						

Except for portfolios designed to replicate a market index, most funds typically hold many fewer securities than are represented in the benchmark. Contribution analysis not only identifies the value added return from holding securities in a different proportion than the index weight, but it can also show the value added by *not* holding a benchmark constituent at all. For example, Exhibit 17.7 shows the value added from not holding Security A, when Security A had a return lower than the benchmark average return. In fact, in this example the majority of the value added over the period came from the decision not to buy Security A.

This example also illustrates why we use the benchmark return when calculating the contribution to value added. In this case the fund had no position in and thus no return for Security A. The use of benchmark rather than fund returns does, however, lead to a problem: We are implicitly assuming that the fund and benchmark security returns are the same over the period. This assumption might hold when the fund is not trading heavily. But if the fund is trading then the assumption might not be a good one. For example, if the fund is trading a lot and the market is volatile, the security returns to the fund and benchmark will be different because of trades done at prices different than the end of day price used in the calculation of the benchmark returns.

OPPORTUNITY COST ANALYSIS

The contribution to value added made by a particular security holding is an important performance measurement metric. It allows us to dissect the relative performance of a fund and its benchmark. Let's take a closer look at what makes up the contribution to value added. In Exhibit 17.6 the contribution for Security D is 2% for the fund and 2.5% for the benchmark. The contribution to relative return for Security D was 0.125%. We can dissect this relative value added into two pieces; one being the value added to the fund by investing in this security as opposed to investing in the benchmark total return, and the second being the value added to the benchmark by having this security versus the benchmark average total return. Referring to cell B15 in Exhibit 17.8, we can see that the opportunity cost of having a weight in Security D is 2.5%, which is the weight in Security D, 20%, multiplied by the benchmark average return, 12.5%. We can interpret this as the *opportunity cost* of having invested in Security D, rather than just holding the benchmark.

If we subtract the opportunity cost from the contribution to return earned we get the economic value added by the fund's investment in Security D, which is 2% − 2.5% = −0.5%. But, this does not tell us the whole story because the benchmark also had a position in Security D. We can also calculate the value added over the opportunity cost of the benchmark holding. The opportunity cost is calculated in the same way as for the fund, we take the Security D weight and multiply it by the total benchmark return (25% × 12.5% = 3.125%). Subtracting the opportunity cost from the value added gives us the value added to the benchmark for having Security D, which is −0.625% (2.5% contribution −3.125% opportunity cost).

Next, we can derive the 0.125% relative value added for Security D by taking the difference of the fund and benchmark value added over the opportunity cost (−0.5% − −0.625%). The contribution to value added made by any one security holding within a portfolio is equal to the relative difference between the absolute value added and the opportunity cost of holding the benchmark instead. The total benchmark return can be thought of as a neutral investment, because if the manager had no special insight or information as to the relative value of different securities, he might instead choose to invest in the market itself.

EXHIBIT 17.8 Opportunity Cost Analysis

	A	B	C	D	E	F	G	H
1			Fund				Benchmark	
2	Security	Weight	Return	Contribution		Weight	Return	Contribution
3	A	40.00	20.00	8.000		25.00	20.00	5.000
4	B	20.00	10.00	2.000		25.00	10.00	2.500
5	C	20.00	10.00	2.000		25.00	10.00	2.500
6	D	20.00	10.00	2.000		25.00	10.00	2.500
7	Total:	100.00	14.00	14.000		100.00	12.50	12.500
8					=((H6/100)-((F6/100)*(G7/100)))*100			
9								
10			Value Added over Opportunity Cost					
11	Security	Fund	Benchmark	Difference				
12	A	3.000	1.875	1.125				
13	B	(0.500)	(0.625)	0.125	=B15-C15			
14	C	(0.500)	(0.625)	0.125				
15	D	(0.500)	(0.625)	0.125				
16	Total:	1.500	0.000	1.500				
17				=(D6/100-((B6/100)*(G7/100)))*100				

EXHIBIT 17.9   Single Period Contribution to Value Added

	A	B	C	D	E	F	G	H	I	J
1	Period 1		Fund				Benchmark			
2	Security	Weight	Return	Contribution		Weight	Return	Contribution		Value Added
3	A	40.00	20.00	8.000		25.00	20.00	5.000		1.125
4	B	20.00	10.00	2.000		25.00	10.00	2.500		0.125
5	C	20.00	10.00	2.000		25.00	10.00	2.500		0.125
6	D	20.00	10.00	2.000		25.00	10.00	2.500		0.125
7	Total:	100.00	14.00	14.000		100.00	12.50	12.500		1.500
8										
9	Period 2		Fund				Benchmark			
10	Security	Weight	Return	Contribution		Weight	Return	Contribution		Value Added
11	A	42.10	20.00	8.420		26.68	20.00	5.336		1.131
12	B	19.30	10.00	1.930		24.44	10.00	2.444		0.137
13	C	19.30	10.00	1.930		24.44	10.00	2.444		0.137
14	D	19.30	10.00	1.930		24.44	10.00	2.444		0.137
15	Total:	100.00	14.21	14.210		100.00	12.67	12.668		1.542

MULTIPERIOD CONTRIBUTION TO VALUE ADDED

The analysis presented here will capture the value added by weighting differences for a single period, which might be a day or a month. We are, of course, usually interested in analyzing fund management decisions over multiple valuation periods. So we can extend the single period analysis of the contribution made by different securities to the value added over the benchmark in a way similar to the way that we extended the contribution analysis to multiple periods. We do make some adjustments, however, when we are calculating a multiperiod contribution to value added.

Let's take an example where we have a fund invested in the same securities as the benchmark, but in different proportions. If the manager does not trade or rebalance the portfolio, the beginning weights in Period 2 will be calculated using the Period 1 begin market values multiplied by the Period 1 growth rate. Exhibit 17.9 shows the fund and benchmark weights, returns, contributions and value added over the benchmark for the two periods.

To determine the contribution to value added made by holding each security over the two periods we need to compound the single period value-added statistics over the two periods. We saw before how we could compound the cumulative prior period contribution to return at the current period total fund return to derive the multiple period contributions to return. Here we are interested in compounding only the benchmark relative value-added component over time. To do this we add each period's value added scaled by the growth rate of:

1. The fund total return for prior periods.
2. The benchmark total return for subsequent periods.

EXHIBIT 17.10 Multiperiod Contribution to Value Added

	A	B	C	D	E	F	G	H	I	J
17				=((J6/100)*(1+G15/100))*100						
18	Period 1-2		Fund	Benchmark			Contribution to Multiperiod Value Added			
19	Security	Return	Contribution	Return	Contribution		P1	P2	Period 1-2	
20	A	44.000	17.558	44.000	10.969		1.268	1.289	2.556	
21	B	21.000	4.214	21.000	5.261		0.141	0.156	0.297	
22	C	21.000	4.214	21.000	5.261		0.141	0.156	0.297	
23	D	21.000	4.214	21.000	5.261		0.141	0.156	0.297	
24	Total:	30.199	30.200	26.752	26.752		1.690	1.758	3.448	
25				=(J14/100)*(1+C7/100)*100		=G23+H23				
26										

Exhibit 17.10 shows how we can calculate value added over multiple periods. Taking Security D as an example, in Cell G23 we have taken the 0.125% value added for Period 1 and compounded it at the Period 2 total benchmark return, 12.67%. Then in Cell H23 we took the 0.137% value added in Period 2 and compounded it at the Period 1 total fund return, 14%. The sum of the two monthly scaled values is 0.297%, which is the multiperiod contribution to value added made by holding Security D.

Why did we compound the value added in this way to derive the multiperiod values? One way to think about this is that we use the benchmark return for subsequent periods because subsequent period fund returns *already include* the subsequent period value added, and we use the fund return for prior periods because it is the fund return that is invested into the value added for subsequent periods.

CHAPTER **18**

Attributing Value Added to Management Decisions

Now that we have calculated the fund's security and segment returns, compared them to those of the benchmark, and determined which securities have contributed to the value added over the benchmark, we might think that we have a complete understanding of why the portfolio performed as it did. But for funds that are managed via a top-down process of asset allocation to market segments, such as countries or industries, we can derive additional information as to the success of these weighting decisions via return decomposition techniques. In this chapter we discuss the generic return decomposition techniques, which are appropriate for many, but not all investment strategies. In Chapter 19 we discuss some extensions to the basic analysis to cover important factors in the management of multicurrency and fixed income portfolios. The two chapters together introduce some of the most common performance attribution techniques.

MEASURING THE CONSEQUENCES OF MANAGER DECISIONS

The contribution to return made by the individual security holdings held by a portfolio tells us why the fund behaved as it did over the period. The contribution to value added over the benchmark made by each of the fund's holdings quantifies the sources of benchmark relative returns earned by positioning the fund differently than the benchmark during the period. If the fund outperformed its benchmark, the positive contributions to relative return might be taken as an indication of the manager's security selection skill. If we take the security level contribution to value-added statistics in aggregate and over time as a sign of manager skill, we are making several implicit assumptions. First, we assume that the benchmark selected for the analysis is relevant to the asset class and style of management for the portfolio. So the most important requirement for performing any kind of comparative analysis is that the benchmark is appropriate. A second assumption we make is that the manager has a bottom-up investment process or strategy. That is, he forms portfolios by selecting individual stocks first and then weights them to maximize the anticipated return for a given level of risk. This might be a good assumption for some managers, for example, an active equity manager with a pure stock picking process. For analyzing the performance of this manager we can use contribution analysis to determine which "bets" worked and which ones did not. We can look at the consistency of value added over time and make some inferences as to his stock selection abilities.

But there are many other investment strategies where security selection is not the primary goal of the fund, or selection takes place within the context of a larger strategy. For example, the manager of a balanced fund with a tactical asset allocation program might have a model that decides when to overweight or underweight asset classes. He might overweight equity or fixed income, given the anticipated relative attractiveness of the asset class, but seek to match the index returns within the asset class. Or we might have the opposite situation, where a manager seeks to maintain a broad asset allocation that accords with the client's strategic asset allocation requirement, but seeks to add value through security selection within the asset class. Or a manager might have an eye for the selection of attractive countries within an international stock fund, or industry segments within a domestic equity fund. We can describe these strategies as "top-down" strategies, where the manager adds value by making broad asset allocation positioning decisions. There are also hybrid strategies, where the manager combines a top-down and a bottom-up process. For example, we could have a global stock fund where the manager selectively over- or underweights countries as compared to the index, but also over- or underweights particular securities *within* each country.

Let's take a look at what happens when we use contribution analysis to determine the sources of value added for a global stock fund that seeks to approximate the benchmark weighting of the countries represented in the index, but select attractive securities within each country. Exhibit 18.1 shows a contribution analysis for this strategy. Notice that there is an overweight to Security A compared to its weight in the index, and Security A did worse than the benchmark average return of −1.1%.

EXHIBIT 18.1 Contribution Analysis

	A	B	C	D	E	F	G	H	I	J
1			Fund				Benchmark			
2	Security	Weight	Return	Contribution		Weight	Return	Contribution		Value Added
3	A	50.00	(5.000)	(2.500)		30.00	(5.000)	(1.500)		(0.780)
4	B	20.00	(7.000)	(1.400)		40.00	(7.000)	(2.800)		1.180
5	C	20.00	10.000	2.000		20.00	10.000	2.000		0.000
6	D	10.00	12.000	1.200		10.00	12.000	1.200		0.000
7	Total:	100.00	(0.700)	(0.700)		100.00	(1.100)	(1.100)		0.400

EXHIBIT 18.2 Contribution Analysis by Country

	A	B	C	D	E	F	G	H	I	J
1			Fund				Benchmark			
2	Security	Weight	Return	Contribution		Weight	Return	Contribution		Value Added
3	Japan	70.00	(5.571)	(3.900)		70.00	(6.143)	(4.300)		
4	A	50.00	(5.000)	(2.500)		30.00	(5.000)	(1.500)		(0.780)
5	B	20.00	(7.000)	(1.400)		40.00	(7.000)	(2.800)		1.180
6	Canada	30.00	10.667	3.200		30.00	10.667	3.200		
7	C	20.00	10.000	2.000		20.00	10.000	2.000		0.000
8	D	10.00	12.000	1.200		10.00	12.000	1.200		0.000
9	Total:	100.00	(0.700)	(0.700)		100.00	(1.100)	(1.100)		0.400

The overweight of Security A, which did poorly relative to the average stock return, took away 78 basis points of value added. Now, with some knowledge of the strategy, we want to see how the fund performed on a country-by-country basis. In Exhibit 18.2 we have grouped each of the securities by country and performed the same analysis.

Security A and Security B are both Japanese stocks. If our goal was to maintain the same country weights as the benchmark, then we needed to maintain a 70% weighting in Japan. If we had just the Securities A and B to select from, clearly we made a good decision to overweight Security A because it had a higher return than Security B and, thus, the return to the average Japanese stock during the period. So, knowing that that strategy of the manager was to select attractive securities within countries, we would want to come up with a method of analysis that would assign a positive contribution for decisions like this, instead of the negative contribution to value added that the security level contribution analysis assigns to Japan in this analysis.

This example actually illustrates an important factor to consider in using performance attribution analysis techniques: To get anything out of the analysis, we have to know something about the strategy or style of the manager and design an analysis around this strategy.

Although we cover in this chapter several methods of quantifying the value added due to the actions of the manager, not every strategy is amenable to this kind of analysis, and we need to carefully interpret the results in the context of the fund's strategy. Having said that, analysts use performance attribution techniques to analyze many kinds of portfolios and have creatively adapted the tools presented here to meet the requirements of particular situations. The aspects of active management, whose results we are seeking to quantify, can be called *management effects*. Depending on the strategy, we would expect to have a positive management effect from various activities. In this example, we are interested in whether the manager added value by picking good stocks, or *security selection*, within countries. Different strategies will have different management effects that are important to measure. In the rest of this chapter, we consider three management effects: security selection, asset allocation, and an interaction effect.[1] We can measure additional effects that depend on the particular strategy, some of which are covered in the next chapter.

MEASURING SECURITY SELECTION DECISIONS

The problem presented by Exhibit 18.2 is that we want to ascribe a positive contribution to total value added from a decision to overweight a security that outperformed the other securities within a segment, but the segment happened to perform poorly during the period. One way to approach the problem is to first look at why the contribution analysis assigns a negative value added for Security A. It does this because when we calculate the value added, we are comparing the security return, -5%, to the total benchmark return, which was -1.1%. So the contribution formula looks at any overweight to a security that had a return below the benchmark average and assigns a negative value added. But because the manager has a mandate to select securities *within* countries, and maintain benchmark country weights, we should instead compare the Security A return to the average Japanese stock return, not the total benchmark return. If we compare the Security A return of -5.000% to the Japanese stock return that we earned with the fund (-5.571%) we get a positive 0.571% contribution to Security A ($-5.000\% - -5.571\%$).

---

[1] The value-added decomposition approach in this chapter is sometimes called "Brinson"-style attribution. Variations of this analysis were used in the following two papers to develop the thesis that much of the variability in pension plan performance is due to asset allocation decisions. See Gary Brinson, Randolph Hood, and Gilbert Beebower, "Determinants of Portfolio Performance," *Financial Analysts Journal* (July 1986); and Gary Brinson, Randolph Hood, Brian Singer, and Gilbert Beebower "Determinants of Portfolio Performance II: An Update," *Financial Analysts Journal* (May 1991).

To determine the effect that this decision had on the value added of the whole portfolio, we multiply the value added by the weight of the Japanese stocks in the fund, 70%. So the value added from selecting good stocks within Japan was positive 0.40% (70% weight × 0.571% value added), and since this decision was the only source of value added during the period, the Japan stock selection effect equals the total value added over the benchmark during the period.

Because our strategy calls for adding value via security selection within a country, we are interested in the country segment level value added from security selection within each country. We can derive this *security selection effect* by taking the difference between the fund and benchmark returns earned within the segment and multiplying it by the weight of the segment within the benchmark.

> Security selection effect
> = (Fund segment return – Benchmark segment return)   (18.1)
>   × Benchmark segment weight

We will discuss the reason for using the benchmark weight rather than the fund weight in the section on the interaction effect, but in this example it is not relevant which weight we use, because the fund and index segment weights are the same. Exhibit 18.3 shows the calculation of the security selection effect for our sample fund.

Here we earned a higher return than the benchmark in Japan because of our overweight in the better performing stock during the period. We take the return differential and weight it by the proportionate weight of Japan within the index in order to derive the value added due to security selection equal to 0.40%.

EXHIBIT 18.3 Security Selection Management Effect

	A	B	C	D	E	F	G	H
1			Weights				Returns	
2	Country	Fund	Benchmark	Difference		Fund	Benchmark	Difference
3	Japan	70.00	70.00	0.00		(5.571)	(6.143)	0.57
4	Canada	30.00	30.00	0.00		10.667	10.667	0.00
5	Total:	100.00	100.00	0.00		(0.700)	(1.100)	0.40
6								
7							Value Added	
8				Country		Selection		
9				Japan		0.400	=(H3/100)*(C3/100)*100	
10				Canada		0.000	➤=(H4/100)*(C4/100)*100	
11				Total:		0.400	=SUM(F9:F10)	

EXHIBIT 18.4 Asset Allocation Effect

	A	B	C	D	E	F	G	H
1			Weights				Returns	
2	Country	Fund	Benchmark	Difference		Fund	Benchmark	Difference
3	Japan	25.00	30.00	(5.00)		5.000	5.000	0.000
4	France	15.00	20.00	(5.00)		7.000	7.000	0.000
5	Canada	60.00	50.00	10.00		10.000	10.000	0.000
6	Total:	100.00	100.00	0.00		8.300	7.900	0.400
7								
8							Value Added	
9				Country		Selection	Allocation	
10				Japan		0.000	0.145	
11				France		0.000	0.045	
12				Canada		0.000	0.210	
13				Total:		0.000	0.400	
14			=(D5/100)*(G5/100-G6/100)*100					

MEASURING ASSET ALLOCATION DECISIONS

Now, consider the opposite investment strategy: to select countries on the basis of their investment prospects, but allocate assets within the market in proportion to the index. Such a strategy should deliver similar returns to the market for each country, but a higher return than the benchmark as a whole because of the positive contribution due to overweighting attractive countries. We can quantify value added due to this strategy via the *asset allocation effect*, which is the difference between the fund and benchmark segment weights multiplied by the differential segment return.

> Asset allocation effect
> = (Fund segment weight – Benchmark segment weight)   (18.2)
>   × (Benchmark segment return – Benchmark total return)

Exhibit 18.4 illustrates the asset allocation management effect. Here we have a country selection fund, which was overweighted in Canada at the beginning of the period, and Canada outperformed the average country. So we had a positive asset allocation effect in Canada equal to 0.21%, which is the 2.1% difference between the return in Canada and the benchmark total return (10% – 7.9%) weighted by the 10% incremental overweight in Canada (60% – 50%). Given the overweight in Canada we underweighted something else. In this case we underweighted both Japan and France, leading to positive asset allocation effects in both countries. The positive effects are due to the underweight in countries that did worse than the average benchmark return during the period.

INTERACTION BETWEEN THE TWO TYPES OF DECISIONS

What if we were evaluating the performance of a portfolio where the manager has a strategy that consists of a combination of both asset allocation and security selection techniques? Many times investment advisory firms have a multilevel decision-making process for allocating assets *within* the fund. For example, one team makes country weighting and another team makes local market security selection decisions. Here we would expect the successful firm to demonstrate value added via both the security selection and the asset allocation management effects. The calculation of these effects in tandem is straightforward, but by trying to quantify the efforts made by two separate decision making processes we have a problem: the assignment of value added in situations where there is both a gain due to security selection *and* a gain due to asset allocation within a segment. This is because there is an *interaction* between the two management effects.

This problem is analogous to the problem we had calculating currency return in Exhibit 15.12, where we showed how the base currency return to a security was comprised of a local return, currency return, and an interaction effect between the local and currency returns. Here we will see that there is an interaction effect between the asset allocation and security selection effects that cannot be attributed to either decision without having prior knowledge of the manager's strategy.

Consider a portfolio where the manager has added value through both security selection and asset allocation techniques. Exhibit 18.5 shows a global stock fund during a period in which Canada had a higher return than the other two countries. The benchmark return in Canada was 10%, and the weighted average country return was 7.9%.

EXHIBIT 18.5   Interaction Effect

	A	B	C	D	E	F	G	H
1			Weights				Returns	
2	Country	Fund	Benchmark	Difference		Fund	Benchmark	Difference
3	Japan	25.00	30.00	(5.00)		5.000	5.000	0.000
4	France	15.00	20.00	(5.00)		7.000	7.000	0.000
5	Canada	60.00	50.00	10.00		12.000	10.000	2.000
6	Total:	100.00	100.00	10.00		9.500	7.900	1.600
7								
8			=(D5/100)*(H5/100)*100				Value Added	
9					Country	Selection	Allocation	Interaction
10					Japan	0.000	0.145	0.000
11					France	0.000	0.045	0.000
12					Canada	1.000	0.210	0.200
13					Total:	1.000	0.400	0.200

We see that the manager overweighted Canada, which leads to an asset allocation effect on value added equal to 0.210% (60% – 50% = 10% overweight × 10% – 7.9% = 2.1% excess return). The fund also had a higher return in Canada than the benchmark. This is presumably the result of selecting securities with a better return during the period than the average Canadian stock. The security selection effect on value added was 1.00% (50% benchmark weight × 2% differential return). But if we add these effects along with the value added due to underweighting France and Japan, we derive a 1.4% total value added due to security selection and asset allocation decisions. But the value added by the total portfolio was 1.6% (9.5% fund return – 7.9% benchmark return). So we have missed a component of value added.

If we look at the Canada segment, we can see that value added over the benchmark was achieved by allocating assets to an attractive country and by selecting better securities *within* the country. The interaction between these two decisions led to another 0.2% of value added, computed by taking the difference between the returns and multiplying it by the difference between the fund and benchmark weights.

> Interaction effect
> = (Fund segment weight – Benchmark segment weight)   (18.3)
>   × (Fund segment return – Benchmark segment return)

The interaction effect is a cross product between the asset allocation and security selection effects. It can be interpreted as the incremental gain to security selection on top of the gains due to asset allocation. Because it is the product of two differences, it will be small if the weight and return differences are small. If the interaction effect is large, it is because one or both of the return and weighting differences is large. If there are persistent large interaction effects, it is possible that the benchmark is not an appropriate benchmark for the portfolio. Here the 0.2% interaction effect combined with the other effects accounts for the total value added over the benchmark.

Depending on the manager's strategy, we may want to combine the interaction effect with either of the two other effects. For example, if the primary mandate of the fund is the selection of attractive stocks, and not asset classes, industries, or other market segments, it would be appropriate to combine the interaction effect with the stock selection effect. We can modify the calculation of stock selection in Equation (18.1) to automatically include interaction by multiplying the difference in returns by the fund segment weight instead of the benchmark segment weight.

> Security selection effect including interaction
> = (Fund segment return – Benchmark segment return)   (18.4)
>   × Fund weight

EXHIBIT 18.6   Pension Plan Value-Added Analysis

	A	B	C	D	E	F	G
1			Begin Weights			Returns	
2		Fund	Bench	Weight Diff	Fund	Bench	Return Diff
3	Cash	10.00	10.00	0.00	0.35	0.55	-0.20
4	Fixed Income	30.00	40.00	-10.00	-1.00	-1.00	0.00
5	Equity	60.00	50.00	10.00	4.00	3.00	1.00
6	Total	100.00	100.00		2.135	1.155	0.980
7					=SUM(D12:F12)		
8							
9				Selection	Allocation	Interaction	Total
10			Cash	-0.020	0.000	0.000	-0.020
11			Fixed Income	0.000	0.216	0.000	0.216
12			Equity	0.500	0.185	0.100	0.785
13			Total	0.480	0.400	0.100	0.980
14					=SUM(G10:G12)		

EXHIBIT 18.7   Analysis of Attribution Effects

Segment	Effect	Contribution
Equity	Selection	0.500
Fixed Income	Allocation	0.216
Equity	Allocation	0.185
Equity	Interaction	0.100
Cash	Selection	-0.020
Fixed Income	Selection	0.000
Cash	Allocation	0.000
Cash	Interaction	0.000
Fixed Income	Interaction	0.000
	Value Added:	0.980

Analyzing Value Added

A complete single period value-added decomposition analysis is presented in Exhibit 18.6. Given our understanding that this fund is being managed across asset class lines, we have attributed the value added equal to 0.98% to asset class allocation and then stock selection decisions within each asset class.

Notice that we cannot add the effects within a *segment* to back into the return difference by *segment*. At the segment level, the effects are segment level contributions to *total* value added over the benchmark. Notice that the total return difference in cell G6, 0.98% is attributed by the sum of the factors in cell G13. The total value added adds across by factor (0.98 = 0.48 + 0.40 + 0.10) and down by asset class (0.98 = −0.02 + 0.216 + 0.785). Assuming that the portfolio is managed along asset class lines, the result clearly summarizes how the value added was achieved.

We can analyze the results by sorting the effects by the absolute value of the impact, as in Exhibit 18.7. We can see that the biggest contributor to excess return was security selection within the equity segment, followed by the asset allocation underweight to fixed income.

EXHIBIT 18.8   Single Level Attribution

	A	B	C	D	E	F	G	H
1		**Begin Weights**				**Returns**		
2		Fund	Bench	Weight Diff		Fund	Bench	Return Diff
3	Financial	40.00	30.00	10.00		11.00	12.92	-1.92
4	Technology	60.00	70.00	-10.00		-0.67	-1.25	0.58
5	Total	100.00	100.00			4.000	3.000	**1.000**
6								
7						**Value Added**		
8						Allocation	Selection	Total
9				Financial		0.992	-0.767	0.22
10				Technology		0.425	0.350	0.78
11				Total		1.417	-0.417	**1.000**

MULTILEVEL DECOMPOSITION

The decomposition of value added into asset allocation, security selection, and interaction management effects can be done using any appropriate portfolio segmenting scheme. For example, we can analyze performance by asset class, industry, attractiveness rating, market capitalization, and other factors. One drawback to the analysis performed so far is that we are attributing performance one factor at a time. If assets are allocated within the fund using a multilevel security classification hierarchy, we can derive more information by calculating additional asset allocation effects at each level.

Let's begin with a single level example. Exhibit 18.8 shows a single period return decomposition where stocks are classified by economic sectors, and we perform the attribution at this level.

For brevity we show only two sectors and combine the selection and interaction effects into the selection effect. There was 1.00% of value added over the benchmark, earned primarily by the combined effects of underweighting the technology sector (0.425%) and earning a better return on the stocks within the technology sector (0.350%). Now, suppose we know that the manager also looks at individual industries within the economic sectors when making asset allocation decisions. We expand the segments to the industry level in Exhibit 18.9.

We have three industry segments within each economic sector. Taking a top-down view of the performance of the portfolio we find the following:

1. There was value added due to economic sector weighting decisions. The fund is overweight in financial stocks, and financial stocks did better than the benchmark as a whole (12.92% versus 3.00%). The underweight to the technology sector when technology did worse than the average sector also added value (−1.25% versus 3.00%). Column D shows the contributions from the sector decisions. We calculate the

allocation statistic in the same way as in Exhibit 18.4, by comparing the total benchmark return to the economic segment level returns and multiplying the difference by the over or underweights.

2. Value was also added from weighting decisions *within* the economic sectors. For example, we have an underweight to communications stocks when communications stocks did worse than the average technology stocks. Cell E23 shows how we earned 0.138% from this decision. The calculation is the same for the asset allocation effect performed at the sector level, except we modify the formula to replace the total level return with the appropriate sector level return. Here we compare the communications return with the total technology return and weight it by the underweight of communications within the portfolio to find the effect at the total fund level. Notice that when we perform the analysis at only the sector level, the total industry effect, 0.136%, was embedded in the security selection effect. When we perform a multi-level decomposition, we take contributions to return that are attributed to security level decisions and move them up to higher levels of the analysis. We can do this with knowledge of the appropriate hierarchy of decision making used to allocate assets within the fund, in this case economic sectors broken down by industrial segments.

EXHIBIT 18.9   Multi-Level Attribution

	A	B	C	D	E	F	G
1							
2		Begin Weights				Returns	
3		Fund	Bench	Weight Diff	Fund	Bench	Return Diff
4	Financial	**40.00**	**30.00**	**10.00**	11.000	12.917	-1.917
5	Banks	15.00	10.00	5.00	12.000	13.000	-1.000
6	Brokers	15.00	10.00	5.00	15.000	12.750	2.250
7	Insurance	10.00	10.00	0.00	3.500	13.000	-9.500
8	Technology	**60.00**	**70.00**	**-10.00**	-0.667	-1.250	0.583
9	Computers	20.00	25.00	-5.00	-2.000	-1.300	-0.700
10	Communications	15.00	20.00	-5.00	-5.000	-4.000	-1.000
11	Semiconductors	25.00	25.00	0.00	3.000	1.000	2.000
12	Total	**100.00**	**100.00**		4.000	3.000	1.000
13							
14	=(D4/100)*(F4/100-$F$12/100)*100					=SUM(D17:F17)	
15					Value Added		
16				Sector	Industry	Selection	Total
17			Financial	0.9917	-0.0042	-0.7625	0.2250
18			Banks		0.004	-0.150	
19			Brokers		-0.008	0.338	
20			Insurance		0.000	-0.950	
21			Technology	0.4250	0.1400	0.2100	0.7750
22	=D21+D17		Computers		0.003	-0.140	
23			Communications		0.138	-0.150	
24			Semiconductors		0.000	0.500	
25			Total	1.417	0.136	-0.553	1.000
26	=(D10/100)*(F10/100-$F$8/100)*100						
27							
28			=(B11/100)*(G11/100)*100				

EXHIBIT 18.10   Multiple Single Period Value-Added Decomposition Results

	A	B	C	D	E	F	G	H	I	J	K	L
1	Month 1	Begin Weights				Returns				Value Added		
2		Fund	Bench	Diff.		Fund	Bench	Diff.		Sel.	Alloc.	Total
3	Cash	10.00	10.00	0.00		0.35	0.55	-0.20		-0.020	0.000	-0.020
4	Fixed Income	30.00	40.00	-10.00		-1.00	-1.00	0.00		0.000	0.216	0.216
5	Equity	60.00	50.00	10.00		4.00	3.00	1.00		0.600	0.185	0.785
6	Total	100.00	100.00			2.135	1.155	**0.980**		0.580	0.400	**0.980**
7												
8	Month 2	Begin Weights				Returns				Value Added		
9		Fund	Bench	Diff.		Fund	Bench	Diff.		Sel.	Alloc.	Total
10	Cash	9.82	10.00	-0.18		0.35	0.55	-0.20		-0.020	0.001	-0.019
11	Fixed Income	29.08	40.00	-10.92		-1.00	-1.00	0.00		0.000	0.235	0.235
12	Equity	61.10	50.00	11.10		4.00	3.00	1.00		0.611	0.205	0.816
13	Total	100.00	100.00			2.188	1.155	**1.033**		0.591	0.441	**1.033**
14												
15	Month 3	Begin Weights				Returns				Value Added		
16		Fund	Bench	Diff.		Fund	Bench	Diff.		Sel.	Alloc.	Total
17	Cash	9.65	10.00	-0.35		0.35	0.55	-0.20		-0.019	0.002	-0.017
18	Fixed Income	28.17	40.00	-11.83		-1.00	-1.00	0.00		0.000	0.255	0.255
19	Equity	62.18	50.00	12.18		4.00	3.00	1.00		0.622	0.225	0.847
20	Total	100.00	100.00			2.239	1.155	**1.084**		0.603	0.482	**1.084**

3. After considering the industries, we calculate the security selection effect as the difference between the industry level returns weighted by the industry weight within the portfolio. In our case, security selection decisions led to a detraction of 0.553% from the total value added.

MULTIPERIOD VALUE-ADDED DECOMPOSITION

The examples in the previous sections allow us to derive the value added over the benchmark for a single valuation period. To extend the analysis over multiple periods, we need to take into account the fact that the beginning of period weights change with each new valuation period, unless the fund is continually rebalanced.

Suppose that we want to analyze value added over a quarter where the fund is valued at each month end. Exhibit 18.10 shows the result of decomposing the returns for each monthly period. We have assumed that we earned the same asset class returns each period, and that the fund was not rebalanced, i.e., the fund asset class weightings were allowed to drift with the returns. In this case, the change in total fund performance from month to month is entirely due to the reinvestment into the next period of the gains earned in the prior period.

Notice that the value added for each single monthly period is fully accounted for by the attribution effects. Quarterly returns for the fund and benchmark are shown in Exhibit 18.11. The segment and total returns are calculated by compounding the monthly segment and total returns. After compounding the returns and taking the difference, we determine that the quarterly total value added over the benchmark equals 3.201% (6.706% − 3.505%).

We are interested in attributing the quarterly value added to the various management effects. Unfortunately, we cannot add the single period attribution factors to derive the quarterly attribution factors. The reason for this is the same reason we cannot add the three monthly returns to derive the quarterly return. We multiply returns in order to account for the reinvestment of gains earned in prior periods. Our first instinct might be to adjust for this problem by performing the analysis using the beginning of the quarter weights and the quarterly returns. Exhibit 18.12 shows the results generated using this method.

The total of the management effects does not reconcile the value added over the benchmark. The reason they do not is that by using only the beginning of quarter weights, we are not accounting for the fact that the asset class weights have changed over the period.

One way to perform a multiperiod analysis is to scale the management effects to account for the compounding over multiple periods. We start by observing that our sample fund has a return higher than the benchmark return, or positive value added, in each of the three monthly periods. We calculate the total value added in the first month as the fund return less the benchmark return

EXHIBIT 18.11   Quarterly Returns and Value Added

		Returns	
Months 1-3	Fund	Bench	Return Diff
Cash	1.05	1.66	-0.61
Fixed Income	-2.97	-2.97	0.00
Equity	12.49	9.27	3.21
Total	6.706	3.505	**3.201**

EXHIBIT 18.12   Quarterly Value-Added Decomposition Using Begin of Quarter Weights

Month 1 Begin Weights			Quarterly Returns			Value Added		
Fund	Bench	Diff.	Fund	Bench	Diff.	Sel.	Alloc.	Total
10.00	10.00	0.00	1.05	1.66	-0.61	-0.061	0.000	-0.061
30.00	40.00	-10.00	-2.97	-2.97	0.00	0.000	0.648	0.648
60.00	50.00	10.00	12.49	9.27	3.21	1.928	0.577	2.505
100.00	100.00		6.706	3.505	**3.201**	1.868	1.224	**3.092**

$$VA_1 = FTR_1 - BTR_1 \tag{18.5}$$

where VA = Value added, FTR = Fund total return, BTR = Benchmark total return, and the subscripts symbolize the monthly period. In terms of our example, Month 1 value added equals 0.98%. (2.135% – 1.155%). Value added for any single period is calculated in this way:

$$\begin{aligned}
VA_1 &= FTR_1 - BTR_1 \\
VA_2 &= FTR_2 - BTR_2 \\
VA_3 &= FTR_3 - BTR_3
\end{aligned} \tag{18.6}$$

To calculate quarterly fund and benchmark returns, we compound the single period fund and benchmark returns.

$$\begin{aligned}
FTR_{1\text{-}3} &= [(1 + FTR_1) \times (1 + FTR_2) \times (1 + FTR_3)] - 1 \\
BTR_{1\text{-}3} &= [(1 + BTR_1) \times (1 + BTR_2) \times (1 + BTR_3)] - 1
\end{aligned} \tag{18.7}$$

So value added over the quarter is impacted via the process of compounding.

$$\begin{aligned}
VA_{1\text{-}3} &= [(1 + FTR_1) \times (1 + FTR_2) \times (1 + FTR_3)] \\
&\quad - [(1 + BTR_1) \times (1 + BTR_2) \times (1 + BTR_3)]
\end{aligned} \tag{18.8}$$

Or multiperiod value added equals the difference between the compound fund returns and compound benchmark returns—in our case, we earned a value added of 3.201% for the quarter (6.706% – 3.505%). Because of the compounding effects, Equation (18.6) breaks down when we are using returns calculated over multiple periods.

$$VA_{1\text{-}3} \neq VA_1 + VA_2 + VA_3 \tag{18.9}$$

The value added equal to 3.201% is greater than the sum of the single period value added figures (3.097% > 0.98% + 1.031% + 1.084%) because of the reinvestment of the value added from previous periods in subsequent periods.

We can account for multiperiod value added by compounding the management effects. The value added over two periods includes both the value added in periods 1 and period 2. But it also includes the effect of taking the period 1 value added and reinvesting it, plus the period 1 fund return invested in the value added for period 2, or

$$VA_{1\text{-}2} = [VA_1 \times (1 + BTR_2)] + [VA_2 \times (1 + FTR_1)] \tag{18.10}$$

Single period value added is compounded into a multiperiod value added by scaling value added by two compounding factors:

1. Periodic value added is invested at the benchmark return for subsequent periods; and
2. Periodic value added is scaled up by the fund returns in prior periods.

We use the benchmark return for subsequent periods because subsequent period fund returns include the subsequent period value added, and we use the fund return for prior periods because it is invested into the value added for subsequent periods. We extend the analysis over three periods by:

$$
\begin{aligned}
VA_{1\text{-}3} = {} & [VA_1 \times (1 + BTR_2) \times (1 + BTR_3)] \\
& + [(1 + FTR_1) \times VA_2 \times (1 + BTR_3)] \\
& + [(1 + FTR_1) \times (1 + FTR_2) \times VA_3]
\end{aligned}
\qquad (18.11)
$$

Notice that the value added in the second period is scaled by both the period 1 fund return and the period 3 benchmark return. We add the scaled single period effects to derive the multiperiod value added.

Exhibit 18.13 summarizes the three monthly periods to show the value added over a quarter. This approach to multiperiod value added decomposition is a commonly used approach. But there is more than one way to extend the single period analysis to multiple periods.[2] Notice that we have been attributing the arithmetic value added to the various management effects. That is, it is the difference between the fund and index return that we have decomposed into the various effects. Another approach would instead be to decompose the geometric difference between the fund and benchmark returns. This is usually called *geometric attribution*. The geometric value added is the ratio between the fund and index growth rates. The geometric approach to value added decomposition provides some advantages in that it implicitly accounts for the growth in value added over multiple periods, but it is generally considered more difficult to communicate and interpret.[3]

---

[2] For additional methods of extending the single period attribution to multiple periods see David Carino, "Combining Attribution Effects over Time," *Journal of Performance Measurement* (Summer 1999) and Andre Mirabelli, "The Structure and Visualization of Performance Attribution," *Journal of Performance Measurement* (Winter 2000/2001).

[3] For more on geometric attribution see J. Stephen Burnie, James Knowles, and Toomas Teder, "Arithmetic and Geometric Attribution," *Journal of Performance Measurement* (Fall 1998).

EXHIBIT 18.13   Multiperiod Value-Added Decomposition

	F	G	H	I	J	K	L	M	N	O
1	M1 Returns			Value Added				Contrib. To Quarterly		
2	Fund	Bench	Diff.	Sel.	Alloc.	Total		Sel.	Alloc.	Total
3	0.35	0.55	-0.20	-0.020	0.000	-0.020		-0.020	0.000	-0.020
4	-1.00	-1.00	0.00	0.000	0.216	0.216		0.000	0.221	0.221
5	4.00	3.00	1.00	0.600	0.185	0.785		0.614	0.189	0.803
6	2.135	1.155	**0.980**	0.580	0.400	**0.980**		0.593	0.409	**1.003**
7	=I5 * (1+$G$13/100) * (1+$G$20/100)									
8	M2 Returns			Value Added				Contrib. To Quarterly		
9	Fund	Bench	Diff.	Sel.	Alloc.	Total		Sel.	Alloc.	Total
10	0.35	0.55	-0.20	-0.020	0.001	-0.019		-0.020	0.001	-0.019
11	-1.00	-1.00	0.00	0.000	0.235	0.235		0.000	0.243	0.243
12	4.00	3.00	1.00	0.611	0.205	0.816		0.631	0.211	0.843
13	2.187	1.155	**1.032**	0.591	0.441	**1.032**		0.611	0.456	**1.067**
14	=I12 * (1+$F$6/100) * (1+$G$20/100)									
15	M3 Returns			Value Added				Contrib. To Quarterly		
16	Fund	Bench	Diff.	Sel.	Alloc.	Total		Sel.	Alloc.	Total
17	0.35	0.55	-0.20	-0.019	0.002	-0.017		-0.020	0.002	-0.018
18	-1.00	-1.00	0.00	0.000	0.255	0.255		0.000	0.266	0.266
19	4.00	3.00	1.00	0.622	0.225	0.847		0.649	0.235	0.883
20	2.239	1.155	**1.084**	0.602	0.482	**1.084**		0.629	0.503	**1.132**
21	=I19 * (1+$F$6/100) * (1+$F$13/100)									
22										
23				Returns				Quarterly Value Added		
24		Months 1-3	Fund	Bench	Diff.			Sel.	Alloc.	Total
25		Cash	1.05	1.66	-0.61			-0.06	0.00	-0.058
26		Fixed Income	-2.97	-2.97	0.00			0.00	0.73	0.730
27		Equity	12.49	9.27	3.21			1.89	0.63	2.529
28		Total	6.706	3.505	**3.201**			1.833	1.368	**3.201**
29			=M5+M12+M19							

VALUE-ADDED DECOMPOSITION CONSIDERATIONS

Value-added decomposition can be used to partition the value added into various management effects for many, but not all, investment situations. There are several considerations to keep in mind when using this technique:

- Selection of the appropriate benchmark.
- Data input requirements.
- Single factor attribution.
- Accounting for additional management factors.

Benchmark Selection

We saw in Part II of the book that the value added over the benchmark is only one aspect of performance evaluation. We also consider the relative risk taken to achieve the value added over the benchmark. An important caveat to value-added decomposition approaches is that we have implicitly assumed that the level of risk inherent in the benchmark is approximately the same as that in the portfolio.

The interpretation of the various management effects depends on the selection of an appropriate benchmark for analyzing the manager's strategy. If the fund is a small company stock fund, and the attribution is performed against the S&P 500, then the results will be meaningless. Style is also important. If the manager is a value manager, then the appropriate benchmark would be a *value-style benchmark,* whose constituents more closely match the universe of stocks that the manager selects from than a more broad-based benchmark. There may not be an appropriate market index for every investment strategy; therefore many times we create a custom benchmark for performance attribution purposes.

Inputs to the Analysis

To perform the attribution analysis, we had to first calculate the security and segment level returns for the portfolio and the benchmark. One implicit assumption here is that we had access to information about the positions held by the fund during the period. Many times we are interested in evaluating the performance of a manager, and we do not have access to the actual positions that the manager held during the period. One example of this is where a pension consultant or other third party is charged with analyzing a portfolio, or where an investment advisory firm is interested in reverse engineering the performance of a portfolio managed by a rival firm. When we cannot access the portfolio holdings, we cannot use value added decomposition techniques to analyze management decisions. But there are additional tools available for analyzing performance in these situations.

Style Analysis is a technique used to discover the management style of a portfolio, using an analysis of the fund's *historical returns.* The results of a style analysis are a list of market indices that best represent the historical performance of a portfolio, weighted by their implied influence on the funds return. Style analysis was developed by William Sharpe[4] and has become a popular methodology with several applications for analyzing portfolios. Enhancements have been made to the basic methodology for the purpose of performance attribution. Attribution using style analysis is sometimes used to isolate the effects of the manager's security selection ability from results attributed to the fund's investment style over the period. Style analysis has the advantage that

---

[4] See William Sharpe, "Determining a Fund's Effective Asset Mix," *Investment Management Review* (November/December 1998).

we do not need to know the actual holdings of the portfolio; we instead infer the asset weightings within the portfolio by reference to the fund's covariation with a set of indices. This is one of the advantages of style analysis, as compared to other attribution techniques, and makes it particularly useful for analyzing the results of competing money managers. Given that we want to perform an attribution analysis using the manager's long-term investment style, we can also use style analysis to determine the appropriate benchmark for a portfolio.

Multifactor Attribution

One problem with the value-added decomposition is that the analysis is performed one *factor* at a time. In other words we can perform the analysis by country or by sector or by P/E range, but for each analysis we will get a separate set of management effects that cannot be combined together. One way to deal with this problem is to perform a separate attribution analysis for each effect, and rank the results according to their contribution to return. For example, we can perform the single level analysis by country and also by P/E range, rank the results, and see that, for example, asset allocation to Canada and security selection within value stocks contributed more to value added than other effects.

Another approach is to decompose the return of *each security* into multiple factors and then aggregate the results to the portfolio level. A *multifactor model* is a statistical model of security behavior within a particular market. The model decomposes individual security returns into a set of factor exposures. The multifactor model is a regression equation that describes the way a particular security reacts to industry sector, stock fundamental, macroeconomic, and market influences. For example, an equity multifactor model captures the sources of equity returns by factors including interest rates, industry, market cap, P/B ratio, P/E ratio, price volatility, and the like. The multifactor model is an equation like Equation (18.12), where the Beta coefficients are the sensitivities of the security returns to the factors.

$$R_i = B_1 F_1 + B_2 F_2 + ... B_N F_N \qquad (18.12)$$

Where R_i is the expected return to the security, B_i are the factor Betas, and F_i are the factors that have effects on the return of the security, and the combination of Beta's best explains the security returns over a period of time. The security's responsiveness to a change in the Beta factor is its *factor exposure*. The factor exposures and the factors used in the model change over time. There are multifactor models for particular asset classes and markets. The factor exposures are derived from a historical analysis of the covariance of proxies for the individual factors and the security returns. The security level factor exposures are then summed to determine the portfolio and benchmark relative returns to the factor. This method of attribution is sometimes called *return attribution* in order to differentiate it from the performance attribution techniques based on observing the portfolio's actual weightings and returns over the period.

Accounting for Additional Factors

Finally, there are additional considerations in the management of many investment portfolios that are not captured by the basic return decomposition approach. Extensions of the basic value-added decomposition methodology to cover the particulars of multicurrency and fixed income investing is the subject of the next chapter.

CHAPTER 19

Strategy-Specific Return Decomposition

The value-added decomposition approach to performance attribution presented in the previous chapter was originally developed to analyze the sources of return to pension plans investing in multiple asset classes, but has been proven useful in the analysis of relative return in many other investment situations. The allocation, selection, and interaction effects best relate to actual management decisions when the investment process proceeds along the lines of a top-down segment allocation and bottom-up selection of individual securities within segments, where the segments represent the appropriate asset allocation factors for the strategy. The information value of these component effects diminishes when there are factors important to the management of the portfolio that are not captured in the analysis. For example, currency exposures are an important consideration in the management of portfolios holding foreign securities. But the general framework has proved so useful for performance analysis that practitioners have extended the basic methodology to capture additional factors important in the management of funds investing in particular asset classes. In this section we consider the extension of value-added decomposition techniques to the analysis of funds investing in foreign and fixed income securities. The manner in which we extend the methodology is similar in both cases, so the approach informs the route to follow for further extending the analysis to the needs of other situations.

EXHIBIT 19.1   Base Currency Value-Added Decomposition

	A	B	C	D	E	F	G	H	I	J	K	L
		Begin Base Weights				Base Returns				Value Added		
1		Fund	Bench	Diff.		Fund	Bench	Diff.		Selection	Allocation	Total
2												
3	United States	20.00	20.00	0.00		3.250	3.000	0.250		0.050	0.000	0.050
4	France	35.00	40.00	-5.00		-3.818	-3.818	0.000		0.000	0.290	0.290
5	Japan	45.00	40.00	5.00		7.263	7.263	0.000		0.000	0.264	0.264
6	Total	100.00	100.00			2.582	1.978	**0.604**		0.050	0.554	**0.604**

DECOMPOSING THE VALUE ADDED BY MULTICURRENCY PORTFOLIOS

Suppose that we are analyzing the performance of the portfolio in Exhibit 19.1. The fund is a global equity portfolio, where the primary strategies are to overweight attractive countries and to also select superior stocks within each market. Using the return decomposition approach from Chapter 18 we can see that:

■ The manager produced 0.604% of value added over the benchmark during the period.
■ 0.05% of the value added was attributable to selecting stocks within the United States that outperformed the average U.S. stock (here the interaction effect is combined with the selection effect).
■ Most of the value added, however, was attributable to asset allocation. Specifically, the underweight to France when France performed worse than the average country, and the overweight in Japan, which performed better than average, added 0.554% of return over the benchmark.

This analysis provides some valuable information as to the sources of value added. But, given that the fund holds assets denominated in multiple currencies, we might have some additional questions:

■ What portion of the value added was attributable to the fluctuation in the value of the foreign currency over the period? In other words, how much of the asset allocation gain was due to investing in *currencies* that outperformed rather than markets within *countries* that outperformed?
■ Assuming that currency was an important factor in the management of the portfolio, how much of the value added due to currency fluctuation can be credited to the actions of the manager?

■ Did the manager hedge any of the currency exposures accompanying the investment in foreign countries? Did the hedging activity impact the value added achieved?

These questions are specific to the management of portfolios invested in markets whose securities are traded in currencies different than the investor's home, or *base* currency. Because the exchange rate between two currencies fluctuates over time, currency translation is an important factor in the management of multicurrency portfolios. One way to think about a multicurrency portfolio is that it is really *two* portfolios, a portfolio of assets and a portfolio of currencies. This is a useful framework because the manager cannot achieve the local currency return when he invests overseas, as measured in the investor's base currency. He can either achieve the local currency return adjusted by currency translation gains and losses or the local currency return, with some of the currency gains and losses eliminated by the effects of hedging activity.

Analysts have developed several frameworks that extend the generic value-added decomposition methodology to help answer questions specific to the analysis of value added by multicurrency portfolios. In this section we summarize a popular multicurrency value-added decomposition methodology, which is credited to Ernest Ankrim and Chris Hensel.[1] This methodology helps in the analysis of multicurrency performance by adding several new effects to the generic model:

■ A Currency Effect, which serves to isolate the local market selection and allocation effects from the currency translation effects.
■ An anticipated component of currency return called the Forward Premium, and an unanticipated element called Currency Surprise.
■ An effect representing the influence on value added of any currency Hedging Activity during the period.

We take each effect in turn.

---

[1] Ernest Ankrim and Chris Hensel, "Multicurrency Performance Attribution," *Financial Analysts Journal* (March/April 1994). For additional approaches see Gregory Allen, "Performance Attribution for Global Equity Portfolios," *Journal of Portfolio Management* (Fall 1991); and Brian Singer and Denis Karnofsky, "The General Framework for Global Investment Management and Performance Attribution," *Journal of Portfolio Management* (Winter 1995).

EXHIBIT 19.2 Currency Returns

	A	B	C	D
8		Spot Exchange Rates		
9		Begin	End	Return
10	U.S. Dollar	1.00	1.00	0.000
11	Euro	0.87840	0.88000	0.182
12	Yen	0.00760	0.00800	5.263
13		=((C12-B12)/B12)*100		

CURRENCY EFFECT

The first step in extending the value-added decomposition methodology to multicurrency portfolios is to isolate the effects of exchange rate gains and losses from the local market selection and allocation effects. We do this to get an understanding of the pure impact of allocating assets amongst markets and then selection of assets within each market. To isolate local market effects we calculate local, base, and currency returns for each fund and benchmark segment. In our example, we break down performance using country segments, but the analysis can be performed using any segment structure, such as industry sectors. The portfolio from Exhibit 19.1 is invested in securities trading in three countries, each of whose securities trade in a different currency. The United States securities trade in the dollar, French securities the euro, and Japanese securities the yen. Assuming the fund's base currency is the U.S. dollar, the fund is exposed to U.S. dollar to euro (USD/EUR) and U.S. dollar to yen (USD/YEN) exchange rate fluctuations. So the United States country segment returns will be the same in both local and base currency, but the France and Japan local and base returns will differ if there was any fluctuation in exchange rates during the period. Exhibit 19.2 shows the beginning and end of period spot exchange rates from the U.S. dollar to these currencies and the resulting currency returns over the period.

We measure the currency return using the change in the spot exchange rates over the period. The *spot exchange rate* is the current quoted exchange rate for near term delivery of the currency. Here we have quoted the exchange rates in dollars per unit of foreign currency. So at the beginning of the period it cost 0.8784 dollars to buy one euro and at the end of the period 0.88 dollars to buy one euro. Given that it took more dollars to buy the same amount of foreign currency, we can see that the dollar fell against both euro and yen over the period. This change in the relative value of currencies led to a gain to a portfolio from holding assets denominated in euro or yen, as viewed by an investor with a U.S. dollar base. For example, the USD/YEN exchange rate rose from 0.0076 USD per yen to 0.0080 USD per yen. If we had a holding worth 100,000 yen at the beginning of the period, its value in dollar terms rose from 760 USD to 800 USD (100,000 × 0.0080). While the base currency returns in Exhibit 19.1 were calculated taking into account any transactions during the period and the current exchange rate at the time of these transactions, the beginning and ending exchange rates give us an indication as to the impact of currency fluctuations on fund returns over the period. If the fund did not trade over the period, the difference between the local and base fund returns would equal the return calculated by referencing the beginning and ending exchange rates. Exhibit 19.3 shows the local and base currency returns for the fund and the benchmark over the period. Measured in the fund's base currency, the positive exchange rate returns served to decrease the local currency loss in France and increase the local currency gains in Japan.

By replacing the base returns with local returns and recalculating the management effects, we can isolate the exchange rate effects on return from the local market selection and allocation effects. Exhibit 19.4 shows the decomposition of the local market returns.

The total security selection effect measured in local currency is the same as when calculated in base currency in Exhibit 19.1, because the value added due to security selection was in the United States segment, and the U.S. segment had no currency return. But notice that the total allocation effect is now 0.30% rather than the 0.554% as when measured in base currency. So the pure market impact of the decision to overweight Japan and underweight France is 0.30%. The difference between the local and base allocation effects is attributable to currency translation gains. The difference between the effects calculated in local currency and the total base currency value added is the currency effect for the period. The *currency effect* is the portion of value added due to investing the portfolio in a mix of assets with a net currency exposure different than that of the currency exposure implied by the benchmark.

EXHIBIT 19.3   Local and Base Currency Returns

	A	B	C	D	E	F	G	H	I	J	K	L
1		Begin Base Weights				Local Returns				Base Returns		
2		Fund	Bench	Diff.		Fund	Bench	Diff.		Fund	Bench	Diff.
3	United States	20.00	20.00	0.00		3.250	3.000	0.250		3.250	3.000	0.250
4	France	35.00	40.00	-5.00		-4.000	-4.000	0.000		-3.818	-3.818	0.000
5	Japan	45.00	40.00	5.00		2.000	2.000	0.000		7.263	7.263	0.000
6	Total	100.00	100.00			0.150	-0.200	0.350		2.582	1.978	0.604

EXHIBIT 19.4   Local Currency Value-Added Decomposition

	A	B	C	D	E	F	G	H	I	J	K	L
1		Begin Base Weights				Local Returns				Value Added		
2		Fund	Bench	Diff.		Fund	Bench	Diff.		Selection	Allocation	Diff.
3	United States	20.00	20.00	0.00		3.250	3.000	0.250		0.050	0.000	0.050
4	France	35.00	40.00	-5.00		-4.000	-4.000	0.000		0.000	0.190	0.190
5	Japan	45.00	40.00	5.00		2.000	2.000	0.000		0.000	0.110	0.110
6	Total	100.00	100.00			0.150	-0.200	0.350		0.050	0.300	0.350

EXHIBIT 19.5   Multicurrency Value-Added Decomposition with Currency Effect

	A	B	C	D	E	F	G	H	I	J	K	L	M
1		Begin Base Weights				Base Returns				Value Added			
2		Fund	Bench	Diff.		Fund	Bench	Diff.		Sel.	Alloc.	Curr.	Total
3	United States	20.00	20.00	0.00		3.250	3.000	0.250		0.050	0.000	0.000	0.050
4	France	35.00	40.00	-5.00		-3.818	-3.818	0.000		0.000	0.190	0.100	0.290
5	Japan	45.00	40.00	5.00		7.263	7.263	0.000		0.000	0.110	0.154	0.264
6	Total	100.00	100.00			2.582	1.978	**0.604**		0.050	0.300	0.254	**0.604**
7						=(D5/100)*((D12/100)-(J13/100))*100							
8		Spot Exchange Rates				Local Returns				Bench. Curr. Contribution			
9		Begin	End	Return		Fund	Bench	Diff.		Return			
10	U.S. Dollar	1.00	1.00	0.000		3.250	3.000	0.250		0.000			
11	Euro	0.87840	0.88000	0.182		-4.000	-4.000	0.000		0.073	=SUM(J10:J12)		
12	Yen	0.00760	0.00800	5.263		2.000	2.000	0.000		2.105			
13	Total					0.150	-0.200	0.350		2.178			
14						=(C5/100) * (D12/100) * 100							

Local Selection:	0.050
Local Allocation:	0.300
Currency Effect:	0.254
Value Added:	**0.604**

We can expand the analysis by calculating a currency effect for each country segment. Segment level currency effects are derived by comparing the benchmark segment currency return to the total average benchmark currency return, and then weighting the difference by the fund segment over- or underweight at the beginning of the period.

Currency effect
$$= \text{(Fund segment weight − Benchmark segment weight)}$$
$$\times \text{(Benchmark segment currency return}$$
$$- \text{Benchmark total currency return)} \tag{19.1}$$

Exhibit 19.5 shows the decomposition of base currency value added into local selection, local allocation, and currency effects.

Because both the euro and the yen appreciated against the dollar, an overweight in foreign currency-denominated assets would have produced a positive total currency effect for the period. The magnitude of the effects is dependent on the size of the weighting difference and the currency return to each segment for the period. In our example, most of the currency effect is due to the foreign currency exposure associated with the overweight to the Japanese market during the period.

CURRENCY MANAGEMENT EFFECT

Assuming that the manager intentionally overweighted Japan in anticipation of superior performance, we can attribute 30 basis points of value added during the period (0.19% from underweighting France and 0.11% from overweighting Japan) to the asset allocation decision. But how do we interpret the 0.254% currency effect? One way to interpret the currency effect is similar to that of the allocation effect, where we credit the manager with a gain due to allocating assets to markets that outperformed during the period. One problem with this interpretation, however, is that currency returns actually have two components: an expected return given the difference in interest rates at the beginning of the period, as well as an unexpected return. In this section we discuss a method to isolate the expected from the unexpected return in order to credit the manager only with the return that could not have been anticipated at the beginning of the period.

The reason for a component of currency return that can be anticipated at the beginning of the period is that currency returns are influenced by the difference between interest rates in the two markets on either side of the exchange rate. The difference in interest rates prevailing within two countries is called the *interest rate differential*. For example, if interest rates in Japan were higher than interest rates in the United States at the beginning of the period, we would expect that the Japanese yen would depreciate versus the dollar during the period. Over time we expect high interest rate currencies to depreciate relative to low interest rate currencies. This must be so in order to eliminate an arbitrage opportunity whereby, for example, investors could earn a risk-free return by borrowing at the risk-free rate in the United States during the period, exchange dollars for yen, and then invest in Japanese risk-free investments during the period. To eliminate the arbitrage opportunity, holding all other influences on exchange rates constant, the value of the yen will fall during the period, as measured in U.S. dollars, in an amount required to offset the interest rate differential.

Because of the relationship between interest rate differentials and expected currency returns, a portion of the currency effect might have been expected at the beginning of the period, given the funds over- or underweight in a particular currency relative to the benchmark. We could take the position that we should not credit the manager with the portion of the currency effect that is due to the anticipated return, and instead only credit the manager with the portion of the currency return not already priced into the market at the beginning of the period. We can observe the priced-in return effect by observing the difference between the spot and forward rates at the beginning of the period. In fact, we can lock in the anticipated component of currency return at the beginning of the period by entering into forward contracts to hedge the forward currency exposures.

EXHIBIT 19.6   Forward Premium and Currency Surprise

	A	B	C	D
8			Spot Exchange Rates	
9		Begin	End	Return
10	U.S. Dollar	1.00	1.00	0.000
11	Euro	0.87840	0.88000	0.182
12	Yen	0.00760	0.00800	5.263
13		=((C12-B12)/B12)*100		
14				
15			Forward Exchange Rates	
16		Begin	Premium	Surprise
17	U.S. Dollar	1.00	0.000	0.000
18	Euro	0.88000	0.182	0.000
19	Yen	0.00760	0.000	5.263
20	=((B19-B12)/B12)*100			
21		=((C12-B19)/B12)*100		

Forward Premium and Currency Surprise

To segregate the known differential interest rate effect from the active management effects, we need a way of backing out from the currency return the anticipated exchange rate change over the period. We can separate the effects by observing the forward premium embedded in forward contract exchange rates. The *forward premium* is the beginning of period percentage difference between the forward exchange rate and the spot exchange rate, where the forward rate is the market exchange rate for currency contracts with a delivery date at the end of the period.

$$\text{Forward premium} = \frac{\text{Beginning forward exchange rate} - \text{Beginning spot exchange rate}}{\text{Beginning spot exchange rate}} \quad (19.2)$$

After removing the beginning of period forward premium from the currency return over the period, we are left with the currency return in excess of the forward premium. We can call this component of currency return the *currency surprise*. The currency surprise is equal to the difference between the ending spot exchange rate and the beginning forward exchange rate, divided by the beginning spot rate.

$$\text{Currency surprise} = \frac{\text{Ending spot exchange rate} - \text{Beginning forward exchange rate}}{\text{Beginning spot exchange rate}} \quad (19.3)$$

Exhibit 19.6 shows the calculation of the forward premium and currency surprise for each currency that our example fund is exposed to. We can see that the there was no surprise component to the USD/EUR return and that the change in the USD/YEN exchange rate was unanticipated at the beginning of the period. When the interest rates are similar in the two countries on either side of the exchange rate, the forward premium will be small and any currency return will be unexpected.[2]

Decomposing the Currency Effect

We can modify the value-added decomposition to isolate the impact of the forward premium and currency surprise. Because both the fund and benchmark have currency exposure, the impact on value added comes from only the differences in the currency weights between the two entities. To isolate the impacts we first calculate a total benchmark currency premium and benchmark currency surprise return, and then weight the difference between the country segment level and total level effects by the fund over- or underweights. In Cells K10 to K13 in Exhibit 19.7, we calculate the contributions to the benchmark currency premium. Taking the euro forward premium of 0.182% and weighting it by the benchmark weight in France, 40% yields the country segment premium contribution to the total benchmark currency premium, 0.073%. In the same way, we calculate the benchmark currency surprise in Column L.

EXHIBIT 19.7 Value-Added Decomposition Isolating the Currency Management Effect

	A	B	C	D	E	F	G	H	I	J	K	L
1		Begin Base Weights				Base Returns						
2		Fund	Bench	Diff.		Fund	Bench	Diff.				
3	United States	20.00	20.00	0.00		3.250	3.000	0.250				
4	France	35.00	40.00	-5.00		-3.818	-3.818	0.000				
5	Japan	45.00	40.00	5.00		7.263	7.263	0.000				
6	Total	100.00	100.00			2.582	1.978	**0.604**				
7						=(C4/100)*(C18/100)*100						
8		Spot Exchange Rates				Local Returns				Bench. Curr. Contribution		
9		Begin	End	Return		Fund	Bench	Diff.		Return	Premium	Surprise
10	U.S. Dollar	1.00	1.00	0.000		3.250	3.000	0.250		0.000	0.000	0.000
11	Euro	0.87840	0.88000	0.182		-4.000	-4.000	0.000		0.073	0.073	0.000
12	Yen	0.00760	0.00800	5.263		2.000	2.000	0.000		2.105	0.000	2.105
13	Total					0.150	-0.200	0.350		2.178	0.073	2.105
14										=(C5/100)*(D19/100)*100		
15		Forward Exchange Rates								Value Added		
16		Begin	Premium	Surprise			Local			Currency		
17	U.S. Dollar	1.00	0.000	0.000		United States	Sel.	Alloc.		Premium	Management	Total
18	Euro	0.88000	0.182	0.000		France	0.050	0.000		0.000	0.000	0.050
19	Yen	0.00760	0.000	5.263		Japan	0.000	0.190		-0.005	0.105	0.290
20						Total	0.000	0.110		-0.004	0.158	0.264
21							0.050	0.300		-0.009	0.263	**0.604**
22				=(D5/100)*((C19/100)-(K13/100))*100								
23				=(D5/100)*((D19/100)-(L13/100))*100								

---

[2] For more on exchange rate relationships, see Mark Kritzman and Roger Clarke, *Currency Management: Concepts and Practices* (Charlottesville, VA: The Research Foundation of the Institute of Chartered Financial Analysts, Virginia, 1996).

Given the total level benchmark premium and surprise, we can decompose the value added due to currency effects. The *forward premium effect* is equal to the over- or underweight in the segment multiplied by the difference between the benchmark segment forward premium and the benchmark total forward premium.

Forward premium effect
= (Fund segment weight − Benchmark segment weight)
  × (Benchmark segment forward premium
  − Benchmark total forward premium)   (19.4)

The currency surprise is the portion of currency return unanticipated by interest rate differentials at the beginning of the period. The portion of value added to this effect is called the *currency management effect*, which is the currency surprise weighted by the amount of over- or underweight to the segment at the beginning of the period.

Currency management effect
= (Fund segment weight − Benchmark segment weight)
  × (Benchmark segment currency surprise
  − Benchmark total currency surprise)   (19.5)

Cells J18 to K20 in Exhibit 19.7 show the calculation of the forward premium and currency management effects during the period. We can see that most of the currency effect is due to currency management. The currency management added value was due to the decision to underweight assets denominated in euro, which had no currency surprise during the period and overweight yen based assets, where there was a positive currency surprise.

HEDGING ACTIVITY

The currency management effect shows the impact on return of allocating assets by considering the attractiveness of both the underlying local market and the currency in which these assets are denominated. So far we have assumed that the currency allocation to a country was equal to the market asset allocation. But we can also alter the currency exposure of the portfolio by hedging the currency exposures that accompany the investments overseas. For example, if we expected the Japanese local market to be attractive over the next period but did not want to be exposed to the risk of exchange rate fluctuations, we could hedge away the Japanese yen exposure during the period. Many investors modify currency exposures via hedging as either a risk control tool or active management strategy. Currency hedging can be accomplished in several ways: forward contracts, currency futures, options, and swap contracts, with currency forwards being the most commonly used. Currency exposure changes via forward contracts and other instruments create two sets of portfolio and benchmark weights at the beginning of the period: asset weights and currency weights.

Suppose that we altered the currency exposure of our example portfolio by hedging all of our yen exposure by selling yen forward for dollars at the beginning of the period, but that the benchmark remains fully exposed to currency in proportion to the market asset weights. Exhibit 19.8 shows how we derive the currency weights at the beginning of the period from the asset weights and hedging exposures.

Hedging has the impact of eliminating the currency surprise over the period. If we hedge away the currency surprise, the currency return will equal the forward premium during the period. We cannot hedge away the forward premium because it is embedded in the forward exchange rate at which we can enter into the hedge at the beginning of the period. The value added due to hedging, or *hedge effect*, is equal to the difference between the currency surprise of the currency being hedged and the average currency surprise, weighted by the difference between the fund and benchmark segment currency hedge weights.

Hedge effect
$$\begin{aligned}
&= (\text{Fund segment hedge weight} - \text{Benchmark segment hedge weight}) \\
&\quad \times (\text{Benchmark segment currency surprise} \\
&\quad - \text{Benchmark total currency surprise})
\end{aligned} \qquad (19.6)$$

To examine the impact of hedging on benchmark relative returns, suppose that we had no local currency return during the period. In this situation the fund return would be due entirely to exchange rate fluctuation. Also assume that foreign currencies depreciated versus the base currency of the fund during the period, so that any holding of foreign securities would penalize the fund and benchmark returns. Exhibit 19.9 shows the returns and value-added decomposition for the period.

EXHIBIT 19.8   Hedging and Currency Weights

	A	B	C	D	E	F	G	H	I	J	K	L
1		Asset Weights				Hedge Weights				Currency Weights		
2			Fund	Bench	Diff.		Fund	Bench	Diff.		Fund	Bench	Diff.
3	U.S. Dollar	20.00	20.00	0.00		45.00	0.00	45.00		65.00	20.00	45.00
4	Euro	35.00	40.00	-5.00		0.00	0.00	0.00		35.00	40.00	-5.00
5	Yen	45.00	40.00	5.00		-45.00	0.00	-45.00		0.00	40.00	-40.00
6	Total	100.00	100.00				=B5+F5			100.00	100.00	

EXHIBIT 19.9 Multicurrency Return Decomposition with Hedging

	A	B	C	D	E	F	G	H	I	J	K	L
1		Market Weights				Local Returns				Base Returns		
2		Fund	Bench	Diff.		Fund	Bench	Diff.		Fund	Bench	Diff.
3	United States	20.00	20.00	0.00		0.000	0.000	0.000		0.000	0.000	0.000
4	France	35.00	40.00	-5.00		0.000	0.000	0.000		-0.182	-0.182	0.000
5	Japan	45.00	40.00	5.00		0.000	0.000	0.000		0.000	-5.000	5.000
6	Total	100.00	100.00			0.000	0.000	0.000		-0.064	-2.073	**2.009**
7												
8		Spot Exchange Rates				Forward Exchange Rates				Bench. Curr. Contribution		
9		Begin	End	Return		Begin	Premium	Surprise		Return	Premium	Surprise
10	U.S. Dollar	1.00	1.00	0.000		1.00	0.000	0.000		0.000	0.000	0.000
11	Euro	0.88000	0.87840	-0.182		0.87840	-0.182	0.000		-0.073	-0.073	0.000
12	Yen	0.00800	0.00760	-5.000		0.00800	0.000	-5.000		-2.000	0.000	-2.000
13	Total									-2.073	-0.073	-2.000
14												
15		Hedge Weights				Currency Weights						
16		Fund	Bench	Diff.		Fund	Bench	Diff.				
17	United States	45.00	0.00	45.00		65.00	20.00	45.00				
18	France	0.00	0.00	0.00		35.00	40.00	-5.00				
19	Japan	-45.00	0.00	-45.00		0.00	40.00	-40.00				
20	Total					100.00	100.00					
21									=(D19/100)*(H12/100-L\$1\$3/100)*100			
22		Value Added										
23		Local				Currency						
24	United States	Sel.	Alloc.	Premium		Mgmt.	Hedging	Total				
25	France	0.000	0.000	0.000		0.000	0.900	0.900				
26	Japan	0.000	0.000	0.005		-0.100	0.000	-0.095				
27	Total	0.000	0.000	0.004		-0.150	1.350	1.204				
28		0.000	0.000	0.009		-0.250	2.250	**2.009**				

In this example we underweighted the yen, as compared to the benchmark, during a period when the yen fell in value relative to the U.S. dollar. We completely hedged the –5.00% yen currency return because there was no forward premium. We can see in Cells G25 to G28 that we added 2.25% of value by underweighting currencies with a negative currency surprise over the period.

In this example we split the currency hedging effect from the currency management effect, but the two effects combined are the value added due to decisions to allocate currencies differently than the benchmark during the period. Given our example, where the local returns were zero and the forward premiums small, most of the value added over the benchmark was due to these decisions.

FIXED INCOME VALUE-ADDED DECOMPOSITION

Specific characteristics of fixed income instruments give the generically derived allocation, selection, and interaction effects limited insight into the performance of portfolios investing in bonds. We can, however, extend the basic value added decomposition technique to provide a better analysis of the performance of fixed income strategies. There are many types of fixed income securities and strategies for combining them into portfolios. But we can introduce the ideas behind the analysis of fixed income value added by considering three generic active management practices designed to deliver value added over the benchmark return in a diversified fixed income portfolio:

- Positioning of the fund's duration relative to the benchmark duration to better capture the impact of anticipated yield changes.
- Asset allocation to attractive fixed income sectors such as treasuries, corporate bonds, mortgage and agency bonds, and cash.
- Credit analysis and other techniques used to select bonds within sectors that are expected to outperform.

While the latter two practices are conceptually similar to the asset allocation and security selection decisions made for other asset classes, the impact of duration is unique to fixed income. *Duration* is a measure of a bond or bond fund's volatility risk. The number is an estimate of how much a bond's price will move for a given change in market interest rates. If a bond's duration is five, the price of the bond will fall by approximately 5% when there is a 1% rise in interest rates. We can increase our benchmark relative exposure to fixed income segments in two ways:

- By overweighting the fund allocation to the segment.
- By extending the duration of the holdings within the segment.

In other words, we could allocate assets to segments in the same proportion as the benchmark but still achieve a different return if the duration of the fund holdings is different than the benchmark segment duration. Holding all other factors that impact the value of a bond constant, the longer the bond's duration the greater the price volatility we will experience as the general level of interest rates change. Changes in interest rates lead to a change in the yield that investors require to invest in a bond. As interest rates change, the market price of bonds held by the portfolio change to reflect the current required yield. Bond prices and returns have an inverse relationship with interest rates. When interest rates rise, the required yield on bonds rises, and the price of previously issued bonds goes down. The longer the duration the more the bond price will increase as interest rates fall and decrease as interest rates rise. We can estimate the return to a bond given a change in required yields by multiplying the yield change by the inverse of the bond's duration.

$$\% \text{ change in bond price} = -(\text{Duration} \times \% \text{ change in yield}) \quad (19.7)$$

There are other factors that influence bond price changes, but duration provides a good estimate as to how the value of a prototypical bond will change given small changes in the level of interest rates.[3] The same holds true for the total and segment levels of the portfolio and its comparison index: the longer the duration the greater the expected return as interest rates fall.

DURATION EFFECT

Given the important influence of duration on fixed income returns, when we attribute value added over a fixed income benchmark, we seek to isolate the incremental return due to the relative fund and benchmark duration set at the beginning of the period. Suppose that we had a manager with a strategy of taking advantage of interest rate movements that are currently unanticipated by the market. If he foresees a decrease in interest rates, the manager could extend the duration of the portfolio versus the benchmark to produce a higher return than the benchmark as bond prices rise when the interest rates fall. We can measure the impact of decisions to have a different duration than the benchmark via the *duration effect*. The duration effect, together with the segment asset allocation and security selection effects, can be used to understand the sources of value added over the benchmark. There are several steps to incorporate the duration effect into the decomposition analysis:

1. Calculate the beginning of period durations for each segment of the fund and benchmark.
2. Use the durations to estimate the return due to yield changes for each fund and benchmark segment, where the yield changes are captured by observing the shift in the yield curve of risk-free bonds from the beginning to the end of the period.
3. Calculate the duration effect, which is the duration positioning impact on value added.
4. Calculate the security selection and asset allocation effects by comparing the relative weights and returns.

Suppose we wanted to analyze the value added by the fund in Exhibit 19.10. The fund outperformed the benchmark by 0.685% during the period. The fund is invested in three fixed income sectors, and the manager overweighted the corporate bond sector and under-

---

[3] For more on fixed income pricing relationships see Frank Fabozzi (ed.), *The Handbook of Fixed Income Securities* (New York: McGraw-Hill, 2000).

weighted the mortgages sector, with a neutral weight in treasury bonds during the period. We can also see that the fund outperformed the benchmark in the treasury and corporate segments.

We are interested in understanding the sources of value added over the benchmark. The first step is to isolate the impact of duration positioning, if any, on the value added. We will need, in addition to the return and weight information, the beginning of period segment fund and benchmark durations in Exhibit 19.11.

The fund had a longer duration than the benchmark in the treasury sector but neutral durations in corporates and mortgages. Because of the longer fund duration, we expect the fund to experience a higher return than the benchmark if interest rates decrease. We can estimate the return change to the fund and benchmark given changes in bond yields by observing the change in required yields to a risk-free treasury bond over the period. A line graph of required yields versus duration is called the *yield curve*. Cells B10 to D16 in Exhibit 19.12 show the change in yields at several points along the yield curve over the period. There are several ways to capture these yields; one way to do it is to observe the change in yields to zero-coupon treasury bonds that mature at each point on the curve.

Bond yields dropped over the period, but not by an equal amount at each point in the curve. Cells G10 to H12 show how to use the segment level durations and corresponding yield changes to estimate a return to due to yield changes, or *duration return*, for the period.

EXHIBIT 19.10   Fund and Benchmark Returns and Weights

	A	B	C	D	E	F	G	H
1		Begin Weights				Returns		
2		Fund	Bench	Diff:		Fund	Bench	Diff:
3	Treasuries	50.00	50.00	0.00		8.000	7.300	0.700
4	Corporates	40.00	35.00	5.00		8.500	8.300	0.200
5	Mortgages	10.00	15.00	-5.00		3.200	3.200	0.000
6	Total	100.00	100.00			7.720	7.035	**0.685**

EXHIBIT 19.11   Fund and Benchmark Duration by Segment

	A	B	C	D
8		Duration		
9		Fund	Bench	Diff:
10	Treasuries	7.000	6.000	1.00
11	Corporates	6.000	6.000	0.00
12	Mortgages	2.000	2.000	0.00
13	Total	6.10	5.40	0.70

EXHIBIT 19.12   Duration Return

	A	B	C	D	E	F	G	H	I
1		**Begin Weights**						**Duration**	
2		**Fund**	**Bench**	**Diff:**			**Fund**	**Bench**	**Diff:**
3	Treasuries	50.00	50.00	0.00		Treasuries	7.000	6.000	1.000
4	Corporates	40.00	35.00	5.00		Corporates	6.000	6.000	0.000
5	Mortgages	10.00	15.00	-5.00		Mortgages	2.000	2.000	0.000
6	**Total**	100.00	100.00			**Total**	6.10	5.40	0.70
7									
8		**Yield Curve**				=-G3*D16		**Duration Return**	
9	**Duration**	**Beg Yield**	**End Yield**	**Change**			**Fund**	**Bench**	**Diff:**
10	1.00	4.00	3.00	-1.00		Treasuries	7.000	6.300	0.70
11	2.00	4.20	3.10	-1.10		Corporates	6.300	6.300	0.00
12	3.00	5.20	4.00	-1.20		Mortgages	2.200	2.200	0.00
13	4.00	6.20	4.90	-1.30		**Total**	6.240	5.685	0.555
14	5.00	7.20	6.00	-1.20		=-H5*D11			
15	6.00	8.30	7.25	-1.05					
16	7.00	9.20	8.20	-1.00					

Duration return

$$= -(\text{Segment duration} \qquad\qquad (19.8)$$
$$\times \% \text{ change in yield given the segment duration})$$

In this case, there is a positive 0.70% return differential in the treasury segment due to the fund having a longer treasury duration than the benchmark.

Given the duration return, we can calculate the impact of duration positioning on value added. The duration effect is equal to the difference between the weighted segment level duration returns.

Duration effect

$$= \text{Fund segment weight} \times (\text{Fund segment duration return} \qquad (19.9)$$
$$- \text{Benchmark segment duration return})$$

Cells F17 to F19 in Exhibit 19.13 show the calculation of the duration effect for our sample fund. As expected, we achieved 0.35% of value added due to the longer duration in the treasuries segment.

Cells J10 to K12 of Exhibit 19.13 show how to use the duration return to isolate the return not attributable to yield changes, or *excess return*, for the period. There are several components to the excess return. These include the income return and return due to changes in the relationship between the yields on treasuries and the yields on riskier bonds. The difference between the yield on a treasury bond and the yield on a bond with credit risk is called the *yield spread*. Yield spreads compensate for the risk of default and other risks inherent in corporate and other types of bonds. When yield spreads contract or expand, there will be a return over and above that due to the duration return. A manager might overweight a segment in anticipation of a narrowing of spreads, which will lead to an increase in return over that of the benchmark. We calculate the asset allocation effect to capture the return differential due to yield spread changes and other segment allocation factors. The asset allocation effect is calculated by comparing the segment benchmark excess return to the total benchmark excess return, weighted by the relative weight of the fund and benchmark in each segment. For example, in our fund we overweighted corporates, and the benchmark corporate segment had a higher corporate excess return than the benchmark average excess return, leading to 0.063% of value added due to asset allocation to corporates.

The security selection effect is calculated by comparing the fund and benchmark segment excess returns, weighted by the fund weight (here we incorporate the interaction effect into the selection effect). We earned a small security selection effect in corporates by achieving a higher excess return than the benchmark excess return in that segment. We can interpret the security selection effect as the value added due to selecting bonds that perform better than the average bond within the corresponding index segment. For example, if we successfully select bonds that we believe will receive an upgraded credit rating, we would pick up excess return relative to the benchmark because a higher credit rating leads to a lower required yield, increasing the bond's return.

EXHIBIT 19.13   Value-Added Decomposition Isolating Duration Effect

	A	B	C	D	E	F	G	H	I	J	K	L
1		Begin Weights				Returns						
2		Fund	Bench	Diff.		Fund	Bench	Diff.				
3	Treasuries	50.00	50.00	0.00		8.000	7.300	0.700				
4	Corporates	40.00	35.00	5.00		8.500	8.300	0.200				
5	Mortgages	10.00	15.00	-5.00		3.200	3.200	0.000				
6	Total	100.00	100.00			7.720	7.035	**0.685**				
7						=F3-F10						
8		Duration				Duration Return				Excess Return		
9		Fund	Bench	Diff.		Fund	Bench	Diff.		Fund	Bench	Diff.
10	Treasuries	7.000	6.000	1.00		7.000	6.300	0.700		1.000	1.000	0.000
11	Corporates	6.000	6.000	0.00		6.300	6.300	0.000		2.200	2.000	0.200
12	Mortgages	2.000	2.000	0.00		2.200	2.200	0.000		1.000	1.000	0.000
13	Total	6.10	5.40	0.70		6.240	5.685	0.555		1.480	1.350	**0.130**
14	=(B3/100)*((F10/100)-(G10/100))*100											
15						Decomposition of Value Added						
16						Duration	Sel.	Alloc.	Total			
17				Treasuries		0.350	0.000	0.000	0.350			
18				Corporates		0.000	0.080	0.063	0.143			
19				Mortgages		0.000	0.000	0.192	0.192			
20				Total		**0.350**	**0.080**	**0.255**	**0.685**			
21			=(B4/100)*(L11/100)*100									
22			=((G4/100)-(G6/100))*(D4/100)*100									
23												

EXHIBIT 19.14 Value-Added Decomposition without Duration Effect

	A	B	C	D	E	F	G	H	I	J	K	L
1		Begin Weights				Returns				Attribution of Value Added		
2		Fund	Bench	Diff:		Fund	Bench	Diff:		Selection	Allocation	Total
3	Treasuries	50.00	50.00	0.00		8.000	7.300	0.700		0.350	0.000	0.350
4	Corporates	40.00	35.00	5.00		8.500	8.300	0.200		0.080	0.063	0.143
5	Mortgages	10.00	15.00	-5.00		3.200	3.200	0.000		0.000	0.192	0.192
6	Total	100.00	100.00			7.720	7.035	**0.685**		0.430	0.255	**0.685**

For our fund, the total duration effect, 0.350%, accounts for the majority of the value added over the benchmark during the period. Exhibit 19.14 shows why it is important to isolate the effect of value added due to duration positioning. In this exhibit we calculate the selection and allocation effects using the generic methodology.

Here the selection and allocation effects are distorted because they do not take into account the duration positioning of the portfolio. Exhibit 19.13 provides a better indication as to the sources of value added in a fixed income portfolio.

The methodology presented in this section for isolating the impact on return due to yield curve shifts can be further modified to take into account yield curve shape changes and other effects. There are also other approaches to attributing the difference between returns earned on a fixed income portfolio and its benchmark. One approach, sometimes called *multifactor return attribution*, to differentiate it from performance attribution, decomposes the source of return for each bond held by the fund and benchmark into a set of factors.

The factor results often include coupon, yield curve shift, twist, and butterfly-shape change effects, convexity effects, and other factors. In one approach to performing multifactor return attribution, the security level factors are calculated by iteratively repricing each bond held by the portfolio, changing one pricing factor at a time. The difference in the theoretical price calculated for the bond between each change is the factor return for that change. By taking a weighted average of the security level factors we can derive segment and portfolio level factors. The algorithms required by the valuation approach include bond and option pricing models. While return attribution provides a more detailed breakdown of the sources of bond returns, the approach presented here has the advantage of only requiring durations, in addition to returns and segment weights, in order to derive information as to the sources of value added.

The methods for extending the generic value added decomposition to multicurrency and fixed income securities can be used to further customize the methodology to meet the needs of other situations. The underlying procedure is to isolate the relative impact on return of factors specific to the asset class or strategy, and then attribute the value added over the main factors impacting return. The examples presented here were also for only a single period. We can extend the analysis over multiple periods using the same techniques presented in Chapter 18, except we will have additional management effects to compound over time.

Performance
Presentation

AIMR- and GIPS-Compliant Performance Presentations

The competition between money managers to attract assets from investors is intense. Thousands of organizations offer funds with a myriad of styles. It is also a dynamic industry with frequent mergers of existing companies and the emergence of new and niche firms. Institutional investors are also continually hiring and changing investment managers. Investors might look for a new manager because investment objectives, constraints, and resulting asset allocations change over time. Investors might also look for a new manager if they are unhappy with the existing one. A manager search is performed to identify suitable managers meeting the objectives for the new fund. There may be many suitable candidates even after narrowing a prospect list to firms with investment products with the desired asset class, style, and investment process characteristics.

How do plan sponsors and other institutional investors go about selecting from this list? And how do money managers market themselves to prospective clients? Personal and business relationships, trust, fees, quality of advice, and other factors are important in the selection and retention of an investment manager. But a firm's performance history is a major consideration in the hiring of investment managers. The manager with a superior absolute or risk-adjusted performance record has an advantage. Active money managers with poor performance can find themselves rapidly losing business. In a manager search, institutional investors review and compare the candidate manager's absolute, risk-adjusted, and benchmark relative performance histories. This is not just with the intention of identifying top performing managers, but also to determine if the manager's track record reflects his stated style and strategy.

In this chapter we review the institutional investment industry standards for the presentation of returns in the marketing process. We sum up the key provisions of the standards, review some common issues related to maintaining compliance with the standards, and finally examine the calculation of composite returns and other required statistics according to the standards.

Performance Records

Assuming that an investment advisory firm manages more than one portfolio and periodically offers new strategies, what performance data is available to prospective clients? There are several types of returns that could be presented as part of the marketing process.

- For a manager who is currently managing money for multiple clients, a *representative* client account could be selected that demonstrates the performance experienced by the average client or client similar to the prospect.
- The manager may maintain a *model* portfolio that tracks the managers intended strategy. Individual client funds are traded and rebalanced according the model account strategy.
- Backtesting the manager strategy or models could generate *hypothetical* performance numbers. A new manager or a manager with a new strategy will test how the strategy would have theoretically performed in the past.
- The performance of each of the firm's strategies can be presented using the aggregated or *composite* performance of all of the accounts following the same strategy.

For each of these alternatives the manager could also choose to present the account performance over particular time periods. Given these alternatives, prospective investors need to know exactly what the performance record represents. What is to stop a manager from offering up as a representative account the best performing account instead of the average account? Government regulations attempt to guard against the unscrupulous money manager or advisor. But, institutional investors want not only honest, but also comparable and independently verified performance figures for use when evaluating the suitability of a manager.

AIMR AND GIPS STANDARDS

To help provide comparable, verified performance figures a set of voluntary standards for investment performance presentation has evolved under the guidance of the *Association for Investment Management and*

Research, or *AIMR*. The main industry association for investment professionals, AIMR is a nonprofit association of portfolio managers, analysts, and other participants in the investment process. An important goal of the association is to maintain and enhance the reputation of the investment management profession and its practitioners. In this role AIMR has developed a code of ethics and standards for professional conduct outlining member responsibilities to the profession, employers, clients, prospects, and the general public. The standards promote self-regulation of the investment management industry and cover such matters as disclosure of potential conflicts of interest, priority of client transactions over manager transactions, and the maintenance of client confidentiality. AIMR's professional conduct standards include provisions for the fair, accurate, and complete presentation of individual or firm performance information to prospective clients. Misrepresentation of past performance is prohibited.

In addition to promoting the performance measurement standards, AIMR holds conferences on investment subjects, publishes the *Financial Analysts Journal*, sponsors and publishes original research, and runs the *Chartered Financial Analyst*, or *CFA* program. The CFA program is a self-study course for investment professionals with a program that covers a body of knowledge fundamental to the field, including performance measurement. Many of the topics covered in this book are part of the CFA curriculum.

AIMR PERFORMANCE PRESENTATION STANDARDS

The *AIMR Performance Presentation Standards*, or *AIMR-PPS*, are detailed guidelines for presenting performance to prospective customers. Goals for the PPS include:

- Full and fair ethical disclosure of historical performance.
- Industry-wide uniformity of performance presentation along with appropriate disclosures in order to support the valid comparison of the historical performance delivered by investment managers and other advisors.

Compliance is voluntary as the AIMR-PPS are a form of industry self-regulation. No law requires the adoption of the AIMR-PPS, but if a firm claims that their performance results are in compliance with the AIMR-PPS and they are not, the SEC may consider this a "material misrepresentation" and the firm may be liable for damages. Evidence of fraud, such as a presentation that overstates returns, may lead to regulatory action. Where local law and regulation applicable to the presentation of performance records does exist, the AIMR requires compliance with these rules in addition to those specified in the standards. Most large money managers claim compliance with the AIMR standards.

The AIMR-PPS are applicable to investment firms. Other entities that manage money, for example, pension plans with internal management capability, may choose to calculate and report numbers according to the standards. The AIMR standards are widely accepted and many institutional investors require compliance as a basic qualification to be considered in a manager search. Most investment management RFPs (Requests for Proposals) ask for data on the performance of the investment strategy under consideration, and whether the performance has been presented in compliance with AIMR-PPS. This is one reason the AIMR guidelines have become industry standard.

The AIMR-PPS are concerned with the calculation and reporting of composite returns, where the inputs are the returns of all the funds managed according to a particular strategy. But the influence of the AIMR standards goes beyond the presentation of returns for marketing purposes. The process of producing performance statistics for AIMR presentation purposes has trickle-down effects to the rest of the performance measurement process. Returns and other statistics calculated to AIMR standards are used not only for performance presentations to prospects, but also for client reporting, and internal performance, attribution, and risk analysis. The original standards were developed in 1987 and have had several subsequent revisions. The standards covered here were adopted in 2001.

Since 2000 the Investment Performance Council, or IPC, has overseen the AIMR-PPS. The *IPC* is a committee of fifteen members representing key investor and industry groups including pension funds, investment managers, consultants, accounting firms, and systems suppliers. The IPC has a global mandate and members represent European and Asian countries in addition to North America. The mission of the IPC is to promulgate the *Global Investment Performance Standards*, or GIPS. *GIPS* is a set of standards that is intended to form the core of individual country standards.[1] GIPS is the starting point for the AIMR-PPS used primarily by U.S. and Canadian investment managers. The AIMR-PPS and other country standards such as UK-IPS (United Kingdom) and SAAJ-IPS (Japan) include all of the GIPS standards as well as additional local or country specific standards, including:

---

[1] See the AIMR *Global Investment Performance Standards* (Charlottesville, VA: Association for Investment Management and Research, 1999).

■ Local legal and regulatory requirements.
■ Longstanding local industry practices.
■ Translations of the standards into the local language.

The local country standards are a superset of the GIPS standards. As GIPS evolves, the AIMR-PPS will reflect these changes and enhancements. Exhibit 20.1 shows the relationships between the various standard-setting bodies and the standards.

SUMMARY OF THE STANDARDS

Here we focus on the AIMR-PPS, which is the superset of the core GIPS standards that applies in the U.S. Both GIPS and the AIMR-PPS are the sets of required and recommended practices regarding the performance information presented to prospective customers for investment management services. The standards cover:

■ The accounting data inputs to the performance calculations.
■ The methodology used to calculate the returns.
■ Construction methodology for composites of funds.
■ Disclosures of information about the strategy, the composite, and the firm.

EXHIBIT 20.1   AIMR and GIPS Standard Setting

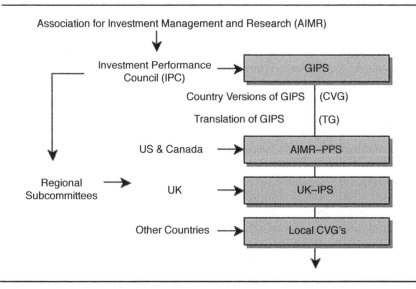

The standards contain generic provisions applicable to all managers and asset classes and some requirements specific to particular asset classes such as Real Estate and Venture Capital. In addition there are supplements covering the independent auditing of the presentations and rules on making claims of compliance within advertisements.

Performance presented according to the standards is for a composite, or an aggregate, of portfolio returns where there is one composite return presented for each investment strategy offered by the firm. The standards presume that the firm manages one or more investment strategies with one or more client account or funds invested in a particular strategy. The composites serve to aggregate performance for each fund managed according to the same objective. The standards require that all of the firm's assets under management be accounted for in a composite wherever the manager has investment discretion over the assets and there is a client paying fees for the management of the account. Simulated or model accounts are not included in composites. AIMR composites are not subject to survivorship bias. If a client left the firm, the terminated portfolio cannot be dropped out of the historical record of the composite. It is included in the composite results for all of the historical periods that it was managed by the firm.

For each fund in a composite, single period returns are calculated using accounting data representing the market value of the assets, including cash balances. Accounting is done on an accrual, not cash, basis. Security transaction adjustments are made on trade date and income is reflected as it is earned. For example, dividend income accrues on ex-date rather than payable date. Transaction amounts are recorded net of all trading expenses such as commissions. The valuation frequency is at least monthly and time-weighted, not dollar-weighted, returns are required. If valuations are not available at the time of every external cash flow, then approximations of the true time-weighted return are allowed. Composite returns are calculated by market value weighting the returns of the individual portfolios. This has the result that the performance of smaller portfolios will have a smaller proportional impact on a composite return than those of larger portfolios. As portfolios leave the composite or new ones join, we reflect the change in composite membership in the current period and moving forward, we do not go back and restate prior period composite returns. This has the effect of eliminating survivorship bias from composite return calculations.

After single period composite returns have been calculated, they are compounded to form multiperiod composite returns. Annual returns are presented for the previous ten years. Presentation of a measure of the dispersion in fund returns, such as the standard deviation of returns, around the average composite return is required. The fund returns are compared to relevant benchmark returns for each period.

CONSIDERATIONS IN MAINTAINING AIMR COMPLIANCE

The process of attaining and the procedures for maintaining AIMR compliance can be time consuming and difficult for some firms. Most of the challenges have more to do with the collection and maintenance of the data required for compliance rather than any difficulty imposed by the calculation methodology. For the firm that is not yet AIMR compliant, the most difficult issue is likely to be the gathering of the historical data required. The requirement to present 10 years of historic returns, which include the returns for clients that subsequently left the firm, may require reconstitution of account histories in order to place the funds in the appropriate composites. Firm mergers and acquisitions, fund manager changes, fund mergers, and strategy evolution contribute to the difficulty.

Definition of the Firm

No manager can claim that the reporting of a particular strategy, composite, or fund is AIMR compliant. Instead, the whole firm must be compliant with the standards in order for it to claim compliance. But many financial services companies have multiple independent business units that provide money management services, often to different markets and in locations around the world. These subsidiaries can claim compliance by defining the subsidiary as the firm, i.e., a particular unit of the firm may claim compliance even if the parent company and other subsidiaries are not. Many investment organizations have more than one firm for AIMR purposes, and this is allowed if the subsidiary is held out to clients as a distinct business unit with a separate investment process. In addition, the firm may define itself as a stand-alone entity for AIMR purposes if it is registered as such with the regulator with jurisdiction over the firm. Once the firm has been defined, all of the fee-paying discretionary assets within the firm must be included in a composite and all of the composites have to be maintained according to the standards. Claims of compliance are made at the firm, not the composite level.

Definition of the Composite

A composite is a group of portfolios managed according to the same style or strategy. All discretionary portfolios managed by the firm must be included in at least one composite. Composites are defined based on several factors, including strategy, style, and benchmark. An example of a composite definition is:

The U.S. Large-Cap Growth/Private Client Composite includes all fully discretionary, taxable portfolios managed according to the fund's growth stock investment strategy, benchmarked against the Russell Growth stock index, with a minimum asset size of $1 Million. The composite is restricted to private clients because they are taxable accounts, and typically hold more cash and more concentrated positions than the funds institutional clients.

A portfolio is *nondiscretionary* if the client maintains a degree of control over management decisions affecting their account. There is a continuum of control that a firm might exert over its client accounts, from merely providing asset allocation and other advice to complete fund management. For AIMR purposes, discretion is more of an investment management rather than a legal concept. The firm therefore defines what it considers to be discretion, and then this definition must be employed consistently. An example of a nondiscretionary account might be one where the manager is managing an equity strategy, but the investor requires the manager to maintain a proportion of the fund in fixed income instruments. Another example of a fund that is not required to be included in a composite is a fund where the manager is restricted from selling a concentrated stock position that comprises a large portion of the portfolio. A composite can also be defined with regard to a minimum asset size; in order to segregate accounts that the manager deems to be too small to fully implement his strategy. Accounts that invest in multiple asset classes, or balanced funds, are placed into a composite with accounts that have a similar range of target allocations. For example, accounts that are allowed to have a large allocation to equities would not be put in the same composite as an account that must hold large cash or fixed income positions. Accounts are not allowed to move from one composite to another unless there has been a documented change in the way the fund is managed.

Carve-outs

A balanced fund manager might want to report the performance of the equity segments of the balanced portfolios under management. By *carving out* the equity segment of individual portfolios and building a composite of these segments the manager can calculate his equity return. AIMR has allowed such *carve-outs* as long as the equity return was adjusted to reflect the proportion of the parent portfolio that was invested in cash. Starting in 2005, the standards will allow carve-out portfolios only if the carve-out is actually managed as a separate portfolio, with its own cash allocation.

Gross of and Net of Fee Returns

Composite returns can be presented either gross (before) or net of fees, together with required disclosures for each case. If the manager has a strategy available via several different investment vehicles, each with different fee structures, this can be problematic. When there is more than one fee schedule, then a net-of-fee composite return loses meaning. The standards recommend that wrap accounts be placed in separate composites. Mutual funds, however, can be maintained in the same composite as other fund types managed with the same strategy. Because mutual fund NAVs, and therefore returns, are calculated on a net-of-fee basis, the returns need to be grossed up for inclusion in a gross-of-fee composite. In Chapter 6 we showed how to gross up a mutual fund return that is to be included in a composite with other gross-of-fee returns.

Large Cash Flows

There are three issues relating to cash flows into or out of an investment account that are significant in size as compared to the investment balance:

1. The impact on the time-weighted versus dollar-weighted return calculation.
2. The impact of the large cash flow on the composite return.
3. The impact to the management of the investment strategy.

AIMR requires the use of time-weighted returns for the purpose of manager comparison. When the manager uses the linked MWR approach to approximate a TWR the single period MWR could be distorted because of a large client cash flow during the period. AIMR recommends revaluation of the portfolio when there is a large cash flow in order to eliminate this distortion and by 2010 AIMR is likely to require that valuations be performed at the time of any external cash flow.

The second issue relates to the calculation of the composite return. Composite returns are calculated as a weighted average of the individual fund returns. The weighting can be performed either using beginning of period or average market values. The use of beginning of period market values will distort the composite return when there are large cash flows during the period. It is more accurate to use the average balance over the period.

The third issue is more of a concern. Suppose we have a strategy where the manager invests in relatively illiquid markets, such as the small cap stocks of an emerging market. Due to liquidity concerns, if the manager receives a large cash flow, he may take some time to fully invest the client account according to the fund's strategy. If during this time the account is invested in cash or cash equivalents and the market is rising, the manager will likely be penalized if the account is included in the composite. AIMR allows two ways for eliminating this distortion. The first method is the use of a temporary new account. Using this method, the cash flow is invested in a temporary account, and then when the account is fully invested the assets are transferred into an account that is defined as being part of the composite. In the second approach, the client's entire account can be excluded from the composite calculation for the period when it is felt that the strategy cannot be fully implemented. Either method must be accompanied by disclosures of the firm's policy regarding significant cash flows.

Independent Verification

Verification is confirmation by an independent party that the performance presentation accurately represents the actual performance of the investment manager. Currently, investment firm performance records are not subject to the level of independent scrutiny of, say, public company accounting statements. Unlike these statements, which are attested by an independent auditor, firms can make independent claims that their performance records are AIMR compliant. But AIMR strongly encourages independent verification. Effectively, there is a requirement for an independent check of the performance presentation because prospective and current clients ask for it. The majority of investment firms have had their performance records independently verified.

CPA firms typically perform these verifications. But what does verification mean? With GIPS, AIMR has revamped the verification requirements. Before GIPS, and effective until 2003, there were two levels of verification, Levels I and II. A Level I verification essentially ensures that all of the firms accounts are included in a composite. Level II is more like a traditional audit, and is what most people expect from a verification. Where the firm itself can be Level I verified, Level II is applied at the composite level.

GIPS are moving away from the idea of two levels of verification. Instead there will be one level, simply called "verification." It is more similar to today's Level I, than Level II. Firms will however be able to claim that they have had individual composite results "examined" or "audited." GIPS verification is focused on checking whether or not:

■ Composites have been constructed according to GIPS on a firmwide basis; for example, all fee-paying discretionary accounts are included in a composite.

■ The firm has processes and procedures in place to calculate and present the numbers according to the standards.

The standards include a set of minimum tasks that the verifier must perform in the process of verification. These include a review of the policies and procedures for such things as determining whether an account is or is not discretionary. The verifier must also test a sample of composites to make sure that accounts have been added and dropped from the composite appropriately and that the returns are calculated accurately. The Level II audit is a more detailed audit of the composite results; including such things as checking that the security prices that went into the return calculation are reasonable. Many firms have their composite presentations verified on an annual basis.

Advertising Compliance
Over and above local market regulation concerning advertisement of performance results, the AIMR-PPS include guidelines for advertising that include performance results and claims of compliance. Firms are allowed to advertise their claim to be compliant with the AIMR-PPS. These advertisements must include certain statements, including the offer to send the prospect a complete list of the firm's composites, and a presentation of results that adhere to the standards. Advertisements that present performance data must also include various disclosures along with the returns.

Portability of Records
When a manager, or group of managers moves from one investment firm to another, or two firms combine via a merger or acquisition, the question arises as to ownership of the historical performance record, i.e., can the prior firm results be linked to the new firm results? The AIMR position is that a performance record belongs to the firm and not the individual. When an individual manager moves from one firm to another, the new firm cannot link in the new managers prior performance, but it can provide it as supplemental information to the presentation.

When one firm buys another there are guidelines as to whether the new firm can merge the prior firms history into a new combined composite. To combine the track records, all of the decision makers and substantially all of the clients must migrate to the new firm.

Beyond the Standards
The AIMR standards state broad requirements for performance presentation and are not intended to spell out detailed rules that cover every

possible situation. The standards are the minimum requirements for a compliant presentation. Behind the specific requirements lie the concepts of "fair representation" and "full disclosure." These two concepts serve as guides to the firm when dealing with issues not specifically covered in the standards. The firm may need to make various disclosures about their historical performance to keep within the spirit of the standards. Many of the issues that come up in practice, however, are common to many firms. AIMR offers a help line, and a Q&A database, as additional resources for clarification of the standards.

The Appendix to this book summarizes the PPS, but the PPS are an evolving set of standards, and there are occasional changes to the rules. Because the standards evolve over time, the AIMR Web site (www.aimr.com) is the place to check for up-to-date documentation of the AIMR-PPS.

CREATING COMPOSITES

The first step in creating an AIMR performance presentation is to define each of the firm's strategies that will require a separate composite. We then collect all of the portfolios that belong to that composite. We note each portfolio's inception date, and closing date, if it has been liquidated. We also record any intermediate periods where the portfolio needs to be removed from the composite because of a change in strategy, discretionary status, account size (if the composite has a minimum), or other reason. Using this list of composite/fund start and stop dates, we then calculate the various composite return, dispersion, and other statistics required for an AIMR-PPS compliant performance presentation. In this section we illustrate the calculation of these statistics.

Exhibit 20.2 contains market value and return data for ten funds we will use to demonstrate composite statistic calculations. We assume that the funds are all discretionary portfolios managed with the same strategy, so they will need to be aggregated together for AIMR-PPS compliant performance reporting. Our sample funds have an extreme range of returns for a group of funds managed according to the same strategy, but this is done with the intent of demonstrating the calculation of the dispersion statistics. Although the standards require ten years of annual returns, here we demonstrate the calculations using two monthly periods.

The first step in calculating composite returns is to determine the members of the composite. Composite membership is determined on a period-to-period basis. If valuations and returns are being calculated monthly, then each fund is evaluated each month as to whether its strategy continued to meet with the definition of the composite. The funds that we determine should be members of the composite for the month are the composite's *constituent portfolios* for the period. For each composite the constituent list could change from month to month. Most changes to the composite constituent list are made because a new fund has opened or a fund has closed. Funds are typically added to a composite for the *first full measurement period* after the inception of the fund. Using our sample funds in Exhibit 20.2, if the returns are being calculated on a monthly basis and the inception date for Fund 6 was during the month of November, then this fund will be added to a composite starting in December. The same convention is used for funds that are terminated. Assuming Fund 7 was closed during December, November is the last full month that it is included in the composite return calculation. In addition to fund openings and closings, there are several other reasons why a fund might be included as a composite constituent for some periods but not others:

- The fund or client strategy may have changed.
- The fund may not have been managed according to the stated strategy during the period. For example, if an equity fund is undergoing funding it might be invested primarily in cash during a startup period. The performance of the fund for this period is not representative of the investment strategy represented by the composite.

When it is determined that a fund does not belong within a composite for a period, the returns of that fund are not included in the composite return. In our examples we are calculating monthly composite returns, so we use a full month rule to determine when funds are to be included in the composite. Some firms use a quarterly rule, where the fund is included in the composite in the first full quarter after inception.

EXHIBIT 20.2 Fund Data used in Composite Calculation Examples

	A	B	C	D	E	F	G
1		November		December			Nov - Dec
2	Fund	BMV	% Return	BMV	% Return		% Return
3	1	276.2	21.72	308.8	0.94		22.86
4	2	263.9	11.40	294.7	-8.88		1.51
5	3	264.3	19.66	220.0	11.79		33.77
6	4	125.9	10.37	129.8	-4.54		5.36
7	5	18.6	7.77	18.8	7.34		15.68
8	6	-	-	499.6	7.44		7.44
9	7	124.2	3.43		-		3.43
10	8	89.4	0.94	90.2	0.94		1.89
11	9	93.9	13.50	87.2	-7.10		5.44
12	10	26.5	0.58	24.2	-8.88		-8.35
13			=((1+C12/100)*(1+E12/100)-1)*100				

COMPOSITE RETURNS

Once we determine the composite constituent list for each period, we can calculate the return for the composite. We do this by first calculating single period returns for each of the composite constituents for that period. We then calculate the composite return equal to the weighted average of the returns to the constituent portfolios. Then we link the single period composite returns to derive cumulative and annualized multiperiod returns.

The periodicity of single period returns is required to be monthly, at a minimum. The standards have evolved over time to require more frequent valuations. Monthly fund returns that are used in the composite can be calculated using portfolio returns that are calculated on a more frequent basis. For example, we can calculate portfolio performance on a daily basis and then use the compressed daily linked returns for the month as input to the composite return calculation.

The returns of the individual funds within the composites are weighted by asset size, i.e. larger funds will have a bigger impact on the composite return than smaller funds. There are two methods for calculating a single period asset-weighted composite return: the aggregate and weighted-average methods.

Aggregate Asset-Weighted Return

Using the *aggregate composite method*, all of the holdings and cash flows from the underlying portfolios are combined and treated as if they were the holdings of and transactions for a single portfolio. The return calculation is performed using a time-weighted or approximation of the true time-weighted return methodology. Once the holdings and cash flows are aggregated the calculation procedure is the same as that for a single portfolio. For example, we could aggregate all of the holdings and transactions for each of the nine portfolios in the composite constituent list for our sample funds in November and then calculate a Modified Dietz return using the methodology described in Chapter 3. The aggregate method creates a size-weighted return because the market values (and transactions) of the smaller funds will have a lesser impact on the total composite return than those of the larger funds.

Weighted-Average Asset-Weighted Return

Alternatively, the most commonly used way to calculate single period composite returns is the weighted-average method. Using the *weighted-average method*, we weight the individual fund returns, where the weights are determined using the constituent total fund market values. The market values that we use for weighting the returns can be either:

1. Beginning of period market values.
2. Average invested market value or balance for the period.

The *average invested balance* is the fund's beginning market value plus the day-weighted external cash flows for the period. The average balance is preferred over the beginning market value. It is more accurate because it includes the effect of interperiod cash flows. For example, a fund with a large contribution on the second day of the month will have a larger weight in the composite using the average balance than if the beginning market value is used.

To calculate a single period asset-weighted composite return:

1. Take either beginning market value or the average invested balance.
2. Sum the balances to compute the composite total market value.
3. Calculate the fund weight by dividing each fund's value by the total.
4. Multiply the fund weight by the fund return to calculate a *contribution to composite return* for each constituent fund.
5. Sum the contributions to obtain the composite return.

In Exhibit 20.3 we calculate the November asset-weighted return for our sample composite, using the weighted-average method. The composite return for November is 13.60%. It was calculated using a weighted average of the nine constituent portfolios under management for the full month.

EXHIBIT 20.3   Single Period Composite Weighted-Average Return

	A	B	C	D	E	F
1			November			
2	Fund	BMV	Weight	Return	Contrib	
3	1	276.2	0.22	21.72	0.047	
4	2	263.9	0.21	11.40	0.023	
5	3	264.3	0.21	19.66	0.041	
6	4	125.9	0.10	10.37	0.010	
7	5	18.6	0.01	7.77	0.001	
8	6	-	-	-	-	
9	7	124.2	0.10	3.43	0.003	
10	8	89.4	0.07	0.94	0.001	
11	9	93.9	0.07	13.50	0.010	
12	10	26.5	0.02	0.58	0.000	
13		=B12/$B$15	↱ =C12*(D12/100)	↰		
14						
15	Composite	1,282.90	1.00	13.60		
16			↑ =SUM(B3:B12)	↳	=SUM(E3:E12)*100	

EXHIBIT 20.4 Weighted-Average Composite Return

	F	G	H	I	J	K	L
				December			Nov - Dec
1							
2	Fund	BMV	Weight	Return	Contrib		Return
3	1	308.8	0.18	0.94	0.002		22.86
4	2	294.7	0.18	-8.88	-0.016		1.51
5	3	220.0	0.13	11.79	0.016		33.77
6	4	129.8	0.08	-4.54	-0.004		5.36
7	5	18.8	0.01	7.34	0.001		15.68
8	6	499.6	0.30	7.44	0.022		7.44
9	7	-	-	-	-		3.43
10	8	90.2	0.05	0.94	0.001		1.89
11	9	87.2	0.05	-7.10	-0.004		5.44
12	10	24.2	0.01	-8.88	-0.001		-8.35
13			=((1+D15/100)*(1+I15/100)-1)*100				
14							
15		1673.3	1.00	1.66			15.49

Exhibit 20.4 shows the composite return calculation for December. The December composite return is 1.66% and was calculated using the weighted-average method. The standards require the presentation of yearly composite returns for the past ten years or since the inception of the strategy if it is not yet ten years old. Composite returns can also be calculated for any other cumulative time period. Managers commonly calculate monthly, quarterly, year-to-date, 3-year, 5-year, 10-year, and since-inception composite returns. Composite returns for periods longer than a year can be calculated either on a cumulative or annualized basis. By weighting the fund returns, larger funds have a greater impact on the overall composite return than smaller funds with similar returns. For example, in December Funds 2 and 10 had the same return, −8.88%, but Fund 2 is much larger and therefore had a larger impact on the December composite level return.

To derive multiperiod asset-weighted composite returns, we compound the single period asset-weighted returns over multiple periods and then take the annualized average if required. Exhibit 20.4 also illustrates the calculation of multiperiod weighted-average composite returns for the sample composite.

The two-month composite return, equal to 15.49%, was calculated by chain linking the two monthly composite returns. Notice that Fund 6 is included in the composite return for December and Fund 7 for November. Multiperiod composite returns are calculated using the constituent portfolio returns where the constituents are determined separately each period. We do not remove a fund from a multiperiod weighted-average composite return just because it did not exist in the composite for the full linked period. By doing this we ensure that all of the funds actually managed by the advisory firm are included in the performance presentation, even if some of the accounts subsequently left the firm. This is also consistent with the way that we calculate fund returns. We include those securities that are in the fund for each single period return, then we link the single period returns to form the multiperiod returns. We do not go back and recalculate prior period single period returns to remove the effect of a security sold in a subsequent period. The multiperiod weighted-average return is a summary statistic representing the return on the average dollar managed by the firm over the period.

COMPOSITE DISPERSION

Notice that the composite return for our sample composite over the two-month period was 15.49%, but no constituent portfolio actually earned this return. One fund came close, Fund 5 with a 15.68% return, but the other fund returns ranged from −8.35% to 33.77% over the period. This is an extreme example, but given that the reported composite return is a weighted average, it may not be representative of the returns actually experienced by the clients invested in the strategy represented by the composite. We can quantify the variability around the average return with various *composite dispersion statistics*. Dispersion within a composite is sometimes called *internal risk*. A high degree of dispersion may be a cause for concern. Unexplained dispersion in results might be evidence of a "quality control" problem. Managers monitor return dispersion as a measure of their success in implementing particular strategies across their client base. The standards require the reporting of a dispersion statistic together with the asset-weighted returns. There are two types of dispersion statistics, asset-weighted and equal-weighted. *Asset-weighted* dispersion statistics show the dispersion of returns to the average dollar invested in the composite. These are the appropriate statistics to use if we are interested in the dispersion of returns unaffected by how the assets were grouped into portfolios. For example, if a composite had one very large fund and nine smaller funds, the asset-weighted composite dispersion statistics would not be greatly influenced by the performance of the smaller accounts. Alternatively, we could calculate *equal-weighted* dispersion statistics. These are indications as to the variability in returns experienced by the owners of the individual portfolios. Small and large funds have an equal influence on these statistics. We look at some asset-weighted statistics first.

Asset-Weighted Standard Deviation

We are interested in measuring the variability of the individual fund returns for a particular period around the composite average return for that period. The standard deviation of the portfolio returns around the weighted average composite return is an indication of the variability of fund returns within the composite. With the standard formula for calculating standard deviation, we divide the deviations from the mean by the number of returns for the period. This has the effect of equal weighting the deviations from the mean. We can instead calculate an *asset-weighted standard deviation* that is consistent with the composite return. We do this by asset-weighting the deviations from the mean return. Equation (20.1) is the formula for calculating the asset-weighted standard deviation.

$$\sqrt{\sum W_i \left[R_i - \left(\sum W_i R_i \right) \right]^2} \qquad (20.1)$$

where W_i is the individual fund constituent weight and R_i are the individual fund returns. Exhibit 20.5 illustrates the calculation of the asset-weighted standard deviation for the sample composite for November.

The asset-weighted standard deviation for November is 7.00%. Because this standard deviation is asset-weighted, larger funds contribute more to this variability measure than smaller funds with a similar return. For example, Fund 10 has the worst return, 0.58%, and the return furthest from the average, but it is a small fund that comprises only 2% of the composite. The effect of Fund 10's return is lessened because the squared return deviation is weighted by the asset size. The higher the asset-weighted standard deviation, the more variability there was in the return to the average dollar invested in the strategy. With an average return of 13.60% and a standard deviation of 7.00%, we would expect the returns to approximately 2/3 of the dollars invested in the strategy to fall in between 6.60% and 21.60%.

EXHIBIT 20.5 Single Period Asset-Weighted Standard Deviation

	A	B	C	D	E	F	G	H
1						November		
2	Fund	BMV	Weight	Return	Contrib			
3	1	276.2	0.22	21.72	0.047	8.12	65.94	14.20
4	2	263.9	0.21	11.40	0.023	-2.20	4.84	1.00
5	3	264.3	0.21	19.66	0.041	6.06	36.73	7.57
6	4	125.9	0.10	10.37	0.010	-3.23	10.43	1.02
7	5	18.6	0.01	7.77	0.001	-5.83	33.98	0.49
8	6	-	-	-	-	-	-	-
9	7	124.2	0.10	3.43	0.003	-10.17	103.42	10.01
10	8	89.4	0.07	0.94	0.001	-12.66	160.26	11.17
11	9	93.9	0.07	13.50	0.010	-0.10	0.01	0.00
12	10	26.5	0.02	0.58	0.000	-13.02	169.51	3.50
13						=D12-$D$15	=F12^2	=C12*G12
14								
15	Composite	1282.9	1.00	13.60		=SUM(E3:E12)*100		48.96
16					→	=SUM(H3:H12)	↗	
17	Asset Weighted Standard Deviation: 7.00					=SQRT(H15)		

EXHIBIT 20.6   Multiperiod Asset-Weighted Standard Deviation

	A	B	C	D	E	F	G	H
1					November-December			
2	Fund	BMV	Weight	2M Return	Contrib			
3	1	276.2	0.24	22.86	0.055	8.14	66.23	15.79
4	2	263.9	0.23	1.51	0.003	-13.22	174.72	39.79
5	3	264.3	0.23	33.77	0.077	19.04	362.60	82.71
6	4	125.9	0.11	5.36	0.006	-9.37	87.73	9.53
7	5	18.6	0.02	15.68	0.003	0.95	0.91	0.01
8	6	-	-	-	-	-	-	-
9	7	-	-	-	-	-	-	-
10	8	89.4	0.08	1.89	0.001	-12.84	164.79	12.71
11	9	93.9	0.08	5.44	0.004	-9.28	86.20	6.99
12	10	26.5	0.02	-8.35	-0.002	-23.08	532.56	12.18
13							↓	
14						=D12-$D$16	=F12^2	=C12*G12
15								
16	Composite	1158.7	1.00	14.73		=SUM(E3:E12)*100		179.72
17					⟶			
18		Asset Weighted Standard Deviation:			13.41	=SQRT(H16)		

While Exhibit 20.5 shows how to calculate the asset weighted standard deviation for a single period, there is a problem introduced when we calculate the statistic over multiple periods. The formula uses a weight to establish the individual fund's contribution to the composite standard deviation. We can use the beginning of period weight, but there may be portfolios that start or leave the composite after the first period. Because of this, when we calculate a multiperiod asset-weighted standard deviation, we typically include only the portfolios that are in the composite for the complete time period. Exhibit 20.6 illustrates the calculation of a multiperiod asset weighted standard deviation over the two-month period.

The two-month composite asset-weighted standard deviation is equal to 13.41%. Only the eight funds present in the composite for both months are included in the calculation, i.e., the summation in the standard deviation calculation is over all the constituents that have been in the composite for the whole period. The individual fund returns are the subperiod linked returns for the two-month period. Notice that the average composite return used to determine the deviations from the average is 14.73%. This is different from the actual reported composite return equal to 15.49%. This is because the mean return used for calculating the multiperiod asset-weighted standard deviation includes only the funds in the composite for the complete period.

Quartile Dollar Dispersion

In addition to the asset-weighted mean and standard deviation, we can further describe the asset-weighted distribution of returns by calculating asset-weighted first and third quartile returns. *Quartile dollar dispersion* is the rate of return for the best and worst performing 25% of dollars invested in the composite during the period. The return on the best performing 25% of dollars is sometimes called Quartile Dollar Dispersion 1, or QDD1. The return on the worst performing 25% of dollars is Quartile Dollar Dispersion 4, or QDD4. To calculate the Best QDD, we

1. Select the funds that were in the composite for the whole period.
2. Order the fund returns from high to low.
3. Calculate a quarter of the composite market value.
4. Starting with the best performing fund, accumulate the portfolios up through the quarterly value from step 3.
5. Weight the portfolio returns by their percentage of the quarterly value. For the fund that puts the accumulated market value over the quarterly market value, use only the portion of the market value required to foot to the quarterly market value.
6. Calculate the QDD by summing the weighted returns.

We calculate the Worst QDD in the same way, except that we use the mirror of the process to accumulate the worst performing portfolio returns. Exhibit 20.7 shows the calculation of the best and worst quarter dollars under management for our sample composite over the two-month period.

Notice that in our example, the Best QDD equals the contribution of the best performing fund plus a portion of the next best performing fund.

EXHIBIT 20.7   Quartile Dollar Dispersion

	A	B	C	D
1		November-December		
2	Rank	BMV	Weight	2M Return
3	1	264.3	0.23	33.77
4	2	276.2	0.24	22.86
5	3	18.6	0.02	15.68
6	4	93.9	0.08	5.44
7	5	125.9	0.11	5.36
8	6	89.4	0.08	1.89
9	7	263.9	0.23	1.51
10	8	26.5	0.02	-8.35
11				
12	Composite	1,158.70	1.00	
13				
14		Quartile Dollars:	289.68 → =B12/4	

EXHIBIT 20.7 (Continued)

	F	G	H	I	J
1					
2	Best QDD:				
3	264.30		264.30	0.91	30.81
4	540.50	250.83	25.37	0.09	2.00
5			↓		
6	=B4+F3	=F4-C14	=B4-G4	=H4/H8	=I4*D4
7					
8			289.68		32.82
9			=SUM(H3:H4)		=SUM(J3:J4)
10	Worst QDD:				
11	290.40	0.73	263.18	0.91	1.37
12	26.50		26.50	0.09	-0.76
13					
14			289.68		0.61

Equal-Weighted Composite Statistics

One of the drawbacks to using a weighted-average return statistic to represent the historical performance of an investment strategy is that not only is it possible for a particular fund to achieve a return different than the reported weighted-average return, but it is also possible that no client actually got a return close to the reported return. Because managers usually do not disclose the individual constituent fund returns and weights in their presentations to prospective customers, we need additional statistics to understand dispersion of performance around the average experienced by individual clients during the period (Assuming that each investor has a separate portfolio).

To do this, we can calculate composite average and dispersion statistics on an equal-weighted basis. While the asset-weighted average statistics provide a measure of the average dollar invested during the period, the equal-weighted statistics measure the dispersion of performance to the average fund. We measure equal-weighted dispersion using standard descriptive statistics including:

■ Mean and standard deviation of returns (equal weighted).
■ High, low and range of returns.
■ First quartile, median, and third quartile returns.

Exhibit 20.8 illustrates the calculation of equal-weighted composite descriptive statistics over the two-month period. Notice that we continue using the convention of including in the calculations only those funds that were in the composite for the entire two-month period. The mean return of 9.77% is the equal-weighted average return using the eight funds that were constituents of the composite over both months. The dollar weighted average return for the composite was significantly higher at 15.49% because several large portfolios did better than the rest during the two-month period, and therefore heavily influenced the weighted-average composite return.

Cumulative Equal-Weighted Return

The statistics calculated in Exhibit 20.8 use only the funds that are in the composite for the complete period; thus we excluded funds 6 and 7. We can also calculate an equal-weighted return that includes all of the portfolios. To calculate a *cumulative equal-weighted return* including all of the portfolios:

1. Calculate an equal weighted composite return for each period.
2. Link the equal weighted composite returns across periods.

Exhibit 20.9 illustrates the calculation of the cumulative equal-weighted return using all of the constituent portfolios.

EXHIBIT 20.8   Equal-Weighted Composite Descriptive Statistics

	A	B	C	D	E	F
1		Nov - Dec			% Return	
2	Fund	% Return		High:	33.77	=MAX(B3:B10)
3	1	22.86		Low:	-8.35	=MIN(B3:B10)
4	2	1.51		Range:	42.12	=D2-D3
5	3	33.77				
6	4	5.36		Equal Weighted Mean:	9.77	=AVERAGE(B3:B10)
7	5	15.68		Equal Weighted Std Dev:	12.65	=STDEVP(B3:B10)
8	8	1.89				
9	9	5.44		First Quartile:	17.48	=QUARTILE(B3:B10,3)
10	10	-8.35		Median:	5.40	=MEDIAN(B3:B10)
11				Third Quartile:	1.79	=QUARTILE(B3:B10,1)

EXHIBIT 20.9   Linked Equal-Weighted Return

	A	B	C	D	E
1		November	December		Nov - Dec
2	Fund	% Return	% Return		% Return
3	1	21.72	0.94		22.86
4	2	11.40	-8.88		1.51
5	3	19.66	11.79		33.77
6	4	10.37	-4.54		5.36
7	5	7.77	7.34		15.68
8	6	.	7.44		7.44
9	7	3.43	.		3.43
10	8	0.94	0.94		1.89
11	9	13.50	-7.10		5.44
12	10	0.58	-8.88		-8.35
13					
14	Equal Weighted Return:	9.93	-0.11		9.81
15		=AVERAGE(C3:C12)			
16					
17		=((1+B14/100)*(1+C14/100)-1)*100			

EXHIBIT 20.10 Composite Summary Statistics

	A	B	C	D
1		**November**	**December**	**Nov - Dec**
2	**Asset Weighted Statistics**			
3	Asset Weighted Return	13.60	1.66	15.49
4	Asset Weighted Std Dev	7.00	7.22	13.41
5	First Quartile QDD	21.43	9.73	32.82
6	Fourth Quartile QDD	4.09	-8.38	0.61
7	**Equal Weighted Statistics**			
8	High Return	21.72	11.79	33.77
9	First Quartile Return	13.50	7.34	17.48
10	Median Quartile Return	10.37	0.94	5.40
11	Third Quartile Return	3.43	-7.10	1.79
12	Low Return	0.58	-8.88	-8.35
13	Range of Returns	21.14	20.67	42.12
14	Linked Equal Weighted Return	9.93	-0.11	9.81
15	Equal Weighted Std Dev	12.65	7.29	12.65
16	**Composite Membership**			
17	Funds Added	0	1	1
18	Funds Removed	0	1	1
19	Funds in Complete Period	9	9	8
20	Funds at End of Period	9	9	9
21	% of Firm Assets	100.00	100.00	100.00

COMPOSITE MEMBERSHIP STATISTICS

For some of the dispersion statistics we calculated, we only used the funds that were constituents of the composite over the entire linked period. To assist in the analysis of the performance presentation we can include other statistics about the number of portfolios that were included in the calculation of the composite statistics, including the number of portfolios that were added to, removed from, and remaining in the composite for the complete period. These *composite membership* statistics can provide some insight into the rate of client turnover or strategy changes. It is possible for a composite to have the same number of portfolios at the beginning and end of a yearly period, but given client turnover the actual funds used in the computation of the composite returns and descriptive statistics could have changed drastically during the period. Finally, the AIMR-PPS requires disclosure of the percentage of the firm's total assets represented by the composite at the end of the period. Care must be taken to avoid double counting when the total net assets are calculated. Exhibit 20.10 summarizes our sample composite average-, equal-weighted, and composite membership statistics for each of the two months and the two-month compound period.

EXHIBIT 20.11   Different Composite Standard Deviations

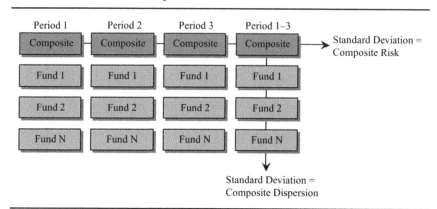

COMPOSITE RISK STATISTICS

Along with composite returns, the standards recommend that managers present appropriate composite risk statistics. The most commonly used measure is volatility, or the annualized standard deviation of the composite returns. Analytics such as the average P/E of an equity composite or the duration of a fixed income composite also help disclose the historical risk associated with the composite. When quoting or using the composite standard deviation it is important to differentiate between the two types of standard deviation commonly reported in an AIMR-PPS presentation, Exhibit 20.11 illustrates the calculation of the two types:

1. The standard deviation used as a proxy for the investment risk inherent in the composite is a measure of the variability in the total composite returns over time. It is calculated by first taking the weighted average composite return for each period. Then we take the standard deviation of the periodic returns. We calculate the standard deviation, as well as the other risk statistics covered in Part II, to provide an indication as to the absolute and relative risk of the composite strategy.
2. The standard deviation used as a measure of dispersion. This is a measure of the variability in the cross section of fund returns within a composite over a particular time period. The period can be either a single period or a cumulative return over multiple periods. This standard deviation is calculated by deriving the standard deviation of the individual constituent fund returns around the composite average return for the period.

The AIMR Performance Presentation Standards

This section summarizes the AIMR-PPS standards effective January 1, 2002. This was the first version of the AIMR-PPS based on the GIPS and several areas where AIMR and GIPS differ are noted. The standards are broken up into nine main areas, and each are has requirements that must be met by the manager to maintain AIMR compliance, and also some recommendations.

1. Input Data – Required

1.A.1.   All data and information necessary to support a firm's performance presentation and to perform the required calculations must be captured and maintained.

1.A.2.   Portfolio valuations must be based on market values (not cost basis or book values).

1.A.3.   Portfolios must be valued at least quarterly. For periods beginning January 1, 2001, portfolios must be valued at least monthly. For periods beginning January 1, 2010, it is anticipated that firms will be required to value portfolios on the date of any external cash flow.

1.A.4.   Firms must use trade-date accounting for periods beginning January 1, 2005.

1.A.5.   Accrual accounting must be used for fixed-income securities and all other assets that accrue interest income.

1.A.6.   Accrual accounting must be used for dividends (as of the ex dividend date) for periods beginning January 1, 2005.

Input Data – Recommended

1.B.1.   Sources of exchange rates should be the same for the composite and the benchmark.

2. Calculation Methodology – Required

2.A.1. Total return, including realized and unrealized gains plus income, must be used.

2.A.2. Time-weighted rates of return that adjust for cash flows must be used. Periodic returns must be geometrically linked. Time-weighted rates of return that adjust for daily-weighted cash flows must be used for periods beginning January 1, 2005. Actual valuations at the time of external cash flows will likely be required for periods beginning January 1, 2010.

2.A.3. In both the numerator and the denominator, the market values of fixed-income securities must include accrued income.

2.A.4. Composites must be asset weighted using beginning-of-period weightings or another method that reflects both beginning market value and cash flows.

2.A.5. Returns from cash and cash equivalents held in portfolios must be included in total-return calculations.

2.A.6. Performance must be calculated after the deduction of all trading expenses.

2.A.7. If a firm sets a minimum asset level for portfolios to be included in a composite, no portfolios below that asset level can be included in that composite.

Calculation Methodology – Recommended

2.B.1. Returns should be calculated net of non-reclaimable withholding taxes on dividends, interest, and capital gains. Reclaimable withholding taxes should be accrued.

2.B.2. Performance adjustments for external cash flows should be treated in a consistent manner. Significant cash flows (i.e., 10 percent of the portfolio or greater) that distort performance (i.e., plus or minus 0.2 percent for the period) may require portfolio revaluation on the date of the cash flow (or after investment) and the geometric linking of subperiods. Actual valuations at the time of any external cash flows will likely be required for periods beginning January 1, 2010.

3. Composite Construction – Required

3.A.1. All actual fee-paying discretionary portfolios must be included in at least one composite.

3.A.2. Firm composites must be defined according to similar investment objectives and/or strategies.

3.A.3. Composites must include new portfolios on a timely and consistent basis after the portfolio comes under management—unless specifically mandated by the client.

3.A.4. Terminated portfolios must be included in the historical record of the appropriate composites up to the last full measurement period that the portfolio was under management.

3.A.5. Portfolios must not be switched from one composite to another unless documented changes in client guidelines or the redefinition of the composite make switching appropriate. The historical record of the portfolio must remain with the appropriate composite.

3.A.6. Convertible and other hybrid securities must be treated consistently across time and within composites.

3.A.7. Carve-out returns excluding cash cannot be used to create a stand-alone composite. When a single asset class is carved out of a multiple-asset portfolio and the returns are presented as part of a single-asset composite, cash must be allocated to the carve-out returns and the allocation method must be disclosed. Beginning January 1, 2005, carve-out returns must not be included in single asset class composite returns unless the carve-outs are actually managed separately with their own cash allocations.

3.A.8. Composites must include only assets under management and may not link simulated or model portfolios with actual performance.

Composite Construction – Recommended

3.B.1. Separate composites should be created to reflect different levels of allowed asset exposure.

3.B.2. Unless the use of hedging is negligible, portfolios that allow the use of hedging should be included in different composites from those that do not.

4. Disclosures – Required

4.A.1. The definition of "firm" used to determine the firm's total assets and firmwide compliance.

4.A.2. Total firm assets for each period (Under the AIMR-PPS standards, firms must disclose total firm assets retroactively for all periods presented).

4.A.3. The availability of a complete list and description of all of the firm's composites.

4.A.4. If settlement-date valuation is used by the firm.

4.A.5. The minimum asset level, if any, below which portfolios are not included in a composite.

4.A.6. The currency used to express performance.

4.A.7. The presence, use, and extent of leverage or derivatives, including a description of the use, frequency, and characteristics of the instruments sufficient to identify risks.

4.A.8. Whether performance results are calculated gross or net of investment management fees and other fees paid by the clients to the firm or to the firm's affiliates.

4.A.9. Relevant details of the treatment of withholding tax on dividends, interest income, and capital gains. If using indexes that are net of taxes, firms must disclose the tax basis of the composite (e.g., Luxembourg based or U.S. based) versus that of the benchmark.

4.A.10   For composites managed against specific benchmarks, the percentage of the composites invested in countries or regions not included in the benchmark.

4.A.11   Any known inconsistencies between the chosen source of exchange rates and those of the benchmark must be described and presented.

4.A.12   Whether the firm has included any non-fee-paying portfolios in composites and the percentage of composite assets that are non-fee-paying portfolios.

4.A.13   The AIMR-PPS standards require that firms disclose whether the presentation conforms with local laws and regulations that differ from AIMR-PPS requirements and the manner in which the local standards conflict with the AIMR-PPS standards. (GIPS requirement: Whether the presentation conforms with local laws and regulations that differ from GIPS requirements and the manner in which the local standards conflict with GIPS.)

4.A.14   The effective dates for AIMR-PPS compliance are provided in the AIMR-PPS Introduction, Section I.B. For any performance presented for periods prior to the applicable effective dates, the period of non-compliance and how the presentation is not in compliance with the AIMR-PPS standards. (GIPS requirement: For any performance presented for periods prior to January 1, 2000, that does not comply with GIPS, the period of non-compliance and how the presentation is not in compliance with GIPS.)

4.A.15   When a single asset class is carved out of a multiple-asset portfolio and the returns are presented as part of a single-asset composite, the method used to allocate cash to the carve-out returns.

4.A.16   The AIMR-PPS standards require firms to disclose the firm's fee schedule(s) appropriate to the presentation (GIPS recommendation: firms should disclose the fee schedule appropriate to the presentation, see Section II.4.B.3 below).

Disclosures – Recommended

4.B.1.   The portfolio valuation sources and methods used by the firm.

4.B.2.   The calculation method used by the firm.

4.B.3.   The AIMR-PPS standards require that firms disclose the fee schedule appropriate to the presentation (See Section II.4.A.16). (GIPS recommendation: When gross-of-fee performance is presented, the firm's fee schedule[s] appropriate to the presentation.)

4.B.4.   When only net-of-fee performance is presented, the average weighted management and other applicable fees.

4.B.5.   Any significant events within the firm (such as ownership or personnel changes) that would help a prospective client interpret the performance record.

5. Presentation and Reporting - Required

5.A.1.   The following items must be reported:

5.A.1.a   (a) The AIMR-PPS standards require firms to present, at a minimum, ten years of annual performance history. See Introduction, Section I.B, for a discussion on the Effective Dates and Retroactive Compliance. (GIPS requirement: At least five years of performance [or a record for the period since firm inception, if inception is less than five years] that is GIPS compliant. After presenting five years of performance, firms must present additional annual performance up to 10 years. [For example, after a firm presents five years of compliant history, the firm must add an additional year of performance each year so that after five years of claiming compliance, the firm presents a 10-year performance record.])

5.A.1.b   (b) Annual returns for all years.

5.A.1.c   (c) The number of portfolios and amount of assets in the composite and the percentage of the firm's total assets represented by the composite at the end of each period. (For all periods after January 1, 1997, the AIMR-PPS standards require firms to provide the number of portfolios and amount of assets in the composite and the percentage of the firm's total assets represented by the composite at the end of each period. Prior to January 1, 1997, firms may choose to report these figures as of the beginning of the period or as of the end of the period, as long as the method prior to January 1, 1997, is consistently followed.)

5.A.1.d   (d) A measure of the dispersion of individual component portfolio returns around the aggregate composite return.

5.A.1.e   (e) The AIMR-PPS standards require firms to use the approved AIMR-PPS "Compliance Statement" provided in the AIMR-PPS Introduction, Section I.B, indicating firmwide compliance with the AIMR-PPS standards. (GIPS requirement: The standard Compliance Statement indicating firmwide compliance with the GIPS.)

5.A.1.f   (f) The composite creation date.

5.A.2   The Effective Dates of Compliance and Retroactive Compliance Guidelines for the AIMR-PPS standards are provided in the AIMR-PPS Introduction, Section I.B. (GIPS requirement: Firms may link non-GIPS-compliant performance to their compliant history so long as firms meet the disclosure requirements of Section 4 and no non-compliant performance is presented for periods after January 1, 2000. For example, a firm that has been in existence since 1990 that wants to present its entire performance history and claim compliance as of January 1, 2000, must present performance history that meets the requirements of GIPS at least from January 1, 1995, and must meet the disclosure requirements of Section 4 for any non-compliant history prior to January 1, 1995.)

5.A.3   Performance for periods of less than one year must not be annualized.

5.A.4   Performance results of a past firm or affiliation can only be linked to or used to represent the historical record of a new firm or new affiliation if

5.A.4.a   (a) a change only in firm ownership or name occurs, or

5.A.4.b	(b) the firm has all of the supporting performance records to calculate the performance, substantially all the assets included in the composites transfer to the new firm, and the investment decision-making process remains substantially unchanged.
5.A.5.	If a compliant firm acquires or is acquired by a non-compliant firm, the firms have one year to bring the non-compliant firm's acquired assets into compliance.
5.A.6.	If a composite is formed using single-asset carve-outs from multiple asset class composites, the presentation must include the following:
5.A.6.I	(i) a list of the underlying composites from which the carve-out was drawn, and
5.A.6.ii	(ii) the percentage of each composite the carve-out represents.
5.A.7.	The total return for the benchmark (or benchmarks) that reflects the investment strategy or mandate represented by the composite must be presented for the same periods for which the composite return is presented. If no benchmark is presented, the presentation must explain why no benchmark is disclosed. If the firm changes the benchmark that is used for a given composite in the performance presentation, the firm must disclose both the date and the reasons for the change. If a custom benchmark or combination of multiple benchmarks is used, the firm must describe the benchmark creation and rebalancing process.
5.A.8.	The AIMR-PPS standards state that composite results may not be restated following changes in a firm's organization.

Presentation and Reporting – Recommended

5.B.1.	The following items should be included in the composite presentation or disclosed as supplemental information:
5.B.1.a	(a) composite performance gross of investment management fees and custody fees and before taxes (except for non-reclaimable withholding taxes),
5.B.1.b	(b) cumulative returns for composite and benchmarks for all periods,
5.B.1.c	(c) equal-weighted means and median returns for each composite,
5.B.1.d	(d) volatility over time of the aggregate composite return, and
5.B.1.e	(e) inconsistencies among portfolios within a composite in the use of exchange rates.
5.B.2.	Relevant risk measures—such as volatility, tracking error, beta, modified duration, etc.—should be presented along with total return for both benchmarks and composites.

6. Real Estate - Required

6.A.1.	Real estate must be valued through an independent appraisal at least once every three years unless client agreements state otherwise.
6.A.2.	Real estate valuations must be reviewed at least quarterly.
6.A.3.	Component returns for participating or convertible mortgages must be allocated as follows:

6.A.3.a	(a) basic cash interest to income return,
6.A.3.b	(b) contingent interest (current receivable) to income return,
6.A.3.c	(c) basic accrued interest (deferred) to income return,
6.A.3.d	(d) additional contingent interest (deferred, payable at maturity, pre-payment, or sale) to appreciation return,
6.A.3.e	(e) return that is currently payable from operations to income return, and
6.A.3.f	(f) all other sources of income that are deferred or realizable in the future to the appreciation component.
6.A.4.	Returns from income and capital appreciation must be presented in addition to total return.
6.A.5.	The performance presentation must disclose:
6.A.5.a	(a) the absence of independent appraisals,
6.A.5.b	(b) the source of the valuation and the valuation policy,
6.A.5.c	(c) total fee structure and its relationship to asset valuation,
6.A.5.d	(d) the return formula and accounting policies for such items as capital expenditures, tenant improvements, and leasing commissions,
6.A.5.e	(e) the cash distribution and retention policy,
6.A.5.f	(f) whether the returns are: based on audited operating results, exclude any investment expense that may be paid by the investors, or include interest income from short-term cash investments or other related investments,
6.A.5.g	(g) the cash distribution and retention policies with regard to income earned at the investment level.

Real Estate - Recommended

6.B.1.	Income earned at the investment level should be included in the computation of income return regardless of the investor's accounting policies for recognizing income from real estate investments.
6.B.2.	Equity ownership investment strategies should be presented separately.
6.B.3.	When presenting the components of total return, recognition of income at the investment level, rather than at the operating level, is preferred.

7. Venture and Private Placements - Required

7.A.1.	All discretionary pooled funds of funds and separately managed portfolios must be included in composites defined by vintage year (i.e., the year of fund formation and first takedown of capital).
7.A.2	For general partners:
7.A.2.a	(a) Cumulative internal rate of return (IRR) must be presented since inception of the fund and be net of fees, expenses, and carry to the general partner.
7.A.2.b	(b) IRR must be calculated based on cash-on-cash returns plus residual value.
7.A.2.c	(c) Presentation of return information must be in a vintage-year format.

7.A.3   For general partners, the performance presentation must disclose:

7.A.3.a   (a) changes in the general partner since inception of fund,

7.A.3.b   (b) type of investment, and

7.A.3.c   (c) investment strategy.

7.A.4   For intermediaries and investment advisors:

7.A.4.a   (a) For separately managed accounts and commingled fund-of-funds structures, cumulative IRR must be presented since inception of the fund and be net of fees, expenses, and carry to the general partners but gross of investment advisory fees unless net of fees is required to meet applicable regulatory requirements.

7.A.4.b   (b) Calculation of IRR must be based on an aggregation of all the appropriate partnership cash flows into one IRR calculation—as if from one investment.

7.A.4.c   (c) The inclusion of all discretionary pooled fund-of-funds and separately managed portfolios in composites must be defined by vintage year.

7.A.5   For intermediaries and investment advisors, the performance presentation must disclose:

7.A.5.a   (a) the number of portfolios and funds included in the vintage-year composite,

7.A.5.b   (b) composite assets,

7.A.5.c   (c) composite assets in each vintage year as a percentage of total firm assets (discretionary and nondiscretionary committed capital), and

7.A.5.d   d) composite assets in each vintage year as a percentage of total private equity assets.

Venture and Private Placements - Recommended

7.B.1.   General partners:

7.B.1.a   (a) Industry guidelines should be used for valuation of venture capital investments,

7.B.1.b   (b) Valuation should be either cost or discount to comparables in the public market for buyout, mezzanine, distressed, or special situation investments, and

7.B.1.c   (c) IRR should be calculated net of fees, expenses, and carry without public stocks discounted and assuming stock distributions were held.

7.B.2.   Net cumulative IRR (after deduction of advisory fees and any other administrative expenses or carried interest) should be calculated for separately managed accounts, managed accounts, and commingled fund-of-funds structures.

7.B.3.   For general partners, the following should be disclosed:

7.B.3.a   (a) gross IRR (before fees, expenses, and carry), which should be used at the fund and the portfolio level, as supplemental information,

7.B.3.b   (b) the multiple on committed capital net of fees and carry to the general partners,

7.B.3.c   (c) the multiple on invested capital gross of fees and carry,

7.B.3.d   (d) the distribution multiple on paid-in capital net of fees to the general partners, and

7.B.3.e   (e) the residual multiple on paid-in capital net of fees and carry to the limited partners.

7.B.4   For intermediaries and investment advisors, the number and size should be disclosed in terms of committed capital of discretionary and nondiscretionary consulting clients.

8. Wrap-Fee Accounts - Required

8.A.1.   Wrap-fee performance must be shown net of all fees charged directly or indirectly to the account (unless transaction expenses can be determined and deducted).

8.A.2.   When a firm includes portfolios as part of a wrap-fee composite that do not meet the wrap-fee definition, the firm must disclose for each year presented:

8.A.2.a   (a) the dollar amount of the non-wrap-fee portfolios represented and

8.A.2.b   (b) the fee deducted, which should be the highest applicable wrap fee.

8.A.3.   Pure gross-of-fees performance may only be presented as supplemental information (in addition to the required net-of-fees performance). Such supplemental information must disclose:

8.A.3.a   (a) fees,

8.A.3.b   (b) investment style, and

8.A.3.c   (c) the information that "pure" gross-of-fees return does not include transaction costs.

Wrap-Fee Accounts - Recommended

8.B.1.   Wrap-fee portfolios should be grouped in separate composites from "non-wrapped" composites.

9. After-Tax Performance - Required

Following are provisions that apply to firms that wish to show after-tax performance results in compliance with the AIMR-PPS standards. Currently, firms are only recommended to present after-tax performance.

9.A.1.   For after-tax composites:

9.A.1.a   (a) Taxes must be recognized in the same period as when the taxable event occurred.

9.A.1.b   (b) Taxes on income and realized capital gains must be subtracted from results regardless of whether taxes are paid from assets outside the account or from account assets.

9.A.1.c   (c) The maximum federal income tax rates appropriate to the portfolios must be assumed.

9.A.1.d   (d) The return for after-tax composites that hold both taxable and tax-exempt securities must be adjusted to an after-tax basis rather than being "grossed up" to a taxable equivalent.

9.A.1.e   (e) Calculation of after-tax returns for tax-exempt bonds must include amortization and accretion of premiums or discounts.

9.A.1.f   (f) Taxes on income are to be recognized on an accrual basis.

9.A.2.   The performance presentation must disclose:

9.A.2.a   (a) for composites of taxable portfolios, the composite assets as a percentage of total assets in taxable portfolios (including nondiscretionary assets) managed according to the same strategy for the same type of client,

9.A.2.b   (b) the tax rate assumptions if performance results are presented after taxes, and

9.A.2.c   (c) both client average and manager average performance if adjustments are made for nondiscretionary cash withdrawals.

After-Tax Performance – Recommended

9.B.1.   Portfolios should be grouped by tax rate.

9.B.2.   Portfolios may be grouped by vintage year, or similar proxy, to group portfolios with similar amounts of unrealized capital gains.

9.B.3.   Cash-basis accounting is to be used if required by applicable law.

9.B.4.   Calculations should be adjusted for nondiscretionary capital gains.

9.B.5.   Benchmark returns should be calculated using the actual turnover in the benchmark index, if available; otherwise, an approximation is acceptable.

9.B.6.   If returns are presented before taxes, a total rate of return for the composite should be presented without adjustment for tax-exempt income to a pretax basis.

9.B.7.   If returns are presented after taxes, client-specific tax rates may be used for each portfolio (but composite performance should be based on the same tax rate for all clients in the composite).

9.B.8.   The following presentations should be made for composites:

9.B.8.a   (a) beginning and ending market values,

9.B.8.b   (b) contributions and withdrawals,

9.B.8.c   (c) beginning and ending unrealized capital gains,

9.B.8.d   (d) realized short-term and long-term capital gains,

9.B.8.e   (e) taxable income and tax-exempt income,

9.B.8.f   (f) the accounting convention used for the treatment of realized capital gains (e.g., highest cost, average cost, lowest cost, FIFO, LIFO), and

9.B.8.g   (g) the method or source for computing after-tax benchmark return.

index

341

Printed and bound by CPI Group (UK) Ltd, Croydon, CR0 4YY

23/04/2025

14660929-0001